MW00512781

HISTORY

OF

McHENRY COUNTY

ILLINOIS

BY

SPECIAL AUTHORS AND CONTRIBUTORS

VOLUME I

ILLUSTRATED

CHICAGO
MUNSELL PUBLISHING COMPANY
PUBLISHERS
1922

In the first century of the Christian era, Tacitus (perhaps the greatest of Roman historians) wrote that the object of history was ' to rescue virtuous acts from the oblivion to which the want of records would consign them."

OUTLINE MAP OF

McHENRY COUNTY

ILLINOIS

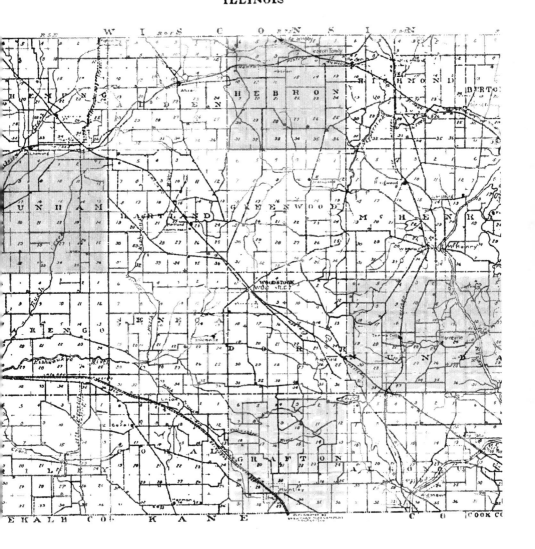

FOREWORD

One of the conspicuous evidences of modern progress is manifested in the increased interest in local and personal history. In a general sense, real history is the record of past events, while biography is the history of individual life. The close relationship of these two branches of history is recognized by the brilliant essayist and historian, Carlyle, in the statement that "History is the essence of innumerable biographies," and that, "in a certain sense, all men are historians," in the fact that they furnish the material facts which constitute true history.

In the formative period of each new community the attention of its members is largely absorbed by the present—the necessity of securing means for personal and family support—the study of natural resources and planning for future development. But as time advances and conditions change, there comes a change in the popular mind and an increased interest in the past. That such has been the condition within the last century in McHenry county, as well as in the Middle West generally, is apparent to the general observer.

These evidences of change and development are taken note of, and in the preparation of the forty chapters, it has been the object to present, in compact form and under appropriate topical headings, the main facts of county history from the earlier settlements and political organization to the present time. Various topics and localities have been treated with reasonable fulness under their appropriate chapter headings by contributors especially selected for that purpose. Of the large number of contributers to these and other departments, it is not necessary here to make special mention as their names are attached to their respective contributions in the body of the work. For the value of such it has rendered thanks are hereby cordially expressed.

With the feeling that the work, as a whole, has been prepared with special care, and with full appreciation of the interest already manifested and patronage pledged by the citizens of McHenry county in its success, it is submitted to its many patrons and the general public in the hope that it will prove of permanent and personal value to a large class of readers.

THE PUBLISHERS

INDEX

CHAPTER I

TOPOGRAPHY, GEOLOGY AND NATURAL FEATURES

CHAPTER II

INDIAN OCCUPATION

CHAPTER III

EARLY SETTLERS AND SETTLEMENTS

CHAPTER IV

LAND TITLES

BY GEORGE W. LEMMERS

CHAPTER V

ORGANIZATION AND GOVERNMENT

By William Desmond

CHAPTER VI

POLITICAL REPRESENTATION

By M. F. Walsh

CHAPTER VII

EDUCATION

By Richard W. Bardwell

CHAPTER VIII

CHURCHES

CHAPTER IX

COURTS, BENCH AND BAR

By Judge Charles P. Barnes

CHAPTER X

MEDICAL PROFESSION

By Dr. C. M. Johnson

CHAPTER XI

JOURNALISM .

By Charles F. Renich

CHAPTER XII

BANKS AND BANKING

By Fremont Hoy

CHAPTER XIII

AGRICULTURE AND COUNTY FAIRS

By George A. Hunt

CHAPTER XIV

DAIRY AND LIVE STOCK INTERESTS

By W. J. Kittle

CHAPTER XIX

FRATERNAL SOCIETIES AND ORGANIZATIONS

CHAPTER XX

PUBLIC LIBRARIES

By Ida L. Gehrig.

CHAPTER XXI

WOMAN'S CLUBS

By Mrs. W. H. Doolittle.

CHAPTER XXII

MISCELLANEOUS

CHAPTER XXIII

ALDEN TOWNSHIP

CHAPTER XXIV

ALGONQUIN TOWNSHIP

CHAPTER XXV

BURTON TOWNSHIP

CHAPTER XXVI

CHEMUNG TOWNSHIP

CHAPTER XXVII

CORAL TOWNSHIP

CHAPTER XXXIII

HEBRON TOWNSHIP

CHAPTER XXXIV

MARENGO TOWNSHIP

CHAPTER XXXV

McHENRY TOWNSHIP

CHAPTER XXXVI

NUNDA TOWNSHIP

CHAPTER XXXVII

RICHMOND TOWNSHIP

PORTRAITS

ILLUSTRATIONS

History of McHenry County

CHAPTER I

TOPOGRAPHY, GEOLOGY AND NATURAL FEATURES

GENERAL SURFACE FOX RIVER PISTAQUA LAKE THE NIPPERSINK—THE
KISHWACKEE SMALL LAKES CAUSE OF PRAIRIES —GEOLOGICAL FEA-
TURES STONE QUARRY GOOD CLAY GRAVEL AND SAND PLAT BEDS
REGENT DRAINAGE

GENERAL SURFACE

The surface of the county is varied, consisting of prairies, both level
and undulating, wooded ridges, and hills of considerable elevation. The
configuration is such that artificial drainage is rendered comparatively
easy, while nature has provided ample water courses. The Fox River,
rising in Wisconsin, flows south, in Lake and McHenry counties, keeping
near the county line. This is a noble stream, one of the finest in the
country Ultimately it unites with the Illinois River. The Fox enters
McHenry County about eight miles from the Wisconsin state line, flowing out of the Pistaqua Lake, which body lies in both counties, and is
but the expansion of the river itself. A little over two miles further
south, the river bends westward into McHenry County, this time coming
from Lake County. From this point it courses down the line until the
southern line of the county is reached again at Algonquin. The Nippersink, a tributary of the Fox, rises in McHenry County and traverses the
northeastern part of the county This county is also the source of the
Kishwaukee River, its chief branches rising in the central and western
part of the county. This stream flows westward into Rock River. There
are other smaller streams throughout McHenry County.

Small lakes or ponds, were originally quite numerous in this county,
but to a great extent these have disappeared through drainage systems

17

of the last half century. There are, however, several left yet. Some of these are ... young ... being ... w ... as ... for ... ...
d ... ... this ... years ... ...

CONTINENTAL S

The soil and other features of ... ans of a survey, of late ... ...
survey ... preseng of the county after the Civil War, precise...
sets ... the following features ... t appearance and condition.

"The soil and climate very nearly approximate to those in the
State ... and is known for a certainty that the standing tap of the
Woodstock was ... baron the highest point in Illinois ...
which further accounts for the wholesomeness of its climate. The county
is ... evenly and equally divided into woodland and prairie ... latter ...
much in excess. Good timber is quite plentiful, and the people are supplied at once with all that is required for fuel and ... me ... and
ornamental building purposes. In 1880 it was believed that there was fully
as much timber in the county as when first settled in the thirties. The
prairies stretching their broad grassy surfaces between the groves present
an interesting natural phenomenon, and as as much more than half of
McHenry County is composed of them, the question of their origin cannot
fail to interest the local reader. Much speculation has been made upon
this subject, the results of which may be summed up in two distinct
theories.

The first theory presupposes that the soil of the prairies was formed
by the decomposition of vegetable matter under water, with attendant
conditions unfavorable to the growth of timber. Those who hold to this
theory maintain than prairies are even now forming along the rivers and
shores of lakes. River channels are constantly changing, by reason of
freshets. The heaviest particles transported by the water fall near the
channel, and here repeated deposits first cause banks to be elevated above
the floods. Trees spring up on the natural levies, serving to strengthen
them and render them permanent. When an overflow takes place these
barriers keep subsiding waters from returning to the river bed; and by
frequent inundations the bottom lands become sloughs or swamps. The
water is usually shallow and stagnant, and is thus soon invaded by mosses
and aquatic plants, which grow beneath the surface and contain in their
fibers silica alumina and lime, the constituents of clay. To these plants
mollusks and other small aquatic animals attach themselves and find in
them their subsistence. Hence a constant decomposition, both of animal

and vegetable matter, ensues, and finally forms a stratum of clay, like the
underlying prairies.

"The marshy bottoms are thus gradually built up to the surface of
the water; vegetable matter becomes more abundant, rushes, reeds and
coarse grasses being added to other forms of plant life. These plants,
rising above the water, absorb the carbonic acid gas of the air and convert
them into woody fiber, which by decomposition first forms the clay mold
and afterward the black mold of the prairie. Such agencies, now operating in the ponds which skirt river banks, originally formed all the prairies
of the Mississippi Valley. According to geologists, the surface of the
land was submerged toward the close of the drift period, and as it slowly
emerged afterward it was covered with extensive ponds of shallow water
which finally became swamps, and then prairies. One remarkable feature
about the prairies, namely, the absence of trees, is accounted for first by
the formation of ulmic acid, which is favorable to the growth of plants,
but retards that of the trees; second the roots of trees require air, which
they cannot obtain when the surface is under water or covered by a compact sod; third, marshy flats offer no solid points to which the trees may
attach themselves. But when the land becomes dry, and the sod is
broken by cultivation, almost all varieties of native woods grow and thrive
upon the prairie. The uneven surface of some of the prairies is due to the
erosive action of subsiding waters. The drainage following the creeks
and rivers, finally resulted in the formation of rolling prairies.

The foregoing theory is based upon a large and constant water supply;
another theory, which is accepted by many, assumes a very different
aqueous condition in accounting for the prairies. It is a well-known fact
in physical geography that the chief continents of the globe are generally
surrounded by belts of timber, while further inland are areas of treeless
tracts, and centrally extensive deserts. On the eastern coast of North
America, from the Gulf of Mexico to the Hudson Bay, as well as on the
Pacific slope of the continent, timber grows thickly and spontaneously.
These two zones of timber approach each other at the north and south,
and within them lie the wide prairies of the Mississippi Valley. Farther
west are those arid regions which have caused them to be designated as
the "Great American Desert." Other portions of the earth have likewise
their areas of forest, treeless lands and barrens. In Africa, the Sahara; in
Europe, the Steppes; in Asia, the rainless wastes; in South America, the
Ateama, all serve to illustrate that the operation of physical laws such as
have caused the diversification of the United States has been general in
all countries.

"Upon investigation it will be found that the alternation of woods, prairie and desert corresponds with the variations in the amount of rainfall. The ocean is the great source of moisture, and the clouds are the vehicles which transport it over the land. Actual investigation has proved that most of the water taken from the ocean in form of vapor or cloud is discharged upon the rim of the continent; that the amount of rainfall is much less toward the interior, until finally, almost total aridity is found. Upon applying this theory to the American continent, it will be found that in going from New York to San Francisco, the amount of rainfall very nearly coincides with the alterations of woodland prairie and desert. At New York the average rainfall is forty-two inches; the region extending thence to Ann Arbor, Mich., where the annual rainfall is twenty-nine inches, is well timbered; thence to Galesburg, Ill., where the rainfall is twenty four inches, the country is prairie interspersed with occasional clumps of woodland; thence to Ft. Laramie, having only twenty inches of rainfall, the country rapidly changes to continuous prairie; thence to Ft. Youma, having three inches, it becomes a desert; and then to San Francisco, where the rainfall is twenty-two inches, it changes back to thick forests. Illinois lies within the region of alternate wood and prairie.

"Still further some scientists claim that the treeless tracts are due to the nature of the soil. It is highly probable that each of the forces named in these theories may have had something to do with the formation of our beautiful and productive prairies."

GEOLOGICAL FORMATIONS

It is not the object of this chapter to go far into the detailed account of the geological formation of this county, but merely to give a general idea of the common geological formations as have been determined by state and other geologists, especially Prof. Worthen, former state geologist.

The geological formations in this county consist largely of drift. The bedrock, which is rarely exposed, belongs chiefly to the Niagara group. Along the western border of the county, is a narrow strip running north and south, the underlying formation belongs to the Cincinnati group. The drift deposits consist of clay and hardpan, with occasional beds of sand and gravel, and boulders frequently scattered throughout the mass cover the whole surface of the county for an average depth of about seventy feet. The mighty agencies of nature at work during the glacial period ground away and transformed all of the original formations above the Silurian rocks, and buried these rocks themselves beneath a mass of debris of heterogeneous character.

There are no good opportunities afforded for observing sections of drift in this county. There being no natural exposures, excavations for wells afford about the only data accessible, and this is meagre. Wells are seldom sunk to a greater depth than forty feet, and in that distance little is found except blue clay, or hardpan, with an occasional pocket or irregular seam of quicksand and gravel. Boulders are found both on the surface and in excavations. They are of varying size and of all sorts of material, such as granite, senite, trap, greenstone, limestone and sandstone. Near the Fox River the ridges contain large quantities of rolled limestone boulders, evidently derived from the Niagara rocks of Wisconsin. The mass of the drift, however, appears to be clay and hardpan, with occasional boulders. Logs of wood and other vegetable remains have frequently been found beneath the surface at distances from fifteen to fifty feet.

With the exception of the narrow belt along the western line of the county, already referred to as belonging to the Cincinnati group, the underlying formation probably belongs wholly to the Niagara group. The outcrops, however, are so few as to render absolute knowledge of the formation impossible. In the northeastern corner, in section 17, township 44, range 9, nearly on the county line between Lake and McHenry, the limestone is exposed in an excavation by the roadside. It is unstratified and contains no well-preserved fossils. At the Sand Hills on the Kishwaukee, in the southwest part of section 21, township 44, range 6, a bed of limestone was found in an excavation, fourteen feet below the surface. This is probably of the Niagara group.

The exposures of the Cincinnati formation are limited to one locality, about two miles east of Garden Prairie station, of the Galena division of the Chicago & Northwestern Railroad, about one-fourth of a mile south of the main wagon road between that station and Marengo. This rock has been quite extensively quarried here. It is a bluff limestone, thinly bedded, and containing considerable chert in some part of the quarry. Frequently it has a slight bluish tinge. Fossils are scarce and very imperfect.

The only extensive stone quarry in the county is the one just mentioned. The rock being thin-bedded, and containing chert, is not calculated to serve all purposes of a building stone, yet it becomes very useful in foundation and for the rougher kinds of masonry. Along the

Fox River the boulders found in the ridges have been quarried to some extent, and a rough building material obtained therefrom. Lime has been burned from the limestone boulders in some places, but no extensive manufacture of it has ever been attempted.

Good clay for brick making is quite abundant in McHenry County. Its prevailing color when burned, is red, or reddish brown. At Woodstock and McHenry, however, a white straw colored brick is made. The clay for the white brick is obtained at Woodstock under a peat bed, and it was formerly supposed to be a sedimentary formation more recent than the drift. That at McHenry, geologists tell us, belongs to the drift period proper. At Woodstock the same clay used in making brick has also been profitably employed in making drain tile.

Peat is abundant in the county, but the most extensive deposits are the north half of the county. It is found in the sloughs or bogs, in varying depths and of various qualities. Many years ago it was thoroughly tested and found to be excellent for fuel. In 1880 it was estimated that there were between 4,000 and 5,000 acres of sloughs containing peat in the counties of Lake and McHenry. One of the largest peat sloughs was situated near Hebron station, in sections 7 and 8 in township 46, range 7. This bed, with slight exceptions, extends several miles to the southwest, to the Nippersink, probably covering an area of about three square miles. The average depth appears to be from six to ten feet. It was stated in the seventies, that these peat beds afforded an almost inexhaustible fuel supply, stored for future ages. Peat was used for fuel in Durfee's brick and tile works at Woodstock, where it proved very successful. But from the fact that coal and wood were to be had here, but little practical attention was ever given to the use of peat. Many of the sloughs where it exists, have been drained and are today "pastures of living green," more valuable to its owner than for fuel, it is believed. Hence it will be observed that McHenry County does not possess great mineral wealth and depends largely on what its rich soil will produce, rather than from anything to be taken from beneath its surface.

CHAPTER II

INDIAN OCCUPATION

ORIGIN OF THE INDIAN

Archeologists and ethnologists differ materially with reference to the origin of the North American Indian, the Red Man. Some contend that he is the direct descendant of the two lost tribes of Israel; others that he is but the climatic development from the original man; and still others that with the scattering of mankind at the fall of the Tower of Babel, some found their way across Asia into North America at a period long antedating recorded history aside from the preserved parchments of Sacred Writ. However, no matter what is the origin, the American Indian was found on this continent when its wonders and possiblities were revealed to the Old World. By right of possession, he was the owner of this vast country, and many believe that shame will ever rest on the White Man that the Aborigine was grievously deprived of his birthright.

ILLINOIS TRIBES

The tribes found in what later became the State of Illinois, are usually grouped under the name Illini, from whence comes our name Illinois. The leading tribes in the Illini confederation were the Sac, Fox, Winnebago, Chippewa, and Pottawatomi. The latter were friendly, and gave little or no trouble to the white settlers, very friendly relations existing between the Indians and the pioneers. The government had considerable trouble with the Sac and Fox Indians, making several treaties with them, which were regarded by the ignorant savages as "mere bits of paper," something in the same manner as a once powerful nation was to later treat similar sacred obligations, without the extenuating excuse of ignorance. Black H[illegible] the [illegible] leader of the Sacs, resenting the [illegible] 18[illegible] [illegible] 1831 [illegible] [illegible] in [illegible] [illegible] W[illegible] and Black Hawk with his people [illegible] the river, [illegible] the village [illegible] Prophet's Town [illegible] ently [illegible] along [illegible] the Black Hawk War.

[illegible]K HAWK [illegible]

[illegible] R[illegible] [illegible] volun[illegible] [illegible] Br[illegible] S[illegible] W[illegible] regular army [illegible] General At[illegible] and [illegible] companies under Ma[illegible] Stillman. A[illegible] Prophet was burned, there was a small engagement [illegible] Run. There were engagements at Apple River Fort [illegible] expedition against Rock Island, the battle of Bad Axe, and finally Black Hawk was captured together with his son and the Prophet, and sent to Washington, D. C. [illegible] prisoners to Fortress M[illegible] [illegible] Black Hawk was confined until July 4, 1833, when he was set at liberty by order of the President, and together with his companions returned to Rock Island, where with impressive ceremonies they [illegible] and crossed the Mississippi River for the last time. [illegible] Black Hawk built [illegible] a white man's dwelling [illegible] Des Moines [illegible] engaging in hunting, fishing and agricultural pursuits. His death occurred October [illegible] 1838, and [illegible] six [illegible] hand [illegible] the banks of the Father of Waters [illegible] separated [illegible] the [illegible] Civil War, possibly [illegible] Iowa [illegible] of Black Hawk [illegible] years later [illegible] were [illegible] other [illegible]

Charles T. Allen

THE INDIAN IN THIS COUNTY

As McHenry County did not become a separate unit until after the Indians were finally exiled from this part of the state, as a corporate body, it had no part in the Indian troubles, nor did any of its settlers participate in the Black Hawk War, save as residents of some other section. Prior to the coming of the first permanent white settler in 1834, roving bands of Indians hunted over this territory, and camped along its streams. It is claimed that Indian traders frequently came up the Fox River with their goods which they bartered in exchange for the pelts the Indians secured from their hunts.

INFLUENCE OF THE INDIAN

As long as the nomenclature of the State of Illinois remains as it is, the Indian will not be forgotten. The beautiful Fox River recalls the powerful Fox tribe that for so many years spelled terror to the settlers in some parts of the state. Algonquin, Nippersink, Kishwaukee are also reminiscent of the days when the Red Man reigned supreme.

INDIAN MOUNDS

No one has satisfactorily explained the origin of the mounds found in various parts of the country, known as Indian Mounds. They have been given the name Indian, although relics found in them prove that they were originally built by some peoples antedating the Red Man. That the Indians used them for interment purposes, and also for storing away of implements and articles of value to them, is admitted. Some claim that these mounds were watchtowers of the tribes, from which the advance of hostile tribes could be watched. At any rate they are interesting and their value as monuments of a period in our history, would seem to suggest that they be preserved for posterity by the government.

INDIANS OF TODAY

Gone is the warrior of old. His arrows with his bow, are but curiosities to be handed down to his children as heirlooms of the past. Few of the Indians now wear their tribal garb. Many of the racial characteristics have disappeared. The younger generations have been, and are being, educated at Carlisle and other government schools. Many of the Indians are wealthy and honored members ... tal of the western states ... they are living in the grants of land from the government. In a few ... the descendants of the older time warriors will be as true Americans, different at most perhaps by ... and there are those who ... al the ... rebels in the capital at Washington, ... a dusky pioneer ... down to this day, ... the Red Man had been ... protected from the onslaught of the ... of a river ... the ... summer.

CHAPTER III

EARLY SETTLERS AND SETTLEMENTS

FRONTIERSMEN— PRIMITIVE CONDITIONS—THE NEW HOME—EARLY ROADS—
EARLY MILLS—PASTIMES—FIRST RECORDED SETTLERS—PREVENTING CLAIM
JUMPING—PIONEER CONDITIONS—OLD SETTLERS' ASSOCIATION—RE-
UNIONS—PIONEER SETTLERS.

FRONTIERSMEN

The history of each county of every state has its own distinguishing features, but there are certain facts common to all of them. Before any permanent settlements could be made, explorations had to be set on foot by those fitted by nature and training for such arduous work, and from the reports brought back by them, those seeking new homes made their decisions. The hardy frontiersmen who traveled at different periods over the fertile prairies now included in McHenry County, brought back glowing accounts of the advantages to be had in this section of Illinois territory, but owing to Indian disturbances, no permanent settlements were made here until 1834. As soon as it was found that settlers could come here with impunity, others flocked to get a title to some of the land the more foresighted saw soon would be very valuable, and the results prove that they knew their business thoroughly.

PRIMITIVE CONDITIONS

No one of this generation has any conception of the conditions prevailing when the pioneers entered what was to become one of the most important divisions of the state. At that time there were no railroads, and travel on the rivers, canals and the lakes was slow and expensive. For this reason, many preferred to load their possessions into a covered wagon, drawn either by horses or oxen, and travel across country, driving their stock before them. There were no conveniences then along the way. When night came, the hardy emigrants camped by the wayside, having to depend upon their scanty stores for food, although occasionally

27

the men folks were able to bring down birds or game of some kind. If
t___ ___ d ___ s___ l som___ ___ l so___bt a___ ___li___s___ to t___ food
s___p___ ___ ___ ___ ___s s___ ___ms ___ut ___ose w___re ___ ___ that would ___v___
___d___ ___ ___t ___r Hoover ___ ___ ___tainly food conser___ation ___ ___s practic___d ___nd
___l___ ___no ___ ___ any kind. It was a period when only t___ ___t
sur___ ___d ___ ___ th___ ___ ___s show. Many of little fir___ flame flick___red ___nd
w___ ___ ___at ___ut ___ lo___ ___ ___arn___y from th___ old home t___ the new ___nd more
than ___ne a___ed person found life too difficult, and so laid down its bur___ ___n
and made the way___ide a permanent abiding place until summon___d ___t
the last ___all upon judgment day.

THE NEW HOME

When the journey was over with all its dangers and hardship___ ___the
wagon that had been the family shelter for so many weary week___ br___g___t
to ___ standstill. and the household goods covered with a makeshift shelter
on the land sel___ted for the claim, the difficult___es had only commenced
The f___od, brought in the wagon naturally ran low, and until a crop
could be put in, the pioneers had to depend chiefly on what could be
garnered from the woods and streams. Fortunately nearly all of them
knew the value of wild growths and could find palatable and nourish-
ing foods in what their great grandchildren would consider weeds. It
was not long, of course before the energetic settlers had crops and from
them ground their own meal, and made their own products. The homes
of the pioneers were crudely fashioned from rough logs, and the furniture was homemade. Glass was a luxury, and stoves unknown. Clothing was made from cloth woven from flax and wool spun and carded
by the women and all of the stockings and sox were knit by them. The
women generally planted and took care of the gardens; they made ___ ___ ___di-
cines from berries and roots, and in the very earliest days had to minister
to and nurse the sick. The men cut down the forest growths, grubbed
out the stumps, and then plowed the land and planted the crops. They
also hunted and fished, for in those days stock was too valuable to be
killed to furnish meat. and when wild game was plentiful, the pioneers
did not suffer.

EARLY ROADS

Of course at first there were no roads of any kind, save the dim
Indian trails. As settlements increased, however, of course the pioneers

made trails of their own, as convenience or preference suggested, and in time some of these were developed into well defined roads. In the early days all travel was done on horseback or in the wagons of the periods. Carriages and buggies were unknown, and it was many years after the first settlers of McHenry County had located there before the railroads were built.

EARLY MILLS

The first settlers had to grind their own meal, but it was not long after the pioneers had assembled before one and then others, erected crude horse-mills, and later water ones by means of which a certain amount of service could be secured, although the process was tedious and the trip a long one for some who lived far distant from the nearest of these mills. Going to mill was quite a journey in those days, and the grain was carried in saddle bags on horseback, and the meal taken back in the same way.

PASTIMES

It must not be thought, however, that because there was plenty of hard work and hardships, that the pioneers failed to enjoy themselves, for they had their dancing and games, their spelling matches and singing schools, their barn and house raisings, their apple-parings and quilting bees. Whenever a religious teacher could be found, there were services either in the homes or at the log schoolhouses, and because of their scarcity, these meetings were all the more appreciated. No weather was severe enough to keep any of the pioneers away from a "preaching." They were kind-hearted, generous and sympathetic, always willing to lend a hand or listen to a tale of woe, and the advice given was generally sound and always well meant. The pioneer has passed, but his influence lives on in the lives of the community his foresight and persistent hard work established.

FIRST RECORDED SETTLERS

James Gillilan came to what is now Algonquin Township in November, 1834, bringing his family with him from West Virginia, and he was the first to locate here permanently. Mrs. Gillilan was the first white woman in McHenry County. In 1835, two settlements were made

in this county, on ... ... as The V... ... C..., ... cated in wh.t is
r... ... ... of Dorr T... ... ... a... th... Pl...sant Grov...
... ... low ... ... nt ... f Ma... ... T... ... t ... t...s ...
t... ... ... h... Ob... ... Cr...ff...n, C.l...s p... ... P...
C... t... Ru... D... ns R...a... Stoop... as ... d... B. Gal...
T... ...tl...s ... N...b...a C... w...a ... ... d... D...b...
C... ... W. k... Jos..h W. ...p, William H...man J...... G...s...
J... M...t ... and S... ...d Gill...n, all of w... ... ...1 1855.

S... aft... the ... ... ti... ... McHenry C... ... ...
in a... ... ... rapi... ra... M... came in on ... ... h... s ba... ...
horse t...ms an... ...o... with ox teams. But ... th... ... ... r... t
h...d n...t y...t made his app...aran..., each man ...ould ...nly ... s... prai...
or ...mber s...ly, ...ak... ...ut his "...laim" or pl... s aroun... ... ... ho...l a
pl... t... do w...h, put ap h...s cabin and ...sider himself at h...m... A...
cordin... t... Henry Clay the whol... mass f...rm...d "... .... ba... l...
squa...."

The human disposition b...ing the same th..., a... now, it ... ...
ne...ss...y t... pr...v...h s...m... mode ...f proving ...nd ...c...rd...g... th... ...l... ...s
as a s...urity against those disposed to "jump." Accordingly the s...t
t...rs f...rmed themselves int... an association for mutual p...t...ction, ...g...l
izing a sort of ...ourt ... cl...ims.   In pursuance of this ...j...t th...
territory was divided int... "...laim districts."

E...ch district was then subdivided into subdistricts i... ...ach, ...
wh...h three commissi...ners were appointed t... record claims and h...ar
and d...t...rmine all contests in that regard. Th...s... claims wh...n r...c...rd...d
b...came evidenc... of title. It do...s n...t appear th...t the claim ...mm...s
si...n...rs had much t... do with what is now McHenry C...unty but ... w...ll
did th...y p...rform their duty in th... Lake precincts th... but littl... tr...ubl...
aros... and what did, was ...asily and quietly adjusted. The surv...y ...f
th... land c...mprised in the county proc...eded from the Third principal
meridian ...astward reaching th... west rang... 5 in 183... and finishing Lak...
County four years later when these courts of claims b...ing no long...r
n...eded, ...eased t... exist.

Th...s... emi...rants wer... a n...ighborly set, coming as th...y s...metimes did
in strings of from six to ...ight covered wagons, the inmat...s ...f which
wer... s...eking to b...tter their ...ondition by putting t... some use the im-
m...ns... wast... ...f timb...r and prairi... stretching away ...n ...very sid... as far

as the range of human vision. The trouble of choice was increased by
the extent of unoccupied, beautiful country, still they could not wander
on forever; they must have land, water and timber the last all important
to them, as the first thing to be provided was shelter. The spot having
been selected and claim satisfactorily adjusted, they formed themselves
into a co-operative society for the purpose of house building, putting
up the first house for the one who seemed to them to stand the most in
need of shelter. Thus all in a short time were provided with such dwell-
ings as the materials at hand afforded.

PIONEER CONDITIONS

Mills, log schoolhouses and villages soon made their appearance
and if unlike in that respect, to those who in December, 1620, left the
Mayflower for the bleak coast of New England, they brought no minister with them, that necessary element of organized society, was not
long behind the forerunners of civilization, and preaching in barns,
school and private houses was done to audiences more attentive, if less
fashionable than now. These itinerant ministers found beneath every
"shake" roof a hearty welcome to the table and a no less hearty one to
the "shakedown" for the night unless the host provided with that
rarity in those days, a spare bed.

The rate of taxation for the early settlers was one percent on the
following schedule: slaves, or indentured, or registered negroes or
mulatto servants, stock in trade, horses, mules, asses, and neat cattle
above three years of age, swine, lumber, and one-horse wagons, clocks,
watches, etc., but none was levied on bank or railroad stock, piano or
silverware. The tax of 1837 for this county realized $370.86.

Among the curiosities of ancient legislation is a tavern license of
1837, costing eight dollars. So that the landlord might not swindle
his thirsty customers, the board established the following prices for
liquors: brandy, rum or gin, pints, 25 cents; wine, $37\frac{1}{2}$ cents; whisky,
$12\frac{1}{2}$; beer or cider the same meals, $37\frac{1}{2}$ cents; lodgings, $12\frac{1}{2}$ cents;
while a span of horses could chew hay all night for 25 cents.

OLD SETTLER'S ASSOCIATION

Not until 1868 was there any successful effort at organizing an old
settler's or pioneer's society in this part of the state. Indeed it is
singular that with the class of American-born people who settled this

county that such a society was not formed long before 1868. And
t   (e agin of with Lake County   The ri...d me ng w s
a. Libertyvlle, Lake County. The mmitte in arge c...ded that
th   should b held in McHenry Wednesda   S pn n s 1869, a
r ..... d the old settlers of the two counties. Th s meeting w s held
and f   the Woodstock Sentinel said the ne.. y   The lar st
ass   .. . . people at that ev r ss mbled i   cll ry Coun .
ent rly xceeding the most sanguine expectations of its originators and
ast. shm t all pres nt by the brilliantly successful man   r in which all
th   ...... me nts we re con... d and carried out.

"The officers of the meeting were: William M. Jac... pres dent;
H. N. ...... secretary; J. H. Jo...son, marsal, n   Ge rg   Gag
cra' r. Four bands of music were in attendance. The meeting was
called to order and a song, "Way Out West." very effectively sung. Hon.
George Gage delivered an eloquent oration, treating of the history and
the pioneer life of the counties of Lake and McHenry.

"At the end of the oration, the audience partook of two barbecued
oxen and other light refreshments. Toasts were offered and several
short witty and at times very pathetic speeches were made."

On October 14, 1875, the pioneers of these two counties held a
reunion at McHenry. The officers that season were: William A. Mc-
Connell, president; Charles H. Bartlett, Nelson Landing and E. Gridley,
vice presidents for Lake County; E. G. Ayer, George Gage, N. Donnelly,
vice presidents for McHenry County. J. H. Johnson was marshal and
that celebrated Illinois character, Hon. John Wentworth, "Long John,"
delivered the address. Several bands of music were present; the crowd
was large, but a rain set in and this marred the occasion. The exercises
closed with a ball at the Riverside Hotel in the evening.

No regular organization had been effected, however, until May 10
1876, when at a meeting held at McHenry village the Old Settlers
Association of McHenry and Lake counties was organized and adopted
a constitution.

The second reunion was held at McHenry, June 14, 1877.

The next meeting was held June 13, 1878, on the Fair Grounds at
Woodstock. There were fully 5,000 people present. The reunion was
opened by singing the Star Spangled Banner. Rev. R. K. Todd offered
the prayer. The address was by Joel H. Johnson, but the oration of the
day was by Hon. John F. Farnsworth. Other speakers were B. W. Raymond and Judge Morrison of Chicago. Mrs. Margaret Gillian, the first
white woman who came to this county, was present, and naturally re-

Charles R. Barnes

ceived much attention. A ball game and an evening dance concluded the exercises.

On February 26, 1880, officers were elected for the ensuing year and the reunion that season was held at Wauconda.

On September 6, 1883, the reunion was held at McHenry and was a grand success. An original poem composed for the occasion by Peter Goff, of Chicago, was presented but not read on account of the time being short.

The ninth annual reunion and picnic of the Association was held at Slausser's Park, Hainesville, August 21, 1884. Hon. L. L. Mills, State's Attorney from Cook County, was the chief speaker. Portions of his address, all so full of true sentiment, must here find space for they will interest the present-day reader of local history, even as it will those yet unborn. While it has been said that "History Repeats Itself," this is not true in the instance of pioneer life, for remember there is but one set of pioneers or first settlers in any given community, hence let us recall the beautiful words of the speaker as they fell from his lips on that hot day in August, thirty-five years ago:

"Fifty years ago this was a wilderness, without roads, except Indian trails; with forests deep and dark; with prairies of tall grass; with only jealous savages to welcome, and a cabin of logs for the home of the immigrant. Here, then, came and began this intense history of development, the young pioneer. He had journeyed from the rock-bound coast of New England, or neighboring places; his conveyance was a rude wagon; his companions, the young wife and prattling babe; his weapon of defense, the implement of his industry, the ax with the honest blade.

"Every age has its type of manhood: the ancient sculptured beauty and the philosopher; the Middle Ages painted the battles of rival countries and placed their heromaking art in the gallery of time. The hero of the nineteenth century is the pioneer. He seeks discovery all round the world. He is Livingstone in Africa, the Arctic explorer, foolish or wise in the enthusiasm of his time, facing the freezing storm to find the open sea; above all, he is the sturdy youth who cleaves the forests, wins lands waiting with fertility, builds towns and cities and creates States.

"The old settlers of Illinois are of the class whose type is the heroism of the age. They laid the foundation of the State. Their spirit and toil none ever now can know; the Western wilds of half a century ago are beyond our horizon; the Indian almost seems like a figure in a romance,

the log cabin is supplanted; the ax and the plow are minor implements compared with .... nties. The .... ods of the pio .... h .... k and s .... inspir....
.... to.

.... per .... by ..... us a th.... les.... ns. They we.. brave enough for Western wilds, persistent enough to .. k.. u and w ...... and dang.... as journey.. th...... a stra.... land a l.... st...... d....tia..n. The h.... tl.... h........si.... kn w .... limitless p.....bilities t .. the W... th.. spir... develop th.... .... l th...... .... and persist.... ....

From this beautiful pla..... .... look a..... today ...... ey..... eye is cl.... to s.. th.... grand result .... great wide-spreading farms with homes .... barns filled with cattle, and granaries .... sp.... .... harv....... the d... k w..ds made beautiful .... past ....., the s n.... l hous.... in every hamlet and the church b.......ning th.... hearts of m.... t.... higher things.

"The enjoy.... nt .... the old s....tlers is an inspiration to the young By toil and bravery and manly character they won this day and have the right to claim its triumph. To us the lesson .... that enterprise is the true spirit of the tim.... bravery the h....noring characteristi.... of the Amer ican, patient industry the foundation of his success, and the sch....l and the .... l the climax of his civilization. In the atmosph.... of this .... le bration we learn that there is no maxim higher than manhood, no .... g.... superior to industry and courage, and no success greater than a .... munity composed of men and women who love labor, erect homes, and in law and p.... are friends together under the protecting guidance .... t re ligious sentiments.

"To Lake and McHenry counties we may say your beginnings w.... made by splendid men, your woods were hewed by their industrious f.... estry, your fields were tilled and made fallow for the future by th.... toil, your schools and churches were builded by their sentiments.

"And in all the story .... this magnificent growth no fact is a greater continuation of the pioneers endeavors than the patri....ism of these coun ties. How many hundreds rushed to the defense of the flag in th.... sad days when the nation's life was threatened.... Regiments went forth from Lake and McHenry counties, and in them today there is not a graveyard where a soldier does not lie, dead from his country's battle. There is scarcely a home from Waukegan to the western limits of McHenry county that does not mourn a boy or man who died for his nation.

"Thus the spirit of the pioneer expressed itself in the heart of the patriotic son; and the sentiment of the ax and plow in the early advances of the first settlers, to make the state, was proclaimed again by the voices and sustained by the stout arms of the farmer boys who fought for and saved the nation."

PIONEER SETTLERS OF McHENRY COUNTY

From the secretary's book of the Old Settlers' Association in 1884, the subjoined list of names indicates the county's first settlers, together with the date of their coming to this county:

A. Carmack	1831	S. T. Eldridge	1838
J. H. Giddings	1832	C. O. Parsons	1838
Allen Sisson	1833	John Snowden	1839
J. W. Salisbury	1833	D. E. Barrows	1839
Richard Gillian	1834	T. J. Richards	1839
Adam Musgrove	1834	Rebecca Howard	1839
F. Diggins	1835	C. Hastings	1839
A. W. Beardsley	1835	O. W. Owen	1840
A. H. Hanley	1836	William Moore	1841
Susan Hanley	1836	C. Rhodes	1842
George Gage	1836	C. M. Pendleton	1842
Mrs. M. P. Gage	1836	Henry Drake	1843
E. A. Beers	1836	L. M. Woodard	1843
Esther M. Beers	1836	C. R. Brown	1844
Samuel H. Walker	1836	Martin Metcalf	1844
Mark Hicock	1836	Rev. R. K. Todd	1847
Mrs. B. H. Hicock	1836	Harriet Owen	1848
Job Toles	1836	C. Kuhnert	1848
Samantha Toles	1836	Wm. Hutson	1849
W. H. Huffman	1836	Peter Whitney	1849
Mary S. Huffman	1836	John M. Crane	1850
Joel H. Johnson	1836	Russell Diggins	1836
Alvin Judd	1836	T. S. Carr	1836
H. D. Judd	1836	J. M. Kimball	1837
Wm. A. McConnell	1836	J. F. Moore	1837
Neill Donnelly	1838	W. Whittemore	1837
John F. Huffman	1838	Lewis Hatch	1837
E. W. Smith	1838	S. S. Chappell	1837
E. M. Owen	1838	C. H. Tryon	1837

James B. Church 1851   Erastus Richards   ..187?
Ro...d Dic...   . ...1.ol   St.....n C... r...   ..1. ?
F t Ri 1.82

Of re... ...rs other matters seem to have ... ded m upon th.
minds and r...ous of the old pear... and wn.d ... a o .n...r annual,
at th.. old ..tlers gatio.ri..s. and no meetin., h.. . .bl.   ..
is a matt r.. .... t. many

CHAPTER IV

LAND TITLES

By George W. Lemmers

ORIGINAL OWNERS—PECULIAR INSTANCES—ORIGINAL DOCUMENTS—EARLY
DEEDS

ORIGINAL OWNERS

That the most of the land in McHenry County was originally taken
up from the government by speculators, is a statement that can easily
be verified by the records of the county. Of course there were settlers
who came here to find homes in obedience to the admonition of Horace
Greeley, "Go West, young man, go West," but the large majority who
came were either imbued with the spirit of the adventurer or those who
saw in this new Eldorado the opportunity to acquire "easy land" at little
expense.

PECULIAR INSTANCES

Again there were others who came to the county and to this then
virgin wilderness to escape the hand of the law for some trivial mal-
feasance in their old homes or to get away from matrimonial entangle-
ments that were irksome and unpleasant. An instance of this latter kind
is found in the case of William Walmsley, who came to McHenry County
sometime during the year 1845, from the State of New York, and who
purchased from the government and from individuals 600 acres of land,
said land being that now owned by Helen L. Beach in section 29, township
44, range 9 east, in the township of Nunda; that now owned by Louvain
A. Werden in the same section of the same township; that now owned by
Gilbert J. Baillergeon in section 32, of the same township; that now
owned by John Lenzen in the same section of Burton Township, now
owned by Delbert A. Whiting and Julius D. Smith in section 16, of
McHenry Township; and that owned by Frank L. Wattles in section 28

37

of the same township. Walmsley died, April 24, 1874, having in the meantime sold all said land to various persons. During all of the years that Walmsley lived in this county, near the village of McHenry, he posed and was accepted as a single man and no one ever suspected anything to the contrary, not knowing that he had ever been married; but September 7, 1874, twenty nine years after Walmsley's arrival in the county one Harty Walmsley filed bills for dower against all of the then owners of the land, claiming that she had married William Walmsley November 5, 1828, in the town of Farmington, Ontario County, N. Y., and that they had lived together several years after such marriage. She made out such a strong case that most of the parties who were sued settled with her by paying certain agreed sums of money and she gave them quit claim deeds. Two of the parties, however, dragged the cases along through court until finally Harty Walmsley, who was then seventy five years old when the cases were filed, passed away and of course her cause for action died with her, as no one could inherit her dower.

The only other thing worthy of note, or to which any romance attaches in regard to McHenry County titles is all set forth in the accompanying review of abstract sheets which affect about 4,000 acres of land in McHenry County and also in Boone and Winnebago, just over the county lines. A word painter might build quite a story around the fact that this man, William Taylor, was sent to the country from Scotland to buy land and died here after many peculiar experiences.

The language of the documents left in the recorder's office of McHenry County concerning this man is so peculiar and so expressive that it would be much more interesting to quote it in toto than for the writer to attempt to make a story of his own, and we give it literally as to spelling, punctuation, capitalization, etc. The first document bares no date of execution, but is a power-of attorney given by David Chalmers, William Littlejohn, George Yeates, Robert Catto, Peter Williamson, Alex Fonterton, Alexander Smith, Charles Chalmers, and Nathaniel Farquhar to one Alexander Ferguson to act as the agent for what was known as the North American Investment and Loan Company, of which they were the directors. The said power of attorney reads as follows:

"Whereas by a certain contract in writing, bearing date the 8th and 10th of May A. D. 1839, between (parties of the first part as named above), and William Taylor, who has since deceased, of the other part, it was agreed by and between the said parties, amongst other things, as follows: 'That the Directors of said company having engaged the said William Taylor as Manager of the Company's business in America for

the term of five years from and after the first day of June next in this
present year, the said William Taylor binds and obliges himself to proceed to the United States of America and to leave this country for that
purpose on or before the first day of June next in this present year and
to continue in the service of said Company at such places in North
America as the Directors may from time to time appoint for the period
of five full and complete years from and after that date, during
which said space the said William Taylor binds and obliges himself
faithfully and honestly to act in the capacity of Manager aforesaid in
conducting the business of the Company and in the following forth to the
best of his ability the whole objects thereof as expressed in this contract
of co-partnery, declaring that the said William Taylor shall invest the
sum of Two Thousand Pounds Sterling in the original Capital Stock of
the Said stock Company and shall subscribe the contract of co-partnery
thereof with all convenient speed, it being understood that the said
William Taylor shall be entitled to have stock of the above amount assigned to him by the Directors out of the shares reserved by the Contract
and placed at the disposal of the Directors and this without paying any
premium upon the same and further declaring that as it is in the meantime intended that the investment of the Company's funds in America
are to be made in the name of the Managers and Accountant jointly and
the survivor of them, the said William Taylor hereby binds and obliges
himself, his heirs, executors and successors, whomsoever, without prejudice to his engagement as Manager aforesaid for the above mentioned
period of five years instantly to divest himself of the whole or any part
of the Company's property when required by the Directors so to do and
to convey and transfer the same to any person or persons who may be
appointed by the Directors of the said Company that purpose and to
that end the said William Taylor hereby assigns, transfers, conveys, makes
over to and in favor of the said Company for the time being the whole
property of whatsoever description heritable and movable, real and personal, which he may afterwards acquire in North America as Manager
aforesaid; and he hereby binds and obliges himself, and his heirs and
executors to grant all necessary deeds for fully vesting such property
in the said Directors or in any person they name at any time when
required by them so to do, and further declaring that the said William
Taylor in his capacity as Manager aforesaid, shall at all times and under
all circumstances be bound to conform himself to the instructions of the
Directors in the conduct of the Company's affairs as the same shall be
notified to him through the Cashier's Agents of the Company, and further

declaring that the said William Taylor shall be bound with all convenient speed upon his arrival in America, to sell and dispose of any property which he may at present possess in that country, and that he shall not be entitled to make any fresh investments, or to enter into, or be connected with any transaction whatsoever in business in America, either in his own name or of any person or persons for his behoof and that all investments in America which shall hereafter be made in his name or in the names of any other person or persons for his behoof, shall be understood and held to have been made with the funds and for behoof of Company. And Whereas, the said William Taylor, after the execution and delivery of the said Contract in writing, and in the pursuance thereof, did proceed to the United States of America and in his capacity as Manager and Agent as aforesaid, and for behoof and on account of said Directors and with the funds of said Company, did purchase from the government of the United States sundry tracts or parcels of land, situated, lying and being in the State of Illinois, and described as follows: (Here follow lengthy descriptions of the lands referred to) "And whereas the titles to the said several tracts of land were taken by the said William Taylor in his own name and so remain of record, and whereas the said William Taylor has since departed this life; therefore this indenture made and entered into this ――― day ― ―, in the year 1844, between the said (parties of the first part as named above), of the one part and Alexander Ferguson of the other part, Witnesseth that in consideration of the premises and for the further consideration of $100.00 to the parties of the first part in hand paid by the parties of the second part, the receipt whereof they do hereby acknowledge, they, the said parties of the first part, do by these presents grant, bargain and sell, conform and convey unto the said party of the second part, all the right, title and interest and claim, legal or equitable in possession, remainder or reversion of them, the said parties of the first part in and to the several tracts or parcels of land above described and every part thereof, except to such portion of the same as may have been sold, paid for and conveyed by deed to the parties so purchasing by the said William Taylor during his lifetime. And they, the said parties of the first part, do by these presents, in virtue of the authority vested in them by the Contract aforesaid, require and direct the executors, Administrators or Heirs at law of the said William Taylor, deceased, to convey to the said Alexander Ferguson with all convenient speed, whatever title legal or equitable, they or either of them shall have acquired to said lands or any part of them from said William Taylor be devise, descent or otherwise; And to that end, they,

E. E. Bassett

Cora M. Bassett

the said parties of the first part, do by these presents constitute and appoint the said Alexander Ferguson their true and lawful agent and Attorney in fact, to demand, sue for and receive of and from the Administrators, Executors, and Heirs or other legal representatives of the said William Taylor, deceased. Hereby ratifying and fully confirming whatsoever shall be lawfully done by the said Alexander Ferguson in the premises. In testimony whereof the said parties of the first part have hereto set their hands and affixed their seals at the City of Aberdeen, in Scotland, this ——— day of -———, 1844.''

Following this comes the signatures, but none of them conform to the full given names inscribed above, the difference easily being recognized in D. Chalmers and Nathe Farquhar. This document was acknowledged December 31, 1844, before Jno. Braihie, Provost and Chief Magistrate of the City of Aberdeen, Kingdom of Great Britain (under official seal).

Then follows a conveyance by commissioner's deed which indicates that some litgiation followed the strange adventures of William Taylor in America and we quote the same as indicating the peculiar processes of those early days in Northern Illinois, as well as the peculiar phraseology that prevailed in those times:

"Deed recites that, whereas David Chalmers, William Littlejohn, George Yeats, Robert Catto, Peter Williamson, Alexander Fonlerton, Alexander Smith, Charles Chalmers and Nathan Farquhar, as Directors of the Aberdeen North American Investment and Loan Company lately, to wit: On the 8th day of February, in the year 1845, filed their bill of Complaint on the Chancery side of the said Circuit Court of Winnebago County against Isabella Taylor, George Taylor, William Primrose, and Elizabeth Primrose, his wife, George Porter and Elspet, his wife, Alexander Ferguson and the unknown heirs and devisees of James Duncan, deceased, therein setting forth, among other things, that one William Taylor, late of the City of St Louis, deceased, did in his lifetime, as the agent of the Complainant in said Bill of Complaint named, with the money and for the benefit of themselves and the said Company, but in his own name, purchase all the tracts and parcels of land hereinafter mentioned and described: That after the purchase of the said land as aforesaid, the said William Taylor died seized of the legal title of said land, but as Trustee for the said Complainant as Directors of said Company, as in said Bill mentioned, leaving as his heirs at law Isabella Taylor, George Taylor, Elizabeth Primrose, wife of William Primrose, Elspet Porter, wife of George Porter; that said William Taylor in his

life time by his last Will and Testament, devised all his real estate to
Alexander Ferguson, situate and lying . . . .
. . . .
the . . . . William Primrose and Jas. Durason and
. . . .
. . . .
. . . .
William Primrose and Elizabeth, his wife, George Porter and Elspet
his wife, Alexander Ferguson and the unknown Heirs and Devisees of
James Durason, deceased . . . .
released . . . . Alexander Ferguson
or . . . . of the persons Trustees as the said Complainants . . .
the . . . . . maintaining such decree designate in trust for the said Complainants as the Directors of the said Aberdeen North American Investment . . . . and further . . . . . as the
nature of the case might require and should be agreeable to equity as
and by said Bill of Complaint filed with the Clerk of said Court, on the
Chancery side thereof, afterwards to-wit: On the 21st day of April at
the April term of said Court in the said year 1845 such proceedings
were had to the said Court by its Decree in that behalf made fully
established the said trusts in the said William Taylor in his life . . .
and after his death in the said Isabella Taylor, George Taylor, William
Primrose and Elizabeth, his wife, George Porter and Elspet, his wife,
and the unknown Heirs and Devisees of James Durason, deceased, by
the 24th of April, aforesaid, by good and sufficient Deeds of Conveyance
to convey and release to the said Alexander Ferguson in Trust for the
said Complainants in said Bill named, all the right, title, interest, claim
or estate which they or any of them might have had in or to the premises herein mentioned and described tract of land as they were on and by
said Decree required to do, and whereas, in consequence of said . . . .
the said party of the first part hereto, was afterwards, to-wit: On the
20th day of the month of April, by a further order and decree of said
Court in that behalf and in pursuance of the Statute in cases such made
provided, appointed a Special Commission to make, seal and execute
for and in behalf of the said Isabella Taylor, William Primrose and
Elizabeth, his wife, George Porter and Elspet, his wife, and the unknown Heirs and Devisees of the said James Durason, deceased, all
such releases and conveyances as might be necessary to comply with
said Decree and to vest in the said Alexander Ferguson, all the
right, title and interest or estate of the said Isabella Taylor, Wm.

liam Primrose and Elizabeth, his wife George Porter and Elspet, his wife, and the unknown heirs and devisees of said James Duncan, deceased, or which they or either of them had or might have had to or in said hereinafter mentioned and described tracts and parcels of land as by the said Decrees remaining of record in the Office of the Clerk of said Court reference being thereto had, will more fully and at large appear.

"Now, therefore, the said party of the first part, by virtue of the power and authority granted and given to him by the said Decrees of said Court as above mentioned, in pursuance of the Statute in such cases provided, and in behalf of said Isabella Taylor, George Taylor, William Primrose and Elizabeth, his wife, George Porter and Elspet, his wife, and the unknown heirs and devisees of the said James Duncan, deceased, and for and in consideration of the sum of $1.00 to him in hand paid by the said party, granted, hath bargained sold, alien, release and convey unto the said party, to him, and to his heirs and assigns, forever, all those several tracts and parcels of land in said Bill of Complaint and in said Decree particularly mentioned and described, which are known, designated and described as follows:" (Here follows description of the following additional.)

"And also all the estate, right, title, interest, trust, property, claims and demands whatsoever, both at law and at equity in any manner whatsoever accruing of the said Isabella Taylor, George Taylor, William Primrose, Elizabeth, his wife, George Porter and Elspet, his wife, and the unknown Heirs and Devisees of James Duncan, aforesaid deceased, and of each and every of them, of, in and to, or out of said lands, premises, and hereditaments and every part and parcel thereof. Provided, however, upon the Trusts by the above mentioned Decree in the said party of the second part, fully established and declared in favor of and for the benefit of the aforesaid David Chalmers, William Littlejohn, George Yates, Robert Catto, Peter Williamson, Alexander Smith, Charles Chalmers, Nathaniel Farquhar and Alexander Fonlerton as Directors of the aforesaid Aberdeen North American Investment and Loan Company and upon such trusts as they shall from time to time direct and appoint."

From the above it can be seen that there is abundant reason for the numerous bills in chancery and bills to clear titles that thrice a year burden the columns of the newspapers of McHenry County and crowd the docket of the Circuit Court.

CHAPTER V

ORGANIZATION AND GOVERNMENT

By William Desmond

BOUNDARIES ORIGIN OF NAME—ANNEXATION TROUBLES—HISTORIC SITUA-
TION ORGANIZATION OF THE COUNTY SELECTION OF COUNTY SEAT—
POPULATION FIRST ELECTION ROAD DISTRICTS PRECINCTS PRECINCTS
REFORMED TOWNSHIP ORGANIZATION REMOVAL OF COUNTY SEAT
FIRST COURTHOUSE SECOND COURTHOUSE PRESENT COURTHOUSE PRES-
ENT JAIL POOR FARM COUNTY JUDGES SUPERINTENDENT OF SCHOOLS
— SHERIFFS COUNTY TREASURERS COUNTY CLERKS CIRCUIT CLERKS
AND RECORDERS CORONERS SURVEYORS SUPERINTENDENTS OF POOR-
STATES ATTORNEYS COUNTY COMMISSIONERS BOARD OF SUPERVISORS
NEW ASSESSMENT LAW.

BOUNDARIES

McHenry County is the second from the eastern line of the State
it is bounded on the north by Wisconsin; on the east by Lake County;
on the south by Cook, DeKalb and Kane counties; and on the west by
Boone County. It contains seventeen civil townships, the total of which
is 620 square miles.

ORIGIN OF NAME

McHenry County was named in honor of Colonel William McHenry,
who commanded a regiment during the Black Hawk War, marching
through the territory now comprising the county that bears his name
to join General Atkinson at Ft. Atkinson, Wis. This territory once
belonged to the Great Northwest Territory established in 1787, and
while Wisconsin was yet a territory itself, what is now McHenry County,
with thirteen other Illinois counties, desired to become a part of Wisconsin. The account of this affair will be given, before taking up the
real county organization and government questions

44

ANNEXATION TROUBLES

For more than a dozen years before Wisconsin was admitted into the Union of States, many of the citizens and tax-payers living in the northern part of Illinois desired to be annexed to Wisconsin, it really amounted to a movement of secession. In fact this feeling had existed many years back even to the date of Illinois being admitted into the Union in 1818. The story of this struggle forms one of the most interesting stories connected with the Commonwealth. The final adjustment is a perpetual witness to the prophetic genius of Nathaniel Pope, the territorial representative of Illinois in Congress. In the light of subsequent history it was nothing less than genius that enabled this man alone, and unchallenged to add fifty miles to the northern boundary of Illinois, and thus make her with her commercial metropolis on the lake front the keystone of the magnificent arch of great western states. As a statesman and patriot Nathaniel Pope is worthy to be placed at the head of the illustrious column which includes Lincoln, Douglas, Grant, Yates and Logan.

This movement was widespead and the feeling at times was intense, and even bitter. The war cry of "fifty-four forty or fight" did not more thoroughly arouse the enthusiastic democracy over the Oregon boundary line than did this inter-state controversy and kindle the sectional prejudices of the settlers in the disputed territory. The village of Rockford played quite a prominent part in this struggle and its influence was felt as far east as McHenry County, as now described. "There was brought to light in this city a few years ago a copy of the official proceedings of a mass-meeting held in Rockford July 6, 1840. This convention was composed of delegates from the northern fourteen counties of the state. Its purpose was secession from Illinois and annexation to the proposed new State of Wisconsin. History has never fully explained the causes of this movement. Tradition alone has interpreted its true animus. The apparent motive was a restoration of the boundary line as originally established between the two states that might be formed of the territory north of an east and west line running through the southern bend of Lake Michigan. This line, it was claimed, had been arbitrarily and unfairly extended fifty miles north when Illinois became a State." (Winnebago County History of 1884.)

The real reasons for this movement were two. First, the settlers in the northern and southern portions of the state had little or no interest in common. The northern portion was settled mostly by people from

New England and New York. They were industrious, thrifty and progressive, liberal, free and tolerant in their views. These settlers ... still very well educated, came... its ... evident and ... at ... 'ti ... generally ... as th ... of ... and ... in these days to our country's history. This class of poor people came ... others, Illinois from slave-holding states ... the limit or ... of the former poverty. Between the people of the southern and north ... portions of the state was a great gulf fixed. Each misunderstood too ther. The Illinois and Michigan canal was opposed by the people of southern Illinois for fear it would flood the state with Yank... This conflict of interest and opinion was a continuation of the ... be-tween the civilization of Plymouth and Jamestown. The Puritan and the class distinctions of the cavalier had entered the vast open arena where a few years later Lincoln and Douglas fought the hist... battle of the century

The second reason for this sectional divorcement was the desire of the northern people to escape the burden of the enormous state debt which had been created by the gigantic scheme of internal improvements. In 1840 during Governor Carlin's administration the total debt of this state was $14,666,562.42. The treasury was bankrupt; the revenue was insufficient; the people were unable to pay high taxes and the state had borrowed itself out of a good credit. The state never repudiated its debt, but simply could not pay it at that time. Again, the state had little to show for its vast expenditures. Southern Illinois dominated the state, and the people in the sparsely settled northern counties were not responsible for the creation of so great a state debt—hence naturally rebelled, and wished to be annexed to Wisconsin, where taxes were not nearly so great a burden.

HISTORIC SITUATION

In order to fully understand the position at the date of the Rockford Convention in 1840, it is best to briefly refer to the Ordinance of the Northwest Territory, as adopted in 1787. This ordinance provided for the division of this vast area for territorial purposes, which of course had no direct reference to present matters. It provided that not more than two states should be formed from the territory north of an east and west line running through the southerly bend of Lake Michigan.

The public record shows that in 1818 Illinois Territory petitioned Congress for admission into the Union on an equality with the original states. The petition defined the northern boundary of the state in accordance with the provisions of the Ordinance of 1787. When the petition came before Congress, Mr. Pope was instructed by th com mittee to report a bill in pursuance of the petition. Before the bill became a law it was amended by the extension of the boundary line from the southerly bend of Lake Michigan to 42 degrees and 30 min utes. Thus was added to Illinois a territory fifty miles from north to south, which now includes the northern fourteen counties of the State of Illinois. These radical changes were proposed and carried through both houses of Congress by Mr. Pope, entirely on his own personal responsibility. The territorial legislature had not even petitioned for them, but the great and lasting advantage was so apparent that the action of Mr. Pope received the unqualified endorsement of the people.

When Wisconsin began to aspire to statehood, it was upon the lan guage of the Ordinance of 1718, above quoted, which was declared a compact to remain in force forever unalterable, that our northern neigh bor based her claim to the territory north of the original line. This question of boundary became an issue in local politics and it was not until 1848, when Wisconsin became a state, that all the hope of the restoration of the original line was abandoned.

Let it be remembered that had it not been for Nathaniel Pope, Congressman, succeeding in getting the boundary line, as given in the old Ordinance of 1787, changed to take in these fourteen northern coun ties of Illinois, this volume would necessarily be for a county within the State of Wisconsin.

As has been well said by another historic writer: ''The beneficent results arising from the policy of Nathaniel Pope and the failure of the separatists are incalculable. No reflections are cast upon those who desired separation. They acted from worthy motives, but they failed to foresee the future. Time has shown their error to have been that of judgment rather than of heart. The people of Wisconsin, however, never fully became reconciled to the situation. From the standpoint of state pride, it may be said that in the collapse of the movement was the magnificent city of Chicago, the 'Queen of the north and west,' saved to Illinois. The most wealthy and populous, as well as progressive, counties were preserved to our own beloved Commonwealth, which has become the pride of the nation.''

Again, Mr. Pope saw that none of the states in the West could ven ture a dissolution of the Union without the assistance of a state which

ne ture had planned ... and ... be l re ... d ... wer ... Nathaniel Pope was
i ... 'a ...

On J ... ... 1 ... 1 ... ... M. Henry was ... created by
Act f ... ... as Cook County dur-
i ... t p ... ... of the counties ... L. ... Oak ... M ...
H ... ... t W M. Th ... ... the county lead as follows:

... name ..d, that all the tract of country within the following
boun lar es to wit: Be inn... at a point on Lake Michigan where th ...
te ... ... line divid... ... town ps 42 and 43 strikes said lak... and run
... ... n ... t ... ... d line to the east line of range number 4
... ... pal meridian thence north to the boundary lin ...
... St ... ... Lake Michigan, thence east along the shore
... the ... pane of beginning shall constitute a new county to be
... ed "McHenry." The population according to the census of 1920 is
5,3 6 ...

ELECTION OF COUNTY SEAT

The Legislature selected as a commission to locate a county seat to
the n ... county, M. L. Coville, of McLean County; Peter Cohen of
Will County; and Daniel Dunham, of Kane County. The locatirs
suggested were Libertyville, Half Day, McHenry, Crystal La... and
F r Hill. After taking into due consideration the advant rs of each
s th c ounf sug ... s ted, the commissioners decided, May 10 1837, upon
McHen y is being the best suited for the seat of justice as ... was that
the g raphical center of the county, as then constituted ... Ha ng
thirty congressional townships.

FIRST ELECTION

On June 1 1837, McHenry County held its first election at the
house of Hiram Kennecott, near Half Day which is now in the present
County of Lake. As a result of the election, Charles H. Bartl... Matthias Mas n Solomon Nort n were elected county commis'oners, H nr
B. Steele s cret y; Michael C McGuire coror r, Seth Washb urn ... record r, and Ch ... s E. M r surveyor.

J. V. Buckland.

ROAD DISTRICTS

The county was first divided into what were called Road Districts, this division being effected June 10, 1837 and as follows: Oak Precinct, which was that part of the Lake road commencing at line of McHenry County and extending to the north line of Oak Precinct; that part of the Lake road commencing at the north line of Oak Precinct and extending to the north line of McHenry County; that part of the road in Oak Precinct west of the north branch of the Chicago River, commencing on the south line of said county, and extending to the north line of Oak Precinct; that part of the Desplaines road leading from Chicago to Milwaukee, commencing at the south boundary line of said county, and extending to the north line of Ferry Hubbard's claim; that part of the Desplaines road commencing at the north side of Ferry Hubbard's claim and extending to the north side of Wynkoop's claim; that part of the Desplaines road commencing at the north end of Wynkoop's claim, and extending north to where said river crosses the Desplaines road; the road commencing near Washburn's on Indian Creek, and extending west to Bang's Lake; and Fox Precinct.

PRECINCTS

A further division was made in September, 1837, when the Commissioners' Court ordered, "That that tract of the country—viz.: following the south line of said county a distance of twelve miles; thence north twelve miles, thence east to a point two miles east of Fox River, thence south for two miles from the river to the place of beginning - shall constitute a general precinct and magistrate's district to be called Virginia Precinct and Magistrate's District."

On June 1, 1840, "all that part of Virginia Precinct lying north of the north line of township 43, east of Fox River, was attached to McHenry Precinct."

McHenry Precinct, which was set aside on September 4, 1837, originally had the following boundaries, according to the following order: "That the following tract of country—viz.: Commencing at a point two miles east of Fox River, thence west following the north line of the Virginia Precinct twelve miles, thence north to the state line to a point two miles of Fox River, thence south following said river to place of beginning— shall constitute a general precinct and magistrate's district to be called McHenry Precinct and Magistrate's District."

Nipersink Precinct ordered on the same date was the third precinct. The order separating it read as follows: "That the following tract of country viz.: Commencing on the north corner of McHenry Precinct at the State line, thence south following the west line of McHenry Precinct to the southwest corner, thence west to the county line, thence north to the State line, thence east along said State line to the place of beginning shall constitute a general precinct and magistrate's district, to be called Nipersink Precinct and Magistrate's District.

Under the same date, "Ordered by the court, that the following tract of country-viz.: Commencing at the southwest corner of Virginia Precinct, thence west following the south line of said county of McHenry to the west line of said county, thence north following said county to the southwest corner of Nipersink Precinct, thence east to the northwest corner of Virginia Precinct thence south to the county line to the place of beginning shall constitute a general precinct and magistrate's district to be called the Kishwaukee Precinct and Magistrate's District. "

On October 5, 1840, the Commissioners' Court ordered, That a new precinct be formed from McHenry Precinct embracing township 46, range 7, township 46, range 8, and that part of township 46, range 9, which belongs to McHenry County shall be known and designated as and by the name of Independence Precinct."

PRECINCTS REFORMED

With the influx of settlers, came a necessity for a change in the boundaries of the precincts, and on March 1, 1841, the commissioners Court ordered the following reforms:

"Independence Precinct contains township 46, range 7, township 46, range 8, and the west half of township 46, range 9.

"Nipersink Precinct contains range 6, township 46, and range 5, township 46.

"Eagle Precinct contains township 45, range 5 and two miles off from the north part of township 44, range 5."

"Hartland Precinct contains township 45, range 6, and the west half of township 45, range 7, the north half of township 44, range 6, and sections 4, 5, 6, 7, 8, 9, 16, 17, and 18 of township 44, range 7."

"McHenry Precinct contains the east half of township 45, range 7; township 45, range 8; west half of township 45, range 9, and all that part of township 44, range 9, which formerly belonged to Virginia Precinct lying on the east side of Fox River."

"Virginia Precinct contains township 44, range 8, sections 1, 2, 3, 10, 11, 12, 13, 14, 15, and also the south half of township 44, all being in township 44, range 7; and township 43, range 7; township 43, range 8; the west half of township 43, range 9.

"Kishwaukee Precinct contains the south half of township 44, range 6, and sections 13, 14, 15, 16, 17, 18, 19, 20, 21, 22, 23, 24, 25, 26, 27, 28, 29, 30, 31, 32, 33, 34, 35, 36, of township 44, range 5; township 43, range 5, and township 43, range 6."

On March 29, 1841, the Commissioners' Court ordered "That township 45, range 5, be annexed and hereafter form a part of Nepersink Precinct; and that part of township 44, range 5, which heretofore belonged to Eagle Precinct be attached to Kishwaukee Precinct; and that Eagle Precinct (formed at the March term of said court) be and is hereby extinguished from the list of precincts in McHenry County; and that the place for holding elections in Nipersink Precinct be held at the schoolhouse neat Jason N. Jerome's, in said precinct; and that Joseph Metcalf, Nathaniel Smith, and Welby Diggins, be appointed judges of election in said precinct."

Another precinct was added on March 6, 1843, by an order that provided, "That the petition of divers citizens of Independence Precinct (be granted) that the precinct heretofore known as Independence Precinct (be divided) and that a new precinct be formed with the boundaries as follows, to-wit: To consist of the whole of township 46, range 9, and four miles off from the side of township 46, range 8 east of the third principal meridian. That this precinct be known and styled as Wentworth."

On December 5, 1843, the Commissioners' Court ordered, "That a new precinct be formed off from the southeast corner of Virginia with boundaries as follows, viz: "Commencing at the southeast corner of McHenry County, running north to the line between McHenry and Lake counties to the northeast corner of section 5, on the south line of township 44, range 9; thence west six miles to the northwest corner of section 4, township 43, range 8; thence south to the Kane County line; thence east to the place of beginning. Said precinct shall be known by the name of Fox Precinct."

In June, 1844, the boundaries of Fox Precinct were changed as follows: "Commencing at the northeast corner of section 4, running thence south to the southeast corner of section 16, thence west one mile, thence

south to the county line." Under the same date, it was ordered, "That
the ——— Precinct and at ——— ———
w——— —— to ———
——— Precinct ——— ———
——— ———

On ——— 2, 1846, the Commissioners' Court ordered, "the
precinct be formed from Nipersink Precinct, with the boundaries ———
——— township 46 north ——— ———
——— part ——— and precinct ——— ———;

Another precinct was formed on the same date, under the
order, "That a new precinct be formed from the ——— Nipersink
sink Precinct consisting of township 46 north, range ——— and that
said precinct be called Alden."

On June 5, 1845, the Commissioners' Court ordered, "that township
46 north, range 7 east, and the north half of township 44 north, range
7 east, constitute a new precinct, and that said precinct be called Woodstock.

During the June term of the Commissioners' Court in 1846, Virginia
Precinct was given another name, under this order, "That the place of
holding elections in Virginia Precinct be at the house of Henry M. Wait
and S. King in said precinct, and that the name of said precinct be
changed to Cass."

On March 2, 1847, the following order was given: "On the petition
of Paschal Stowell and others Kishwaukee Precinct was divided, and
township 44 north, range 6 east, was constituted a precinct to be known
as Franklin."

On March 2, 1847, a second order is filed, towit: Denying petition
of Ellison D. Marsh and others for the formation of a new precinct to
be known as Coral Precinct.

On December 7, 1847, the Commissioners' Court ordered, "That the
petition of divers citizens residing north of the center line in township
44 north, range 8 east of the third principal meridian and west of Fox
River, asking to have that part of said township above described annexed
to McHenry Precinct be accepted."

The Commissioners' Court ordered under date of June 7, 1848, "That
township 46 north, range 5 east, be, and is hereby, constituted an election
precinct by the name of Chemung."

On June 7, 1848, the Commissioners' Court ordered, "That township
43 north, range 7 east, and the south half of township 44 north range

7 east, be, and is hereby, constituted an election precinct under the name of Grafton Precinct"

Acting on petition of John Purdy and others, on September 5, 1849, Independence Precinct was divided, and the western third of township 46, range 8 taken from Independence and attached to Kishwaukee Precinct.

TOWNSHIP ORGANIZATION

On November 6, 1849, at a general election, the people of McHenry County voted 1,943 in favor of township organization, and the Commissioners' Court therefore ordered, "That Carlisle Hastings, Phineas W. Platt and Frederick W. Smith, be, and are hereby, appointed commissioners to divide the county of McHenry into towns or townships, as is provided by the 5th section of the 1st article of the act to provide for township and county organization. Approved Feb. 12, 1849."

The results of the commissioners in dividing the county into townships are as follows: Benton, Richmond, Hebron, Alden, Chemung, Bryon, Hartland, Greenwood, McHenry, Brooklyn, Center, Seneca, Marengo, Riley, Coral, Grafton, and Algonquin. During 1850, the name of Brooklyn was changed to Nunda, Byron to Dunham, Center to Dorr, and Benton to Burton. From 1850 to the present date, the affairs of the various townships, so far as county government has been concerned, have been in capable, honest hands, for only such have been elected to the board of county supervisors. A list of all members appears at the close of this chapter.

REMOVAL OF COUNTY SEAT

A review of the records of almost any county will show that at some time in its history, agitation has arisen over the location of the county seat. Frequently, as in the case of McHenry, changes in the original boundary lines, makes the first choice undesirable because of its location. When McHenry was selected by the commissioners, as before stated, it was the geographical center of the new county, but when Lake County took all of the country east of the section line running north and south three miles east of Fox River at McHenry; in other words, two thirds of range 9 east, together with all lying east of the line mentioned, McHenry was no longer the center of the county, and dissatisfaction arose with it as

th seat of justice. ... 's objection ... felt in th early days than
it would be if th day ... ... th ... se dependent upon t...
... A ... th
... ...
... ... th
... ...
...

P... ... ...
se... to McHenry ... ... pa... ...
was passed, and approved Fe... ary, 6, 1843 author... ...
of ... ... the s... Crystal Lake, W... p's C... ...
east of Woodstock and Centerville now Woodstock. W... ... ... la...
for the seat of justice. Centerville was ch s... t... p... o... q... s...
quarter of the southwest quarter of section 5, township 44, rang 7, east
of the third principal meridian upon which the courthouse was t... b...
... ed. This selection was ratified by t... ... ll S... ember ...
1843. On account of trouble that Alvin Judd ... t a p... as up... s
claim to the land required for the seat of justice ... ... to ... t... t that
he did not reside upon the above described land in June 1843, no ... upon
it until the fall of that year, the matter had to be finally s... b... ty ...
special act of Congress, be...ab...ng Judd's claim. On December 2, 1844,
the County Commissioners' Court met for the first time at Centerville.
The name Centerville not meeting with the approval of ... m... ty ...
the people of McHenry County, an appeal was made to ... Legislat... t...
Joel H. Johnson and others to change the name t... W... st... ...
Woodstock, Vermont the old home of Mr. Johnson ... d som... this ...
low citizens, and this was ... by special act under date of Feb... y
1845. This name has since been re a... d.

In 1855, another movement was inaugurated t... ... ...
of the county seat to Algonquin Township, within on... ... ile ... t... ...
tra... cr... essing ... the Illinois and Wisconsin a... d... Fox Valley ... l
roads, and between that point and Crystal Lake in said town. Th... ...
tion was put to the people at a general election in Apr... w... h r... sult
that the vote stood, for removal, 1,048; against removal, 2,695.

FIRST COURTHOUSE.

The first courthouse of the county was built at McHen... ... the c... t
being let to William H. Beach, and was occupied f... r the first time by t...
Commissioners' Court on August 5, 1840. Several contracts o...l... t...

by the county, and canceled prior to the completion of this building, but there appears to be no definite description of it. As a new building for it and also for the housing of the prisoners, was soon deemed necessary, it doubtless was not a very imposing structure. Had it been very valuable, the public building would have been moved to Centerville.

SECOND COURTHOUSE

George C. Dean and Daniel Blair erected the second courthouse, which was accepted on September 4, 1844, for said county, and all documents of the county were ordered removed to it. This second courthouse was a plain, two-story frame building, which stood nearly in the center of the public square at Woodstock. The land on which it stood, comprising the public square, was conveyed to the county commissioners and their successors in office for the use of the county by George C. Dean on September 2, 1844. Owing to the fact that the new courthouse was utterly inadequate for the needs of the county, an additional building was erected for the use of the county officers, and it was familiarly known as the "Rat Hole." This name was applied to it after it lost the tin roof with which it was covered. This roof was blown off in a heavy wind storm, leaving the officials exposed to the inclemency of the weather. As they hurried out, a wag exclaimed, "See the rats crawl out of their holes." The name stuck as long as the building stood, although sold by the county on February 25, 1856, to Lindsay Joslyn for $723.

PRESENT COURTHOUSE

As can be easily seen, this county was too important a section of the state to remain long without proper housing of its officials, and on May 21, 1853, the board of supervisors authorized an inquiry into the probable cost of the erection of a proper courthouse and jail, appointing as a committee, C. M. Willard, A. Judd, H. T. Rice, Ira Slocumb and Daniel Stewart. Nothing definite was accomplished until September 14, 1854, when the committee reported to the board in favor of securing the passage of an act authorizing the board to levy a special tax on the assessment of the county during 1855, for the purpose of erecting a suitable courthouse, and such law was passed at the next session of the Legislature.

On May 30, 1855, Neil Donnelly, C. M. Goodsell and A. B. Coon were appointed as a special committee on securing plans and specifiections for the erect... of a joint courthouse and jail. A special tax ... ... Mary McMa... and ... ... the people of We dst... and ... ... county ... ... the tow... We ... st... ... ... be used for tw... purposes. It was later de ... ed by ...

A'f r som ... changes in plans, sealed proposals were re ... d until Jan ... y 21. 18... for the buildings, to be completed by October 1 18 7. Messrs. Donnelly, Kasson and Goodsell were the members of the building committee. George Hebard and Son, of Marengo, received the ... ... for the brick, stone mason, plasterer and stone cutter work, their price being $18,000. Russell C. Mix and James A. Hirds, of Aurora, received the contract for the carpenter, joiner, glazier and iron work, their bid also being $18,000. The entire cost of the third court-house was about $17,000, and the building was completed on time.

The third courthouse is in reality the one still in use. However, when ever it appeared too small to accommodate the needs of the county officers and the many public records, the county board of supervisors has provided additions in either direction, which has given plenty of vault room and more adequate quarters for the convenience of the judges and court same quality of material and stone trimmings, as well as roofing, have been so added that the style of architecture has been kept intact. It is a red brick structure.

JAILS

Until the present jail was erected, McHenry provided for the incarceration of its prisoners within its several courthouses, and the barred windows in the basement of the present courthouse show that at one time the cells within were used to confine those who had offended against the law. Living quarters were also set aside in the courthouse for the sheriff, but with the expansion of the county's business it was found inexpedient to continue these practices and the present jail and sheriff's residence was erected adjoining the courthouse, in 1887, at a cost of $17,-000. It was erected under the supervision of R. J. Beck, a member of the board of supervisors, who had been appointed on the building committee. As the property now stands it has increased very considerably in value owing to the numerous improvements and the increase in building costs. New steelwork for the cases was put in about 1913, and other changes have been made as needed.

McHENRY COUNTY COURT HOUSE, WOODSTOCK

POOR FARM

Until 1884, the county was without a poor farm, although it cared for its paupers from the earliest days. As early as 1859, an Act of Legislature was secured authorizing this county to set apart the necessary funds to purchase at least one hundred acres of land and erect the necessary buildings, but the measure was defeated when put before the people. Up to the securing of a farm, each township cared for its own unfortunate poor under a special act approved February 10, 1853.

In 1884 the board of county supervisors voted $25,000 for the purpose of buying the land and erecting buildings, the money to be provided by the issuance of five per cent bonds. A committee was appointed to select a farm suitable, comprised sufficient acreage to care for the pauper element. The farm of 113 acres was finally purchased for $6,000 from J. C. Allen, and is near Kishwaukee, in Hartland Township.

Proper buildings were erected on the farm and there the poor of the county have been cared for under a superintendent ever since. During the spring of 1919, the supervisors appropriated $9,000 for the building of a more roomy and modern residence on the poor farm. The contract was let June 9 to Andrew Lindquist of Marengo, with other contractors for special portions of the work.

At a special meeting of the board of supervisors held in March, 1921, the following report was made relative to the poor farm by the committee having it in charge, F. A. Walters, chairman, A. H. Hale, H. M. Turner, D. M. Wright, R. E. Haeger, Charles H. Ackman, and E. C. Hughes.

SUMMARY NO. 1

Total for year	$19,153.34
Divided as follows:	
Permanent improvements ....$ 4,579.36	
Running expenses 12,415.34	
Clothing, boots and shoes 952.48	
Tobacco 312.40	
Medicine 252.40	
Medical attendance 416.50	
Undertaking 224.80	
Total	19,153.34

Less farm products sold..... ... . $ 3,062.00
Less board of inmates 123.40

Total 3,185.40

Balance $1,967.94
Supplies on hand March 1, 1920.   2,144.00

Total $18,111.94
Less supplies on hand March 1, 1921.   2,247.73

Balance $11,284.85
Less permanent improvements 4,579.36

Total cost for one year... ..... $11,284.85

Number of weeks 1844.
Number of inmates 48.
Cost per week $6.11.

SUMMARY No. 2

Total expenses for one year............ $19,153.34
Less following items.
Permanent improvements . ... $ 4,579.36
Clothing, boots and shoes... ....   952.48
Tobacco 312.40
Medicine 252.46
Medical attendance 416.50
Undertaking 224.80
Farm products sold 3,062.00
Board of inmates 123.40

Total 9,229.40
Supplies on hand March 1, 1920..............   2,144.00

Total $11,373.94
Less supplies on hand March 1, 1921...........   2,247.43

Total cost dieting one year. .... $ 9,126.51

Number of weeks- 1841.
Number of inmates- 48.
Cost of dieting per week- $4.95.

COUNTY JUDGES

The following have served as county judges. Amory Thomas, elected in 1839; Andrew J. Barnum, 1840; Joel H. Johnson, 1841-42; E. J. Smith, 1843-48; L. Joslyn, 1848-49; Joseph Golder, 1849-54; J. M. Strode, 1854-57; T. D. Murphy, 1858-61; William Kerr, 1862-66; L. S. Church, 1867-69; B. N. Smith, 1870-82; O. H. Gilmore, 1882-90; C. H. Donnelly, 1890-97; O. H. Gilmore, 1897-1906; D. T. Smiley, 1906-20; 1920 Charles P. Barnes.

SUPERINTENDENTS OF SCHOOLS

This official from the organization of the county down to the sixties was styled "school commissioner," but since then the term "superintendent" has been used. Those who have held the offices of both commissioner and superintendent are as follows: Charles Hastings, 1841-43; Peter Dietz, 1843-45; Major T. Irwin, 1845-47; Phineas W. Platt, 1847-49; Rev. R. K. Todd, 1849-54; M. T. Hutchinson, 1854-55; Asa W. Smith, 1855-59; Alvin Brown, 1859-61; Theodore Mead, 1861 63; Thomas Ercanbrack, 1863-65; A. J. Kingman, 1865-69; G. S. Southworth, 1869-73; William Nickle, 1873-77; A. W. Young, 1877-81; D. D. Baldwin, 1881-83; H. R. Baldwin, 1883-84; Lester Barber, 1884-90; W. E. Wire, 1890-1902; Geo. W. Conn, 1902-10; A. M. Shelton, 1910-22.

SHERIFFS

Those who have held the office of sheriff since 1837 are as follows: Henry B. Steele, 1837-39; Andrew B. Cornish, 1839-40; Christopher Walkup, 1840-43; Henry M. Wait, 1843-46; Thomas M. White, 1846-49; Neill Donnelly, 1849-51; John Brink, 1851-53; Carlisle Hastings, 1853-55; G. W. Bentley 1855-57; John Eddy, 1857-58; E. E. Thomas, 1858-60; Lewis Ellsworth, 1860-62; B. F. Church, 1862-64; E. E. Thomas, 1864-66; J. M. Southworth, 1866-69; Austin Badger, 1869-73; Malachi Church, 1873-77; Daniel Stedman, 1877-81; Malachi Church, 1881-83; A. Udell, 1883-85; George Eckert, 1886-90; Asad Udell, 1890-94; George Eckert, 1894-98; Henry Keys, 1898 1902; M. M. Lake, 1902-06; Charles Wandr k, 1906-10; Andrew Hend sso , 1910 14; C arle Wandrack, 1914-1 , R d. Stewart, 191 ... sheriff ... term ... ires in 1922.

COUNTY TREASURERS

Since the organization in 1837 McHenry County's treasurers have been as follows: Andrew S Wells, 1837; Lewis G. Sm th, 18 8 39 Thomas R. Chunn, 1839 40; S. S. Greenleaf, 1840-43; Peter L. Dox, 1843-47; Joseph Golde , 1847 48; George W. Dana, 1848 49 Jam T Pierson, 1849 51; Charles McClue, 1851 53; Gilbert B. Drake, 1853 55; Abel W. Fuller, 1855-56, Samuel Richardson, 1856 58; William H r Jr. 1858-62; Fred J. Mansfield, 1863 66; Alexander S. St wart, 1867 71, James Nish, 1875-86; William H. Stewart, 1886-90; Jame B. Perry 1890 94; Henry Keyes, 1894-98; F. F. Axtell, 1898 1902; E C. Jev tt 1902 06, William S. McConnell, 1906-1910; A A Crisse, 1910 14 Lynn Richards, 1914-18; William S. McConnell, 1918 22.

COUNTY CLERKS

Hamilton Dennison, 1837; Joseph Wood, 1837 39; Ziba S. Beardsley, 1839-43; Joel S. Johnson, 1843-48; Enos W. Smith, 1848-53; Elam M. Lamb, 1853-58, William H. Stewart, 1858-61; Elam M. Lamb, 1861-65; M. D. Hoy, 1865-72; Peter Whitney 1872-82; William Avery, 1882-94; George F Rushton, 1894 1910; Guy E. Still, 1910, whose term extends until 1922, have been the county clerks of this county.

CIRCUIT CLERKS AND RECORDERS

Seth Washburn, 1837; Archimedes Burr Wynkoop, 1838 39; Isaac G. Wilson, 1839; Joel H. Johnson, 1840-56; George T. Kasson, 1856 61; Charles H. Russell, 1861-64; Joseph Dwight, 1864-68; J. M. Southworth, 1869-72; Austin Badger, 1873-76; Erastus C. Richards, 1877-88; W. P. Morse, 1888-96; George B. Richards, 1896-1904; Theodore Hamer, 1904-20; 1920, Charles F. Hayes, have served in the dual offices of circuit clerk and recorder.

CORONERS

This county's coroners have been as follows: Michael C. McGuire, 1837; A. B. Cornish, 1838-39; B. F. Bosworth, 1840-41; Nathaniel Smith,

1842-43; Neill Donnelly, 1844-45; M. L. Huffman, 1846-47; Jesse Slavin, 1848-51; William Pratt, 1852-54; C. H. Shapley, 1855-57; William G. Smith 1858-59; B. A. Wade, 1860-61; P. W. Murphy, 1862-63; David Blair, 1864-65; D. P. Conklin, 1866-74; J. W. Groesbeck 1874-76; W. E. Smith, 1876; John S. Cummings, 1877-78; Howard L. Pratt, 1878, William M. Cook, 1879-84; C. E. Cook, 1884-96; S. C. Wernham, 1896-1904; J. S. Maxon, 1904-9, and the balance of term was held by C. E. Peck, who was elected and held the office until 1920 when Dr. Emil Windmueller was elected.

SURVEYORS

The county's surveyors have been as follows: C. E. Moore, 1837; A. S. Barnam, 1838-42; John Brink, 1842-52; T. McD. Richards, 1853-56; John Brink, 1857-84; W. N. Willis. 1884-88; C. N. Tryon, 1888-1908; Lester Barber, 1908-12; G. L. Tryon, 1912 to the present time.

SUPERINTENDENTS OF POOR

Since the county has had a poor farm on which to care for the unfortunate poor, the superintendents have been as follows: N. S. Robb, 1884-95; Homer Brown, 1895-1902; George R. Mills, 1902-13; Gardner Knapp, 1913 to the present time.

STATES ATTORNEYS

Alonzo Huntington, 1837-40; Edward G. Regan, 1840-43; James Curtiss, 1843-44; William A. Boardman, 1845-49; Alonzo Platt, 1850-51; Amos B. Coon, 1852; M. M. Boyce, 1853-57; Edward S. Joslyn, 1857-61; Amos B. Coon, 1861-63; M. M. Boyce, 1864-69; Charles Kellum, 1870-73; Joseph P. Cheever, 1873-76; Ira R. Curtiss, 1877-84; A. B. Coon, 1884-96; V. S. Lumley, 1896-1900; L. D. Lowell, 1900-08; David R. Joslyn, 1908-16; V. S. Lumley, 1916 to the present time.

COUNTY COMMISSIONERS

From 1837 until the adoption of the township system in 1850, the following men served as members of the Commissioners' Court: 1837—Charles H. Bartlett, Matthias Mason, Solomon Norton, Samuel Sherman; 1838—Solomon Norton, Ransom Steele, William Jackson, B. B. Brown,

Gibson Colby, Robert G. White; 1839—B. B. Brown, R. G. White, D. W. P. Tower; 1840—B. B. Brown, R. G. White, Daniel W. P. Tower; 1841 R. G. White, D. W. P. Tower, H. B. Throop; 1842 D. W. P. Tower, H. B. Throop; 1843 H. B. Throop, B. H. Tryon, Andrew Hayward 1844 Same as 1843, 1843 H. B. Throop, A. J. Hayward William A. McConnell 1846 H. B. Throop, W. G. A. McConnell, Carlisle Hastings; 1847 W. D. A. McConnell, Carlisle Hastings, Dexter Barrows, 1848 Same as in 1847.

After the abolishment of the County Commissioner Court came the present supervisor system whereon each civil township in the county is represented on what is termed the "Board of county supervisors." The men holding such position since the system commenced in 1850 have been: 1850 James C. Thompson, Chemung; Cyrus Allen, Byron. Amos D. Coon, Marengo; Ira E. Searles, Riley; Calvin Pike, Seneca; Olonzo Golder, Hartland; Andrew Easton, Alden; Josiah H. Giddings (chairman), Hebron; Joseph N. Barber, Greenwood; Elzaphan J. Smith, Centre; Elias A. Thomas, Algonquin; William Salisbury, Brooklyn, Charles H. Russell, Richmond; Sylvanus Stillson, Benton; Charles Crego, Coral; Thomas S. Huntley, Grafton; Alex H. Nixon, McHenry

1851 Cyrus Allen, Dunham; Horace Burton, Nunda; Amos B. Coon, Marengo; John Freeman, Alden; Alonzo Golder, Hartland; Oliver H. P. Gookin, Hebron; William Hart, Jr. Chemung; Pliny Hayward, Greenwood; U. T. Hyde, Seneca; Merrit L. Joslyn, Dorr; Darius Kingsley, Burton. Alpheus Kenny, Grafton; Abraham Reynolds chairman Mc Henry; Charles H. Russell, Richmond; Ira A. Searles, Riley; Elias A. Thomas, Algonquin; James M. White, Coral.

1852 Cyrus Allen, Dunham; Horace Burton, Nunda; N. M. Capron, Alden; Wesley Diggins, Chemung; Pliny Hayward, Greenwood; Alvin Judd, Woodstock; Darius Kingsley, Burton; Joseph F. Lyon, Dorr; Myron P. Potter, Algonquin; Abraham Reynolds chairman, McHenry; Henry T. Rice, Hartland; Sam. Richardson, Riley Thomas McD. Richards, Seneca; Daniel Stewart, Marengo; Charles H. Tryon, Hebron; S. T Thompson, Grafton.

1853 Jesse Fellows, Riley; Daniel Stewart, Marengo; H. C. Chandler, Dunham; Wesley Diggins, Chemung; Andrew Easton, Alden; Henry T. Rice, Hartland; T. McD. Richards, Seneca; Anson Rodgers, Coral; W. S Robb, Grafton; O. A. Hitchcock, Dorr; A. Judd chairman,

Woodstock; Ira Slocumb, Greenwood; A. Coggswell, Hebron; John Sibley, Richmond; Alfred Stephens Burton; A. H. Nixon, McHenry; E. M. Lamb, Nunda; J. F. Miller, Algonquin.

1854 Joseph Patterson, Riley; Henry C. Chandler, Dunham; Newton M. Capron, Alden; John Eddy, Coral; George H. Griffin, Dorr; Charles M. Goodsell, Greenwood; William A. McConnell (chairman), Richmond; A. H. Nixson, McHenry; Alexander Keeler, Marengo; C. R. Brown, Chemung; George T. Kasson, Seneca; Sanford Haight, Grafton; Enos W. Smith, Woodstock; Charles H. Tryon, Hebron; John Sanborn, Burton; J. R. Mack, Nunda, Henry T. Rice, Hartland.

1855- Samual Richardson, Riley; Amos B. Coon, Marengo; J. Wells, Dunham; C. R. Brown, Chemung; Stephen Alberty, Alden; Henry T. Rice, Hartland; George T. Kasson, Seneca; Anson Rodgers, Coral; Chauncey Pendleton, Grafton; Nathan Jewett, Dorr; Neill Donnelly, Woodstock; Charles M. Goodsell, Greenwood; William H. Stewart, Hebron; John Sibley (chairman), Richmond; John Sanborn, Burton; P. E. Cassidy, McHenry; William Salisbury, Nunda; Warren Stannard, Algonquin.

1856- -Samuel Richardson (chairman), Riley; Jonathan Wells, Dunham; A. B. Stark, Alden; U. T. Hyde, Seneca; Charles Hubbard, Grafton; Charles M. Goodsell, Greenwood; John Sibley, Richmond; John W. Smith, McHenry; Jesse F. Miller, Algonquin; William Edwards, Marengo; Wesley Diggins, Chemung; Mr. McFarland, Hartland; John Eddy, Coral; Charles M. Willard, Dorr; Josiah H. Giddings, Hebron; John Sanborn, Burton; J. Butler, Nunda; Neill Donnelly, Woodstock.

1857 -Samuel Richardson, Riley; Peter W. Deitz, Marengo; John Wells, Dunham; Mr. Hutchinson, Chemung; Aaron D. Stark, Alden, died Feb. 3, 1858; Andrew Hood, Hartland; U. T. Hyde, Seneca; James M. White, Coral; E. P. Hayden, Grafton; M. W. Hunt, Dorr; M. B. Baldwin, Woodstock; Stephen G. Brittain, Greenwood; Josiah Giddings, Hebron; John Sibley (chairman), Richmond; Richard Wray, Burton; Richard Bishop, McHenry; James McMillen, Nunda; Jesse F. Miller, Algonquin.

1858—M. Butterfield, Riley; Peter W. Deitz, Marengo; George Hebbard, Marengo village; Cyrus Allen, Dunham; Thomas Paul, Chemung; Stephen Alberty, Alden; Andrew Hood, Hartland; Garrett W. Deitz, Seneca; William M. Jackson (chairman), Coral; Thomas S. Huntley, Grafton; William H. Murphy, Dorr; M. W. Hunt, Woodstock; S. G. Brittain, Greenwood; Alphonso Tyler, Hebron; C. H. Russell, Rich-

rond; Richard Wray, Burton; Ri ard Bishop McHenry; C. W. Huʳ,
N ; J F. Miller, Algonquin

  1 M. But to Ri A. B. C s, Marengo; C. Lansi
 , Mar Br ; C s Allen Durham w B. McArt
C Stephen Alberty Alden; An H d Ho an C. W
D a; William Noble Coral Adams Hart Ga ; M W
Hu W stock Pas A De r; H. Burt n p J H.
Geldings, Hebron. A. P. Wells Richmond; Lewis Hat Burt A C
Th ps n G en d; Ric d Bi q McHenry, C W Hu Nunda
E A T nas, Algonquin.

  1860 A. B. Coon, Marengo; C Lansing hairman, Mar g vil
la D Barrows. Dunham W. B. McArt r, Chemung S. Albe
Alde , A Hood, Hartland; O. Turn r Seneca; S. R. Bartholom w,
Coral, Mr. Cummings. unspecified; I. Slocum Greenwood N ill Don
nelly Woodstock; Mr. Thompson; Mr. Mead Hebron; A P. Wells
Richmond; Lewis Hatch, Burton; Richard Bishop, McHenry; E. M.
Lamb, Nunda; Mr. Kluk, Algonquin; M. Butterfield, Riley

  1861 H. Underwood, Riley, A. B. Coon, Marengo; Ces Lansing
(chairman), Marengo village; D. Barrows, Dunham; W. B. McArthur,
Chemung; S. Alberty Alden; D. Sculley, Hartland; Mr. Parsons. Sen
eca; J. G Templeton, Grafton; I. Slocum, unspecified; M. L. Joslyn,
Dorr; J. Eckert, Greenwood; A. P. Wells, Richmond; E. M. Lamb,
Nunda , James Nish, Algonquin; Richard Bishop, McHenry; S. R. Bar
tholomew, Coral.

  1862 H. Underwood, Riley; A. B. Coon, Marengo; Dexter Bar
rows. Dunham; W. B. McArthur, Chemung; Stephen Alberty, Alden;
D. Sculley, Hartland; Mr. Parsons. Seneca; C. W. H. Card chairman
Grafton; Ira Slocum, Greenwood; J. G. Templeton. unspecified; J
Eckert. unspecified; Mr. Hopkins. unspecified; A. P. Wells, Richmond;
Richard Bishop. McHenry; Mr. Buck, unspecified; James Nish, Algon
quin; M. L. Joslyn, Dorr; Ces Lansing. Marengo village; A. S. Hanchet,
Woodstock.

  1863 W. O. Nichols, Riley; Peter W. Deitz, Marengo; B. A. Wade,
Dunham, T. B. Wakeman. Chemung; Stephen Alberty. Alden; Andrew
Hood, Hartland; Uriah T. Hyde, Seneca; Daniel C. Thomas, Coral;
T. S. Huntley (chairman), Grafton; M. L. Joslyn, Dorr; Jacob Eckert,
Greenwood; C. S. Adams, Hebron; Alfred P. Wells, Richmond; Lewis
Hatch. Burton; Richard Bishop, McHenry; Josiah Walkup. Nunda;
E. A. Thomas. Algonquin; William Kerr. Woodstock; E. G. Hackley,
Marengo village.

THOMAS BURNSIDE

MRS. THOMAS BURNSIDE

1864—S. R. Bartholomew, Coral; Stephen Burton, Grafton; Richard Wray, Burton; M. L. Joslyn, Dorr; Harrison C. Smith, McHenry; Henry Underwood, Riley; Peter W. Weitz, Marengo; Dexter Barrows, Dunham; Charles R. Brown, Chemung; Stephen Alberty, Alden; Andrew Hood, Hartland; Thomas M. Hood, Seneca; Geo. H. Garrison, Greenwood; Charles S. Adams, Hebron; James Robbins, Richmond; Francis Harrison, Nunda; E. A. Thomas (chairman), Algonquin; William Kerr, Woodstock; W. H. Messick, Marengo village.

1865—Henry Underwood, Riley; Peter W. Deitz (chairman), Marengo; Dexter Barrows, Dunham; T. B. Wakeman, Chemung; Stephen Alberty, Alden; Andrew Hood, Hartland; L. W. Sheldon, Seneca; S. K. Bartholomew, Coral; Stephen Burton, Grafton; M. L. Joslyn, Dorr; George H. Garrison, Greenwood; Charles S. Adams, Hebron; A. P. Wells, Richmond; Frank Cole, Burton; Richard Bishop, McHenry; F. D. Patterson, Nunda; J. F. Miller, Algonquin; William Kerr, Woodstock; G. B. Adams, Marengo village.

1866—Edward H. Skinner, Riley; Peter W. Deitz, Marengo; Cyrus Allen, Dunham; T. B. Wakeman, Chemung; Stephen Alberty Alden; Andrew Hood, Hartland; T. Bigelow, Seneca; S. W. Bartholomew (chairman), Coral; Elias Wanzer, Grafton; William Kerr, Dorr; Geo. H. Garrison, Greenwood; Charles S. Adams, Hebron; Alfred P. Wells, Richmond; Richard Wray, Burton; Richard Bishop, McHenry; F. D. Patterson, Nunda; James Crow, Algonquin; L. S. Church, Woodstock; G. B. Adams, Marengo village.

1867—E. H. Skinner, Riley; Peter W. Deitz, Marengo; Cyrus Allen, Dunham; J. C. Crumb, Chemung; Stephen Alberty, Alden; Andrew Hood, Hartland; T. Bigelow, Seneca; S. K. Bartholomew, Coral; Elias Wanzer, Grafton; Elam M. Lamb, Dorr; G. H. Garrison, Greenwood; Charles S. Adams, Hebron; W. A. McConnell (chairman), Richmond; Robert Richardson, Burton; Richard Bishop, McHenry; F. D. Patterson, Nunda; John Gillilan, Algonquin; E. M. Lamb, Woodstock; G. B. Adams, Marengo village.

1868—E. H. Skinner, Riley; Peter W. Deitz, Marengo; Dexter Barrows, Dunham; J. C. Crumb, Chemung; Andrew Hood, Hartland; T. McD. Richards, Seneca; D. C. Thomas, Coral; Elias Wanzer, Grafton; M. L. Joslyn, Dorr; George H. Garrison, Greenwood; Charles S. Adams, Hebron; William A. McConnell (chairman), Richmond; Robert Richardson, Burton; F. J. Wheaton, Nunda; John Gillilan, Algonquin; B. N. Smith, Woodstock; J. H. Bagley, Marengo village; E. G. Ayer, Harvard.

1869—E. H. Skinner, Riley; Alexander D. Stewart, Marengo; Dex-

ter Barrows, Dunham; J. C. Crumb, Chemung: Andrew Hood, Hartland; L. W. S... n, Seneca; S. K. Bartholomew Coral; C. W. H.
C.d, G. ton; M. L. J. .ys, Dorr; Ge... H. Gar'.. Gre..w..d:
Charles S. Adam., Hebron; William A. McCon.ll ... man Ri...
m..d L... Hat... Burton David Sol..., McHen..., J... W.
kup. Nund.; Jam.. Nish Algonquin. M. D. Hc.. W.. iste... J. C.
Crumb, Harvard; G. B. Adams, Marengo village

1870 W. H. G..esb..k Alden; R. D. C... y Hartland Coral;
O. Par..s, S..ca S. K. Bartholomew Co.. Thomas S. Huntley
Grafton Mer..d L. Joslyn, Dorr; George H. Garrison, Greenwood Sam
W. Br..wn, Hebron; William A. McConnell chairman., Ri.... d
Robert Richardson Burton; F. K. Granger McHenry; James M. M. I
len Nunda; James Crow, Algonquin; H. Underwood, Riley; A. D.
Stewart Marengo; G. B. Adams Marengo village; J. A. West Dun-
ham R. Gardner, Harvard; E. E. Richards Woodstock.

1871 William H. Groesbeck, Alden; R. D. Cooney, Hartland; C. O.
Parsons, Seneca; S. K. Bartholomew Coral; T. S. Huntley, Grafton;
M. L. Joslyn, Dorr; George H. Garrison, Greenwood; S. W. Brown
Hebron; W. A. McConnell chairman Richmond; Robert Richardson,
Burton; F. K. Granger, McHenry; J. McMillen, Nunda; James Nish,
Algonquin; H. Underwood, Riley; A. D. Stewart Marengo; Seth Lewis,
Marengo village; O. C. Diggins, Dunham; J. C. Crumb, Chemung; R.
Gardner, Harvard; E. E. Richards Woodstock.

1872 Henry Underwood, Riley; A. D. Stewart. Marengo; Orson
C. Diggins, Dunham; J. C. Crumb, Chemung; William H. Groesbeck,
Alden; R. D. Cooney, Hartland; Thomas McD. Richards, Seneca; S. K.
Bartholomew. Coral; James G. Templeton, Grafton; M. L. Joslyn, Dorr;
George H. Garrison, Greenwood; Sam W. Brown, Hebron; William A.
McConnell chairman., Richmond. Lewis Hatch, Burton; F. R. Granger,
McHenry; Amos D. Whiting. Nunda; M. Butterfield, Marengo village;
L. H. Davis, Woodstock; A. E. Blake, Harvard.

1873 Lewis Hatch, Burton; Z. E. Goodrich, Marengo; O. C. Dig-
gins, Dunham; Robert Gardner, Chemung, R. O. Southmayd, Alden;
Rodderick B. Cooney, Hartland; Charles O. Parsons Seneca; S. K.
Bartholomew, Coral; James G. Templeton. Grafton; Elam M. Lamb,
Dorr; Henry Eckert Greenwood; Charles S. Adams, Hebron; William
A. McConnell (chairman., Richmond; Lewis Hatch, Burton; J. W.
Christy, McHenry; Albert H. Colby, Nunda; Edwin H. Benson, Algon-
quin; M. Butterfield, village; unspecified, H. W. Axtel, J. S. Wheat.

1874 H. N. Axtel, Riley; Z. E. Goodrich, Marengo; O. C. Diggins,

Dunham; James Thompson, Chemung; R. O. Southmayd, Alden; R. D. Cooney, Hartland, Orsamus Turner, Seneca; S. K. Bartholomew, Coral; George Van Valkenburg, Grafton; Elam M. Lamb, Dorr; George H. Garrison, Greenwood; Sam W. Brown, Hebron; William A. McConnell chairman, Richmond; J. H. Cooley, Burton; J. W. Cristy, McHenry; B. F. Peck, Nunda; Edwin H. Benson, Algonquin; unspecified, Henry Baker, M. Butterfield.

1875 Ira E. Searles, Riley; Z. E. Goodrich, Marengo, O. C. Diggins, Dunham; James Thompson, Chemung; R. O. Southmayd, Alden R. D. Cooney, Hartland; C. O. Parsons, Seneca; S. K. Bartholomew, Coral; George Van Valkenburg, Grafton; M. L. Joslyn, Dorr; G. H. Garrison, Greenwood; S. W. Brown, Hebron; William A. McConnell chairman, Richmond; Jos. H. Cooley, Burton; J. W. Cristy McHenry; D. F. Peck, Nunda; James Nish, Algonquin; unspecified, S. S Crandall, Henry Baker.

1876 Ira E. Searles Riley; Z. E. Goodrich, Marengo; O. C. Diggins chairman, Dunham; James Thompson, Chemung; R. O. Southmayd, Alden; R. D. Cooney, Hartland; Charles O. Parsons, Seneca; Calvin Gilbert, Coral; D. E. Wood, Grafton; M. L. Joslyn, Dorr; George H. Garrison, Greenwood; Sam W. Brown, Hebron; Marcus Foote, Richmond; Joseph H. Cooley, Burton; John M. Smith, McHenry; B. F Peck, Nunda; C. F. Dike, Algonquin; unspecified, R. M. Patrick.

1877 Ira E. Searles, Riley; Z. E. Goodrich, Marengo; O. C. Diggins chairman, Dunham; James Thompson, Chemung; Sam Cutter, Alden, R. D. Cooney, Hartland; C. O. Parsons, Seneca; Lester Barber, Coral; George Van Valkenburg, Grafton; M. L. Joslyn, Dorr; George H. Garrison, Greenwood; Alfred Wilcox, Hebron; Marcus Foote, Richmond; Robert Richardson, Burton; J. W. Christy, McHenry; B. F. Peck, Nunda; John Gillilan, Algonquin; unspecified, R. M. Patrick.

1878 Henry Underwood, Riley; Thomas W. Porter, Marengo; O. C. Diggins Dunham; James Thompson, Chemung; Sam Cutter, Alden William Conklin, Hartland; C. O. Parsons, Seneca; Lester Barber, Coral; John S. Cummings, Grafton; M. L. Joslyn, Dorr; George H. Garrison, Greenwood; A. Wilcox, Hebron; W. A. McConnell (chairman, Richmond; Chauney Sweet, Burton; J. W. Cristy, McHenry; B. F. Peck, Nunda; G. S. Frary, Algonquin; unspecified, G. B. Adams. A. E. Axtell, Alfred Wilcox.

1879—Henry Underwood, Riley; Z. E. Goodrich, Marengo; O. E. Diggins, Dunham; James Thompson, Chemung; Samuel Cutter, Alden; William G. Conklin, Hartland; C. O. Parsons, Seneca; Lester Barber,

Coral; John S. Cummings, Grafton; Elam M. Lamb, Dorr; G. H. Garrison, Greenwood; Amos Wires, Hebron; W. A. McConnell chairman, Richmond; Chauncey Scott, Burton; J. W. Cristy, McHenry; B. F. Peck, Nunda; G. F. Frary, Algonquin; unspecified, R. Curtis, A. E. Axtell.

1880 H. Underwood, Riley; Z. E. Goodrich, Marengo; O. C. Duggins, Dunham; James Thompson, Chemung; Samuel Cutter, Alden; William G. Conklin, Hartland; G. W. Goodrich, Seneca; Lester Barber, Coral; William G. Sawyer, Grafton; Elam M. Lamb, Dorr; G. H. Garrison, Greenwood; Alfred Wilcox, Hebron; W. A. McConnell chairman, Richmond; Lewis Hatch, Burton; J. W. Cristy, McHenry; B. F. Peck, Nunda; G. S. Frary, Algonquin; unspecified T. R. Curtis, B. A. Wade.

1881 Amory Barber, Riley; Z. E. Goodrich, Marengo; John Snowden, Dunham; H. S. Williams, Chemung; Samuel Cutter, Alden; Daniel Flavin, Hartland; G. W. Goodrich, Seneca; Lester Barber, Coral; William G. Sawyer, Grafton; Elam M. Lamb, Dorr; George H. Garrison, Greenwood; Alfred Wilcox, Hebron; William A. McConnell chairman, Richmond; Charles Mead, Burton; J. W. Cristy, McHenry; Henry Keller, Nunda; G. S. Frary, Algonquin; unspecified, I. R. Curtis.

1882 Amory Barber, Riley; Z. E. Goodrich, Marengo; John Snowden, Dunham; H. S. Williams, Chemung; Sam Cutter, Alden; D. H. Flavin, Hartland; G. W. Goodrich, Seneca; Lester Barber, Coral; W. G. Sawyer, Grafton; Elam M. Lamb, Dorr; George H. Garrison, Greenwood; H. W. Mead, Hebron; W. A. McConnell chairman, Richmond; Fred Hatch, Burton; Joseph W. Cristy, McHenry; Harry Keller, Nunda; G. S. Frary, Algonquin; unspecified, I. R. Curtis, Owen McGee.

1883 John Hadsall, Riley; Ira R. Curtiss chairman, Marengo; John Snowden, Dunham; H. S. Williams, Chemung; W. H. Groesbeck, Alden; D. H. Flavin, Hartland; G. W. Goodrich, Seneca; Lester Barber, Coral; W. G. Sawyer, Grafton; Elam M. Lamb, Dorr; G. H. Garrison, Greenwood; H. W. Mead, Hebron; A. R. Alexander, Richmond; Archdale Wray, Burton; Richard Bishop, McHenry; William Butler, Nunda; C. F. Dike, Algonquin; unspecified, B. S. Parker.

1884 John Hadsall, Riley; Ira R. Curtiss chairman, Marengo; John Snowden, Dunham; H. S. Williams, Chemung; W. H. Groesbeck, Alden; D. H. Flavin, Hartland; G. W. Goodrich, Seneca; Lester Barber, Coral; W. G. Sawyer, Grafton; Elam M. Lamb, Dorr; George H. Garrison, Greenwood; H. W. Mead, Hebron; A. R. Alexander, Richmond; Fred Hatch, Burton; Richard Bishop, McHenry; J. H. Palmer, Nunda; C. F. Dike, Algonquin.

1885 Amory Barber, Riley; Ira Curtiss Marengo; R. J. Beck, Dunham H. S. Williams Chemung; W. H. Groesbeck Alden; Daniel H. Flavin Hartland; G. B. Richards, Seneca; Z. E. Goodrich, Coral; W. G. Sawyer Grafton; Elam M. Lamb, Dorr; George H. Garrison, Greenwood. H. W. Mead, Hebron; A. R. Alexander, Richmond; Fred Hatch, Burton; F. K. Granger, McHenry; J. H. Palmer, Nunda; C. F. Dike, Algonquin.

1886—Amery Barber, Riley; R. M. Patrick, Marengo; A. J. Shurtleff chairman, Village of Marengo; R. J. Beck, Dunham; H. S. Williams, Chemung; M. W. Lake, Harvard village; Samuel Cutter, Alden; Daniel H. Flavin, Hartland; George B. Richards, Seneca; Z. E. Goodrich, Coral; W. G. Sawyer, Grafton; Elam M. Lamb, Dorr; George H. Garrison, Greenwood; H. W. Mead, Hebron; A. R. Alexander, Richmond; Fred Hatch, Burton; F. K. Granger, McHenry; J. H. Palmer, Nunda; C. F. Dike, Algonquin.

1887- John Hadsall, Riley; A. B. Coon, Marengo; Loren Woodard chairman, Village Marengo; R. J. Beck, Dunham; H. S. Williams, Chemung; M. W. Lake, Harvard; Sam Cutter, Alden; D. H. Flavin, Hartland; G. B. Richards, Seneca; T. E. Stevens, Coral; John Weltzein, Grafton; Elam M. Lamb, Dorr; George H. Harrison, Greenwood; Henry W. Mead, Hebron; A. R. Alexander, Richmond; Fred Hatch, Burton; F. K. Granger, McHenry; John H. Palmer, Nunda; C. F. Dike, Algonquin.

1888- John Hadsall, Riley; A. B. Coon, Marengo; Loren Woodard, Village of Marengo; R. J. Beck, Dunham; H. B. Williams, Chemung; M. W. Lake, Harvard Village; W. H. Groesbeck, Alden; Daniel H. Flavin, Hartland; G. B. Richards, Seneca; F. E. Stevens, Coral; John Weltzein, Grafton; Elam M. Lamb, Dorr; Samuel E. Clark, Greenwood; G. W. Coon, Hebron; Fred Hatch, Burton; F. K. Granger, McHenry; John Gracy, Algonquin.

1889- Amory Barber, Riley; A. J. Shurtleff, Marengo; Loren Woodard, Village Marengo; R. J. Beck, Dunham; H. S. Williams, Chemung; William H. Groesbeck, Alden; Daniel H. Flavin, Hartland; George B. Richards, Seneca; F. E. Stevens, Coral; John Weltzein, Grafton; L. T. Hoy, Dorr; Erastus Richards, City Woodstock; Samuel E. Clark, Greenwood; G. W. Conn, Hebron; A. R. Alexander, Richmond; L. W. Howe, Village Richmond; Fred Hatch, Burton; F. K. Granger, McHenry;

J. H. Gracy, Nunda; Lafe Benthusen, Village Nunda; W. P. Thompson, Algonquin.

1890 Amory Barber, Riley C. P. Wright Marengo; Loren Woodard, Corporation of Marengo; R. J. Beck Dunham; H. S Williams Chemung; M. W. Lake, Corporation of Harvard; W. H. Groesbeck Alden; Daniel H. Flavin, Hartland; G. B. Richards, Seneca; F. E. Stevens, Coral; John Weltzein, Huntley; L. T. Hoy Dorr, Erastus Richards, Corporation of Woodstock; George H. Garrison, Greenwood; G. W. Conn, Hebron; A. R. Alexander, Richmond; Fred Hatch, Burton; F. K. Granger, McHenry; J. H. Gracy, Nunda; W. P. Thompson, Algonquin.

1891— Amory Barber, Riley; C. P. Wright, Marengo; R. M. Patrick, Corporation of Marengo; R. J. Beck, Dunham; H. S. Williams Chemung; W. H. Groesbeck, Alden; William Desmond, Hartland; G. B. Richards Seneca; F. E. Stevens, Coral; John Wiltzein, Grafton; L. T. Hoy, Dorr; George H. Garrison, Greenwood; G. W. Conn, Hebron; A. R. Alexander, Richmond; A. B. Stevens, Burton; F K. Granger, McHenry; J. H. Gracy, Nunda; W. P. Thompson, Algonquin.

1892- Amory Barber, Riley; C. P. Wright, Marengo; S. K Bartholomew, Corporation of Marengo; R. J. Black, Dunham; F F. Axtell, Chemung; W. H. Groesbeck, Alden; William Desmond, Hartland; George B. Richards, Seneca; F. E. Stevens, Coral; John Wiltbzein, Grafton; L. F. Hoy, Dorr; S. E. Clark, Greenwood; G. W. Conn, Hebron; George McConnell, Richmond; B. A. Stevens, Burton; F K. Granger, McHenry; J. H. Gracy, Nunda; W. H. Thompson, Algonquin.

1893- Nathan Brotzman, Riley; C. P. Wright Marengo, E. D. Shurtleff, Corporation of Marengo; R. J. Beck, Dunham; F. F Axtell, Chemung; George Ruston, Alden; William Desmond, Hartland; G. B. Richards, Seneca; F. E. Stevens, Coral; John Weltzein, Grafton, L. T. Hoy, Dorr; S. E. Clark, Greenwood; G. W. Conn, Hebron; George McConnell, Richmond; J. N. Burton, Corporation of Richmond; A. M. Wray, Burton; William Cristy, McHenry; J. H. Gracy, Nunda; W. P. Thompson, Algonquin.

1894 D. A. Seamor, Riley; C. P. Wright, Marengo; A. R. Thompson, Dunham; F. F. Axtell, Chemung; J. N. Woodbury, Alden; William Desmond, Hartland; F. E. Stevens, Coral; John Weltzein, Grafton; S. E. Clark, Greenwood; George McConnell, Richmond; J. H. Gracy, Nunda. In 1895 the practice was adopted and continued of electing the supervisors for a period of two years so that from that date on one-half of the board was composed of newly elected members each year.

1895-96—N. Brotzman, Riley; Robert J. Beck, Dunham; W. D. Cornue, Alden; George B. Richards, Seneca; L. T. Hoy, Dorr; H. F. Jones, Hebron; A. M. Wray, Burton; W. A. Cristy, McHenry; W. P. Thompson, Algonquin; E. D. Shurtleff, Marengo; William Desmond, Hartland; F. E. Stevens, Coral; John Weltzein, Grafton; S. E. Clark, Greenwood; George W. McConnell, Richmond; J. H. Gracy, Nunda.

1897-98—N. Brotzman, Riley; R. J. Beck, Dunham; W. D. Cornue, Alden; J. S. Mills, Seneca; L. T. Hoy, Dorr; H. F. Jones, Hebron; Frank W. Hatch, Burton; W. A. Cristy, McHenry; James Nish, Algonquin; Ed. D. Shurtleff, Marengo; James Lake, Chemung; William Desmond, Hartland; J. H. Gracy, Nunda; F. E. Stevens, Coral; S. E. Clark, Greenwood; L. B. Covell, Richmond; John Weltzein, Grafton.

1899-1900—N. Brotzman, Riley; R. J. Beck, Dunham; W. D. Cornue, Alden; J. S. Mills, Seneca; L. T. Hoy, Dorr; Henry M. Turner, Hebron; F. W. Hatch, Burton; William A. Cristy, McHenry; L. E. Mentch, Algonquin; E. D. Patrick, Marengo; James Lake, Chemung; William Desmond, Hartland; F. E. Stevens, Coral; John Weltzein, Grafton; S. E. Clark, Greenwood; L. B. Covell, Richmond; J. H. Gracy, Nunda.

1901-02—N. Brotzman, Riley; C. M. Stevenson, Dunham; John Baldock, Alden; J. S. Mills, Seneca; L. T. Hoy, Dorr; H. M. Turner, Hebron; Frank W. Hatch, Burton; William A. Cristy, McHenry; L. E. Mentch, Algonquin; J. M. Marks, Marengo; James Lake, Chemung; William Desmond, Hartland; J. H. Calbow, Coral; John Weltzein, Grafton; S. E. Clark, Greenwood; L. B. Covell, Richmond; Ben. Throop, Nunda.

1903-04—H. E. Whipple, Dunham; John Baldock, Alden; F. D. Perkins, Seneca; William S. McConnell, Dorr; H. M. Turner, Hebron; Frank W. Hatch, Burton; Simon Stoffel, McHenry; L. E. Mentch, Algonquin; A. A. Crissey, Marengo; James Lake, Chemung; William Desmond, Hartland; J. H. Calbow, Coral; John Weltzein, Grafton; M. Long, Greenwood; L. B. Covell, Richmond; Ben Throop, Nunda.

1905-06—N. Brotzman, Riley; H. E. Whipple, Dunham; John Baldock, Alden; F. D. Perkins, Seneca; W. S. McConnell, Dorr; H. M. Turner, Hebron; Jesse B. Richardson, Burton; James C. Ladd, McHenry; L. E. Weltzein, Algonquin; A. A. Cristy, Marengo; James Lake, Chemung; William Desmond, Hartland; J. H. Calbow, Coral;

H. F. Heinemann, G....on; C. W. Th.....son, G.....od; L. B. Covell,
Richmond; ....Pr.....

.......Br......R....; H. E. W.....pl., D.....; John B.
do..., A.....D. P.....s, S.....ca; F. J.....l. H. M. T...
H.....B.....C.lad.....H.....L. J...
A.....A. A.....v, M.....; W. H. Wa.....a....;.....
D.....H.....J. E. W.....Coral, H. S. H.....C.
t.....T.....G.....L. B. C.....l, R.....G......
N.....

1909-10 N. Br.....a. Ri.. D..les M. Wri.....M.....H. E.
Whipple Dunham; John Baldock, Alden; F. D. Perkins, S....., E. C.
Jewett, Dorr; H. M. Turner, Hebron; J. B. Richards..., B....o; H.
F.....McHenry, I. E. Ment.l. Algonquin, D.les M. Wr.....Ma-
r.....k H. Ward, Chemung, William Desmond, Hartlan.....J. E.
Williams, Coral; H. F. Heinemann, Grafton; E. C. Jew.....Dorr;
C. W. Thompson, Greenwood; L. B. Covell, Richmond; Ber....rcep
Nunda

1911-12 N. Brotzman, Riley; H. E. Whipple, Dunham; J.....Bal
dock, Alden; F. D. Perkins, Seneca; H. M. Turner, Hebron; J. B.
Richardson, Burton; S. H. Freund, McHenry; Robert E. Haeger, Al-
gonquin; D. M. Wright, Marengo; W. H. Ward, Chemung; William
Forrest, Hartland; J. E. Williams, Coral; John Donoahue, Grafton;
John E. Harrison, Greenwood; L. B. Covell, Richmond; A. H. Hale,
Nunda.

1913-14 N. Brotzman, Riley; H. E. Whipple, Dunham; John Bal
dock, Alden, F. D. Perkins, Seneca; Fred H. Walters, Dorr; H. M.
Garner, Hebron; J. B. Richardson, Burton; S. H. Freund, McHenry;
Robert E. Haeger, Algonquin; D. M. Wright, Marengo; W. H. Ward,
Chemung; William F. Forrest, Hartland; P. A. Raenie, Coral; John
Donahue, Grafton; John E. Harrison, Greenwood; L. B. Covell, Rich
mond; Alva H. Hale, Nunda.

1915-16 N. Brotzman, Riley; H. E. Whipple, Dunham, John Bal
dock, Alden, Ed. F Knecker, Seneca; F. A. Walters, Dorr; H. M.
Turner, Hebron; W. F. Pierce, Burton; S. H. Freund, McHenry; Robert E. Haeger, Algonquin; D. M Wright, Marengo; W. H. Ward, Chemung; W. H. Forrest, Hartland; Charles Ackman, Jr., Coral; John
Donahue, Greenwood; L. B. Covell, Richmond; Alva H. Hale, Nunda.

1917-18 H. Stanley, Riley; H. C. Whipple, Dunham; H. G. Durkes,
Alden; E. F. Knecker, Seneca; F. A. Walters, Dorr; H. M. Turner,
Hebron; W. F. Pierce, Burton; S. H. Freund, McHenry; Robert E

A. J. Cole

Haeger, Algonquin; D. M. Wright, Marengo; W. H. Ward, Chemung; Earl C. Hughes, Hartland; Charles H. Ackman, Jr., Coral; John Conley, Grafton, John E. Harrison, Greenwood; L. B. Covell, Richmond; A. H. Hale, Nunda.

1919-20 H. Stanley, Riley; D. M. Wright, Marengo; H. E. Whipple Dunham; W. H. Ward, Chemung; H. G. Durkee, Alden; E. C. Hughes, Hartland; E. F. Knecker, Seneca; Charles Ackerman, Jr. Coral; John Conley, Grafton; E. A. Walters, Dorr; J. E Harrison Greenwood; H. M. Turner, Hebron; L. B. Covell, Richmond; W. F Pierce, Burton; Stephen H. Freund, McHenry; A. H. Hale, Nunda; R. E. Haeger, Algonquin.

The present board is composed of the following: H. H. Barber, Riley; D. M. Wright, Marengo; H. E. Whipple, Dunham; W. H. Ward, Chemung; H. G. Durkee, Alden; E. C. Hughes, Hartland; E. F. Kucker, Seneca; Charles Ackerman, Jr., Coral; John Conley, Grafton; F. A. Walters, Dorr; L. N. Thompson, Greenwood; H. M. Turner, Hebron; F. B. McConnell, Richmond; Frank May, Burton; Stephen H. Freund, McHenry; A. H. Hale, Nunda; R. E. Haeger, Algonquin.

NEW ASSESSMENT LAW

The Legislature of Illinois in the winter of 1918-19, enacted a law which has changed the old rate of assessment in the State which was one-third of the actual value of real estate, to one-half. So that now where the assessor places the amount of "assessed valuation" on a given property to be $1,000, it signifies that such property has a supposed actual cash value of $2,000.

This law went into immediate effect and this caused quite an extra burden upon the part of county officials in order to comply with the new enactment. In most cases the assessor's books had already been turned over to the county clerk and now this officer is compelled to assist the board of review in carrying out or extending a new column in all books relating to realty in the several townships, in order that the "valuation" be in accord with the provisions of the new law. This does not mean, necessarily, that the taxes will be any higher than heretofore. This is a matter of the disposition of the people in each county. The former provision was one by which there could not be raised at the legal amount of levy allowed on each dollar's worth of property, a sufficient amount to meet the demands in some of the counties in the commonwealth. But by giving a higher "assessed value" a larger sum can be obtained within the constitutional tax limit per dollar.

In McHenry County there has in reality not been much change of "assessed valuations" for the last ten years. The board of review had complex work in adjusting the assessments to correspond with the times and with the new valuation law above named.

CHAPTER VI

POLITICAL REPRESENTATION

By M. F. Walsh

SEVERAL APPORTIONMENTS—EARLY REPRESENTATIVES—LATER REPRESENTA-
TIVES—A CAPABLE OFFICIAL—MEMBERS OF THE GENERAL ASSEMBLY—
STATE SENATORS—STATE REPRESENTATIVES—POLITICAL STATISTICS—
PRESIDENTIAL VOTE.

Under the constitution of 1848 McHenry County became a part of the Twenty-fourth Senatorial district with Boone and Winnebago counties, and with Boone County formed the Fifty-first Representative District. In 1854 it was associated with Lake County in a Senatorial and with Boone in a Representative District. In 1861 it was made a part of the Twenty-third Senatorial District, with Boone, Winnebago and Lake, and this political unit existed until the apportionment of 1872, which ushered in what became known as the minority system of representation, each district being entitled to one senator and three representatives.

McHenry and Lake counties formed the Eighth District, Boone having been added in 1882 and this political division had made up the Eighth Senatorial District to the present time.

EARLY REPRESENTATIVES

McHenry County obtained its first resident representative in the general assembly in 1848, when John F. Gray was elected to the lower house. Two years later the county had two representatives at Springfield in the persons of A. H. Nixon and George Gage, the former being re-elected for the third term in 1854, when George Gage, after a service in the lower house, was elected to the State Senate, thus being entitled to the distinction of being the first state senator elected from McHenry County.

Westley Diggins was elected to the lower house in 1856 and Lawrence S. Church in 1858, 1860 and 1862, in which year Thaddeus B. Wakeman was elected to the lower house. Merritt L. Joslyn was elected to the lower house in 1864 and was succeeded by T. B. Wakeman in 1866. Peter W. Deigan was elected in 1868. [...] W[...] A. McC[...]ll and Ira R. Cu[...]s were [...] d [...] l in 1870 [...] [...]k [...]n a [...] Ninety-third dist[...].

R[...]d B[...]p [...]s the [...] at Demo[...]ti[...]er [...] [...]on McHenry C[...]w[...] [...]ah [...] he [...] g[...]s [...] 1[...]2. [...] f K. Grange v[...] a Republ[...] r [...]elected. Mr Granger w[...] r[...]lected in 1871. Me[...]ri[...] L. Joslyn was elected to the state senate in 1876 and Mr. Granger re-turned to the house in 1878

LATER REPRESENTATIVE

Orson C. Dig[...]ins, a Republican, and James Thompson, a Demo[...]rat were both elected to the lower house in 1880. Charles H. Tryon was elected in 1882 and Ira R. Curtiss elected state senator in 1884. Gardner S. Southworth was elected to the house in 1888 and Robert J. Beck chosen at a special election to succeed E. M. Haines, deceased, July 15, 1890. Mr. Beck served in two later sessions of the general assembly, hav-ing been elected in 1892 and 1894. John C. Donnelly was elected to the house in 1890, re-elected in 1892 and 1898.

Edward D. Shurtleff was elected in 1900 and has served continuously for twenty years, his first election to the house taking place in the autumn of 1900, making ten terms he has served this county and district. James H. Vickers was elected to the house in 1910, re-elected in 1914, 1916 and 1918.

A CAPABLE OFFICIAL

While McHenry County has always been fortunate in the high type of men it has chosen as its representatives at Springfield it is not dis-paraging to any of them to say that to Edward D. Shurtleff belongs the distinction of exerting the greatest influence as a legislator and attaining the greatest reputation.

For three terms Mr. Shurtleff was elected speaker of the lower house and made an enviable record. When seeking renomination in the primary campaign of 1918 and when it appeared as if his candidacy was in danger, Governor Lowden, without knowledge of Mr. Shurtleff, paid the latter the following high tribute when a country newspaper sought the Gover-nor's estimate of Shurtleff:

Springfield, Ill., Sept. 4, 1918.

Mr. W. J. Smith,
    Waukegan, Ill.
    Edward D. Shurtleff was my dependence in the house of Representatives in enacting my program into law in that general assembly.

There will be much important legislation for the consideration of the coming general assembly and Mr. Shurtleff will be of more use to the people of the State of Illinois than a dozen ordinary men.

I hope the Eighth senatorial district will again send this useful veteran legislator to Springfield as one of its representatives.

I would regard it a great misfortune if, for any reason, Mr. Shurtleff were not sent back to the legislature.

Signed: Frank O. Lowden, Governor.

MEMBERS OF THE GENERAL ASSEMBLY

The following is a list of the state senators and representatives for the districts in which McHenry County has been located since its organization as a county—1838 to 1919:

State Senators: 1838-40, Ebenezer Peck; 1840-42, John Pearson; 1842-47, Ira Minard; 1846-48, Elijah Wilcox; 1848-50, Alfred E. Ames; 1850-54, Thomas B. Talcott; 1854-58, George Gage; 1858-62, Henry Blodgett; 1862-66, Cornelius Lansing; 1866-72, Allen C. Fuller; 1872-76, Clark W. Upton; 1876-80, Merritt L. Joslyn; 1880-84, George Kirk; 1884-88, Ira A. Curtiss; 1888-90, Charles E. Fuller; 1890-92, Charles E. Fuller; 1892-94, Reuben W. Coon; 1894-96, Reuben W. Coon; 1896-98, Flavel K. Granger; 1898-1900, Flavel K. Granger; 1900-02, D. F. M. Fuller; 1902-04, D. F. M. Fuller; 1904-06, A. N. Tiffany; 1906-08, A. N. Tiffany; 1908-14, Alb. J. Olson (deceased).

State Representatives: 1838-40- Colson Kercheva, Richard Murphy and Joseph Naper for Cook, Will and McHenry Counties.

1840-42—Albert C. Leary, Richard Murphy and Ebenezer for Cook, Will and McHenry Counties.
Kalb; Henry Madden for Boone, DeKalb, McHenry and Kendall.

1842-44—William M. Jackson for Kane, McHenry, Boone and De-
McHenry, Boone and DeKalb.

1844-46—William M. Jackson, E. Jewell, James L. Loop for Kane.

1846-48-—Under the Constitution of 1848, until the next apportionment, Boone and McHenry Counties formed the fifty-second district,

entitled to two representatives. James Harrington, George W. Kest-
singer, James T. Pierson for Kane, McHenry, Boone and DeKalb, all
served from the district in order given.

1848-50—John F. Gray McHenry; Selby Leach, Boone.

1850-52—A. H. Nixon, McHenry; H. C. Miller, Boone.

1852-54—A. H. Nixon, McHenry; H. C. Miller, Boone.

1854-56—Under the apportionment of 1854 Boone and McHenry
Counties constituted the forty-fourth district S. W. Lawrence and W.
Diggins

1856-58—L. S. Church, McHenry; Stephen A. Hurlbut, Boone.

1858-60—L. S. Church, McHenry; Stephen A. Hurlbut, Boone.

1860-64—The apportionment of 1861 made McHenry the fifty fourth
district, with Thaddeus B. Wakeman as representative.

1864-66—Merritt L. Joslyn.

1866-68—Thaddeus B. Wakeman.

1868-70—Peter W. Deitz.

1870-72—In 1870 McHenry County was made the ninety-third district and had two representatives—William A. McConnell and Ira R.
Curtiss.

1872-74—By the apportionment of 1872 McHenry and Lake Counties became the eighth district, entitled to three representatives—Richard
Bishop, McHenry County; Flavel K. Granger, McHenry; Elisha Gridley, Lake County.

1874-76—Flavel K. Granger, McHenry; William A. James, Lake;
Elijah M. Haines, Lake.

1876-78—Flavel K. Granger, McHenry; William A. James, Lake;
Edward M. Dennis, Lake.

1878-80—Frank K. Granger, William A. James, Lake; William Price,
Lake.

1880-82—Orson C. Diggins, McHenry; James Thompson, McHenry;
James Pollock, Lake.

1882-84—In 1882 McHenry and Boone became the eighth district,
entitled to three representatives—Charles H. Tryon, McHenry; E. M.
Haines, Lake; Charles Fuller, Boone.

1884-86—James Pollock, Charles Fuller.

1886-88—Charles E. E. Fuller, Charles A. Patridge and Geo. Waite.

1888-90—Charles A. Patridge, G. S. Southworth and Elijah Haines.

1890-92—John C. Donnelly, Charles A. Patridge, George Reed.

1892-94—J. C. Donnelly, Robert J. Beck, George Reed.

1894-96—George Reed, T. J. Beck, P. H. Delaney.

Thomas D Cole & Family

1896-98—D. F. M. Fuller, G. R. Lyon.
1898-1900—Geo. M. Lyon, D. F. M. Fuller.
1900-02—Ed D. Shurtleff, George R. Lyon, C. V. Connor.
1902-04—Ed D. Shurtleff, George R. Lyon, William Desmond.
1904-06—Frank R. Covey, Ed D. Shurtleff, D. E. Gibbons.
1906-08—Frank R. Covey, Ed D. Shurtleff, D. E. Gibbons.
1908-10—A. K. Stearns, Ed D. Shurtleff, Thomas F. Burns.
1910-12—Ed D. Shurtleff, James H. Vickers, Joseph E. Anderson.
1912-14—Ed D. Shurtleff, Thomas E. Graham, Fayette S. Munro.
1914-16—Ed D. Shurtleff (McHenry County).
1916-18—Ed D. Shurtleff (McHenry County).
1918-20—Ed D. Shurtleff (McHenry County).

POLITICAL STATISTICS

At the first election held in McHenry County, June 1, 1837, the whole number of votes cast was 115. The election for county officers was held at the store of Hiram Kennicott, near Half Day, on the Desplaines River, within the present county of Lake.

In 1838 the county chose its first representative to the State Legislature, electing Dr. Richard Murphy, Democrat, over Giles Spring, Whig, by a considerable majority. The convention which nominated the successful candidate was held the first Monday in March, 1838. About sixty delegates were present, among whom were the following from McHenry County: William M. Jackson, Proctor Smith, William Sponable, Russell Diggins, C. Canfield, William A. McConnell and A. B. Coon. Of the entire number of delegates, only four were living in the early eighties, of whom Messrs. Coon and Jackson of this county were survivors.

This county was solidly Democratic from its infancy until 1856, when the impending crisis changed the majority to the Republican side, where it has remained ever since.

PRESIDENTIAL VOTE

The vote for presidential electors from 1844 to the present is given below:

1844—Polk, Democratic, 668; Clay, Whig, 488; scattering, 77.

1848—Cass, Democratic, 1,096; Taylor, Whig, 660; Van Buren, Freesoil, one vote.

1852—Pierce, Democratic, 1,198; Winfield Scott, Whig, 886; Hale, Freesoil, 645.

1856 John C. Fremont, Republican, 2,869; James Buchanan, Democratic 945; Fillmore, Know-nothing, 43.

1860 Abraham Lincoln, Republican, 3,063; Stephen A Douglas, Democratic, 1,444.

1864 Abraham Lincoln, Republican, 2,951. Geo. B. McClellan. Democrat, 1,188

1868 U. S. Grant, Republican, 3,296; Seymour, Democratic 1,388

1872 U. S. Grant, Republican, 2,895; Horace Greeley, Liberal, 1,080. O'Connor, Democratic, 21.

1876 Rutherford B. Hayes, Republican, 3,465; Samuel J. Tilden, Democratic, 1,574; Peter Cooper, Greenback, 34.

1880 James A. Garfield, Republican, 3,516; W S Hancock Democratic, 1,799; James B. Weaver, Greenback, 194.

1884 James G. Blaine, Republican, 3,697; Grover Cleveland, Democratic 2,077; St. John, Prohibitionist, 145.

1888 Benjamin Harrison, Republican, 3,563; Grover Cleveland, Democratic, 2,002; Fisk, Prohibitionist, 322.

1892—Benjamin Harrison, Republican, 3,204; Grover Cleveland, Democratic, 2,317; Bidwell, Prohibitionist, 263.

1896—William McKinley, Republican, 5,047; William Jennings Bryan, Democratic, 1,910; Gen. John Palmer, Gold Democrat, 48; Levering, Prohibitionist, 102.

1900—William McKinley, Republican, 5,118; William Jennings Bryan, Democratic, 2,058; Wooley, Prohibitionist, 132.

1904- Theodore Roosevelt. Republican, 5,409; William Jennings Bryan, Democrat, 1,309.

1908 William Howard Taft, Republican, 5,331; Democratic, 1,887.

1912 William Howard Taft, Republican, 2,370; Woodrow Wilson, Democratic, 1,913; Theodore Roosevelt, Progressive, 3,046.

1916— Charles E. Hughes, Republican, 9,000; Woodrow Wilson, Democratic, 3,265.

1921 Warren G. Harding, Republican, 9,885; James M. Cox, Democrat, 1,536.

CHAPTER VII

EDUCATION

By Richard W. Bardwell

ORIGIN OF SCHOOLS—PIONEER SCHOOLHOUSE—FIRST SCHOOLS—EARLY INSTI-
TUTES—COUNTY INSTITUTES—INCREASE IN SCHOOLS—EARLY SCHOOLS
BY TOWNSHIPS — OTHER EDUCATIONAL INSTITUTIONS — TEACHERS INSTI-
TUTES—SCHOOL STATISTICS—GROWTH OF COMMON AND HIGH SCHOOLS—
MC HENRY COUNTY SCHOOL PRINCIPALS ASSOCIATION—COUNTY SUPERIN-
TENDENT OF SCHOOLS—TODD SEMINARY.

ORIGIN OF SCHOOLS

As the people of the world began to emerge from the chaos of the
savage state, they commenced to think and plan, not entirely for themselves, but for their children. Originally tillers of the soil, they recognized the fact that if they were to hope for better conditions for those
to come after them, they must have a good soil to grow crops. That,
after they had provided for stronger and more perfect bodies, they
must train the minds of their offspring. Gradually they recognized
the fact that if they banded together to hire some one to teach all of
the children together, a much wiser person could be secured, than if
each family tried to provide instruction. As the value of schools became recognized, the state took up the matter so as to provide the instruction for those children who were orphans, or whose parents were not
possessed of sufficient means to pay their quota into the common educational fund. Gradually, with annual improvements, the present public
school system has come to obtain in this country. It commenced about
1835-40. Now, parents the world over in civilized parts, feel that
there is no purpose, no real good in their lives, unless the miracle shall
come to their children, that they enjoy advantages denied to the
fathers and mothers.

It was this spirit of sacrifice for the next generation that made the
pioneers struggle so earnestly to get some kind of educational forces

at work, almost before they had grubbed out a stump, or turned a furrow of their new land. Of course, at first the schools had to be held in private homes or in a rude log cabin erected for school purposes, and by scrimping at home, the good parents would deny themselves much in order to properly clothe, and furnish necessary schoolbooks in order that their children might be sent to school.

THE PIONEER SCHOOLHOUSE

No matter how many times one reads of the little old log school-house built in the forest, or on the wild prairie's sod, where first the tiny tots attended schools in which their A, B, C's were mastered, another description of the same old rude schoolhouse written by one seeing the hard benches and dirt floors, gives a different angle, but the story is ever of deep interest to both old and young.

Picture a small building, so small that it might easily be set down in the ordinary living room of today, fashioned of rough logs, fastened together, with mud plastered in the chinks between the logs. At one end was an opening, sometimes protected by a slab door, but oftentimes left without any cover. At the other end was a crude fireplace, which was liable to throw into the room as much smoke as was carried away by the mud and stick chimney. The floor sometimes was merely hard dirt; again, it was constructed of split logs, with the bark side laid down. The furniture was all homemade, consisting of puncheon seats for the pupils, and a slab with longer pegs in it as a desk for the teacher. There were no blackboards, no globes, no scientific apparatus, no marble statues, pictures or maps. Indeed, ofttimes there were mighty few books for either the pupils or teacher, and yet how those children did absorb information, and lay in these primitive temples of learning, a lasting foundation for magnificent superstructures. Some of the best men this country ever produced, attended just such a school as the one above described.

As the community increased in importance, so did the schools, frame structures gradually replacing the log buildings, and then came handsome brick and stone schoolhouses of today. The early history of the schools of this county is similar to that of most other sections, but after the close of the Civil War, a radical change set in for the uplift of the common schools, and today every citizen worthy the name, boasts of, and duly appreciates, the excellent schools we are enjoying at this time.

COMMUNITY HIGH SCHOOL, WOODSTOCK

FIRST SCHOOLS

It appears that the first schools in the county were taught in the year 1836, in Burton and Dorr townships, which answered the above description of the log school. In 1837 another small school was opened in Coral Township; another in Algonquin, in 1838; Marengo had one in 1839; Seneca, McHenry and Chemung in 1840 and Richmond in 1841; Alden's first school started in either 1840 or 1841.

The first schoolhouse of which there appears to be any official record is the one built in section 1, township 45, range 9, Dunham Township, which was completed in June, 1839. The first official mention of the public schools in this county appears upon the county records under the date of June, 1841. Carlisle Hastings was then appointed School Land Commissioner, and boards of school trustees were appointed for each township in the county. These boards and the townships, as they are now named, are given below:

Riley—A. E. Smith, R. Bates and Samuel Johnson;

Marengo—Marcus G. White, John Poyer, Daniel Steward;

Dunham—Jonathan Fellows, J. N. Jerome, Thomas Finey;

Chemung—Nathaniel Smith, William Hart, Rodolphus Hutchinson;

Coral—A. F. Randall, Selah Markham, E. N. Frink;

Seneca—William M. Jackson, Leander H. Bishop, Wm. Wattling;

Hartland—George Stratton, Appolos Hastings, George H. Guffing;

Alden—Thaddeus B. Wakeman, Ransom Parrish, Orry Barrett;

Grafton—Prescott Whittemore, John B. Oakley, Louis Holdridge;

Dorr—Allen Dufield, Solomon Keyes, Michael Best;

Greenwood—Andrew J. Hayward, Amos Scofield, M. B. Gwinns;

Hebron—Josiah H. Giddings, Jacob Gilbert, Bela H. Tryon;

Algonquin—Allen Baldwin, Hosea B. Throop, E. J. Smith;

Nunda—Josiah Walkup, Charles Patterson, William Huffman;

McHenry—Aromy Thomas, Gideon Colby, Benjamin Tuttle;

Richmond—William A. McConnell, J. W. White, Samuel Merrick;

Township 43, range 9, now a part of Algonquin--Thomas R. Chunn, William D. Carey, Joseph Clink;

Township 45, range 9, now within McHenry Township, Alden Harvey, Alfred Stone, Chauney Beckwith.

Township 46, range 9, Burton Township—S. S. Stilson, Jonathan Kimball, Alfred Stephens.

From that date on schoolhouses were built and schools supported wherever the population was sufficiently dense to bear the expenses. As the county grew more thickly settled, new districts were formed so that in a very few years every settler was within a short distance of a school-house. It is related that the greatest obstacle to the development of the schools was found in the lack of competent teachers. Many seemed fairly well qualified, and labored earnestly, but others who were employed in the absence of better material were sadly deficient both in education and aptitude. The teachers, too, worked against hardship of not having suitable and uniform text-books, so that real classification was impossible.

In 1855, the records say that Mr. Jewett, member of the board of supervisors, and on the committee on education, presented resolutions declaring:

"1st. That there is a sad deficiency of properly and legally qualified teachers in and for your said county.

"2nd. That there is a lack of interest and zeal on the part of said teachers to discharge those weighty responsibilities incumbent upon them in a becoming manner.

"3rd. That there is a lamentable lack of uniformity in the plan of instruction which is so desirable in every county.

"4th. That there have been considerable sums of money expended for the purpose of maintaining and supporting teachers' institutes, the object of said institutes being to remedy the difficulty above named.

"5th. That these institutes have come far short of the object for which they were established, etc.

"To improve the then existing state of the public schools, Mr. Jewett proposed the establishment, at the county seat, of an institute to be called the McHenry County Normal School; but alas, his suggestion was never acted upon by the board of supervisors."

EARLY INSTITUTES

The pioneers as a class were favorable to education and supported the district schools manfully, as well as fostered and encouraged in all ways private educational institutions, the chief institutes being located at Lawrence, Marengo and Crystal Lake, though several others were started in other parts of the county.

Lawrence Academy, in the northwestern part of the county, was one of the earliest and most successful schools of its kind. It had able instructors, and many afterward prominent men were students there. It gradually waned and finally ceased to exist, better conditions of the public schools of the county supplying its place.

At Crystal Lake village a flourishing seminary was maintained for some years under the name of Nunda College.

COUNTY INSTITUTE

The County Institute organized in 1856, perhaps aided more than any other single factor in bringing about an improved condition of the public school system in the county. For, it is seen by reference to public records, as well as to an interesting article in a former history of the county, that in 1885 there were many valuable school libraries in the school districts of McHenry County. A paragraph from this book may be useful in this connection:

"Constant and well directed efforts have wrought their results, and now the people of McHenry may justly be proud of their public schools. It is doubtful if there can be found anywhere in the country a country no older than this which has better schools. While these schools are not perfect, yet in excellence of school buildings, convenience of arrangement, competent supervision and thorough instruction, the county will compare favorably with any of like age and population. The county superintendents, the teachers, the taxpayers and the pupils are all interested in their work, and the results are apparent. The county institutes are well attended and play an important part in keeping alive the interests of education in our county."

INCREASE IN SCHOOLS

In 1860 the number of schools in the county was 142; number of schoolhouses, 139; number of teachers, 218; number of male scholars, 4,036; female scholars, 3,778. In 1870 the number of pupils was 11,890, of whom 7,000 were enrolled. In 1875 the number of school-houses in this county was 150, but the work did not advance with other elements of growth in the county in the next years following those just named, for it is found that in 1884 there were only 138 schoolhouses, though it was said that 175 were badly needed. In 1883-84 only 270 teachers were employed, and school property was only valued at $186,-285.

EARLY SCHOOLS BY TOWNSHIPS

The first school taught in Alden Township was in 1841, by Miss Clarissa Nelson, of Geneva Lake. The school was held in the first schoolhouse built in the township. It was a log structure located near the present site of the railroad station. This building was erected in the spring of 1841, its dimensions being 12x14 feet, but small as it was, it was plenty large enough to accommodate the little band of nine pupils. A report of the schools of the township in 1884 gave the enrollment of pupils as 313 of school age, and there were then nine schoolhouses within the township. The school property was valued in 1882 at $3,340. For present day school statistics the reader is referred to the table in this chapter, the same being extracted from the county superintendent's annual report.

In the early eighties Algonquin Township was in the lead in the number of schoolhouses, the number being ten, valued at $12,000. The number of persons of school age in the township was 630. The circulating library then contained 200 volumes. The first schoolhouse in the township was a log building at Crystal Lake in which Miss Hannah Beardsley taught in 1838.

In Burton Township a school was taught in 1846 by Miss Case, in the "red schoolhouse" in Section 8. It was built by the patrons of the school and the teacher was paid on the subscription plan and usually "boarded 'round." The first school, however, was taught in 1836 in a log building on Nippersink Creek, by Wm. Stearns.

In Chemung Township the first school was taught in the village of Chemung about 1840. In 1880 the number of persons of school age in the township was 978, or ninety more than any township within the county. It paid at that date next to the highest wages for teachers of any of the townships. The school property of seven schoolhouses was then valued at $16,500. The first school in Harvard was taught in 1859; J. E. Young was the first principal, assisted by Miss Mary Ballou. In the eighties the attendance was large and more building room had to be provided. The old reports show the village had 457 pupils in school in 1884.

In Coral Township the first schoolhouse was erected in 1838, on Section 8. William Jackson taught the first term of school and he took his pay in 4,000 rails for his four months' work. His patrons split 1,000 rails a month, so that when the school ended they had paid in full, all in good rails. At the end of the term in a frolic, the "big boys" tore down the schoolhouse. In 1884 this township had eleven schoolhouses in use and that was more than any other township then had. There were on an average 409 pupils in attendance. School property was valued at $10,000.

ST. MARY'S SCHOOL, WOODSTOCK

In Dorr Township the first school was taught by Alvira Cornish in the house of Uriah Cattle in 1836. The school consisted of seven pupils. In 1883 the value of school property of this township was $55,200; the annual salaries paid were $5,677; number of children of school age were 880.

In Dunham Township the first school was taught in the schoolhouse built in 1838, on the farm of Mr. Jerome. It was a small log structure which was also used for religious and political purposes. Miss Edna Jewett was the first to teach there. A. M. Disbrow was the new teacher. In 1881 the township had seven substantial school buildings, and paid annually about $1,800 for teachers.

In Grafton Township a third of a century ago there were eight fairly good school buildings and persons of school age upwards of 500. The first school here was taught in a log cabin erected in 1842 in District No. 7 (old number), and the first teacher was Cynthia Thompson.

In McHenry Township the first school was taught in 1840 by a Miss McOmber, in a small log house erected on the banks of the Fox River. This was also the first school building in the township. In the early eighties reports show seven fairly well-built frame schoolhouses in the township which property was valued at $9,000 and there was a school population of 658. The township also had a small, but most excellent library. In the village of McHenry the first school was taught in a frame building on the present public square. It cost $2,000. Another schoolhouse was built in 1859, in the east side of town and its cost was $6,000. The West side building was burned in 1862.

In Marengo Township the first school was taught by Caroline Cobb in 1839, but prior to this O. P. Rogers taught in a small log schoolhouse, nearly opposite the Calvin Spencer residence in the village of Marengo. The school taught by the lady was held in a building erected for a shoe shop, and her pupils numbered nine the most of the term.

In Seneca Township the first school was taught by Mrs. Roxy Stevens in 1840, at her home which was one mile south of Franklinville. In Franklinville the first schoolhouse of the township, a frame building, was erected in 1845.

In Woodstock the first school was taught in 1846, by David Richardson, who paid $2.00 a month for the privilege of holding school in the old courthouse. The next year, 1846, the first school building in Woodstock was erected on the same site still used for school purposes. In 1866 this house was deemed too small, and it was sold and a new building provided in 1867. A new building was erected in 1906 at a cost of

$25,999, and a four-room school building was erected that same year on Clay street. The large building burned to the ground December 2, 1919. In January, 1921, the Clay street school was enlarged and improved, making it a modern, eight-room grade building. In the same year an eight-room grade building was erected on the corner of Dean street and Forrest avenue

In Richmond Township the first school was taught by the daughter of Elder Pease, of Crystal Lake, in the Montelona schoolhouse. This was built in 1841, on the corner of William A. McConnell's farm, west of the village. In 1842 a school of forty-two pupils was taught at Solon by Charles Knapp. The graded school at Richmond was first opened in the fall of 1861, with Dr. S. F. Bennett as its teacher.

OTHER EARLY EDUCATIONAL INSTITUTIONS

Here in this county there have been several attempts at founding and maintaining religious training schools among which was the Presbyterian Academy at Marengo. It had quarters in the basement of the then new church of that denomination. E. B. Conklin was its first principal and he was, after two years, succeeded by Professor Scudder. The enrollment was from eighty to 120 pupils. This academy was in existence some five or more years, when in the financial collapse of 1857, an "Educational Institute" was formed. A large five-story brick building was erected for the purpose of carrying on the institution. It had scarcely been in operation for one year, when, for want of sufficient endowment, it fell into the hands of other parties and soon was discontinued.

TEACHERS' INSTITUTES

Teachers' institutes and normal schools have been in existence a long time in this county. It is not the purpose of this article to go far into detail concerning these helpful adjuncts to the public schools, but simply to give a brief account of the establishing of such factors. That excellent educator and grand old Presbyterian clergyman, Rev. R. K. Todd, organized a teachers' institute in the autumn of 1849, during the first year of his first term as school commissioner. It was held in the old courthouse, continued for one week, had an average attendance of 150. During each succeeding fall for his term of office, a similar institute or teacher's meeting was held, but during his successor's term.

the movement dwindled down until A. W. Smith, on assuming the office in 1855, had some trouble in re-awakening the teacher's dormant interest in this means of improvement. His institutes were held for two weeks, and at his third meeting, in the fall of 1856, a constitution was adopted and the institute began to assume a more perfect form. Mr. Smith was the first to go out of the county to secure instructors, he having at his second meeting, the state superintendent as one of them.

School Commissioner Hutchinson was succeeded in 1855, by Asa W. Smith, who wrote as follows:

"In the fall of 1855, I was elected school commissioner, and, upon accepting the office, found it to be one of my legal duties to visit schools fifty days in a year, with a compensation of $2.00 per day. There were at that time somewhat over 200 schools in the county. Notwithstanding it was "big work and small pay," I resolved to undertake the task, which was performed by visiting two schools daily, and lecturing at night in the most convenient places for the patrons of the two schools just visited that day.

"In October, 1856, the present organization known as the McHenry County Teachers' Institute was formed.

"In 1857, we had the most successful and interesting institute of my time as active member thereof. It was quite generally attended by the best teachers of the county, among whom were Rev. R. K. Todd, John A. Parrish, S. F. Bennett, Theo. Mead, M. F. Ellsworth, the two Misses Thomas, Miss Jewett, Miss Achsee Smith, Miss Thompson, Miss H. S. Corey, Mrs. C. M. Smith, and many others."

In 1877 the records show that after 1857, the institute did not meet regularly. Its meetings were then generally held at Woodstock, but occasionally at McHenry, Richmond and Nunda.

As the years passed by and state school laws made it obligatory upon the part of teachers to attend these institutes, they were, of course, more regular in their meetings. Later the state normal schools sprang into existence, and many teachers were greatly benefited by such educational institutions.

SCHOOL STATISTICS

The following table is made up from items found in the annual report of the county school superintendent for McHenry County, giving the name of districts and their numbers in the several townships of the county, the report for the same items in the incorporated villages and cities of the county, and enrollment of districts:

	Dist. Number	Pupils Enrolled		Dist. Number	Pupils Enrolled
Riley Township—			Oak Grove	98	11
McGovern			Lawrence	125	21
District	142	11	City Harvard ..	125	760
Fay	143	25	Chemung	127	51
Driver	144	9	**Hartland Township—**		
Java	148	14	Cooney	65	17
Williamson	145	22	Delanty	95	12
Riley Center ..	146	33	King	99	18
Anthony	147	16	Newman	100	13
Dunham Township—			Deep Cut	102	19
County Line ...	7	11	Hughes	103	35
Carmack	101	30	Desmond	104	23
North Dunham..	128	22	**Seneca Township—**		
Barrows	129	15	Pleasant Ridge..	74	29
Island	133	14	Evergreen	105	25
Alden Township—			Bayard	106	11
Cash District ..	97	9	Kanalay	107	11
Shields	96	15	Fuller	112	14
Manly-Leo	94	8	Diggins	108	22
Teeple	93	22	Vermont	109	25
Hardscrabble ..	87	10	Franklinville ..	110	19
Alden Village ..	92	67	Maple Hill	111	19
Wilson	91	16	**Coral Township—**		
Bordwell	89	13	Harmony	4	30
Kingsley	88	35	Union Village ..	113	92
Marengo Township—			Seward	114	7
Olcott District..	134	11	O'Rourke	115	18
Burr Oak	135	16	Heath	116	16
McGavern	137	11	Coral Center ..	117	10
Thorne	141	15	Oak Grove	118	7
Poyer	138	20	Brown Town ..	119	16
Wilson-Pringle	139	26	**Burton Township—**		
City Marengo ..	140	370	English Prairie.	9	16
Chemung Township-			Creek	10	29
Big Foot	90	32	Spring Grove ..	11	25
State Line	123	24	**Greenwood Township -**		
White Oak	124	19	Howe District..	35	12

HIGH SCHOOL AND GYMNASIUM, CRYSTAL LAKE.

	Dist. Number	Pupils Enrolled		Dist. Number	Pupils Enrolled
Thayer	63	21	Ford	52	18
Greenwood			South Prairie ..	51	20
Village	64	71	Munshawville ..	49	19
Queen Ann ...	67	12	Crystal Lake		
Reed	66	14	(City)	47	496
Fosdick	71	14	Cary Village ..	26	108
Charles	69	17	Hager	1	25
McHenry Township—			Oak Glen	27	12
Harrison-Marsh	36	10	Fox River Grove	149	45
Ostend	37	15	West Harmony	122	16
Sherman Hill ..	39	11	Grafton Township—		
Lily Lake	16	9	Halligus	81	25
McHenry			Huntley Village.	85	245
Village	15	273	Dorr Township—		
Johnsburg	12	141	Oak Grove	73	35
Ringwood	34	51	Pleasant Valley.	80	25
Lincoln	14	17	Ridgefield		
Nunda Township—			Village	48	44
Emerald Park			Cold Spring ..	70	18
District	17	14	Woodstock	72	898
Burton's			Gregory	75	12
Bridge	22	14	McConnell	76	8
Clemens	40	10	Walkup	77	13
Cherry Valley .	41	12	Lucas	78	19
Prairie	42	11	Hebron Township—		
Holcombville ..	43	17	Hebron Village.	57	221
Terra Cotta ...	44	23	Burgett	56	17
Barreville	45	15	Turner	58	17
Prairie Grove ..	46	11	Glass	59	16
Griswold Lake..	19	14	Vanderkarr	60	17
Algonquin Township—			Stone's Corner.	61	9
McManaman ..	23	25	Tryon's Corner.	62	20
Wienke	55	15	Richmond Township—		
Algonquin			Richmond		
Village	54	129	Village	29	241
Miller	53	5	Meyers-		
Silver Lake ...	24	16	Monteloma ..	30	10

Dist.	Pupils		Dist.	Pupils
	Number Enrolled			Number Enrolled
Keystone	31	23	Solon Mills ...	35	34
Hardscrabble ..	32	9	Washington ...	13	16

The total expenditure for school purposes in the county (1900) was $356,562.17, and of this amount $247,403.61 was spent for payment of teachers.

The average length of the school year is eight and six-tenths months. The number of pupils enrolled in the county averages 6,245, which includes 963 high-school pupils; and the number of children of school age in the county is 8,932.

GROWTH OF THE COMMON AND HIGH SCHOOLS

In the organization of the forces for rural education in this county, the succession of county school superintendents has been a notable one. The high standard of educational ideals existing generally throughout the county was first manifested in the selection by the popular vote of the county's chief educational officer, and sustained especially in the election of Prof. Lester Barber of Marengo; W. E. Wire, George W. Conn, Jr., and Prof. Addison M. Shelton.

During the terms of these four educators the rural schools progressed with general uniformity, and the high standards existing at the present are due in a great measure to their leadership.

In the city school system of the county, modern methods of organization and administration have been constantly introduced and in the selection of studies and methods of teaching, those in authority have constantly improved and kept abreast of the times. Buildings and grounds have been provided in each city as its growth warranted. Among the city superintendents of note who have served in this county may be mentioned R. G. Jones, of Harvard, now superintendent of the Cleveland, Ohio, schools; C. M. Bardwell, of Marengo, now superintendent of the Aurora, Ill., schools, and C. E. Douglas, of Woodstock, who is now superintendent of the Erie, Penn., schools. The influence of these and other successful superintendents, is apparent in the present city school system of McHenry County.

The development of the high schools of the county has been during the past twenty-five years, a wonderful growth. The enrollment has been doubled many times over, and in the present year, several of the city high schools, notably Woodstock, Harvard, and Marengo, find themselves con-- fronted with the necessity of erecting new high school buildings to meet the needs of their districts. In Crystal Lake, the high school building and equipment are of the finest in the county. These improvements were secured though the aid of a large amount of back taxes received in the set- tlement of a local estate. Crystal Lake and Woodstock both have ex- cellent courses in normal school training and domestic science. Wood- stock, Harvard, Crystal Lake, Marengo, and McHenry high schools all give up-to-date commercial training. McHenry and Crystal Lake have fine high-school gymnasiums for the physical training of their students.

The only available records at hand for securing the names of the superintendents of schools in the various cities and villages of the county, are those for Woodstock, which show that the first high school was taught in 1878 and the superintendents since the organization of the high school have been: Professors Warren Wilkie, 1878; A. E. Bourne, 1880; S. B. Hursh, 1888; J. A. Kelly, 1890; John R. Kellogg, 1891; L. B. Eas- ton, 1894; G. W. Conn, 1896; C. W. Hart, 1897; C. E. Douglas, 1907; E. C. Thomas, 1911; and R. W. Bardwell who took charge of the schools in 1914.

The three public school buildings in Woodstock were built as follows: the first one, the old brick school, was built in 1867; the new brick one, attached to or adjacent to the old building, is a handsome structure built in 1906 at a cost of $25,000; the third one is the Clay Street build- ing, built in the northern portion of the city, in 1907, at a cost of $20,000, exclusive of the grounds.

MC HENRY COUNTY SCHOOL PRINCIPALS ASSOCIATION

During the past fifty years one of the most potent influences in the progress of education in the county has been an organization of the princi- pals of the city or village schools of the county, known as the McHenry County School Principals Association. This group of earnest educators has fostered in many ways the welfare of the county's public schools. They have met regularly at the county seat during the school term, some- times to receive inspiring messages from the eminent men from outside the county; at other times to discuss the problems which confronted them in their schools. The membership in 1921 is: Oswell G. Treadway, Mc- Henry, president; A. M. Shelton, county superintendent, secretary; H. A. Dean, Crystal Lake; C. W. Hill, Marengo; R. W. Bardwell, Wood- stock; C. O. Haskell, Harvard; Frank Ben, Hebron; C. H. Duker, Hunt- ley; C. W. Minard, Richmond; and P. H. Willey, Alden.

Charles Hastings, 1841-43; Peter Dietz, 1843-45; Major T. Irwin, 1845-47; Phineas W. Platt, 1847-49; Rev. R. K. Todd, 1849-54; M. T. Hutchinson, 1854-55; Asa W. Smith, 1856-59; Alvin Brown, 1859-61; Theodore Mead, 1861-63; Thomas Ercanbrack, 1863-65; A. J. Kingman, 1865-69; G. S. Southworth, 1869-73; William Nickle, 1873-77; A. W. Young, 1877-81; D. D. Baldwin, 1881-83; H. R. Baldwin, 1883-84; Lester Barber, 1884-90; W. E. Wire, 1890-1902; George W. Conn, 1902-10; A. M. Shelton, 1910 to present date.

TODD SEMINARY

Todd Seminary is a private school at Woodstock for boys only. Its early history was well written up for a former history of McHenry County by its founder's son, Henry Alfred Todd, who brought out the following historic points, in a lengthy biography of the Todd family: Rev. R. K. Todd, founder of this school, was a graduate of Princeton College, N. J., and was educated for the Presbyterian ministry, married a Miss Clover of New York, and, being impressed with the missionary spirit, started on a long trip with his young bride. This was in 1847 and they headed for the "far West." Railroads, generally speaking, had not yet come into common use and so they traveled by the Erie Canal, and by steamer over the Great Lakes to Milwaukee, Wis. Because of a few young friends who had located in McHenry County, Ill., he was led to come here. A Presbyterian Church had just been organized at Woodstock with thirteen members, and he was induced to become its pastor. He was soon selected as superintendent of the McHenry County public schools and held that position a number of years. Subsequently, he established a school of his own at Woodstock

Finding it necessary at the end of a long term of years, on account of an affection of his throat to relinquish in a large part his public speaking, he threw his whole energies into the building up of an institution of advanced education to stimulate, as well as satisfy the needs of the then rapidly growing West. He had already been one of the prime movers in the permanent foundation of the Marengo Collegiate Institute, but that institution was entirely destroyed by fire, from which loss it never recovered. Again a similar calamity confronted Mr. Todd in the burning of the well-equipped building erected by him at Woodstock. Yet despite these losses, he gathered about him,

PUBLIC SCHOOL, HARVARD

as president, a large and efficient corps of instructors, obtained from the Illinois Legislature a generous charter, and inaugurated a long and highly prosperous period of collegiate work, the annual enrollment ranging from 151 to 200 students, from whom the ranks of teachers in Northern Illinois were for many years largely recruited. Late in the seventies, feeling the need for rest, Mr. Todd concluded to limit his efforts to the care of a classical home school for boys. The spacious grounds and buildings, situated at the edge of the city, afforded a beautiful country retreat for a family of about twenty boys in their teens, nearly all of whom came from city homes. Some even came in from distant states. Such was the foundation of the present excellent institution now known as "The Todd Seminary for Boys." Rev. Todd, the founder, feeling that he could no longer undertake the general management of the school, called to his assistance a young, vigorous man from New England, the present proprietor of the institution, Noble Hill, Ph. B., who came in the autumn of 1888, and in 1890 took complete charge. Mrs. Todd, wife of the founder, died, and Rev. Todd went to California to reside with his only son. In 1892 Prof. Hill purchased the property and has ever since owned and conducted a boys' school of a most remarkable and unique character.

The former buildings, in fact the entire institution, has been allowed to run down until it was almost a hopeless task to place it back in the class to which its founder had aspired, but Prof. Hill knew no such word as fail and went to work with a right good will and did what few other men could have accomplished in so short a time, if indeed ever. The old buildings were remodeled, rebuilt and converted to other uses from those of former days and in time new buildings were erected on the beautiful campus which now comprises about eleven acres. During the last school year there were enrolled 110 pupils, coming in from seventeen states and territories, and one was booked from Cuba. The average age of these boys is about twelve years, with several no older than seven. It is estimated that fully three-quarters of these boys come from homes in the City of Chicago. Ten grades are taught, and this course of instruction qualifies the youth to go out into active life a finished scholar in his class, or to enter higher institutions of learning. The West and Middle West furnish the greater number of students. Ten instructors are usually employed, at this date half of them being men and half women. The school year of nine months is between September and June. The motto of this school is "*Add to Virtue Knowledge.*"

This is a strictly non-sectarian school; moral character is all that is insisted upon in taking in students. Again it is strictly a Christian institution, for no instructor is ever employed unless he is a professed Christian, but no Christian denomination is barred, Catholic not excepted.

The ideal of the faculty is "for every Todd boy a good citizen." And this means what it says, a living active principle in the daily life of the Todd boys. The crowning glory of this school is the fact that it is a place where prohibition positively prohibits, a place of respect for authority and obedience to the law, where locks and keys are unknown and individual and property rights are respected.

A more healthful spot cannot be found on the continent, for its altitude is 1,000 feet above sea level, the highest point in all Illinois. During the seventy years of its existence not one death has occurred among the hundreds and thousands of pupils who have been in attendance. Climate, pure air, pure water, proper exercise and observance of sanitary rules have all combined to bring about this unequalled result.

The buildings found on the superb campus are: Wallingford Hall, Clover Hall, Rogers Hall, Grace Hall, the Gymnasium, Headmasters Cottage, West Cottage, Cozy Cottage, and North Cottage, used for hospital purposes.

The following practices are strictly prohibited: Use of cards or any form of gambling; use of tobacco; use of profane or vulgar language; use or possession of fire-arms; reading of trashy books or papers; contracting debts; going off the grounds without permission; going down town unless accompanied by a teacher; and leaving the buildings after evening prayers.

The instructors 1920 and 1921 are as follows:

Principal— Noble Hill, Ph. B.

Associate Principal- -Roger Hill, A. B.

Secretary and Treasurer- -Ross Taylor, A. B.

Headmaster—A. E. Johnson, A. B.

History— H. A. Hunter, A. B.

Latin- F. J. Roubal, A. B.

Geography -S. L. Coover.

Music- -K. Crilly, A. B.

English and Librarian—Miss Grace Libey

Reading and Spelling- Miss Pearl Fidler.

Primary Department- Miss Hazel Macdonald.

Primary Department- Miss Edith Divilbess.

Mathematics—Mrs. F. J. Roubal.
Art—Miss Mary E. Newman.
Secretary to Principal—Miss Selma Rowe.
Dean of the Home—Mrs. Ross Taylor, A. B.
House Mother—Miss Lillian Kauffman.
House Mother—Mrs. A. E. Johnson.
Nurse—Mrs. G. C. Trevarthen.

When Prof. Hill first came to Woodstock he was a single man, but two years later he brought his bride to the institution and to them were born a son and a daughter, both of whom have been educated primarily in this institution. The daughter, Miss Carol Hill, now Mrs. Ross Taylor, is the only girl who has ever attended the school. Both are now connected with their father's institution.

CHAPTER VIII

CHURCHES

RELIGIOUS SPIRIT

Man has ever sought to draw near to his Creator, and never does this tendency become so strong as when he feels the lack of something material in life. As long as his creature comforts are assured, his happiness is intact, he appears able to exist without much thought of a future life, but let trouble or misfortune visit him, and instinctively he longs for some assurance of a power above his own. Just as a nation is purified and elevated through a period of great affliction, so are its people brought into proper religious frame of mind when misfortune falls upon them heavily.

LACK OF FACILITIES

Perhaps no one facility was more deeply felt, not only by individuals, but the communities they formed, in pioneer days than that which in the old homes afforded proper observance of religious duties. The pioneer had no churches, nor could they at first come in contact with religious teachers. The lack of the religious element in the early settlements had much to do with the lawlessness which prevailed in some communities. It appeared impossible to properly curb this until churches were established and a regular religious routine installed. Therefore not only was it important for the peace and happiness of each individual that some religious services be provided, but also for the growth of the neighborhood from a frontier settlement into the home of law-abiding citizens to which desirable people and additional capital would be drawn. Because of these and many other cogent reasons, it is easy to see why the settlers exerted themselves to raise sufficient funds to guarantee a certain regularity of religious services, and their efforts met with ample and gratifying results.

FIRST SERVICES

It matters not upon what exact date some certain sect held services, in a given community. The fact that such services were held is the important fact. It is found that several Protestant and at least two Catholic churches were very early in the field in this county. They all had to hold services in some private home and put up with such accommodations as could be provided in a log cabin at first. Sometimes a schoolhouse was found in which religious services could be held. Some communities lacked a minister, and then a layman took charge, for they believed in the promise made to the "two or three gathered together in my name," even though they were in the wilderness where the sound of the church-going bell had never yet been heard. On red-letter days in the history of a settlement, services were held by a traveling clergyman, at which time creeds and differences of doctrine were usually forgotten, and all gathered to drink in the words of warning and comfort which fell from the eloquent lips of one or another of the missionaries, soldiers of the Cross, who went forth, on horseback, into the wilderness and preached and labored for the Master, without thought of reward other than a bare living and the realization that they were living up to their conception of their duty to their Maker and humanity.

FIRST CHURCHES

Ofttimes the log schoolhouse served as a meetinghouse in the early days, but finally, after much effort, in each of the new settlements, the little frame house of worship with its tiny bell in a wooden belfry, began to dot the prairies or grace the beautiful valleys midst the woodland. It was one of such that the poet wrote "The Little Brown Church in the Vale," so popular everywhere now-a-days. Each Lord's day, a stream of people, clad in the best they possessed, might have been seen wending their way, on foot, horseback and with ox teams, to these little country chapels. In time these small frame structures gave way to larger, more appropriate edifices with costly and attractive stained windows and a high steeple with a silver-toned bell within its belfry. Some obtained pipe organs and modern furniture, but the same spirit guided them, the same purpose of worshiping the only true and living God, in both humble and more pretentious edifices.

In order to give the readers of this volume a clear idea of how the religious element developed in every part of this county, the writer has sought to gather together all possible data from all denominations here represented, and place such information in a readable form in one chapter.

BAPTISTS

The MARENGO CHURCH is among the pioneer church organizations in northern Illinois. The first sermon ever preached in McHenry County was by a Baptist minister named Southworth, one Saturday evening in April, 1836, at the home of Calvin Spencer. The audience was composed of less than a dozen people. Reverend Southworth was on his way further west, and perished in the terrible snow storm, near Rock Island in December, 1836. Rev. Lyman B. King, preached at the home of Calvin Spencer in October, 1836, and from that date on as occasion offered, until the autumn of 1838. In 1840, Rev. Isaac Marvin, a graduate of Harvard University, was sent into this region to labor in behalf of the Baptist Home Missionary Society. He and his young wife came in a one-horse wagon with their trunk strapped to the rear of the vehicle. About half-way between Coral and Marengo, a stick caught in one of the wheels and broke it. They stopped at the next house and remained over night. Their host proved to be Orson P. Rogers, who then lived, where afterwards resided William Boies. Through this incident was formed a Baptist Church in this vicinity.

It was August 28, 1852, when the Baptist Church of Marengo was organized by Rev. Isaac Marvin. Its charter members were as follows: Samuel Farnum, Beniah Farnum, Reuben Farnum, Orin Hubbard, John Robinson, Philander Page, Jedadiah Rogers, James Andrews, Rev. Isaac Marvin, Sarah Marvin, Bertha De Wolf, Mary Wilbur, Wealthy Safford, Eliza Page, Eliza Stull, Hannah Hubbard, Sarah Robinson, Phoebe Perry, Nancy Richardson, Orpha Farnum, Sarah Howe, Clark Richardson, Harriet E. Bates. The membership of this church is 241. The first church building, a frame structure, was superseded in 1897 by the present building, which is valued at $15,000.

The various pastors to serve here have been as follows: Revs. Isaac Marvin, Luther W. Lawrence, Z. A. Bryant, David E. Halteman, T. F. Borchers, O. B. Stone, A. B. White, J. K. Wheeler, R. L. Haley, A. G. Dunsford, Ross Matthews, A. J. Morris, W. E. Billings, Vernon S. Phillips, W. M. Embree, Eugene Neubauer, W. F. Bostick, R. M. Morphett and H. B. Stevens.

THE PLEASANT GROVE CHURCH. While this organization does not now exist, it rightfully finds a place in this connection. This church was organized, December 30, 1840, with seven members. For the first year meetings were held in a log cabin and later at the schoolhouse. In 1851 the Pleasant Grove Church changed its name to that of the "Coral Baptist Church" and continued to worship as such until July 28, 1855, when pastor and members all united with the Marengo Baptist Church. The faithful pastors of this church were Isaac Marvin, who after three years, finding it hard to exist on what was possible to be paid him, resigned; early in 1844, Reverend Lawrence was made pastor, and his flock numbered about forty members. He was a farmer-preacher and owned a farm on the Belvidere road, on which he lived. He drove to his appointment every Saturday and back home Monday.

The oldest religious society at Crystal Lake was the Baptist, it having been formed there in 1839, by Joel Wheeler, D. D., of McHenry. They erected a church in 1853 and it burned in 1864. This society is not active today. Among its first members were Hiram Harris, Benjamin Crabtree, Clarinda Crabtree, and Benjamin Crabtree, Jr.

THE FIRST BAPTIST CHURCH OF WOODSTOCK was organized May 12, 1847, by Elder Adams. The charter members were: Asa Churchill, Mrs. Louisa Churchill, Mrs. Submit Enos, Mrs. Nancy (Enos) Swartout, Bela D. Churchill, Freeman Churchill, Elonor Allen, Louis B. Allen, Norman Butts, Jane (Cranston) Stowell, Sarah L. Allen, Mrs. Polly Butts, Louisa Cranston. The first services were held in a hall, but in 1858 a church was erected. This was subsequently sold and in 1866-67 another church was built, costing $7,000 and it is still in good repair and in use. In 1893, improvements were made on the present structure, which cost the society $1,600. The old frame church was sold to the Methodist people in 1862.

The present total membership of the church is 103. A good Sunday school is connected with the church and this has an enrollment of about 150. It is believed the first pastors here were: Revs. Wheeler and Eldridge Whittier. The record furnished for this article by Rev. Herbert H. Smith, runs as follows (since 1850):

Rev. Whittier—From December, 1850, to November 24, 1851.
Rev. Wheeler—From November 24, 1851, to March 31, 1855.
Rev. Eldridge.
Rev. S. M. Brown—From August 1, 1852.
Rev. E. F. Guerney—From October 21, 1855, to October, 1856.
Rev. G. W. Gates—From February 8, 1858, to July 31, 1858.

Rev. S. Washington--From September 19, 1858, to December, 1859.
Rev. N. Colver From January 4, 1861, to July 20, 1861.
Rev. A. C. Hubbard From October 6, 1861, to October 1, 1862.
Rev. E. O Brien From January, 1863, to April 12, 1863.
Rev. Ross From June, 1863, to July, 1863.
Rev. C B. Egan From December, 1863, to April, 1864.
Rev. A S. Foreman From October, 1864, to September, 1865.
Rev. John Young From December 16, 1865.
Rev. William M. Haigh From February 1, 1866, to April 2, 1868.
Rev. J. Sunderland From May 4, 1868 to July, 1868.
Rev. I. N Carman From July 26, 1868 to October 3, 1869.
Rev. Maul From 1870.
Rev. Horace Burnard From April, 1870, to December 1, 1873.
Rev. E. A. Ince From March 15, 1874, to August 1874.
Rev. H. L. Stetson From October, 1874, to January, 1876.
Rev. P. S. Cox From May, 1876, to February, 1877.
Rev. D. S. McEwan From May 20, 1877, to June 7, 1880.
Rev. William Ostler From October 1, 1880, to August 5, 1881.
Rev. J. D. McLean From September 4, 1881, to December, 1881.
Rev. Clark--From 1883.
Rev. L. Parmely From March 6, 1883, to April 27, 1884.
Rev. Henry Happle From September 21, 1884, to September 1, 1886
Rev. Edward McClain.
Rev. G. W. Kemp.
Rev. George P. Wright--From November 4, 1888, to May 11, 1890.
Rev. S. E. Cady--From June 1, 1890, to May 15, 1892.
Rev. John McCaw From November 20, 1892, to June 28, 1896.
Rev. C E. Barker From August 2, 1896, to April 25, 1897.
Rev. E. T. Stevens From June 6, 1897, to October 17, 1898.
Rev. C. C. Markham From November 16, 1897, to October 17, 1898
Rev. W. E. Sawyer- From December, 1899, to December 12, 1900.
Rev. S. P. Morris- From December 16, 1900, to November 7, 1901.
Rev. S. E. Moon- From November 10, 1901, to June 15, 1902.
Rev. W. I. Fowh From July 11, 1902, to June 21, 1903.
Rev. I. T. Underwood From August 9, 1903, to May 1, 1905.
Rev. J. F. Eaker From September 6 1905, to May 1, 1906.
Rev. G. C. Crippen From June 10, 1906, to April 17, 1908.
Rev. L. E. M. Freeman--From October 9, 1908, to January, 1909.
Rev. John Henry Perry—From March 7, 1909, to September 15, 1909
Rev. W. C. Moore From December 7, 1909, to March 30, 1913.

P. E. Corbett

E. Christian Corbett

Rev. Herbert H. Smith—From April 20, 1913, and
Rev. John L. Hess, the present pastor.

CATHOLIC

There are numerous strong and well-directed Catholic churches within this county. The construction of railroads through the county brought many Irish and other foreign-born of this religious faith to the county and many of these, after finishing the railroad work, settled here and formed a strong nucleus which added to those who had settled in and near McHenry village, as early as 1840, made possible the organization of some prosperous parishes.

ST. PATRICK'S CATHOLIC CHURCH, was organized at McHenry, in 1840 by Rev. M. St. Palais, afterwards Bishop of Vincennes. The charter members were: John Sutton, Michael Sutton, George Frisby and James Gibbs.

There are now 480 souls in this parish. The first church was built in 1853 at a cost of $300; in 1872 it was rebuilt at a cost of $2,000; in 1883 it was enlarged and valued at $3,000. The present church edifice and property is valued at $15,000. The rectory, which was built in 1899, with its property is valued at $5,000.

There is at this time an out Mission at Richmond, this county. Mass is said at Richmond on the first and third Sundays of the month.

The following have served as the faithful pastors of this parish: Rev. Fathers: M. St. Palais, Gigwan, McGorick, McMahan, Hampstead Brady, P. Gaffney, James Moran, Andrew Eustace, James Meagher, P. Smith, G. Pendergrast, Peter Birch, John Kilkenny, John A. Wayes, Peter J. Gormley, Michael Welby, P. M. O'Neil, Paul Burke, D. Lehane, H. Hagen, Charles Quinn, J. Lynch, and M. J. McEvoy, who was appointed to St. Patrick's in August, 1915, is the present pastor.

ST. JOHN'S CATHOLIC CHURCH. The first church formed at Johnsburg was St. John's, in 1843, by Father Portman, there being but three families in the parish at that time, those of Nick Adams, Jacob Smith and Nick Frett. There are now 130 families, 705 souls in the parish. At first they worshipped in a log cabin, but soon erected a frame church, and in 1879 erected a stone edifice costing $45,000. The present church, built in 1900, cost $75,000. This is one of the strong churches of the county. Rev. William Weber is the present pastor.

ST. MARY'S CATHOLIC CHURCH, of Woodstock, was organized in 1854 by Father McMahen, who died of yellow fever in the South about five years afterward. Among the more prominent members who assisted in organizing this Church are recalled the names of such faithful souls as Neill Donnelly, who was merchant, mayor and sheriff at sundry times in this county; John Donnelly, Francis Short, John J. Murphy, banker and lawyer.

Previous to building a church here the Catholics of this community worshiped at Hartland. The first church edifice erected in Woodstock was a brick structure in 1856, its cost being about $4,000. In 1881 this building was remodeled and enlarged to meet the pressing needs. This seated over 400 persons. The property was then valued at $12,000. The membership of the parish was one hundred families. The present membership is 1,000. Among the faithful pastors of this church should not be overlooked: Rev. Fathers: Hugh T. Brady, who came in 1852 and left in 1855; Barnard O'Harra, who came in 1855 and remained until 1858, James Meagher, who came in 1859 and continued until 1860; Terrance Fitzsimmons, who served from 1860 to 1867 and was followed by Rev. Lyons. All of the priests above named died prior to 1885. In 1868 came Rev. J. M. Ryan and following him were Rev. P. M. Reardon, assisted by Revs. Peter Sheedy and Rev. Eagan. Rev. T. Quigley, the next priest was followed by Rev. L. Lightner, D. D., who remained till 1870 and was succeeded by Rev. Lawrence Dunne, who remained till 1871, when he was followed by Rev. John Carroll, who arrived in 1871 and remained till November, 1877, after which came Rev. Thomas F. Leyden. Rev. D. J. Conway has been in charge of the parish for many years, and has built up a strong church and fine parochial school. Splendid modern-styled buildings adorn the beautiful grounds in the central part of the city. The present church, erected in 1909, is valued at $75,000. Father Conway has been highly successful in his work and is greatly beloved by all within and without his own church. Public-spirited and true to American ideas, through the late war he proved himself worthy of the highest esteem from all classes.

No point in the state can show a finer Catholic school building than St. Mary's of Woodstock. It was erected in 1916, at a cost of $50,000, and was dedicated in August, 1916. It has ideal lighting and heating arrangements and spacious play-grounds. The main structure, 85 by 120 feet, is two stories above the fine much used basement.

St. Joseph Catholic Church, was formed in 1866 at Harvard. From a beautiful Jubilee book printed on the occasion of the semi-centennial of this parish, the writer is able to glean considerable interesting as well as very valuable history.

In 1866, the ingress of the railroad and the immigration of many of the stalwart sons of Ireland increased the population to such an extent that the church authorities considered Harvard of sufficient importance to have a resident pastor and Father Fitzsimmons was the priest chosen. The little congregation rallied round its pastor and it was not long before they left the store building on Main street for the new log church. The building of the log church was no small task for the few that had it all to do. Father Fitzsimmons did not live long to enjoy the fruits of his labors, and in the year 1869, he passed to his eternal reward. For the next twenty-one years Father Dominic Egan attended to the spiritual needs of the Catholics of Harvard and there are many prominent men and women of today who received their first catechetical instruction from Father Egan. In 1890, this good priest left Harvard for Chicago, to establish the parish of St. Stephens, where he now resides in the vigor and strength of a ripened old age, admired and loved by all.

The little wooden church had now outgrown its usefulness, and Father James E. Hogan was sent to Harvard to bring about a better state of affairs in way of buildings. He succeeded in his work beyond the expectations of all and the present beautiful Gothic church stands as a lasting monument to his faithfulness and good judgment. In July, 1894 the city of Harvard was shocked by the news that Father Hogan was drowned in Lake Geneva and great was the sorrow expressed by all citizens. The sad accident happened in the late afternoon when a strong wind arising capsized the boat, which had contained the crew, Father Hogan, his sister, his brother and his brother's wife. All were drowned.

For the next sixteen years St. Joseph's parish had for its pastors the kind and generous Father Stack and the pious and gentle Father Goulet. On July 12, 1912, the present pastor, Rev. Daniel A. Feely, assumed charge of St. Joseph's Church and the work he has accomplished in the last few years proves his ability. His first and uppermost thought was to add to the comfort of his people. He installed a fine heating system for the church building; he also interested himself in procuring temporary quarters for the parochial residence, and when the debt was liquidated he started that which was nearer to his heart, namely the parochial school. The present enrollment on the parochial school is about 170. It is impossible to estimate the mental as well as physical energy expended on this work by him. The church property is worth at least $150,000. It is stated that in all this work he was greatly assisted by the work of Father Keenan, "a man of gentle and kindly habits, true as steel and as constant as the grace of God.

Other priests who have had charge of Harvard in years long ago were: Revs. Patrick Riordan, and Thomas Quigley. In 1884 the parish of Harvard comprised 200 families. Its present membership is about 250 families and 1,000 communicants.

SACRED HEART CATHOLIC CHURCH was organized about 1867. In its early days it was a part of the Belvidere Parish and Father P. C. Guire and Dr. O'Callahan, with their assistant priests attended it. Not until about 1902 did Marengo became a separate parish. Rev. Father Swanson becoming the first pastor. He was succeeded by Rev. D. J. McCaffrey and still later by Daniel Patrick Dressman the present pastor. The first building was a frame structure once owned by the Methodist people, but sold to the Catholics who used it about ten years. In 1908 the church erected a new handsome church edifice which is valued at $40,000.

The present membership of this congregation is about 450 souls, or 110 families. A church cemetery is located just to the north of the city limits of Marengo.

ST. THOMAS CATHOLIC CHURCH is situated in the village of Crystal Lake. It was organized in June, 1881, by Father Leyden, and its charter members were as follows: John Purvey, James Brannen, Cornelius Malone, James Kelley, Tim Kelley, William Clark, John McGarry, James Gannon, John Riley, Tom Leonard, John Leonard, James Burke, John Callahan, Patrick Bolestry. The church edifice erected in 1881 still stands and is valued with the lot at $10,000. The membership of St. Thomas congregation is 400.

The various priests who have served these people are: Revs. Fathers Leyden, Clancy, Quinn, Fox, Dorney Lonergan and present pastor, Rev. Edwin McCormick.

ST. MARY'S CATHOLIC CHURCH. Through the kindness of Father Edward Berthold, the following facts concerning the organization and development of St. Mary's Church and parish at McHenry have been gathered:

In the early nineties McHenry received a strong influx of Catholic families from Johnsburg and the surrounding villages. To enjoy the accommodations of an attractive river town many farmers retired and built homesteads in McHenry. Old St. Patrick's church was soon overtaxed and headed by Dr. Rogers a delegation of citizens presented the matter and the needs of McHenry to Most Rev. P. A. Feehan, D. D., at that time Archbishop of Chicago. Efforts were made by Father

Mehring of Johnsburg to delay the movement, but the determined people of McHenry succeeded in raising funds and obtained episcopal sanction to purchase the McHenry public school which was for sale at that time. Accordingly, Rev. F. Kirsch was appointed in the summer of 1894 to take charge of the newly formed parish and this young divine became the first resident pastor.

The spacious two-story brick school building accommodated the parish for religious services four years. At the end of that time preparation began for the erection of a pretentious Gothic church edifice, seating five hundred people. The parochial school gradually grew with the increasing parish. Today it accommodates 135 children who are taught by four experienced instructors, sisters whose mother house is in Milwaukee. St. Mary's school is reputed to be a standard school today, teaching eight grades in four large classrooms. It is fully equipped, steam heated, sanitary, efficient, and abreast with the times. During the last few years, under the direction of the present pastor, Rev. Edward Berthold, this private school has made a remarkable stride. Spacious school grounds and play ground apparatus is a notable feature in the physical culture of children attending the McHenry Parochial School. Sister Sydia is superintendent and principal since 1918.

In 1917 larger and more modern accommodations were undertaken in behalf of the school sisters who had been obliged to take quarters in a rented frame house several blocks away. A spacious two-story brick building was erected at a cost of $10,000. The school grounds were enlarged and the property beautified.

During the funeral rites over the deceased Peter Scheid of Crystal Lake, April, 1918, a disastrous fire broke out destroying a beautiful Gothic structure. This church had just been paid for. On account of inadequate water supply a volunteer fire company was unable to save the edifice. Most of the contents were saved and the parish collected $15,000 insurance. War prices made reconstruction difficult and expensive, but the people made signal sacrifice to float the project which cost $25,000. New St. Mary's, more beautiful than the old, was dedicated in September, 1919. It is notable for its red tile roofing, reinforced steel trusses, copper cupola and most especially for its ecclesiastical mural decorations executed by Paul N. Klose of Milwaukee. It is now valued at $50,000.

The church started here with a membership of sixty families and has grown to 181, and 900 souls. The old public school building was purchased by the church for $900, in 1894. In 1895, a parsonage was built at a cost of $2,000. The Gothic church edifice erected in 1898 cost $16,400; it was burned April, 1918; rebuilt at a cost of $25,000. The Sisters' Convent was built in 1917 at a cost of $10,000.

The pastors for this successful parish have been as follows: Rev. Fathers F. Kirsch, M. W. Barth, Anthony Boyer, who died October, 1914, and present pastor, Rev. Edward Berthold, who took charge in 1915.

CHRISTIAN SCIENCE

FIRST CHURCH OF CHRIST, SCIENTIST. Among the later religious organizations in the county is that of Christian Science, which has quite a following at different places, but no regular organized church society outside of the one at Woodstock, known as the "First Church of Christ, Scientist." This was the outgrowth of the Christian Science Society there, and was incorporated January 27, 1916. The first services here were held in the home of Harry Hilands, on North Hoy street, January 5, 1908, and meetings were held there until January, 1911, when the followers went to the supervisors' rooms at the courthouse. There they held services regularly until August 30, 1914, when they moved to the old Belcher residence property at the corner of Dean and South streets, which was purchased December, 1914, and was all paid for by January, 1917. The seating capacity of the building is about sixty persons. A Christian Science reading room was established there in 1915.

The Christian Science Society was organized July 30, 1912, with seven charter members, as follows: Mr. and Mrs. Harry Hilands, Mrs. Carrie Hill, Mrs. Susie W. Clark, Mrs. Louise Eberwein, Mrs. Emilie L. Gall and Mr. Frank Draheim. Services are held each Sabbath; a Sunday school is supported and the reading room is open several days each week.

CONGREGATIONAL

CRYSTAL LAKE CHURCH. Among the oldest churches of this denomination in this part of the country is the Congregational Church at the city of Crystal Lake, which was organized June 10, 1842. The charter members were as follows: Reuben Jenne, Mrs. Susan Jenne, John W. Salisbury, Mrs. Eliza A. Salisbury, Allen Baldwin, George W. Dike and James T. Pierson. The present membership of this church is ninety-five.

A frame building was erected in 1849, the cost of which is now unknown. Another frame edifice was built in 1867, opposite the Park, and is valued at $8,000. It was dedicated in 1868.

The following have served as pastors in the order here noted: Revs. E. G. Howe, Hiram Kellogg, Spencer Balser, John V. Downs, Isaac C. Beach, George Langdon, Elkanah Whitney, John V. Downs, Francis L. Fuller, Henry E. Barnes, James H. Harwood, Norman A. Willard, James H. Harwood, Samuel C. Hay, William F. Rose, Robert Hay, Edwin N. Andrews, Samuel C. Hay, Edwin D. Bailey, Charles J. Adams, Reuben B. Wright, A. E. Allaben, Henry Willard, James R. Kay, Eugene F. Wright, Otho M. Van Swearinger, Winfield R. Gaylord, John E. Evans, J. Vincent Willis, V. Greenwood, H. M. Collecod, W. T. McGann, A. C. Heyman, J. B. Johnston, A. J. Saunders, W. H. Traimem, Theodore Kellogg, F. P. Ford, present pastor.

THE FIRST CONGREGATIONAL CHURCH OF RICHMOND was organized December 23, 1843, by the following charter members: Robert W. Chapman, Walter Jones, Eliza Jones, Daniel Rowe, Joshua Post, Emaline Post and John Brown. Rev. L. Rogers was chosen moderator. The present membership is forty-four. A frame church was erected in 1859, and another built in 1896, valued at $2,000.

The following have served as pastors for this church: Revs. I. K. Hart, J. V. Downs, C. C. Caldwell, Francis J. Douglas, Charles H. Fraser, H. W. Harbaugh, H. O. Spillman, B. C. Preston, J. B. Orr, H. A. Kerns, J. W. Helmoth, Frank B. Hicks, Alex E. Cutler, S. H. Herbert, P. H. Barker, F. A. Williams, Howard Moore, Fred Squires, John Herring, Clay E. Palmer, Ralph T. Cass.

THE ALGONQUIN CHURCH was organized at the village of Algonquin, February 9, 1850, and had for its charter members James Humes and wife, Rosalinda; Ambrose Dodd, Mrs. Ann Kerns, John Van Buren and wife, Livonia; Mrs. Abigail Smock, Mrs. Jane Foster, Wright Warren and wife, Cynthia; Samuel G. Foster. The present membership is 111.

The original church building was dedicated January 17, 1868; it was remodeled, as at present, in 1913 and dedicated November 9, 1913. The first parsonage is still in use. The church is valued at $5,500.

An effort to secure the names of the pastors upon the part of the compiler of this chapter has not met with success. However, from an old publication from church authority, the following incomplete list of pastors has been found and will be here attached: Revs. C. L.

Hall, N. C. Clark, N. Shapely, E. C. Berge, J. D. Davis who came in 1867, I. B. Smith, T. Gulespie, W. W. Cutless, a Miss Newman, Rev. Hill of the Methodist church preached half time for this church and later became a Congregational minister. He was succeeded by Alfred Wray, who came in 1878; next was Rev. Andrich, followed by Rev. Huestis, and he was succeeded by Rev. C. C. Campbell, who in 1885 was still pastor. The present pastor is Rev. J. F. Bishop.

THE HUNTLEY CHURCH was organized in 1852 by the "Congregational Church Society." The early records are not intact at this date, but from a former county history it is learned that the church was formed September 11, 1852, by two clergymen, Revs. Starr and Dickeson. Up to 1865 there was no church building in which to worship, but under the ministration of Rev. C. S. Harrison, a commodious structure was provided. Among the pastors have been Revs. L. Church, Daniel Chapman, W. W. Curtiss, C. H. Abbott, H. W. George, A. K. Wray, T. L. Brown, Charles Hartley, and J. R. Smith.

The membership of the church today is about 156. The same frame edifice erected in 1864-5 is still doing service. It is valued at $19,000.

THE FIRST CONGREGATIONAL CHURCH AT WOODSTOCK. From the present church clerk, Archie W. Hill, and from other sources, it is learned that this church was organized in 1865, with charter members as follows: Caleb Williams, Cordelia B. Williams, Nelson Diggins, Katy M. Diggins, Orvis Gage, Fannie Page, Timothy B. Bidwell, Abner Bidwell, Irwin E. Bidwell, Hattie Baldwin, J. H. Branson, Margaret Kelly, John C. Williams, L. A. Barrows, Emily S. Barrows. The membership today is about 116. The property of the society is valued at $17,000 and consists of a brick church and a frame parsonage. The first church building was a frame one, erected in 1866. The present church was built in 1907. The pastors have included the following, in the order given: Revs. J. J. A. T. Dixon, J. R. Danforth, A. L. Riggs, A. P. Johnson, L. V. Price, T. C. Northcutt, M. A. Stevens, E. J. Alden, J. D. Wells, W. A. Evans, E. B. Boggers, I. N. Adrian, Harry B. Long, C. E. Enlow, W. R. Gaylord, Roy B. Guild, John W. Moore, C. H. Bente, William Kilbourne, V. P. Welch, John W. Herring, and Ira D. Stone.

EPISCOPAL

*CHRIST EPISCOPAL CHURCH. The Episcopalians at one time had more active parishes within this county than at this date. Woodstock, Ma-

L. B. Covell

rengo and numerous places had mission churches planted, but the only really active Episcopal Church in McHenry County now is Christ Episcopal Church at Harvard. The planting of the church here was the accomplishment of an effort begun under very unpromising circumstances, as there were already three Protestant churches here, there did not seem to be any other call for additional work in a religious line. But there were a few families, of the Angelican communion, who felt a desire to see an Episcopal church established here, and by their united and zealous efforts, the end was attained. The initial steps were begun by Rev. Peter Arvedson, who had built a church at Algonquin. Appointed missionary-at-large for some northern counties in this state, he became especially interested in numbers of old-country people settled on farms in McHenry County, and by occasional friendly visits among them won their confidence and esteem. Their number was not large, but they became the nucleus of what afterwards became Christ's Episcopal Church of Harvard. On a petition being signed and sent to Bishop McLaren, asking for a resident priest to hold regular services, Rev. A. A. Fiske was induced to accept the position and serve the little band of believers, beginning his work in the Congregational Church building which was leased for that purpose. The first services were held by Mr. Fiske in January, 1877; the last in May, 1880.

Meanwhile measures had been ripening among the members to build a house of worship of their own. A lot was secured and ground broken for the foundation of the present church, upon which the carpenters began their work in November, 1880, and finished it in the summer of 1881. The new edifice was opened for divine worship in September that year and on Sunday, May 8, 1885, the church was consecrated by Bishop McLaren. The church property, comprising all of the buildings, is valued at $30,000.

In 1886 Rev. Fiske resigned his charge on a call being sent him from the church at Austin, Ill., and other rectors followed him, until Reverend Fiske was called again to his old charge, and continued its faithful pastor until his health failed a few years ago, since which time he has lived a quiet, retired life among the people of other days, when he built up one of the strongest churches of his denomination in this part of Illinois.

The present membership is 153. The church school has a membership of about forty-five pupils, with Mrs. C. J. Hendricks as superintendent.

The following is a list of rectors for this church: Revs. A. A. Fiske,

Francis J. Hall, E. R. Sweetland, J. B. Williams, F. E. Brandt, R. S. Hannah, B. E. Chapman, H. A. Lepper, William Henry Bond, the present incumbent.

The rectory was purchased in 1908 and in 1913 a parish house was erected of brick. St. Mary's Guild is presided over by Mrs. Mary A. Fiske St Catherine's Guild, by Mrs C. M. Johnson; St. Martin's Guild Acolytes, Harry Bosler, Master of Ceremonies Christ Church Men's Club, with 108 members, was organized by Rev. F. E. Brandt in 1907. Hon. J. H. Vickers was elected its first president   The clubrooms of this club were recently built especially with this object in view and are in all ways modern in appointment, having fine reading rooms, billiard parlor and many conveniences. It should here be added in conclusion that whatever success has come to this church has been largely due to the devout men who have been its rectors--men of scholarship and advanced ideas in church work.

At Spring Grove, St. Mary's Episcopal church was formed May 5, 1873, by Rev. Peter Avidson and flourished as long as the English resided in that vicinity.

The first services held in Algonquin township was by the Episcopal people who assembled at the home of Samuel Gillilan, in 1836. St. John's Protestant Episcopal church was organized at Algonquin in 1844. A church was built in 1864 and was clear of debt in 1871. Rev. Avidson, rector, died there in November, 1880. Other denominations have virtually crowded this church out of the field.

LUTHERAN

IMMANUEL EVANGELICAL LUTHERAN CHURCH. This church was organized at Crystal Lake in 1869-70, by Rev. Richmann, then located at Elgin, Ill. The constitution was signed by thirty-six constituent members, only one of whom still survives, John Bohl of Crystal Lake. John Berg, F. T. Reddersdorf, John Lang, F. Wendt, John Ritt, Fred Westphal, Karl Kruse, Carl Kniebusch, William Kniebusch, John Sund, Mr. Zimmerman were also members. The present membership of this congregation is 600.

The first building erected in 1875 by the congregation, was a frame schoolhouse 20x36 feet, John Sund contractor, at a cost of $575. This building is now a part of John Buehler's store at Crystal Lake. In 1877 a church standing near Crystal Lake Park was purchased for $400 and moved to the lot on McHenry Avenue. This was next to the schoolhouse. In 1895 this building was taken down and the present edifice built. It is 80x44 feet, with two steeples 160 feet, and cost $6,000. It is valued at $10,000. The children of the congregation attend the day schools, but for strangers there is maintained a Sunday school, having both German and English departments that is now attended by about twenty nine children. The day school is attended by 114 pupils.

The following pastors have served this congregation: Rev. H. Schmidt, located at Dundee; Rev. Richmann, Elgin, Rev. Adam Beiser, of Desplaines, supplied. The first resident pastor was Rev. Henry Schmidt, 1875-80. He was followed by: Rev. M. Heyer, 1880-83; Karl Schmidt, 1883-97; G. Bertram, 1897-1904; and Rev. F. G. Kuchnert came in 1904 and is the present pastor.

TRINITY EVANGELICAL LUTHERAN CHURCH was organized at Huntley March 1, 1871, by Rev. F. W. Richmann, of Elgin. The charter members were as follows: John Schrader, Henry Heuer, John Frost, John Gutshow, Charles Gruitzmacher, Fred Miller, Fred Zimmerman and Henry Heinemann, Sr., who died at the advanced age of ninety-five years, in 1917. The present membership is 375 souls.

In 1872 they built a fine, large church in which to worship. With alterations and additions the property is valued at $23,000. In 1878, under Rev. J. E. Baumgartner, a steeple was added to the church, the same being 105 feet high, and the bell weighs 545 pounds. The congregation owns a beautiful school property near the church, erected in 1912, a brick structure 46x28 feet, is equipped with all modern improvements and is really an honor and credit to the village of Huntley. Its value is $5,000. The present pastor, Reverend Baumgartner, organized a Sunday school of about seventy-five pupils. He also has charge of the parochial school of the congregation where the Bible and common school branches are taught, and from here pupils are fitted for the seventh or eighth grades in the public schools. As pastor, superintendent and instructor, the present faithful pastor is kept very busy. Besides his congregation at Huntley he also cares for a church at Gilberts, where he holds services monthly.

The following is a list of pastors who have served this congregation: Revs. F. W. Richmann, 1871-73; C. Steinrauf, 1873-75; John E. Baumgartner, 1875-87; J. L. Cramer, 1877-89; G. Guelker, 1889-1903; Daniel Pollott, 1903-10; and Rev. Louis Baumgartner, who assumed charge in 1910, is the present pastor and under whose leadership the congregation is constantly increasing.

ST. JOHN'S EVANGELICAL LUTHERAN CHURCH is situated at the corner of Calhoun and Jefferson streets, Woodstock. It was organized in April, 1874, under direction of Rev. Carl Schmidt. Its charter members were as follows: John Riebe, Wm. Scharrau, Carl Riedel, Joachim Zierk, John K......d W...., William K..k, Fred Albre.. Chr.. V... l..d J..st, John Weiner, Carl Sah. Fred K.. l William Kno bus a, Jul.. Schue t, Sr., Loui. Kirchmann, John Se. uett, Jr., John Nie..nn, Carl Nage. The membership in 1875 was twenty five fami lies. The present membership of this church is about 529 souls divided as follows: ...nty-six voting member, and 253 communicants.

The scho...... connected with this church is as follows: Chr.. an day school, seven grades, R. G. Ern.t teacher; membership thirty nine pupils. Sunday school sixty two pupils. R. G. Ernst teacher. Rev. H. A. Laufer is superintendent of both schools. The Sunday school is conducted entirely in English.

The pastors serving this church have been in the following order: Revs. M. Heyer, Carl Schmidt and H. G. Schmidt, who were nom-esbers coming from various places. The first resident pastor was Rev. H. Engelbrecht, 1894-96; Rev. H. Dannenfeldt, 1897-02; Rev. J. Bertram, 1902-12; present pastor, Rev. H. A. Laufer, came in 1912 and is doing excellent work in both the church and school.

As to the places in which this congregation has worshiped it may be stated that for about the first nine years services were held in the lecture room of the Methodist Episcopal Church of Woodstock. Later the congregation purchased a vacant church, a frame building, on the corner of Calhoun and Jefferson streets for $1,700, which in later years was destroyed by fire. In 1898 a brick veneered church was built for $3,000, but to day is valued at $9,000 with all improvements made since it was first in use. A parsonage and barn erected on the three lots pur chased in June, 1907, are valued at $4,000.

ZION'S EVANGELICAL LUTHERAN CHURCH was formed in 1876 at West McHenry under the direction of Rev. H. G. Schmidt, and in 1884 it had a membership of twenty five. At present it has about twenty one voting members and seventy six communicant members. The Sunday school is conducted by Rev. H. A. Laufer.

The various pastors who have served this congregation are: Revs. Carl Schmidt, M. Heyer and Carl Schneider, up to 1894. Since 1894 the pastors have been: Revs. H. Engelbrecht, 1894-96, H. Dannenfeldt, 1897-1902; J. Bertram, 1902-12, and H. A. Laufer, who commenced his labors here in 1912.

At first this congregation held services in the Baptist church, later in the Methodist Episcopal church. In 1891 the congregation built a frame church costing about $800. It is valued at about $4,000.

St. John's Evangelical Lutheran Church at the village of Algonquin, this county, was formed March 11, 1876, and its first pastor was Rev. J. H. C. Steege of Dundee, who preached in various schoolhouses east of Algonquin. The seventeen original members of this congregation were as follows: Fred Richards, Fred Duensing, Sr., Christian Patsche, William Wodrich, John Colbow, Christian Duehn, Carl Buerkle, Henry Rogahn, Henry Albrecht, Henry Henk, Christian Pinnow, John Zorn, Carl Schoening, J. Wienke, Fred Ahrens, Fred Pruess, Carl Gehr.

Shortly after organizing a congregation the members decided to build a church, which was 22 by 50 feet in size, besides a vestry room 16 by 24 feet. That was also used as a parochial schoolroom.

Rev. Henry Fuss was the first ordained minister, but he remained only one year. Rev. Ludwig von Schenk, who brought new life to the church, faithfully served for three years and was then called to Rockford, Ill. Walter von Schenk was next called, and he proved an able minister and teacher. He was installed June 13, 1882. All debts of the church were paid during his pastorate, also a fine bell was placed in the church tower. On December 6, 1891, Rev. Schenk received a call from a congregation in St. Paul and accepted. Rev. J. Steffen was called to Algonquin in 1892. He was an able man, but much of the time he was an invalid and died after he arrived at Algonquin in about one year. It was during his illness that the parsonage was destroyed by fire and the congregation immediately erected another. The next pastor was Rev. Paul von Torne, who remained until July, 1900, when he resigned. Next came Rev. H. Moldenhauer from Hanson Park, who was installed September 30, 1900. He it was who wisely saw the need of keeping the children in the church and at once gathered them into his school.

The old schoolroom being too small the congregation soon provided a new and better building in which to hold the school. In 1902 he had seventy-six pupils. The pastor was unable to teach and attend to the parish as minister, hence a teacher was employed in the autumn of 1902. Ernst Milizer of Arlington Heights, was called for that position and served well until he met with accidental death by drowning in Fox River, April 8, 1917. Various instructors have been employed since that date.

In 1914 the congregation decided to build a modern church building. The committee finally awarded a contract for the building to Henry Markhoff, of Elgin. The church is valued at $25,000. The present con-

gregation is made up of 100 members. The present pastor is Henry
M....... er.

.... rinity Church was .... ed a M....... o, Ap.. 25, 1....
by R....... k B....... ....
C....... i.... K..f K....... W ..r.. G....... .... H..,
T.... b.. G....r.. l Tr..... W..... Tr.... C.. Z.... d.r.. E.... K..
h.d W.... l K....... t, ...b.... S .b... W..l..m F....... .. t
b.... F.... l..b.... r Z....... .... gr.... t.. ha .... 1....
820 .... th 310 communicants. The church .difi..s .. b ....
cost $19,000; the frame school building cost $3,200; the 'r.... ....
is valu.. .a.. $1,800. This fine propert.... all located on Jackson ....
It is now valued at $30,000.

The p....s ha .... .om .im.. t.. time ..n th. order .ve....... s
follow: Rev. J. E. Baarm..er.ner, 1886-86; J. Cr...m.., 1886-88; O.
Do..derl..m, 1888-91; P. Do..derlein, 1891-1904, ..d .V. C. St.ic... V..
came in 1905.

TRINITY EVANGELICAL LUTHERAN CHURCH. This is one of the stro..g
est church organizations in the county. Its history reaches back to 1884,
when work was begun by Reverend Schenk, who held the first services
in a rented building belonging to the Presbyterian denomination at
Harvard. The mission was really established in February, 1884, when
Harvard had but about 1,700 population. Not until May, 1889, was this
congregation fully organized into a church. A goodly number of families were immigrants from Germany, these numbering certainly as many
as thirty families who helped forward the new church movement at
Harvard. .

The first baptismal ceremony was performed January 27, 1884, the
subject being the daughter of Mr. and Mrs. Fred Nolz.

The first confirmation was on April 20, 1884, when four girls were
confirmed at one time.

The first communion was administered August 26, 1884, when twenty-
seven communed at the Lord's Supper.

The first funeral service was that had in June, 1884. The first wedding was March 31, 1884.

The first regular pastor was Rev. F. Caemmerer, under whose administration the constitution of the church was signed by thirty-nine voting
members of the congregation.

In the month of August, 1885, an attempt was made to start building
operations, but nothing materialized along this line until April, 1892,
when the present frame church edifice was erected. It is a large buil-

ing with a spire surmounting it which is fully 100 feet high. This building was dedicated to the worship of Almighty God, October, 1892. It is valued at $45,000.

The parsonage is also a frame building standing on the same grounds as the church, the premises being a full city block of land in a very sightly part of the city of Harvard. Its street location is East Diggins.

The various pastors who have faithfully served this congregation have been in the order here named as follows: Rev. F. Caemmerer, who served until May 6, 1899, and was succeeded by the Rev. E. A. Behrens, of New York; he continued here five years and six months. Under his administration the influential Ladies Aid Society, with about 150 members was formed. In all, this society.has raised $6,500 for church improvements and for deeds of charity and mercy. The third pastor was Rev. Carl O. Salzmann, of St. Louis, Mo., who served three years and seven months. Under him was built the addition to the church building, used for school purposes. Next came Rev. E. O. Giesel, of Platteville, Wis., who arrived Trinity Sunday, 1908, and served faithfully and well until called by death, December 5, 1912. Under his guidance was added to the parsonage more room and other needed improvements, amounting to an expense of about $1,200, including the splendid basement, hot water heating plant, the cement sidewalks, etc. He it was who started the pipe organ fund with which later the present sweet-toned pipe organ was purchased, and it is highly prized by the congregation and well-trained choir of about twenty voices. Following Rev. E. O. Giesel, Rev. E. A. Giesel, his son, responded to a call from this congregation December 11, 1912. He came from South Haven, Mich. It was he who first introduced the English language in church services here and also in the Sunday school work and Bible classes. He is a strong believer in the use of the English language by all American citizens, whether native or foreign-born.

Under this energetic pastor there was organized a Luther League of 100 members, commencing with the modest number of only twenty-four. This noble band of church workers has been busy in season and out, and have raised and paid into the treasury of this church over $1,589, which has aided a score of needed improvements. The total amount in improvements made under Reverend Giesel is $7,000. The present pastor is John M. Schedler.

The "envelope system" of making collections is employed and was introduced and urged upon the people by the present pastor. The church books and records in general of this congregation show great pains upon the pastor's part, whose every hour is filled with pressing duties as he cares to bear the spiritual and material interests of his large and areat congregation yet seems that be given time and care has he, to keep all of the needs of his flock in good repair form and has indeed an exceptionally clear church record.

When Rev. Giesel came to Harvard he found a church about one-half its present size. There is a membership of 600. The church held its twenty-fifth jubilee anniversary commemorating the dedication of their church edifice in 1917, an illustration of which appears in this volume. At that great gathering Rev. H. K. Doermann, D. D. of St. Paul, was present and delivered the sermon. Up to the date of this jubilee, twenty-five years after the dedication, there had been officiated at by pastors here 1,008 baptisms; couples married, 233; persons buried, 278, and received into the church, 702 persons.

St. John's Evangelical Lutheran Church is located at the village of Union and was organized there November 10, 1887, with charter members as follows: Fred Schneidewind, Charles Miller, Henry Young, Fred Bloedorn, August Kunkle, Fred Martens, Fred Miller, August Kamholz, M. Kolberg, John Hopp, Charles Price, Fred Selchow, Gust E. Hin, Charles Kasten, John Tornow, Alb Gehrke, F. Pries, Charles Winkelmann, F. Dahelke. The present membership is about 103 families with seventy-six voting members. The present buildings of this congregation are the veneered brick church, built in 1901, valued at about $20,000, a parochial school built in 1901, and a parsonage built in 1908.

The pastors who have had charge of this congregation are: Revs. Otto Doederlein, Paul Doederlein, George Lienhardt, August Lobitz and the present pastor Rev. Henry Traub, who came to this church May 1, 1913.

St. Paul's Evangelical Lutheran Church was organized at Crystal Lake in 1896, and reorganized in 1906. It was organized by Rev. E. Rahn, reorganized by Rev. H. Wagner. Under the reorganization the members were: Fr. Mackeben, H. Walther, F. Schulz, H. Dunker, E. Schubbe, K. Tegtmeier, Fr. Kempfert, William Schwarz, Fr. Dreyer, Karl Lange. The present membership includes about thirty families and 600 souls. The Sunday school has four teachers and about thirty children. The Ladies Aid Society has relatively twenty-five members.

The church building is at North Crystal Lake and is a cement structure valued at $10,000. The following have been pastors in the order here given: Revs. H. Wagner, William Kreis, H. Wagner, H.

ROBERT COWAN

ELLEN E. COWAN

Tietke, F. Ernst, Blum J. Heinrich, and F. G. Kuehnert, the present pastor.

St. Paul's Lutheran Church at Harvard, was organized by Rev. R. Reinke about 1904, and now has a membership of relatively 107, with sixty-six communicants. Cary was organized by Rev. Kuehnert in 1911, and now has forty-nine members and twenty-four communicants. Rev. Kuehnert has charge of the church at Harvard as well as at Cary.

Holy Cross Lutheran Church. The Lutheran Church at Cary station was organized in 1910, and has a present membership of thirty souls. There is no church property. Rev. F. G. Kuehnert is the pastor.

Grace Evangelical Lutheran Church is a rather recent religious organization of Woodstock. The church building they now own and occupy is not far from the Catholic Church in the northwestern part of the city. It was built by the old German Presbyterians who disbanded a few years since. In 1919 a large addition was made to the edifice to accommodate the greatly increasing congregation. The church is valued at $20,000. There is a membership of 600 souls. Rev. Roger C. Kaufman is the present pastor.

METHODIST

The First Methodist Episcopal Church of Marengo was among the first pioneer church organizations in this county. It was organized in 1837 by Rev. John Clark and Leander S. Walker. It was during 1837 that the conference formed the Sycamore circuit which embraced all the territory from Sycamore north to the Wisconsin line, running east as far as the Fox River and west to the Rock River. The regular appointed places for holding services were Sycamore, Rockford, Belvidere, Round Prairie, Garden Prairie, Marengo, Harmony, Ridgefield and McHenry, besides many isolated places where occasional services were held. In all this vast region there was not a single church house at that date, private homes being made into "meeting houses." In the autumn of 1837, Rev. William Gaddis preached his first sermon at the house of Dr. Eli Smith, in Riley Township. The audience did not exceed eight persons besides the doctor's family. Sometime in 1838 the minister in charge formed a class at Marengo, holding meetings in the house of Calvin Spencer. The following were the first members of the pioneer society: Eli Smith, class-leader; Asenith Smith, Samuel and Polly Smith, and Eunice Cobb. A few days later the names of O. P. Rogers, Mary S. Rogers and Chester Williams were added to the list.

In consequence of this circuit being 200 miles in circumference,
requiring [illegible] ....
d .... K. L. S. W .... I N ....
t c .... A. first ....
a R and P .... W .... i W. D..
r .O. P. R .... W.2...... I. J.......
a .... -100 a ...... t the ....
w ia .... in Sunday

In the .... of ...... a .... 1830 ....
m........ .... [illegible] this county. As Last
Marengo, ... H. commenced in the second and estab-. H. springer
d. .... p....... Peoples from .. far and near. I....
Was the people were shortly connected. It was in 1855 the ....
erected its taludes .... the same being dedicated and ...spring
Rev. John Demster. A Sabbath school was organ... ... 1840 with ....
pupils but in 1855 the school had over 100 pupils.

The present beautiful brick edifice was built in 1897 at a ...
$20,000 while the parsonage cost $3,500. The membership ... 42.
The Ministers who have faithfully discharged the duty, as pastor of
the church at Marengo are as follows: Revs. William Gehm, N. ....
Jew ... D. A. Wilke, P. Ferry, N. Smith, William Goold's Charles
McClure, E. Brown, A. Hammond, D. Fellows, J. N. Hannan, James
McLane, G. W. Murphy, John Hodges, E. Ransom, E. G. Wood, A.
McWright, A. B. Call, William Skelton, J. P. Nance, D. Cassidy, J. R.
Goodrich, L. S. Walker, David Leed, A. P. Mead, E. W. Adams, Charles
Hanley, George Richardson, N. D. Lanning, Alonzo Newton, H. J.
Huston, A. Schoemaker, J. H. Reever, J. M. Chardoming, W. H.
Smith, J. C. Bigelow, S. H. Wells, C. W. Thornton, E. J. Rose, F. H.
Gardner, C. A. Bunker, Wilmer Jaygard, N. J. Harkness, E. G. Schutz,
A. L. Fisher, C. J. Brady, William Ewing, R. E. Buckey, W. H. Lope
and Chas. J. Dickey.

The RICHMOND CHURCH is one of the county's oldest religious socie-
ties. It was organized November 3, 1838, by Rev. L. S. Lewis, who
preached two years. At that date this formed a part of Crystal Lake
Circuit which comprised about thirty preaching appointments. Among
the earlier ministers here were the following: Revs. Walker, Jewett,
Nathaniel White, Dr. Decker, Whipple, Amos Wiley, L. S. Walker,
John Rhodes, B. F. Jacobs, Calvin Brookins, Edwin Brown, J. H.
Moore, Thomas Corwin, E. M. Battis, G. S. Wiley, Nathan Critchett,
Samuel Earngey, P. C. Steere, W. F. DeLap, Grover C. Clark, and

many more who came at a later date. At first a schoolhouse was used for a house of worship, but in 1855 the society dedicated its own church building on Main street, a frame edifice seating 250 and costing about $2,500. In 1880 the total membership was about forty. The present membership is fifty-three. The Sunday school attendance is about 112. The church property erected in 1902 is valued at $10,500. The present pastor is P. W. Poley.

THE McHENRY CHURCH is also numbered among the pioneer religious societies of this county. It was organized in 1840 and its first members were Ira and Mrs. Mary Colby, Darius Reynolds and wife, Alden and Mrs. M. Harvey, Freeman Harvey, and Mrs. Abigail Harvey, with Freeman Harvey as class-leader. The county seat was then at McHenry and services were held in the courthouse once in four weeks, and also at times in private homes. The circuit then consisted of seven appointments. In 1850 this church, in connection with the Free-Will Baptists, built a brick church and used it alternately. The Methodists built a church for their own use about 1870 and a parsonage in 1879. The church property is valued at $7,300. Rev. Raymond Sanger is the present pastor.

THE WOODSTOCK CHURCH. Methodism in Woodstock was established in 1850 by Reverend Morehouse. The charter members were as follows: Mr. Cotting and wife, Mrs. C. Ramsey, Mrs. Dr. Rose, Miss Mary Sherwood, George Starr and wife, Silas Wilson and wife, William Montgomery and wife. The first officers were: George Starr, class-leader; S. O. Gregory, William H. Murphy, Silas Wilson, James Murphy, John Reider, Andrew Murphy, Owen Murphy were stewards; and Charles McClure and I. H. Fairchilds were local preachers. Services at first were held in the schoolhouse, then in Excelsior Hall, and two years later in Phoenix Hall. The church was organized twelve years before a church edifice was owned. In 1862 they purchased the old Baptist church building for the sum of $1,500. For many years this building served as a place of worship, but finally it was too small to accommodate the increasing congregation and the present frame edifice was erected in 1870 at an expense of $8,000. It seats about 400 persons but is fast going to decay and is soon to be replaced by a larger and more modern building at a cost of $60,000.

The present membership is 350. Franklinville, a country station to the west, belongs to this church.

The pastors who have faithfully served this church are: Revs. Morehouse, Guyer, E. Brown, Joseph Hartwell, Burlingame, D. W. Lynn,

Lyon, W. A. Smith, W. A. Cross, G. S. Huff, M. B. Cleveland, C.
Brookins, S. T. Stow, M. H. Triggs, N. D. Fanning, E. M. Boring, I
H.   , A. Newton, S. Earngey, John Adams, Geo. K. Hoover, 1884;
M. H. Plumb, 1886, Henry Lea, 1888; J. J. Walter, 1889, Frank Mc-
Nurney, 1891; N. A Sunderland, 18   Thomas A. G. C., 1904, J. W.
Hockings, 1906, P. R. Greene, 1909, Charles D. Wilson, 1913, J. A.
Markak 1917, and F. A. Graham, 1918, the present pastor.

The GREENWOOD CHURCH was organized at the village of Greenwood in 1850, but lapsed in 1875 and was reorganized in 1884, the last
organization being made by C. W. Jaycox with charter members as
follows: Mr. and Mrs. Joseph Parker, Alphonso Newman, Mr. and Mrs.
Owen Murphy, Mr. and Mrs. Andrw Murphy, Mr. and Mrs. Stewart.
The present membership is about ninety. This church was one of the
original appointments comprising the old McHenry Circuit which included
in 1852, Highland Prairie, North Hebron, Richmond, Ringwood, Greenwood, East Greenwood, Queen Ann, English Prairie and McHenry.

The first church used by this congregation was the old Presbyterian
building. This was torn down and a new church provided in 1909. A
frame parsonage was built in 1904. The church is valued at $8,500
and the parsonage at $2,500.

The following is a list of pastors who have served at Greenwood:
Revs. Leander S. Walker, Rev. Shepherd, Christopher Lazenby, T. R.
Satterfield, Rev. Stewart, 1863; Rev. Bundoe, M. H. Triggs, Rev. Wil-
son, 1866; S. H. Adams, 1867; L. R. Davis, 1869; Rev. Brookins, 1871;
Byron Alden, 1872-75 no pastor for some time; Rev. Adams, 1880;
Rev. Elkins, 1881; William Nickle, 1881-1884; C. W. Jaycox, 1884;
Rev. William Nickle, 1887; Herbert J. Cocknell, 1897; Homer Lee, 1898;
William Nickle, 1899; Charles E. Coon, 1901; W. H. Whitlock, 1903,
Charles E. Butterfield, 1904; Warren Jones, 1906; J. E. DeLong, 1906;
C. J. Bready, 1908; H. J. Collins, 1910; Seth Baker, 1913; Harry Cul-
bertson, 1917; and C. J. Hewitt.

The RINGWOOD CHURCH was organized in the village of Ringwood
in 1855 as a Union church, made up of Methodist and Congregational
church people. In 1868 the Congregationalists withdrew. The charter
members of this church were as follows: Mr. and Mrs. Samuel Simmons,
Mr. and Mrs. William Mead, Jane Vasey, John Vasey, Richard Vasey,
William Vasey, Frank Vasey, Mr. and Mrs. Joseph Carr, Mr. and Mrs
Matthews Carr, William Forth, William Moody and wife. The present
membership is fifty-one. The present value of church property is $5,000.
Pastors who have served here are as follows: Revs. Nathan Jewett, Chris

topher Lazenby, Matthew Triggs, T. R. Satterfie'd, Rev. Bundock, Simon Hewes, Simon Leek, Andrew Adrian, Wycoff, William Clark W. P. J. Jordan, Cormack, Peal, C. J. Bready, H. J. Collins, Seth Baker, Harry Culbertson Harmon, and D. H. Ross, the present pastor.

THE ALDEN CHURCH. Methodism began in this part of McHenry County very early in the "thirties" and the work in the section now known as Alden belonged with a very extensive circuit and so continued until about 1856, when it was detached from the old field and since that date the pastors who have served are as follows: Five or six whose names do not appear of record, but after that they appear in the pastor's record to be: Revs. J. M. Clendenning, Robert Beatty, William Adron, J. C. Bigelow, 1883-85; E. O. Burch, 1887; T. R. Satterfe'd, 1887-8-90; C. H. Hoffman, 1890-93; J. P. Davies, 1893-95; N. M. Stokes, 1895-98; John Adams, 1898-02; E. H. Beal, 1892; Geo. K. Geoffrey, 1904. John E. Robison, 1908-10; Floyd L. Blewfield, 1910; W. M. Kauffman, 1911; George Wilson, 1913-14; S. R. Smith, 1914, who served until the station was placed in with that at Hebron (see Hebron church for other history). This society has now a membership of about fifty, and a Sunday school enrollment of about eighty.

THE HEBRON CHURCH was organized not far from 1857, when Rev. Calvin Brookins became pastor in charge. There is no record of this church for many years. It now has a membership of about 170, with a Sunday school enrollment of about ninety; the superintendent is Miss Anna Douglas. On this same circuit is Alden village, above mentioned. The church at Hebron is a small frame structure erected in 1861 and dedicated in September, 1862, by Elder Jewett. On October 29, 1896, was dedicated the present comfortable parsonage which had been so generously donated by Henry W. Mead.

Until 1896 Hebron was with Richmond on one circuit, when Rev. William H. Tuttle was appointed to the Richmond-Hebron charge and the following have served as pastors at this point: Revs. W. H. Tuttle, four years; J. B. Robinson, who came in 1900 and remained till 1901; William Ashfield, 1901; G. T. Nesmith, 1902-06; C. S. Clay, 1906-08; A. T. Stevenson, 1908-10; N. P. Tedrick, 1910-14; Enos Holt, 1914-17; W. H. Locke, who came in 1917, and W. E. Royston.

THE HARVARD CHURCH. During the winter of 1857-58, the Methodist Episcopal Church at Harvard was organized with five charter members. In 1860 they erected their first church, the first church edifice to be erected at Harvard. The board of stewards were: William H. Fuller, E. J. Sanford, L. B. Wyant, and L. M. Stephenson. Among the pastors

who have served here are the following: Revs. W. H. Reynolds, 1860;
J. H. Moor, S. F. Penn jr., 1865, C. R. Fox, 1865-67; G. J. W. s,
L. Anderson, 1868-70; L. H. when 1870-71; Samue Cass, R. H. W.
karson, Wm. Cark, John H. she Mc C. Shelde 1870 C. R. Cry
de J. W. Scott, 1878-81, Simo swan John H. Reeos A. S. Mrs
L. Grove C. Clark, W. C. Howard, S. A. Sundert E. D. Hull
T. R. S. w ne. E. K. D. Heste J. A. Ma ck, E. C. Lumsden
C. S. Moore James Potter, and C. H. Newham.

The church has a membership of about 425, with a Sunday school
enrollment of about 225. The present brick church edfee w con
s ructed not many years ago at an expense of $30,000.

The First Methodist Church was established in 1866 at Nort
Crystal Lake and is the oldest in the county. The early records re o
exis nce. The congregation built a frame church at old Crystal Lake,
also a parsonage. In 1898 the church was removed to North Crystal
Lak and remodeled. A new frame parsonage was erected at a cost
of $2,000. This branch, like others in the county, has virtually failed
to maintain itself. Its present membership in regular standing s only
five. Of the pastors who have served this church these are recalled:
Revs. C. B. Ebey, F. D. Brooke, J. D. Kelsey, C. S. Spaulding, P. W.
Newcomer, John Harvey, J. F. Hill, H. Lenz, W. C. McNeil, J. G. Rockenbach, J. H. Polly, J. W. Hill, A. L. Wright, W. G. Hanmer, J. G.
Rockenbach, W. M. Kelsey, H. W. Hills and J. E. Parry.

The Crystal Lake Church was organized as early as 1861, possibly earlier, the records are not clear as to the very early events of
this society. It is shown, however, that S. H. Hamilton, E. Owen and
W. A. Smith are named as among the officers. The minister in charg
was Rev. C. Lazenby, with Presiding Elder J. W. Agard. The present
membership is 200. The present value of the church with lo s $18,000,
recent improvements having been made in it. The parsonage is valued at
$8,000.

The list of pastors who have served at Crystal Lake are: Revs. C.
Lazenbey, C. Hamilton, A. G. Burlingame, W. S. Harrington, W. J.
Rider, I. B. Hansey, S. T. Shaw, R. H. Wilkinson, S. Hemes E. Brown,
J. S. Norris, A. J. Scott, L. Clifford, E. M. Boring, S. Hemes, G. L.
Wilsy, O. E. Burch, J. H. Bacon, J. T. Rubert, J. M. Conlee, O. H.
Cessna, G. H. Wells, W. H. Pierce, J. R. Hamilton, M. H. Plumb, A. H.
Kistler, W. H. Locke, W. H. Smith, W. B. Doble, H. J. Cockerill, R.
H. Pate, T. A. Brewster, W. E. Grase, H. P. Barnes, and Manley J.
Mumford, the present pastor.

THE FREE METHODIST CHURCH at Algonquin was organized as a local branch of the "Free Methodist Church of North America," by Rev. D. P. Baker in 1874. Among the first members here were: R. B. McKee, Emeline McKee, William Head, Mr. Dunn, Olive Dunn, William Williams, Ann Williams, Henry Chandler, Mrs. Chandler, and Sarah Hubbard. The church at one time flourished in this community but of late not so much and there are now but two members left of this organization. A frame church was erected in 1877 costing $1,400, and a parsonage was built in 1884 costing about $1,500.

Pastors who faithfully served this church were: Revs. D. P. Baker, M. L. Vorheis, C. P. Miller, W. W. Kelley, C. W. Frink, F. A. Miller, F. A. Haley, C. H. Rawson, W. P. Ferris, David Seymour, P. W. Newcomer, Daniel Sinclair, Julius Buss, William Wilson, H. W. Fish, P. C. Burhars, John Spencer, S. C. Spaulding, R. F. Brouthers, J. J. Hales, F. M. Fish, J. H. Wortendyke, Peter Zeller, E. G. Cryer, O. V. Ketels, F. M. Campbell, D. M. Smashey, D. W. Finch, J. W. Hill, P. W. Newcomer, C. W. Scalf, John Klein, T. B. Webb, F. H. Stiefkin, H. W. Hills and John E. Parry.

THE CARY STATION FREE METHODIST CHURCH was organized at the same time as the one at Crystal Lake in 1874, by Rev. D. P. Baker, with charter members as follows: M. S. W. West and wife, D. D. and Mariah Harbaek, Abraham Goodwin, Margaret Goodwin, A. L. Weaver and Edwin Crabtree.

This church membership has been decreased by death and removals until today only five members are reported. A church was erected in 1877 costing $1,200. At present there is a Sunday school which has an enrollment of about thirty-one pupils.

As a general rule the same pastor who has had charge at Algonquin has also attended to the affairs of the Cary church, hence it is needless to give the names of pastors in this connection.

THE CARY CHURCH was organized about 1888, with charter members as follows: Mrs. George Siebert, Mr. and Mrs. Wallace Burton, Miss Edith Crabtree, and a few others whose names are not now recalled by church officers. It is not a strong church, for today it only numbers seventeen souls. The church edifice was erected in 1875 for school purposes but since 1889 has been used for religious worship. The church proper including the comfortable parsonage is valued at $5,750.

The pastors who have served here include the following: Revs. I. N. Goodell, L. A. Johnson, William Nickle, Charles Wentworth, F. J. Milnes,

C. F. Greaser, F. S. Holm, Greaser, G. H. Tyler, W. A. Cross, C. D. King, C. I. S........ g J. G. Vance E. E. V........ , R. R. F........ L. G. Dowses., H. P. B........ D.. an S.. .... , ... or.

PRESBYTERIAN

The H..... C......t... s for.... 1 Sep t.... 14, 1844 in a sch.. house.... ar L.......... David Prin.... and Re.. L.. Hall was chosen m.. lerat.. The orig.. al......mbe.. s we.. as follo.. s.: John A. Ehl.... d w.... nd are.. daughte.... Ann Van Alst.... Alfre.. H. Earling John and Ly lia Adams. John Sawyer and w.... Daniel, Mari.. J.... and Elisha Con ne, William F... and Olive Peake, Charolette St.. eator, C.....in.. Weaver, Jane Meyers, David Prime and w.... David Slaw, and Ada.. Phillips. A substantial church was erected in 1868 in the vil.. ge of Hebron, and in 1882 the parsonage was built.. This was rep.. ed in 1909 by the present edifice valued at $1,500. The present membership is 110. The present pastor is Rev. F. B. McDowell.

We.. te.. ck Ch.. ch was o.. ganized in 1846 by Re.. J. B. Plumst.. d, with the following me.. bers: M. B. G.. en, Eli.. beth Given, Allen Dufield, Jesse Sloan, Anna Slavin, Margaret J. Slavin, Nao.. i C. Slavin, Charles Dufield, Andrew Scott, James Scott, Sarah Scott, Caleb Williams, Cordelia Williams, John Givins, J. S. Glvenk.. Thomas Lindsay, Mary A. Lindsay, William Gilbert, Catherine Gilbert, William D. Given and Rachel Given.

This church was the outgrow.. h of.. d.. church at Ridg.. fi.. d, then called the Virginia Settlement. Rev G. K. Todd commenced to preach at Woodstock for the new church in 1847, continuing until 1865. He was followed by Re.. Blood as above noted.

T.. following pastors have served his church: Revs. R. K. Todd, Blood, John Thomas, Kirkwood, E. J. Fish.. r, John D. McCain, S. C.. Hay, who came as pastor in 1883, Revs. Beck, Peck, McDermott and R. B. Guthrie.

At first services were held in the old court house for a year previous to building which was accomplished in 1848. This was a small frame structure capable of seating two hundred. Most of the material was donated. The present church building was erected in 1882 at an expense of $4,500. It is situated on the corner of Calhoun and Tryon stee.. s. This is a frame building accommodating about 350 persons. A mans.. was built the same year as the church. The church property

WILLIAM H. DAVIS

MRS. WILLIAM H. DAVIS

including the pipe organ and manse, is valued at $15,000. Rev. R. B. Guthrie of Arkansas, a former supply, is the present pastor.

THE MARENGO CHURCH was formed in 1850 by Rev. George F. Goodhue. The society is in a flourishing condition, has a good church edifice and parsonage.

THE GREENWOOD CHURCH was formed in 1850, with I. A. Hall as first pastor.

THE HARVARD CHURCH was organized in 1868, with Messrs. H. C. Blackman, Lewis Beaner, and C. Brown as trustees, Rev. Thomas C. Easton being first pastor. Soon the Presbyterians united with the Congregationalists, the two societies using the latter's building. In 1880, the two denominations separated. During the winter of 1868-9, the Presbyterians erected a building of their own at a cost of $3,000. This was replaced in 1912 with the present church which is valued at $20,000. The present membership is 333 souls, and the pastor in charge is Rev. Owen W. Pratt.

THE GERMAN PRESBYTERIAN CHURCH. There is no such denomination in Germany, but in some of the localities in this country where Germans settled whose belief was nearer the religious faith of the Presbyterians than any other denomination, hence they organized what was termed the "German Presbyterian Church." One such society was organized first in Greenwood Township, on Queen Ann Prairie, May 1, 1853, by Rev. Weitzel. The society has long since been abandoned and many of its members took their letters and united with the Presbyterian church of Woodstock. As the charter members will bring up by association many old time names among the devout German families, the list of the first members of this church will be given. With the exception of two or three Swiss families, including the Renics', these members were all Germans: Peter Weidrich, George Herdklotz, Peter Sonnedruecker, Michael Herdklotz, Henry Harmann, Henry Sonnedruecker, Jacob Senger, Peter Frey, Sr., Henry Sonneduecker, George Sonnedruecker, Peter Frey, Jr., Peter Herdklotz, Henry Dietrich, Christian Mueller, Henry Schnider, Henry Schmidt, Jr., George Weidrich, Michael Schmidt, Henry Herdklotz, Mike Frey, Peter Senger, Henry Harmann, Jr., Fred Bertchey, Jacob Werner, Fred Stoffell, Louisa Mueller, Margaretta Weidrich, Saloma Herdklotz, Eva Harmann, Catherine Herdklotz, [illegible] Helena Schmidt, Barbara Frey, Margaretta Senger, Charlotta Sonde [illegible] [illegible] [illegible] Queen Ann [illegible] [illegible] In 187[illegible] the name [illegible] to Queen Ann Church [illegible] Woodstock. Services [illegible] 1881, when they built a house of worship [illegible] Woodstock. This was a frame structure and seated 250 [illegible] present [illegible] Grace Evangelical church [illegible]

[illegible] together as a church body as long as possible, but [illegible] the property was sold and the members [illegible] Among the long to be remembered pastors were Rev. [illegible] Schnell, Phillip Roser and Jacob Kalb. As late as 188[illegible] the church was in a prosperous condition and had sixty-six members.

UNIVERSALIST

In earlier times the Universalist society had numerous organizations in McHenry County, but none are active today. Harvard, Marengo, Woodstock and other places were the homes of Universalist societies which no longer are in existence.

A society was formed at Marengo in 1864, with forty members, but before 1880 they had dwindled down to not over a half dozen. At one time they supported regular pastors, but only for a few years.

A church of this faith was established at Woodstock in 1855 by Rev. Livermore, who for many years edited the *New Covenant* in Chicago. At the time of organization there was a membership of twenty-seven. In 1885 they estimated their property to be worth $2,500. For many years this church has not existed. Many of the New Englanders who came in and settled in this county were of this religious faith.

A Universalist society was formed at McHenry, in January 1853, with Rev. James R. Mack as the first pastor. A building was erected in 1854. The first members included these: R. Bishop and wife, D. Brown and wife, Francis Harrison and wife, C. B. Curtis and wife, Christopher Sieber and wife, George Gage and A. H. Nanly.

CHAPTER IX

COURTS, BENCH AND BAR

By Judge Charles P. Barnes

CIRCUIT COURT—FIRST GRAND JURY—CIRCUIT JUDGES—COUNTY COMMIS-
SIONERS—COUNTY JUDGES—EARLY ATTORNEYS—STATE'S ATTORNEYS—
PRESENT ATTORNEYS—McHENRY COUNTY BAR ASSOCIATION—IN MEMO-
RIAM.

CIRCUIT COURT

Under date of May 10, 1838, pleas were heard before Judge Pearson, judge of the Seventh Judicial District, in and for the County of
McHenry, presiding at a court held at McHenry, in McHenry County,
those present being Judge John Pearson, Alonzo Huntington, state's
attorney, and Henry B. Steele, sheriff of McHenry County.

The men composing the first grand jury of the circuit court for this
county were as follows: Andrew S. Wells, James H. Lloyd, Charles H.
Bartlett, Jeremiah Porter, Willard Jones, Thomas McClure, Daniel
Winters, Richard Steele, Samuel L. Wood, Alden Harvey, Christy G.
Wheeler, Luke Hale, Amos Desmond, Moody B. Bailey, Aaron Randall,
Christopher Walkup, William E. Keyes, John McCollom, and from their
number Charles H. Bartlett was chosen foreman. Of the nineteen cases
brought before this court the first day, three were for trespass, and one
for slander. On the second day the grand jury returned three indict-
ments for larceny and one for assaulting an officer in the discharge
of his duty.

CIRCUIT JUDGES

The following is a list of the circuit judges who have served Mc-
Henry County since its organization: John Pearson, 1837-41; Theopilus
W. Smith, 1841-43; Richard M. Young, 1843-47; Jesse B. Thomas, 1847-
48; Hugh Henderson, 1848-51; Issac G. Williams, 1851-61; Allen C.

Fuller, 1861-62; T. D. Murphy, 1862-78; Charles W. Upton, 1878-82;
Charles Kelums, 1882; C. E. Fuller, 1897, Charles H. Donnelly, 1897;
A. H. Frazier, 1902; Robert W. West, 1908, Charles W. Stuart(?)
1911(?) 1914(?)   R. L. K. W.
E. D. Shurtleff, 1920

Justices of the peace have jurisdiction in all cases where the
damages sought do not exceed $300. They also have jurisdiction in
all cases for violation of the ordinances of cities, towns and villages.

County courts have jurisdiction in all matters of probate, settlement
of estates of deceased persons; also in proceedings against executors, administrators, guardians for the sale of real estate. It has also they
have concurrent jurisdiction with circuit courts in all and civil and criminal
causes where the punishment is not imprisonment in the penitentiary
or death, but an appeal is allowed from justices of the peace to county
courts.

COUNTY COMMISSIONERS

From 1837 until 1849, when township organization was adopted
and put into force in McHenry County, when supervisors assumed
their office the county's affairs were conducted by what was termed
the County Commissioners Court to which three commissioners were
elected. These commissioners were as follows: 1837 Charles H. Bart
lett resigned September term 1837, Matthias Mason, Solomon Norton;
Samuel Sherman, December, 1837, 1838 Solomon Norton, Ransom
Steele, William Jackson; 1839 B. B. Brown, Gideon Colby Robert
G White; 1840 B. B. Brown R. G. White, Daniel W. P. Tower; 1841
- R. G. White D. W. P. Tower, Hosea B. Throop; 1842 D. W. P.
Tower, H. B. Throop, Bela H. Tryon; 1843 H. B. Throop, B. H.
Tryon, Andrew J. Hayward; 1844 Same as in 1843; 1845 H. B.
Throop, A. J. Hayward, William A McConnell; 1846 H. B. Throop,
William A. McConnell, Carlisle Hastings; 1847 William A. McConnell,
Carlisle Hastings, Dexter Barrows; 1848 The same as in 1847.

COUNTY JUDGES

Amory Thomas, elected in 1839; Andrew J. Barnum, 1840; Joel
H. Johnson, 1841-42; E. J. Smith, 1843-48; L. Joslyn, 1848-49; Joseph

Golden, 1849-54; J. M. Strode, 1854-57; T. D. Murphy, 1858-61; William Kerr. 1866-67; L. S. Church, 1867-69; B. N. Smith, 1870-82; O. H. Gilmore 1882-90; C. H. Donnelly, 1890-97; O. H. Gilmore. 1897-1906; D. T. Smiley, 1906 1918; Charles P. Barnes.

EARLY ATTORNEYS

It is generally admitted that the first attorney to practice law in McHenry County was Amory E. Thomas, who came here in 1839, and continued his practice until 1844. The same year saw the advent here of Calvin Searl, who located at Crystal Lake and remained there until 1845.

Hosea G. Wilson located at McHenry in 1842, and died in that village about 1847. Charles McClure was admitted to the bar of McHenry county in 1840, but left it soon thereafter. He returned to the county in 1851 and located permanently at Woodstock. Solomon Baird was another pioneer lawyer who spent two years in active practice at McHenry, which he left in 1845.

The following lawyers were engaged in practice in the county between its first settlement and 1844, and some of these continued in practice for many years succeeding the latter date: Milton Nixon, D. C. Bush, William Bloom, Col. Lawrence S. Church, Amos B. Coon, Henry W. McLean, Anson Sperry, Phineas W. Platt, Col. Alonzo Platt, Amos Cogswell, Col. James M. Strode, Hon. Theodore D. Murphy, Charles M. Willard, Freman Van Wickle. Hon. M. L. Joslyn, Hon. William Kerr, H. S. Hanchett, P. B. Enos, S. R. Paynter, George A. Parrish, William Jackson, Hon. Ira Rozel Curtis. Hon. B. N. Smith, M. L. Ellsworth, James H. Slavin, Hon. O. H. Gilmore, James M. Southworth, Hon. Richard Bishop, C. H. Donnelly, A. B. Coon, Jr., Albert E. Boone. C. P. Barnes, and J. F. Casey.

It doubtless will be of interest to many to learn some special facts concerning the lawyers who have practiced in the courts of McHenry County in the days that are past. A former historical work of the county, as well as other books treating of the Bench and its members in Northern Illinois. have been largely drawn upon for the facts given below:

Hon. Richard Bishop, a native of New York state, was born in 1824. His father was killed by the falling of a tree when he was but seven years old. He soon became his mother's sole support, and worked for ten cents a day, at threshing grain with a flail, and he also cut cord

well, when a little older and stronger, for which latter work he re...
could for twen.. to ... ...s per c... When I re... bu...
... ... and d... ... ...
a... ... ... yes... ... ...
t... ss ... ...ter ... ... m N... ... ...
s... ... ... f y t... ... ...les. He
s... ...tly ... the bl... ... trade ... ...st... ...s
years work while most ... ...'s trade. In the sprin... 1844 ...
completed his apprentic ship, he bade farewell to his moth.., ... set
out to seek his fortune in the much vaunted west. After ... ...
peri... s ...d som... priva.ions, he landed ... foot of McH... Il...
... ... swamps for mil...s on ... s a... ... ...
I a... l ... 1844 ... he found plenty ... emp yme... ... ...
th... ... ...ss... it spr..., first at harvesting during the season and the...
durin... the remainder of the time cutting cord wood a... fty cents per
cord. In the spring of 1845 he began working at the t... ... laid
southing.. and durin... th... first year earned enough money ... buy of the
government eighty acres ... land, for which he paid the c... try ... $1 2...
per acre. He kept on adding to his holdings until at ...e time h... was ...
1,000 acres of McHenry County land, and he was also the ... wh... ...
large wagon factory and grist mill. In 1874 he embarked in the ban...
ing business in Woodstock, and followed it for two years, when he
bought a $1,000 law library, began studying law and was lat... admitted
to the bar. In 1874 he was elected to the State Assembly ... 1876 ...
and he also served as county supervisor for fifteen or more ... years.

Albert E. Bourne born at Kenosha, Wis... n 1849 was educat... ...
the W... nsin Stat... University at Madison, Wis., ...rom w...
gradua.ed in 1872. He was th... engaged in teac'in... sch... ... s...e
term.., when he b... ... me a law student, and in 1880 was ...
th... ...r. A... ...rm... he s... ... as captain in th... Ill'n...s N...
Guard. He was a well-known Mason, and in politics was a ... ...ted
Republican.

D. C. Bush was the first lawyer ... locate at W... ...stock. He came
her... in the autumn of 1844, and remained until ... December, 1872
when he rem...ved to Madison, Wis. Possessing aver...ge ... ...bility
he had a fair practice for his day and generation.

Solom... Baird came from Kentucky to J... ville ... a Il
1843, but after two years of practice, returned to K...

Col. Law...ence S. Church, w... lived ma... y ars ... ...
...

born at Nunda, N. Y., in 1820, and passed his early years on a farm. Possessing strong ambitions, he studied until he fitted himself to be a teacher and during the winter months taught school, and with the money thus earned was able to attend institutions of higher learning during the other months of the year. Deciding upon the profession of law he studied to that end, was admitted to the bar, and in 1843 came West to McHenry County, locating in the village of McHenry. Colonel Church made the long trip in a leisurely manner, riding by stage coach a part of the way and walking the remainder. To defray the expenses of his different rides, he frequently stopped long enough in the various communities through which he passed, to lecture on the Constitution of the United States. Soon after his arrival at McHenry, he went to Springfield, Ills., was there admitted to the bar of this state and at once began to practice law at McHenry. When the seat of justice was moved to Woodstock, he went with it, and continued in active practice during the remainder of his life. During his earlier years he was a radical Whig, and so had no chance in this county for political preferment until 1856, when he, with so many of the former Whigs, gave his support to John C. Fremont, the first man to be candidate for the presidency, of the Republican party. McHenry County went strongly Republican, and Colonel Church was sent as a candidate of his party to the State Assembly. He at once became a noted representative of the people, was re-elected, and was made a leader in the stormy session which followed. Later he was a candidate for Congress, but was defeated at the polls by Hon. E. B. Washburn. Once more he was returned to the Legislature, and was made chairman of the Judiciary Committee. With the outbreak of the Civil War, he displayed great zeal in support of the Union, and aided in organizing the Ninety-fifth Illinois Volunteer Infantry of which he was made colonel, but his health failed, and he resigned. The strenuous exertions he had made in behalf of the cause had so undermined his health that he never recovered, and died in 1866. He was a man of sterling integrity and possessed of a clear, brilliant intellect.

A. B. Coon of Marengo, who in 1883, was accounted the oldest attorney then engaged in active practice in the county, was born in Pennsylvania, in 1815, the youngest of twenty-one children born to his parents. In 1835 he came to McHenry County, opening his law office at the village of Marengo. For a number of years he was a surveyor, as well as lawyer, and from 1846 to 1862, was master-in-chancery in this county. During 1851-52 and 1860-64, he was state's attorney for the circuit in which this county was then included. During 1863-65 he served as prosecuting attorney for his congressional district and at a later date removed to a Dakota city.

J. P. Conley, a disciple of Harvard, served several years of twelve, in 1883 located in this probably in Dakota.

Ira Reed Curtiss was born in New York state in 1836, of New England stock. His father died when he was early twelve years old, and the early life was a hard one, and spent on the country and took a great for the Smith family. At the age of sixteen years he rented a farm in the Genesee Flats, N. Y., and in this connection earned enough money to take him through a three-years' course in Artesel College, where he was under the preceptorship of Horace Mann. Subsequently, he entered Union College, and was graduated therefrom in 1860, with the degree of Bachelor of Arts. In February, 1861 he located in McHenry County, taking up his residence at Marengo, where he continued to reside, becoming one of the honored citizens, successful lawyers and prominent business men of that place. During the Civil War he entered the Union Army, served for a year, but had to resign on account of poor health. Debarred from active service, he entered the provost marshal's office and remained there until the close of the war. Studying law, in June, 1865, he was admitted to the bar, began active practice, and was admitted to be an excellent lawyer. He developed into one of the strong political factors of his day, and in 1870 was elected as a representative from McHenry County to the State Assembly, on the Republican ticket. The same party sent him to the upper house of the Legislature, in 1884, and in 1876 and 1880 elected him state's attorney. He was a zealous Mason, a leader in the Grand Army of the Republic, and one of the best citizens of his day in McHenry County.

M. F. Ellsworth, formerly one of the lawyers of Nunda, was born at Rochester, New York, in 1838. His parents moved to McHenry County in 1843, and here the father became an extensive stockdealer, operating until his death which occurred in 1881. The mother died in 1851. M. F. Ellsworth came of distinguished ancestry, he being a direct descendant of Supreme Judge Ellsworth, who served under General Washington while he was president; and his maternal grandfather, a soldier of the American Revolution, was wounded seven times during that war, and lived to the extreme old age of 108 years. Growing up in McHenry County M. F. Ellsworth here received his educational training, but, after reaching manhood went to Kentucky, and was there successfully engaged in school-teaching until the outbreak of the Civil War,

J. C. Diener

Delia M. Diener.

at which time he enlisted in the Union army, and held various official positions until its termination. After his return home from military service, he studied law with Church & Kerr of Woodstock and in the fall of 1866 entered the law department of the State University at Ann Arbor, Mich., from which he was graduated in 1868, and was admitted to the bar. For a short period thereafter, he was engaged in practice at New Hampton, Iowa, and at Crete, Nebr., and then located permanently at Nunda, now Crystal Lake, this county.

O. H. Gillmore, formerly county judge of McHenry County, was born in St. Lawrence County, N. Y., in 1848. The family moved to this county in 1854, and here he attended the common schools, later entering the law department of the University of Michigan, after preparing himself by study under A. B. Coon and Ira R. Curtiss. He was graduated therefrom in 1873, and commenced practice that same year at Woodstock. He was elevated to the bench of McHenry County in 1882.

Charles M. Willard located at Woodstock in 1851, and formed a partnership with Col. L. S. Church. This connection soon terminated by mutual consent, and Mr. Willard practiced alone for a time. Still later he formed a partnership with James H. Slavin, severing it in 1857, to locate permanently at Chicago, Ill. He was an able lawyer.

Amos Cogswell first was engaged in legal practice at Hebron, where he settled in 1847, but three years later came to Woodstock, where he formed a partnership with Charles McClure, and they enjoyed a large practice for several years. Later he moved away, he and Mr. McClure going to Minnesota in 1859, and in the eighties he was known to be practicing his profession in Clark County, Dak. He was a man of distinction, who, having studied law with Franklin Pierce, was by that statesman, after he was elevated to the presidency, appointed to a government position at Washington.

Col. James M. Strode was well known as one of the ablest lawyers of Northern Illinois during earlier years. He located at Woodstock in either 1850 or 1851, and at that time had already won his reputation at the bar in both Galena and Chicago. From 1854 to 1857 he served as county judge of McHenry County, but during the later year he moved to Missouri, and from thence to Kentucky, where he died. His was a logical and legal mind, and he was forceful in argument. It is claimed that as a story-teller he had but one rival in the state of Illinois, Abraham Lincoln.

Theodore D. Murphy, formerly circuit judge of this district, was

b rn in Virginia, in 18??. He ca e to McHenry C unty in 1845, and
s ttled t W   n d   m   y. [l.   st   t p
t   (?)   d a   :   e   d   ?   ,, |
a   1   y   l   .
a   ??   (?   ?s ?   ?)
t   ?s   ? k?   ?   ?(? ?
l?   ?   ?   ?   ?   ?r?
c?   ?   ?   ? ?   ? ? ? ?   ?
r   ?   ?   h ? ? ?w? ?   ? ?   ? ? ?   ?
v?   ? ? ? ? ? th? ?   ? ?   s? if   ?h?   ?
v?   ?   ?   ? ? k   ?n   ?(? ? ? d?st? ? ? ?   ?
l?   ?   ?   lh? ?s

H ?, M L?   ?a   ? ? ? a d politician and early settl r M H   ?
C r?y, was ? ? m Columbia C ?nty N. Y , in 1808 a s?n, ? ?
S ?ch?an wh? ?ame ? America wh n a y?   m?n and ? s th?
soldier of the American Revolution. Henry W. McLean w s ?eared
o   farm nd wh?? he was twenty-tw? years old he began t ? st??,
?f law, and ?as ?dm?ted to the bar ?f his nat?ve state in 18?4 ??d
h? was the?? ?ngaged in an active practice for two years. H? the?
l?ft New York for Illinois, and settled at McHenry. In 1842 h? was
admitted to the bar of Illinois. With the format?on ?f th? Republican
party h? b??a?? on? ?f its zealous supp?r?ers, and attan?d distin?
tion as ?? ?ampaign w?rk?r. Mr. McLean stood high among his ?ll?w
cit z?ns and was rec?gnized as an excellent and well-balanced lawyer.

Charl?s McClur? was admitted to the McHenry C?unty bar in
1840 and for a ?ew months there?fter was engaged in practice at Mc-
H nry, but l?ft that villag? for La Porte, Ind. Still later h? b?came a
minister ?f ?he M?thodist Episcopal faith, but return?d to ?? law,
and c?ming back to McHenry County. for about seven years was ?n-
gag?d in practic? at Woodst?ck in partnership with Ames C ??w ll.
H? then moved to Minnesota. An earn?st purpos?ful man, he ??t ?n?d
to success in the law.

Calv?n S arl, who wa? the fourth attorney to ?ngag? ?n pra?t??
in McH?nry County, settled at Crystal Lake in 1839, remained there
until 18??, ??d then m?ved to Wisconsin.

Hamilton Nixon, a native of Vermont, was among the first of the
att?rn?ys ?? McH?nry County. He was poss?ssed of brilliant int?ll??t,
but di?d wh?n but a littl? over thirty years of age.

Phineas W. Platt came to Woodstock in March, 1845. He was ?
nat?v? ?f Pennsylvania, wh? studi?d law in Indiana, and commenc?d

his practice at Woodstock. It is said that he was one of the best lawyers who ever tried a case in McHenry County. His strength lay in his logical and careful manner, rather than in his eloquence, and his evident sincerity was very convincing to a jury. He formed a partnership with Alonzo Platt and they operated as Platt & Platt and did a large business. Although possessed of the same surname, there was no relationship between them. Alonzo Platt went to California during the period of the first gold excitement, but Phineas W. Platt remained in Woodstock until 1851, when he went to Texas, and there died several years later.

Col. Alonzo Platt was engaged in the practice of law in McHenry County in partnership with Phineas W. Platt, they having their offices in the historic "Rat Hole" Building on the Square. Going to California in 1850, he had many experiences, and died at Virginia City, Nev., in 1862. He was an excellent lawyer, a strong Democrat, and fine campaigner. His birth took place at Danbury, Conn., in 1816, from whence he later went to Wisconsin, where he served in the State Assembly in 1844. Studying law, he was admitted to the bar, and began the practice of his profession at Woodstock. During the time he lived here he served as state's attorney, and was accounted an excellent lawyer and able man.

Anson Sperry, who practiced law at Marengo, was born in Vermont in 1824. His father was an attorney, who, at an early day moved to Plattsburg, N. Y. In 1841 Anson Sperry came to Illinois, and began the study of law under Judge Skinner, and was admitted to the bar in 1845. He continued with Judge Skinner for two years, and then, May 7, 1847, arrived at Marengo, being the second lawyer to locate there. In the autumn of 1848 he was elected magistrate in a political contest between the northern and southern part of Marengo Township. About the same time he was appointed postmaster of Marengo, and held that position until 1861. In 1853, in company with Cornelius Lansing, he opened a banking house at Marengo, and carried it on until 1863, when he was appointed paymaster in the Army of the Cumberland, during the Civil War. In 1865 he was transferred to Chicago, Ill. He was still a resident of McHenry County late in the eighties.

Freeman Van Wickle came from New York to McHenry County about 1852, and for about nine years was one of the lawyers of this neighborhood. For a time he was associated in a legal partnership

with M. L. Joslyn. During the period of the Civil War he moved to
M. Gregan.

—ert L. Joslyn, for many years one of the foremost lawyers of
Northern Illinois was born in New York, Livingston County in 1827,
and resided in this county until after 1830. He was a Democrat and
an elector for James Buchanan for the presidency. Later on he united
with the Republican forces and became a recognized leader among
the stalwarts of this party. During the Civil War he served as captain of the Thirty-sixth Illinois Volunteer Infantry. During 1874-6
he represented the district of which McHenry County was a part in
the State Assembly, and in 1876 was elected to the State Senate by a
majority of over 3,000. He was recognized as a man capable of holding high and important positions. In the eighties this appreciation
took still more practical form in his appointment to the office of assistant secretary of the interior department at Washington, by President Arthur, July, 1882.

William Kerr, now deceased, was born in Delaware County, Ohio,
in 1819. In 1839 he came to Illinois, and for a time resided in Boone
County. Always from his youth, he had evinced a liking and aptitude
for legal matters, and while still in his teens helped to settle many a
neighborhood dispute, without charge. In 1857 his friend, L. S. Church,
induced him to come to Woodstock, and become his partner in his law
business. Mr. Kerr made an excellent lawyer, and was serving his
second term as county judge, when, July 26, 1866, he died very suddenly, his demise being a great shock to the community, for not only
the members of the bar, but the people at large, had great faith and
esteem in and for this truly excellent man.

H. S. Hanchett, a lawyer of fair ability, came to Woodstock in 1857,
and was a partner of M. L. Joslyn until 1862, when he went into the
Union army, during the Civil War, and being subsequently captured
and confined at Andersonville, there met his death, it is claimed from
starvation.

Flavel K. Granger, of McHenry was another early attorney, although
he was even better known as a business man. He was born in Wayne
County, N. Y., in 1832, and remained on a farm until he was fifteen
years old, at which time he entered the Wesleyan Academy at Lima,
N. Y. At the age of eighteen years he commenced teaching school, and
in the spring of 1853, migrated westward, and immediately began the
study of law after reaching Waukegan, Wis. In the fall of 1855 he was
admitted to the bar, but owing to ill health did not at once begin practice

ing his profession, for some years thereafter being engaged in stockbuying and farming in and about McHenry. As the years passed and he regained his health, he began to put to practical use the legal knowledge he had gained, but continued to look after his other interests as well. In 1870 he was elected county supervisor from his township, and was the first Republican to be elected from it. In 1872 he was elected as a representative to the Illinois State Assembly, and was re-elected for three terms without opposition. During the last two terms he was made speaker of the House, being the first to preside in the new state house.

T. B. Wakeman located in what was then the little hamlet of Alden, in 1839, and is the only member of his profession to make it his place of residence. In 1859 he moved to Harvard, and after a few years went to Chicago, where he died in 1882. In 1868 Mr. Wakeman's son, Thaddeus Wakeman, a graduate of the University of Michigan, became associated with him in his law business.

John A. Parrish, born in New York in 1825, was a member of a well-educated and highly-cultured family. He attended the New York Normal School at Albany, N. Y., and then became a school-teacher, following that calling until his health failed him, in 1859. He had come to Illinois and attained distinction in scholastic circles at Aurora and Woodstock, and at the same time had studied law. Soon thereafter he was admitted to the bar and was engaged in a general legal practice at McHenry until his death in 1882. He was highly esteemed at the bar, but on account of his weak lungs, was not a successful jury lawyer, but as an office attorney was excellent. Mr. Parrish was also very successful as a pension agent and as an attorney in insurance cases. He amassed considerable property.

William Jackson was born in Connecticut in 1808. He accompanied his family to Ashtabula, Ohio, in 1832. In 1843 his father came to McHenry County, Ill., where he lived until his death at the age of seventy-seven years. After obtaining an excellent education in the common schools, William Jackson engaged in lumbering, but in 1828 began reading law with Judge Fisbie, but was not admitted to the bar until 1859. First locating at Algonquin, in 1838, he lived in that village until he moved to Nunda, now Crystal Lake, where he was engaged in a general practice, and for sixteen years served as a justice of the peace. Twice he was elected associate judge, and later was appointed judge vice Judge Carr, deceased. Politically he was a Democrat, and for fifty years he was a consistent member of the Christian Church.

Benjamin N. Smith, a native of McHenry County, was born in 1838,

a son of Nathaniel S___, one of the pioneers of the county. He received
an _____ at ____ _____ as _ ___ ___ _____ of Illinois and
W__ _____ ___ 1862 _____ County E N___ ___ In __
V_____ Int__ at ____ __ C. W_____ __ ____ and
th _____ ____ __ b V__ _t__ ____ __ __ ___ at
t_____ _____ _____ __ ___ _ ___ at Woodstock and was
t___ ____ _____ ___ for man_ ___ __ 1869 he was ___ county
jud_ ___ ___ _ __ that ___ for more than a dozen years, and ____ our
y___ ___ _____ ___ _____cy. He was a zealous Mason, _ __ ___
to the Methodist Episcopal Church, the Grand Army of the R_ ___
and the Ancient Order of United Workmen, and lived up to the ideals
of all these organizations

John M. Southworth, another practicing attorney at Woodstock during its earlier period, was born in Vermont in 1839, settled in McHenry
County in 1858 and became one of its useful citizens. In April 1861,
five days after Fort Sumter was fired upon by the Confederates, enlisted in the Seventh Illinois Volunteer Infantry. Later he re-enlisted
in another infantry regiment, serving for a period of over five years,
and leaving the service with the rank of major. He was elected sheriff
of McHenry County in 1866, and clerk of the circuit court in 1868.
In 1873 he began the practice of law at Woodstock, but during the
eighties was an attorney of Chicago. In August, 1873, he was appointed
commissioner of the Illinois penitentiary.

James H. Slavin ranked among the best lawyers of his day and
generation. He was born and reared in McHenry County, and after
practicing here for fifteen years, on February 6, 1875, he passed away,
aged thirty-eight years. He was a self made man, and rose to a high
position among his fellow men. He had a logical mind, a fine discrimi-
nating power, and a most excellent memory. Although interested in
state and national affairs he kept out of politics, and oftentimes refused
nomination for office, preferring to devote all of his time and energy
to the law.

STATE'S ATTORNEYS

Alonzo Huntington 1837-40; Edward G. Regan, 1840-43; James Curtiss, 1843-44; William A. Boardman, 1845-49; Alonzo Platt, 1850-51;
Amos B. Coon, 1852; M. M. Boyce, 1853-57; Edward S. Joslyn, 1857-
61; Amos B. Coon, 1861-63; M. M. Boyce, 1864-69; Charles Kellum,

1870-73; Joseph P. Cheever, 1873-76; Ira R. Curtiss, 1877-84; A. B. Coon, 1884-96; V. S. Lumley, 1896 1900; L. D. Lowell, 1900-1908; David R. Joslyn, 1908-1916; V. S. Lumley, 1916.

PRESENT ATTORNEYS

The present members of the bar of McHenry County are as follows: Allen, C. T., Woodstock; Barnes, C. P. (county judge), Woodstock; Barnes, C. Percy, Woodstock; Bennett, F. B., Woodstock; Cairns, W. R., Woodstock; Carmack, M. A., Woodstock; Carroll, William M., Woodstock; Donovan, Paul J., Harvard; Donovan, Rupert D., Woodstock; Eckert, Floyd E., Woodstock; Field, George W., Woodstock; Francis, Charles H., Woodstock; Hoy, E. R., Woodstock; Joslyn, D. R., Woodstock; Joslyn, D. R., Jr., Woodstock; Lumley, V. S. (state's attorney), Woodstock; Lowell, L. D., Crystal Lake; Manley, B. F., Harvard; Mullen, A. J. (master-in-chancery), Woodstock; Marshall, R. F., Harvard; McCauley, James J., Woodstock; McConnell, W. S., Woodstock; Northrop, Charles S., Woodstock; Palmer, L. B., Harvard; Pouse, Alfred H., West McHenry; Smiley, D. T., Harvard; Shurtleff, E. D. (circuit judge), Marengo; Whittemore, C. B., Marengo; and Waite, E. H., Woodstock.

MCHENRY COUNTY BAR ASSOCIATION

The McHenry County Bar Association was organized February 15, 1915, and elected officers who are still serving, as follows: President, Hon. Charles H. Donnelly; vice president, B. F. Manley; and Paul J. Donovan, secretary and treasurer. Nearly every member of the county bar belongs to this association. As it is still a somewhat new organization, there is but little history connected with it. The judges and lawyers throughout the entire portion of the state, acknowledge that McHenry County has an exceedingly strong bar and that no better trial lawyers can be found in the entire state than some of the members of the small bar of McHenry County. They are often spoken of as "the fighting bar of McHenry County."

CIRCUIT COURT OFFICERS

The officers of the McHenry County Circuit Court, which is a part of the Seventeenth Judicial District, together with Boone, Lake and

Winnebago counties, are as follows: Edward D. Shurtleff, Claire C. Edwards and Robert K. Welsh ___ ; Arthur J. Mallon, has re... ___ , N. S. ___ ; Charles F. H___ ___ Ro___ ___ , ___

The McHenry County Bar pa___ ___ ___ to be s___ d ___ the court records of the county the following resolution on the death Judge Frost and a number of his fellow lawyers the same, be... ented by attorney J. F. Casey, and the committee of which he was chairman:

"Be it resolved, By the members of the McHenry County Bar and each of us, that with sad hearts, reverence and esteem we assemble today, to pay a tribute, just and fitting to the memory of our departed professional brothers, citizens and beloved friends. Calvin J. Hendricks, John J. Cooney and Joseph L. Land, each of whom have been taken from us by the will and decree of God; and yet we no less deplore their loss to their families, friends and professional brothers, each being called to answer the Divine summons of death in the power and vigor of his young manhood, at a time in life when most useful to all the duties, work and obligations to society and the world.

"Be it further resolved, By the members of the McHenry County Bar, that each of our above mentioned professional brothers possessed excellent personality, good ambition and a trustworthy character that each loved the law for its own sake, and practiced it with a true intent toward justice and the right in all cases which came to them for consideration and adjustment.

"Be it further resolved, That each was successful in the great profession of the law, and that the same could not have been obtained without superior intelligence, energy and a high sense of duty which each possessed in no small degree.

"Be it further resolved, That in the death of Calvin J. Hendricks, John J. Cooney and Joseph L. Lang. that the McHenry County Bar has been deprived of three of its most valuable and efficient lawyers, whom we had admired, confided in and whose companionship we all enjoyed in life.

"Whereas it has pleased God to remove from our midst our late brother, citizen and jurist, Arthur H. Frost of Rockford, Ill., and.

"Whereas Be it resolved by the members of the McHenry County Bar. that while we bow with humble submission to the will of the most

A. B. Driggins

Emma f. Driggins

High, we do not the less mourn for our distinguished brother, citizen and jurist, who has been taken from us.

"Be it further resolved, That in the death of Judge Frost, the members of the McHenry County Bar and each of us lament the loss of a brother whose heart and hand were ever ready to assist in bringing about our welfare and prosperity; a friend and companion who was dear to us all; a citizen of whose upright and noble life was a standard to be followed by his fellow citizens; a lawyer of excellent ability and integrity, possessing a high sense of professional duty and ever striving to do it; a judge who in the trial of the cases before him endeavored to recognize only the law and the evidence and rendered his decisions accordingly.

"Be it further resolved, That the Seventeenth Judicial Circuit of the State of Illinois has suffered the loss of a jurist whose services on the bench did much to promote justice, and give confidence to our courts and to elevate the legal profession."

On the death of Attorney John B. Lyon, of Harvard, in July, 1915, Judge Donnelly paid the following fine tribute to the deceased:

"I regarded Mr. Lyon as a very able lawyer. He was the oldest member of the McHenry County Bar at the time of his death; had a varied and extensive practice and combined with his legal knowledge, he possessed a wonderful fund of common sense. He was a careful advisor, a good and resourceful fighter, a legal adversary to be feared, and better than all, always fair and honorable with the court. The members of the bar as well as the courts will miss him as he was always a source of assistance to each."

After thirty years of continuous service on the Circuit Court bench, on account of ill health, Judge Charles H. Donnelly, of Woodstock, resigned in the month of December 1920, and Attorney Edward D. Shurtleff, of Marengo, was immediately appointed by Governor Lowden to serve out Judge Donnelly's unexpired term.

At the January term of the Circuit Court of McHenry County a large gathering of the lawyers and Judges of the Circuit was held at the Circuit Court room in the City of Woodstock to pay their respects to Judge Donnelly on his retirement from the Circuit Court bench.

A large number of the Rockford, Waukegan and Belvidere lawyers and court officials were in attendance as well as other lawyers from Kane and adjoining counties, and on the occasion the following resolution was passed and ordered spread of record in the court over which Judge Donnelly had been the presiding Judge for so many years:

"WHEREAS, the Honorable Charles H. Donnelly, of Woodstock, Illinois, after a service of thirty years on the Bench, has voluntarily retired as one of the presiding Judges of the Seventeenth Judicial Circuit of the State of Illinois:

AND WHEREAS, we, the present presiding Judges of the said Seventeenth Judicial Circuit and the members of the Bar thereof, have today assembled for the purpose of paying a just tribute of respect and Honor to Judge Donnelly upon his retirement;

AND WHEREAS, it is just that a proper recognition of his long and faithful service and a fitting acknowledgment of his many virtues should be publicly made;

THEREFORE BE IT RESOLVED, by the present presiding Judges and the members of the Bar of the Seventeenth Judicial Circuit of the State of Illinois, that in the retirement of Judge Donnelly we and each of us regret the loss to the Bench of this Judicial Circuit of a Judge who possessed legal qualifications of a high order, a true sense of professional honor and integrity, and who, while ever tempering justice with mercy, performed the duties of his office fearlessly and fairly, yet with a kindness of heart that has endeared him to all whose duties or profession brought them in contact with his Court throughout his long years of public service.

BE IT FURTHER RESOLVED, that in the retirement of Judge Donnelly the Seventeenth Judicial Circuit of the State of Illinois has suffered a loss of a jurist of signal ability, scrupulous honesty and integrity, whose service on the Bench did much to promote justice, increase confidence in our courts and elevate the legal profession.

BE IT FURTHER RESOLVED, by the present Judges and members of the Bar of said Seventeenth Judicial Circuit, that our sincere and heartfelt thanks be and they are hereby extended to Judge Donnelly as a private citizen for the many professional and personal courtesies received by us and the kindly services rendered to us in the past with further assurance that our love, esteem and best wishes go with him in his retirement, together with the hope that he may be spared for many years to enjoy the confidence and respect of his fellowmen for his long and faithful services in their behalf, and that his twilight years be brightened by the consciousness of duties well done.

RESOLVED, that this resolution be spread upon the records of the Circuit Court of the Seventeenth Judicial Circuit of the State of Illinois, and an engrossed copy thereof presented to the Honorable Charles H. Donnelly."

CHAPTER X

MEDICAL PROFESSION

By Dr. C. M. Johnson

THE HEALING ART

From the earliest ages until the present, the art of healing has been recognized as one of the most important agencies in the life of the people of any country, and even the savage tribes pay honor to their "Medicine Men." From the days when his prototype was the only recourse for the sick, until these enlightened days when the physician and surgeon is able, through his science and knowledge, to work what but a few years ago would have seemed an impossibility. But yesterday in the World War, in the midst of the thunder of mighty guns, when every device for the destruction of mankind was employed, it is the triumph for the medical fraternity that the percentage of fatalities at the front was not so measurably higher than those of normal existence, because of the skill of the men who have risen to undreamed of heights in the healing art.

This county has contributed its quota to the noble band of men engaged in the work of counterbalancing the horrors of modern warfare, and from the beginning of its history it has been the boast of the county that its physicians and surgeons have ranked with the best of the country.

EARLIEST PHYSICIANS

It is believed that the first doctor to locate within McHenry County was Dr. Christy G. Wheeler, who settled at McHenry about 1837; he was

145

soon followed, however, by Dr. A. B. Cornish. In order to give the reader a clearer account of the scores of physicians who have from time to time practiced in this county, they will be treated by towns, villages and cities in which they have resided, or are now practicing.

ALDEN

Dr. D. S. McGonigle was the first to practice medicine in Alden, he locating there in 1845. Dr. Allen C. Bingham was in practice here from 1857 to 1865, and was very successful. Dr. D. C. Gilbert located here in 1868, and Dr. Woodworth in 1870. From 1874 to 1881, Dr. A. S. Munson was engaged in practice at Alden, and sold his practice to Dr. G. Ballenger. Other physicians have come and gone from this section of the county, some of whom are mentioned in the biographical section of this work.

ALGONQUIN

The first physician of Algonquin was Dr. David Burton, who located here in 1844, and continued to practice until his death, when he was succeeded by Dr. H. C. Terwilliger. Dr. Reed came in 1850 and remained five years, when Dr. A. Hedger succeeded him. Drs. Winslow, Hunt, Johnston, William Winchester, Bentley and Hait were all engaged in practice at Algonquin for short periods each. Dr. Young was another early practitioner. Drs. William A. Nason, Robinson, Hill and D. H. Merrill were also physicians who located in Algonquin during the seventies.

CARY

But little can be learned of the early doctors of this locality. F. J. Theobold is the only physician practicing in this village today.

CHEMUNG

Doctor Miller was the first physician to locate at Chemung; he came in 1848 and remained until 1856. His successor was Dr. H. W. Johnson, who only remained a short time, and then removed to Harvard. In 1853 Dr. B. A. Wade came to Chemung, but in 1863 he, too, moved to Harvard. Dr. Devine came in 1862, but in 1867 moved away. In 1875 Dr. Chase established himself here, continuing in practice for many years. The medical practice of this community is now attended to chiefly by physicians of Harvard.

CORAL

Doctor Hungerford came to Coral in 1853, moving to Union, the railroad station, after about three and one-half years. Dr. A. McWright came in 1855; Dr. Suiter in 1856, and Dr. Snow in 1858. Dr. Elvin Briggs practiced medicine here from 1840 to 1881. Dr. E. L. Sheldon and Dr. Griffith were also among the pioneer doctors.

CRYSTAL LAKE

The first physician to practice at Crystal Lake was Dr. Erwin, who came in 1842 and remained until 1857. The second doctor was a man named Smith; he died while engaged in practice at Crystal Lake. Drs. Beers, Ballou, Lowell, Graves, Hayes, Hall and Crandall were all among the physicians who practiced here prior to and just after 1884.

GREENWOOD

The first doctor to locate at the village of Greenwood was Doctor McCay, who was succeeded by Doctor White, who died while in practice. Doctor Ballinger was the third physician; he remained until about 1884 and was succeeded by Doctor Hart and the latter remained here for many years and was well and favorably known and recognized as an excellent doctor.

HARMONY

Harmony was never a village, simply a country cross-roads community. Here several physicians have practiced, but usually were residents of some near-by village.

HARTLAND

Doctor Bennett was the earliest doctor in this place, and as the years have come and gone, others have cared for the ill of the community usually from Woodstock or Harvard.

HARVARD

Dr. H. W. Johnson was the first to practice medicine in Harvard. He arrived in 1856, and continued in active practice until his death, about twelve years later. The second physician there was Dr. H. W. Richardson, but after a very few years he moved to Marengo, where he died. Dr. C. A. Bingham was third to enter this field for the purpose of practicing medicine. About the same time Dr. B. A. Wade, Dr. A. C. Bingham, H. T. Woodward, C. M. Johnson and Charles Goddard arrived, and some of them remained for many years.

HEBRON

Dr. Royal Sykes came from Vermont and located in Hebron in 1848. He was successfully engaged in medical practice until 1876, when he moved to Chicago. Dr. J. H. Giddings came here in 1858, and practiced until the beginning of the Civil War, when he enlisted in the Union army. His health failed under exposure, and he returned to Hebron, but remained but a short time. In the autumn of 1865, Dr. E. O. Gratton of New York, settled in Hebron, and here he was engaged in a successful practice for many years. Dr. J. M. Mansfield, Dr. H. R. Chesboro, Dr. Alfred Turner and Dr. Catherine Slater all practiced medicine in Hebron prior to, and some of them after, 1883.

HUNTLEY

The first physician to locate for the practice of his profession in Huntley, was Doctor Ainsworth who came in 1852, but died a few years thereafter of cholera, contracted while attending upon a stranger who had just arrived in the village. His successor was Dr. John Garrison and his partner Doctor Trough, both of whom died soon after coming to the place. Drs. Cale, Perry, Rodman, R. Turner, A. Griffith, Charles E. Cook and a number of others all practiced medicine at Hebron.

MC HENRY

Being the first county seat and among the first settlements in this county, naturally a physician was found among the pioneer band at Mc-Henry. He was also the first to practice medicine in the county. We refer to Dr. Christy G. Wheeler, who soon left the practice of his profession and embarked in mercantile business here. Dr. Luke Hale was his successor and he in turn was followed by Doctor Bosworth, who later developed into a merchant. It is said he was a highly educated man and an excellent physician, but for some reason preferred a business to a professional career. The fourth to practice medicine in McHenry was Doctor McAllister. He continued for four years, and then moved to Oshkosh, Wis. Doctor Coleman remained at McHenry four years, and was soon followed by Doctor Flavel, and Doctor Ballou, who were here for the same length of time. Doctor Mellendy practiced for ten years and went to California where he died. Drs. H. T. Brown, Polly, Cavens, Beers, Brown, Fegers, Howard and Childs were all well-known physicians at McHenry prior to the nineties, as well as Doctor Anderson now of Woodstock. Many changes have been wrought out in McHenry, doctors have come and gone, leaving the present practice in the hands of Drs. A. I. Froehlich, D. G. Wells, and N. J. Nye.

MARENGO

Dr. T. W. Stull was the first medical practitioner of Marengo. Other early and later physicians there have been: Drs. J. W. Green, S. C. Wernham, Edward L. Sheldon, Frederick L. Nutt, and C. C. Miller.

RICHMOND

The first physician to locate at Richmond was Dr. S. Fillmore Bennett who wrote the song "Sweet By and By." Physicians have practiced here whose names are now not readily recalled by the present generation. However, it is known that Dr. Samuel R. Ward and Dr. Josiah Hyde were here many years, and both were excellent men and skilful physicians.

WOODSTOCK

Dr. Almon King, who settled at Woodstock soon after the founding of the village, was its first physician. Following him came Dr. Luke Coon, who arrived and entered the practice of medicine in 1849, and remained for two years. Dr. A. F. Hedger came to Woodstock from Algonquin about 1851, and in 1853 Dr. A. F. Merritt settled at the county seat. Drs. George E. Stone, D. C. Green, W. H. Buck, V. B. Anderson and William W. Cook were among the earlier physicians of Woodstock.

COMMON DISORDERS OF EARLY YEARS

Fever and ague was the chief complaint in the homes of pioneers in McHenry, as in almost all the other western counties. Especially was this true along the valley of the Fox River. Aside from this disease, there was but little sickness. The early settlers were usually men and women of strong, robust bodies and had plenty of outdoor exercise and not much rich food, hence were seldom ill enough to call in a physician. When anyone was very ill they sometimes feared to trust the local doctor, who was usually not the best kind of a medical man to say the least, hence they would send into other counties to physicians on the east side of the Fox River. However, as soon as the county settled up and drains were excavated so that standing pools of filthy water could escape, the fever and ague was not seen to any great extent, but this condition lasted at least until 1850, giving the real pioneer band plenty of genuine "shakes." The doctors who visited the homes of McHenry County after the fifties were of a superior type of physicians. They were schooled in reputable colleges of medicine and were competent to do both doctoring and also act as surgeons.

SIDELIGHTS ON EARLY PHYSICIANS

Dr. Christy G. Wheeler, although not strictly speaking a physician, was the first who bore the title of "Dr." at the old county seat of McHenry. He was born in Dunbarton, N. H., in 1811. His health was failing in his native state, so he decided to move with his family to the West, and did so in the fall of 1836, his family being the first white family to locate at McHenry. The following May, the decision was made fixing McHenry as the county seat. Mr. Wheeler paid $100 for surveying the town site. He purchased a small store and had general merchandise, and was also postmaster, keeping the first post office in McHenry County. Subsequently, he was recorder of deeds, which office he held until the time of his death, March 28, 1842.

Dr. V. B. Anderson was born in Girard, Penn., in 1847, and accompanied his parents to Woodstock, Ill., in 1854. He attended the public schools, read medicine under Dr. J. Northrup, and then entered Rush Medical College, Chicago, from which institution he was graduated in 1871. For two years he was engaged in practice in Ford County, this state; three years more were spent in Buchanan County, Iowa, and he then located at the village of McHenry, this county and here remained

A Duke

Alice H. Duke

in practice till 1883, when he removed to Woodstock, where he is still practicing medicine.

Dr. S. Fillmore Bennett, of Richmond, was born in Erie County, N. Y., in 1836, and was brought to Illinois when two years of age, by his parents. At the age of eighteen years, he commenced teaching school at Wauconda, and in 1858, entered the University of Michigan, from whence he came to Richmond, this county, to accept a position as teacher in the Richmond public schools. He was connected with the newspaper business and served as a soldier in the Union army in the Civil War. Subsequently he was graduated at Rush Medical College, Chicago, in 1874, and at once commenced the practice of his profession at Richmond. For years he was United States pension examiner and surgeon. At one time he was consul to Hamilton, Canada. It was at Elkhorn, Wis., that he became associated with J. P. Webster, author of that famous song book "The Signet Ring." He was publisher of hundreds of excellent songs and hymns. Doctor Bennett composed "The Sweet Bye and Bye," and Mr. Webster set the words to music and since then it has been translated into many foreign languages. Doubtless Doctor Bennett will be remembered more as a musical composer than as a medical man, excellent physician though he was.

Dr. Horace W. Johnson, deceased, was the first physician at Harvard, and came to the county in 1856, when a cornfield marked the present site of Harvard and John Ayers was the only man living in the vicinity. Dr. Johnson was born in New York City, December 16, 1810. He was graduated at Rutgers College, New Brunswick, N. J., and became an excellent physician, practicing first in the City of New York. In 1836 he came West, locating at Kenosha, Wis., and there he remained until he came to Harvard where he continued to practice medicine until his death, February 24, 1871. He was the leading physician in this county of his day. His son, Dr. C. M. Johnson, is a medical practitioner and conducts a hospital at Harvard.

PHYSICIANS OF A LATER DATE

Of the regular-school practitioners since 1884 may be mentioned: Dr. H. T. Woodruff, who practiced until his death, at Harvard; Dr. A. C. Bingham, who also practiced at Harvard, and died there a few years ago; Dr. B. A. Wade, who practiced until his death, at Hot Springs, S. D.

COTTAGE HOSPITAL AT HARVARD

Cottage Hospital, the first established in the county, was of humble origin, and by many was not looked upon with favor, but its founder, Dr. C. M. Johnson, one of the oldest and leading physicians of the city of Harvard, thought differently, and by his sagacity and skill he gained recognition for it, and now no one in, or outside of Harvard, has anything but words of praise for this local hospital.

The present buildings are modern in all fittings, supplied with steam heat, electric lights, electric call bells, bed-side telephones, with well lighted, airy rooms and wards, beautiful private rooms and baths, suites with bath; and has an efficient corps of cheerful trained nurses, unsurpassed by those of any institution. Registered nurses are contantly in charge. A well-equipped operating room done in tile, glass and enamel, with wash and private rooms in connection, is equal to that of any large city hospital. The real homelike air and the genuine courtesy and consideration accorded near relatives of the sick, have added materially to the hosts of friends of this institution.

The founder and present proprietor, Doctor Johnson, is a son of the first physician who practiced medicine in Harvard, and he himself has practiced here for more than forty years. In cases where the patients are too poor to pay for services, necessary aid is given them if they are certified to by proper people in their home towns.

A nurses' "training school" is also connected with the hospital. Any reputable physician may bring his patients here for treatment or operation, and have complete charge of his own cases. The attending physicians are: N. M. Percy, M. D., Chicago; E. E. Irons, M. D., Chicago; W. H. McDonald, M. D., Lake Geneva, Wis.; H. D. Hull, M. D.; W. C. Richardson, M. D.; Charles C. Peck, M. D.; H. D. Eaton, M. D.; G. W. Curless, M. D. The attending physicians are: C. M. Johnson, M. D., surgeon-in-chief; G. W. Foddard, M. D., surgeon C. & N. W. Railroad Company; N. L. Seelye, M. D., ear, eye, nose and throat. Helen E. Johnson, R. M., is superintendent, and Emma Fraase, R. N., is superintendent of nurses.

WOODSTOCK HOSPITAL ASSOCIATION

In 1906 there was a private hospital established in the city of Woodstock by Dr. J. E. Guy, and he continued to operate it until 1912, when it was taken over by Dr. Hyde West, who also conducted it as a private

COTTAGE HOSPITAL, HARVARD

hospital until 1914, when the Woodstock Public Hospital Association was formed and incorporated. This association took over the management and converted this private hospital into a public hospital. It was originally on Clay Street, but in 1915 was moved to West South Street, where the old homestead of the late Judge Murphy was purchased and remodeled for modern hospital work.

This hospital accommodates fifteen patients and the present officers of the association are: Rev. Roger Kaufman, president; Dr. G. E. Wright, vice-president; Dr. C. F. Baccus, secretary; Dr. E. Windmueller, treasurer; and the board of directors is as follows: Floyd E. Eckert (attorney), Dr. E. Windmueller, Dr. W. M. Freeman, Dr. C. F. Baccus, Dr. N. L. Seelye, Dr. H. M. Francis, L. T. Hoy, and Mayor S. E. Olmstead. The superintendent is Miss Ethel Hunt, R. N.

This hospital is a great accommodation for all surgical and medical cases in the vicinity of Woodstock. It is located in a beautiful, quiet and attractive part of the city, away from the noise and unpleasant surroundings found nearer the city's center.

PRESENT PHYSICIANS

The following is a list of the physicians practicing in McHenry County:

Algonquin—Martin H. Hubrig.

Crystal Lake—Harry D. Hull, George H. Pflueger, William H. Rupert.

Harvard—Charles W. Goddard, Howard D. Eaton, J. W. Groesbeck, C. M. Johnson, Charles C. Peck, Henry J. Schmid, Norman L. Seelye, Jesse G. Maxon.

Woodstock—C. F. Baccus, H. C. Thon, William Hyde West, Glen Will Wright, Emil Windmueller, William M. Freeman, E. V. Anderson, A. F. King.

Marengo—Rozel M. Curtis, Walter S. Eshbaugh, G. Watson Fowler, William V. Gooder, Spencer C. Wernham, W. J. C. Casely.

Richmond—Walter E. Foster, Samuel R. Ward, C. W. Klontz.

Hebron—Edward V. Brown, C. W. Bailey.

Huntley—Oliver I. Statler, Arthur W. DeVry.

McHenry—Charles H. Fegers, A. J. J. Froelich, N. J. Nye, David C. Wells.

Ringwood—W. Hepburn.

Spring Grove—John C. Furlong.

Cary Station—Frank John Theobald.
Johnsburg—Arnold F. Mueller.
Union—Phineas Renie.

MEDICAL SOCIETY

The McHenry County Medical Society was organized at Woodstock in 1910. Its first officers were: president, Dr. C. M. Johnson, Harvard; secretary and treasurer, Dr. John F. Guy, Woodstock. The present officers are: president, Dr. E. Windmueller, Woodstock; secretary and treasurer, Dr. Howard D. Eaton, Harvard.

There are at present about forty-two physicians in the county, and of this number all but seven are members of this society. This society meets at various places within the county, each month, and at times has open meetings to which anyone is welcome.

CHAPTER XI

JOURNALISM

By Charles F. Renich

FIRST NEWSPAPER

The first newspaper to be issued in this county was the Illinois Republican, published at Woodstock, in 1846, by Josiah Dwight. This
paper was continued under various names and with several suspensions
for ten years, Mr. Dwight continuing as its editor, but in 1856 the name
was changed to the Woodstock Sentinel. In 1854 the paper was called
the Republican Free-Press.

OTHER EARLY WOODSTOCK PUBLICATIONS

The Woodstock Democrat was the second paper started in the county.
It was issued until 1856, in the interests of the Democratic party, its
editor being F. D. Austin, a very able editorial writer.

M. L. Joslyn and E. W. Smith founded the Woodstock Argus in the
spring of 1856, and with its entrance into the field of journalism, the
Democrat passed out of existence, the stock being bought up by the new
firm. The Argus was later absorbed by the Free-Press, but in turn it
was absorbed by the Woodstock Sentinel, in July, 1857, a Mr. Edson
then being its proprietor.

Mr. Austin, after the purchase of the Argus, revived the Woodstock
Democrat, and published it from August, 1858, to July, 1859, when it
again fell by the wayside, thus leaving McHenry County with but one

155

newspaper. The Democrats, however, desiring an organ during the campaign of 1860, revived the journal, and it was continued until 1862, James L. Martin becoming its editor in October, 1860. With its passage from the history of journalism in McHenry County in 1862, its demise was final.

WOODSTOCK SENTINEL.

The first editors of the Sentinel were G. L. Webb, and T. F. Johnson, and the first issue bore the date of July 17, 1856. The owners were an association of Republicans who recognized the necessity of a strong organ of their party to educate the people in the principles of their platform. Mr. Webb sold his interest in the paper October 9, 1856, and Mr. Johnson was the sole proprietor. He made Josiah Dwight his editor, and the paper was intensely partisan. In April, 1857, J. W. Franks & Son became the proprietors but Mr. Dwight continued as editor in charge. Another change was effected with the purchase of the paper in November, 1858, by Abraham E. and William E. Smith, who edited it as well. In 1862, the junior member of the firm went into the ranks of the Union Army, leaving Abraham E. Smith in sole charge. The Sentinel obtained possession on December 1, 1862, of the McHenry County Union that had been published for about a year, and was owned by J. H. Holder. In January, 1866, Mr. Smith sold to Frank M. Sapp and George B. Richardson, and in February of that year the size was changed from a seven-column folio to nine columns. Once more the paper changed hands. William E. Smith becoming its proprietor and editor. G. S. Southworth bought the paper April 1st, 1872, and enlarged it to a seven-column quarto, with "patent insides." In May, 1873, the paper was changed to a six-column quarto, J. Van Slyke being then associate editor for five years. On June 5, 1879, E. T. Glennon purchased a half interest, and the firm became Southworth & Glennon. From that date on the various changes have been as follows:

On January 1, 1891, a corporation was formed which purchased the paper. This corporation was called the Woodstock Sentinel Company; L. T. Hoy, president and manager; Judge C. H. Donnelly, vice-president; E. C. Jewett, treasurer, and E. T. Glennon, since a prominent capitalist of Chicago. Charles A. Lemmers was local editor and foreman of the office. The active management of the plant continued under Mr. Hoy as manager and Mr. Lemmers as local editor for about twelve years until November, 1902.

After Mr. Lemmers left the Sentinel in 1902, the paper had various editors during the next few years, among the number being Walter T. Wheeler and I. C. Wells.

In 1906 the Sentinel Company purchased the local German paper called Das Volksblatt, which was established in Woodstock in 1885 by Fred Renich. After the death of Mr. Renich in 1890, the publication was continued by his sons, Charles F. and Fred L. Renich. Later, Ernest F. Fues, now assistant cashier of the American National Bank, became the editor and manager, but the ownership remained with the Renich estate, until its sale to the Sentinel Company. The Volksblatt was a prosperous newspaper for many years and at one time had a circulation of 1500 subscribers. With the acquiring of the plant and business of Das Volksblatt, Charles F. Renich, then postmaster at Woodstock, became editor and manager of both the Sentinel and Volksblatt, but the latter publication was discontinued in August, 1916.

With the purchase of the German paper by the Sentinel Company, the capital of the corporation was increased from $6,000 to $12,000. The stock was widely distributed by sale among the prominent men of the community, the records of the company showing the following names as stockholders, on January 1, 1906: L. T. Hoy, Judge C. H. Donnelly, E. C. Jewett, E. T. Glennon (Chicago), Charles F. Renich, G. E. Still, R. J. Beatty, E. B. Losee, G. F. Rushton, Fred G. Schnett, A. K. Bunker, F. A. Walters, W. S. Thorne, A. S. Wright, E. J. Heimerdinger, J. M. Hoy, S. L. Hart, Theo. Hamer, W. S. McConnell, G. W. Conn, Jr., Otto E. Seiler, James F. Casey, Judge D. T. Smiley, Emil Arnold, George L. Murphy, D. F. Quinlan, A. J. Dietz, W. T. Wheeler. L. T. Hoy, was elected president, Judge Donnelly vice-president, Theo. Hamer, Secretary, E. C. Jewett treasurer and Charles F. Renich, editor and manager. With the passing of years the above stockholders all sold their stock to Mr. Renich, the editor.

In 1916 Editor Renich and others associated with him purchased the Woodstock Republican, and in 1917 the subscription list and business of the Republican was merged with the Sentinel.

Woodstock Daily Sentinel, McHenry County's first daily newspaper, was established by Charles F. Renich, as editor and publisher, August 23, 1921. The Daily Sentinel started as the little brother to the weekly Sentinel, which has been published continuously since 1856. From the very beginning the daily received a hearty welcome by the people of Woodstock and vicinity, present indications are that the daily will soon be big brother eventually outstripping-the weekly in size.

J. W. Dyer, formerly of Mount Carmel, Illinois, an experienced daily newspaper man, is city editor and with the hearty co-operation of the publisher and the entire organization of the Sentinel plant, is putting out a newspaper with which the people of Woodstock and McHenry County are well pleased. The Daily is receiving liberal support from the merchants, is filled each day with the day's news, and bids certain to be a success.

On April 1, 1919, the capital stock of the Woodstock Sentinel Company was increased from $12,000 to $18,000. The gross business transacted for 1920 was $34,000. The equipment of the plant consists of two linotypes, models 5 and 8, two two-revolution presses, two jobbers one equipped with Miller automatic self-feeder stitching machine and punching machine, dust-proof type cabinets, large quantities of new job and advertising type, and everything else needed or useful in an up-to-date country newspaper office. Although only printing a twelve-page weekly paper, the company is mechanically prepared to launch a daily paper at any time the company consider the field will warrant such a venture. The property is under the personal management of Charles F. Renich, president of the company and editor.

In 1916 editor Renich received the award and prize money for the best "first-page" newspaper in Illinois, the same being given by the department of Journalism in the Illinois University.

OTHER NEWSPAPERS

The Woodstock Citizen was issued in 1873, but it was published only a part of a year.

The Franklin Printing Company of Chicago founded a paper issued in the interest of the Grange movement, at Woodstock, and named it the Anti-Monopolist. Its first issue bore date of October, 1873, and on November 6, 1873, the Sentinel made notice of its demise.

Another Grange organ was the New Era, founded on Thanksgiving Day, 1873, under the management of Ringland & Price, the latter a clergyman, being the chief organizer. In a short time he left the management, and in February, 1874, W. D. Ringland became its sole proprietor. Later, it embraced the doctrines of the Greenback party, and still later, like all of that class of mushroom newspapers, espoused the cause of the then dominant political party, and the "loaves and fishes" there might be in it, thus it became a Republican paper. In 1876, it suspended publication, for a time, but was resumed later in the year. In October,

Wm. A. Dodge

Nellie L. Dodge

1878, Mr. Ringland moved the plant to Elgin, Ill., and soon thereafter suspended publication. Again he resumed publication at Woodstock, but in March, 1880, the plant was destroyed by fire. The subscription list was then sold to the Sentinel.

MC HENRY COUNTY DEMOCRAT

In April, 1877, the McHenry County Democrat came into existence, being established by A. R. Bradbury, and it passed into the hands of John A. and M. C. Dufield, in October of that year. On August 12, 1882, M. C. Dufield retired, leaving John A. Dufield as sole proprietor. Among the early employes of the Democrat under Mr. Dufield were M. F. Walsh, who in December, 1877, founded the Harvard Herald and whose career is covered in another paragraph. Another employe was Charles A. Lemmers, who for many years afterwards, was destined to play an important part in the newspaper activities of the community. Mr. Lemmers became local editor of the Democrat, which at that time was an influential factor in the political affairs of its party in the northeastern counties of Illinois. On January 1, 1891, Mr. Lemmers left the Democrat, taking up a similar position with the Sentinel, the opposing Republican newspaper. The Democrat continued under Mr. Dufield's ownership, with several changes among its editors, until Mr. Dufield's appointment as postmaster at Woodstock, under President Cleveland's second administration. At about that time John W. Metzger took charge of the paper and conducted it successfully until 1902. At the present time Mr. Metzger is employed with the Sentinel.

In November, 1902, Charles A. Lemmers left the Sentinel and associated himself with seven other men: C. P. Barnes, F. B. Bennett, F. R. Jackman, V. S. Lumley, James F. Casey, D. R. Joslyn and George L. Murphy, in the purchase of the Democrat from John A. Dufield. They changed the name to the Woodstock Republican. With this change the Democratic party lost its only newspaper in this part of Illinois. Mr. Lemmer's co-partners gradually sold out until the ownership of the paper was virtually in his hands. In 1913 Mr. Lemmers was compelled to relinquish the management on account of ill health and removed to Colorado where he has since resided, and is now secretary to Governor Shoop. W. H. Simpson took charge of the Republican when Mr. Lemmers left it, and a year later the paper was sold to George W. Conn, Jr., Mr. Simpson continuing as manager.

In December, 1916, the property was purchased by Charles F.

Renich and Theo. Hamer and April 1, 1917, the Sentinel and the Republican were combined under one management by the Sentinel Company, both papers being continued for a number of months until January 1. 1919, when the name Republican was dropped.

WOODSTOCK AMERICAN

This is the latest newspaper publication in the county. It was established in 1918 by Al F. Hock, of Random Lake, Wis., and James E. Brown, of Sauk Center, Minn., assisted by prominent Woodstock men. It is a well-printed, ably-edited weekly paper which seeks to gather and print all of the important news of the county. Its up-to-date office is opposite the City Building. Its first issue was run from the presses May 31, 1918. In October of that year Mr. Brown withdrew and is now publishing a weekly paper at Walker, Minn. The American's plant is equipped with excellent and thoroughly up-to-date machinery. The subscription rate is $2.00 per year in advance. Al S. Hock is the present editor and manager. This newspaper is of the seven-column eight page quarto class.

McHENRY JOURNALISM

The McHenry Plaindealer was established August 4, 1875, by J. Van Slyke, an early-day newspaper man of this county. It was launched in the interest of the Republican party, and was later purchased and conducted by a company which had for its president the now retired banker, James B. Perry. This company sold the plant to the present owner, November 1, 1906, and since that date the Plaindealer has been published and edited by F. G. Schreiner. In size and form it is an eight-page paper and is half home and half "patent" print and is published in a leased building. Its circulation is largely in McHenry, Johnsburg, Ringwood, Volo, Spring Grove, Solon Mills and Terra Cotta. It has a subscription rate of $2.00 per year in advance. Its publication day is Thursday. The equipment of the office, newspaper and job department, is a 10 by 15 Chandler & Price jobber; a 24 inch paper cutter, hand stapler, Cranston cylinder press, a No. 15 Mergenthaler linotype and the whole is operated by electric motor. Let it be said of the Plaindealer that its name indicates its style. It is a clean local paper which strives in every possible way to build up the interest of the community in which it is published.

The only newspaper now published at the thriving city of Marengo is the Republican-News. This paper is a combination of the old Republican and the News and has in brief the following history: In 1867 the Republican was established by J. B. Babcock, an able writer and publisher and a veteran of the Civil War. The same continued until 1906 when both the News and the Republican were purchased by the Republican-News Company, with Charles Scofield as editor and principal owner. Charles Scofield purchased the News in 1896 from M. C. Dufield.

In the summer of 1919 Mr. Scofield sold the paper to Albert L. Johnson, who had previously been associated with the Sentinel at Woodstock, as manager of the job printing department. Mrs. Albert L. Johnson has personal charge of the editorial and news department, while Mr. Johnson looks after the business and mechanical department. Mrs. Johnson is a gifted writer, and had seven years' experience in newspaper work as associate editor of the Sentinel.

This is a Republican newspaper of the seven-column quarto style. It has six page home and two pages of "patent" print. Its circulation is largely in the southwestern part of the county. Its subscription rate is $2.00 per year; its publication day is Thursday; the power for running the machinery of the printery is electric. The equipment includes a Model 8 Linotype, Potter and Gordon presses, folder, etc. The Republican-News is a bright, snappy and clean home paper, giving all the news of the community in which it is published, that is suitable for insertion in a high class local newspaper.

Marengo had a newspaper as early as 1852, in which year the Marengo Journal was established. It was continued for five years by Edward Burnside, and suspended in 1857. It was succeeded by the Marengo Weekly Press, but it too, passed out of existence in a few years.

In 1867 (one account states) the Marengo Republican was first published, although the plant was located at Belvidere, being moved to Marengo in May, 1868, when D. C. Potter was its editor. In the same year J. B. Babcock became its editor, and continued to hold that position for many years. A large job office was opened when the paper was moved to Marengo. The subsequent history of this paper has already been shown above.

Before Crystal Lake had taken the field of journalism in the southeastern part of McHenry County, the town was styled Nunda and had

several experiences with newspapers and among these early journals
are: the Nunda Herald, established in July, 1880, by I. M. Mallory; the
Weekly Advocate, established in November, 1883, by M. C. Dufield, as a
neutral organ, but in 1884 it became the advocate of the principles of
the Prohibition party, and Rev. George K. Hoover of Woodstock assumed
the editorial duties. It was not many years before these newspapers
ceased to exist, doubtless having partly filled the high mission for which
they were established.

NEWSPAPER OF HARVARD

The city of Harvard, has been the home of excellent local newspapers
from its earliest days. The *Harvard Herald* was founded December 23,
1887, by M. F. Walsh. It has been owned and published continuously
by Mr. Walsh and P. E. Whittleton ever since it was established about
a third of a century ago. At present its form and size is that of an eight
and ten page, seven column paper. It is handsomely printed on electric
motor power propelled presses and is issued each Thursday at a subscription rate of $2.00 a year, strictly in advance. It has a good circula-
tion in Harvard and surrounding territory. It was the first newspaper
within McHenry County to discard the use of "patent" print and has
long since been an all-home-print newspaper. Its equipment is strictly
modern as its pages testify. The office is within a handsome building
erected by Mr. Walsh expressly for a newspaper office. With Mr. Walsh
as its founder and present editor, it goes almost without saying that the
Herald is a Republican newspaper.

'One star differeth from another," and the same is true of newspapers whether published in the city or country towns. The *Herald*
is an exceptionally well edited, well managed, mechanically perfect and
clean local newspaper of which any community may well be proud. Not
alone does it stand high in McHenry County as a first class journal, but
abroad it is appreciated as will be seen by the following production of
an article which appeared in the organ of the Department of Journalism
for the Ohio University, the same being a photo-letter:

HARVARD INDEPENDENT

The Independent at Harvard was established in 1866, just at the end
of the great Civil War, by Rev. H. V. Reed and Lon McLaughlin. It had
many owners within a decade from 1870 to 1880. Among those who
owned and conducted it were J. C. Blake, George H. White, A. M. Leland

PRESIDENT JAMES MELVIN LEE, NEW YORK UNIVERSITY, NEW YORK CITY   VICE PRESIDENT WILL G. DAVID, UNIVERSITY OF TEXAS AUSTIN
SECRETARY MANAGER CARL H. GETZ, SOUTH DAKOTA STATE UNIVERSITY, COLUMBIA

MEMBERS OF EXECUTIVE COMMITTEE FRED NEWTON GETZ, UNIVERSITY OF MICHIGAN, ANN ARBOR
JAMES W. PIERCE, INDIANA UNIVERSITY, BLOOMINGTON

AMERICAN ASSOCIATION OF TEACHERS OF JOURNALISM

OFFICE OF THE SECRETARY

January 23, 1917.

Mr. M. F. Walsh,

President, Harvard Herald Company,

Harvard, Ill.

Dear Mr. Walsh:

The Harvard Herald is the best country newspaper I have ever examined. I can say that without any qualification. By a country newspaper I mean one that is published but once a week in a comparatively small community.

At one time I edited a country newspaper in Western Washington which is today regarded as one of the most creditable weekly newspapers in the west. Because of its clean typographical appearance, our newspaper gained national recognition. I shall be glad to obtain a copy of this paper for you.

The Harvard Herald appeals to me because of its clean, typographical appearance, its splendid makeup, its excellent ad makeup and lastly because of the high quality and clean character of your advertisements. If the people of Harvard are not giving you their unqualified support--a study of your advertising columns would lead to believe that they are--then there is indeed something wrong somewhere. A newspaper such as yours ought to be regarded as the town's principal asset.

I am going to send the copies of the Herald which you sent to me, to friends of mine who are teaching classes in country journalism in some of the state universities.

I would be indebted to you if at some time you would write to me and let me know something about your town, its population, what opposition you have, how far are you from a large city, do city newspapers come into your town, how many men do you employ and how large a plant have you.

With all good wishes.

Yours cordially,

Carl H. Getz

N. B. Burtch, G. W. Hanna & Son, O. M. Eastman, Emerson and Saunders, and M. J. Emerson.

It is now a seven-column quarto, all home-print. It is run from presses propelled by an electric motor. Its publication day is on Thursday of each week, and the yearly subscription rate is $2.00. Its circulation is mostly in Harvard and surrounding towns and country. Politically, the Independent is Republican. The office is fully equipped with modern machinery, such as a two-revolution Potter job and newspaper press; three Chandler & Price Gordon printing presses, each equipped with the Kimble motors; a 33-inch Chandler & Price paper cutter, newest style stapling machine, etc. In every detail the Independent is fitted to do almost any kind of job work that may come to its office.

Concerning some of the men who have helped to make the Independent what it is today the following may be recalled by the older men of the community:

George H. White, now a Chicago lawyer, was city prosecutor during the administration of Mayor Fred Busse; A. M. Leland, was an old time printer who passed away in Woodstock a few years ago; N. B. Burtch, who was a Civil War soldier and deeply interested in politics, died in recent years; O. M. Eastman, an eastern printer, learned his trade in Boston and formerly edited a paper in Fairbury, Ill.; Rev. H. V. Reed, founder of the Independent, was father of the late Myrtle Reed McCulloch, the poet and writer; Lon McLaughlin, who was prominent in state politics; and J. C. Blake, who was a manufacturer and real-estate man.

CRYSTAL LAKE JOURNALISM

The Crystal Lake Herald was established in 1876 as the Nunda Herald, by I. M. Mallory, who conducted it till 1898. The next proprietor was J. V. Beatty who owned and operated the plant until his death, June 11, 1912, after which it was edited and managed by Frank LaTulip, for the widow until July, 1913, when it was purchased by L. W. Cobb and A. M. Shelton who ran the paper until August, 1915, after which Mr. Cobb continued alone until the Herald Publishing Company was incorporated with L. W. Cobb as president and general manager.

It is a Republican organ, runs eight pages, seven columns to the page, 22-inch column. The plant is equipped with a Cotterell cylinder, Chandler and Price jobber; also a Pearl paper cutter and best of all the

Harvey G. Durkee & Wife

Mergenthaler linotype. The office also has a practical folder and other machinery of an up-to-date character.

The Herald circulates in Crystal Lake, Cary, Algonquin and throughout all southeastern McHenry County. Its subscription rate is $2 per year. It is published each Thursday. From six to eight pages of this paper are home print.

It may be stated that the Herald was one of the first papers, if not the first in McHenry County to cast aside self-interest and devote its entire energies to the interest of the country during the World War, regardless of the consequences to itself from a business standpoint. The Herald was an American newspaper, first, last and all the time during the war, having one aim, to stand by our country and devote its energies to the winning of the war.

HEBRON TRIBUNE

This local newspaper was established at the village of Hebron, September 1, 1890, by James H. Turner and Hurley B. Begun. One year later Mr. Begun purchased the interest held by Mr. Turner and conducted it five years; he passing away in about 1897, one year later; George S. Boughton and Dr. E. V. Brown bought the Tribune and conducted the paper for one year, then selling it to Orson Boughton. G. C. Lemmers bought the paper of Mr. Boughton, in 1903, and operated it until 1913. The publication has had a continuous issue, save for a few months in 1913 just before the purchase of the plant by its present owner, Arthur D. Wiseman, in August, 1913.

It has an excellent circulation in Hebron, Alden, Richmond, Greenwood, Dorr, Chemung, Burton townships, and in Walworth County, Wis. Its publication day is Thursday and its subscription rate is $2.00 per year. It is a four-page (sometimes increased to six) journal of home print, and four pages "patent." Its machinery is propelled by electricity and includes a Prouty newspaper press, Gordon Jobbers and power paper-cutter. This is the only newspaper ever established in Hebron and the present business is annually increasing.

RICHMOND GAZETTE

The Richmond Gazette was established in 1876 by H. B. Begun. Among the numerous owners of this local news-sheet may be recalled George Utter, J. Nethercut, P. K. Wright, Fred E. Holmes, Roy E.

Scott, John H. Brill, and present publisher Homer B. Gaston who purchased the plant in 1918.

It is a seven-column, eight to twelve page paper, issued every Thursday at a subscription rate of $2.00 per year in advance. It has a good circulation in this county and also in Walworth County, Wis. Four pages of this journal are "patent" print and the remainder is set up at home. The equipment consists of modern machinery including a linotype and up to date presses both in the newspaper and job departments. Politically, the Gazette is Republican. Its machinery is operated by means of an electric motor.

The Gazette has with the passing years, had many excellent editorials and well selected local news columns and has been greeted at many a fireside as a welcome guest.

CHAPTER XII

BANKS AND BANKING

By Fremont Hoy

FIRST UNITED STATES BANK—FIRST BANK OF CHICAGO—WOODSTOCK BANK-
ING INSTITUTIONS—STATE BANK OF WOODSTOCK—AMERICAN NATIONAL
BANK OF WOODSTOCK—FARMERS' EXCHANGE STATE BANK—WOODSTOCK
NATIONAL BANK—BANKING AT CRYSTAL LAKE—UNITED STATES BANK—
HOME STATE BANK OF CRYSTAL LAKE—HARVARD BANKING INSTITUTIONS
—HARVARD STATE BANK—FIRST STATE BANK OF HARVARD—FINANCIAL
REMINISCENCES OF MC HENRY—FOX RIVER STATE BANK—RINGWOOD
STATE BANK—FIRST NATIONAL BANK OF MARENGO—DAIRYMAN'S STATE
BANK OF MARENGO—STATE BANK OF UNION—HEBRON STATE BANK—
STATE BANK OF HUNTLEY—ALGONQUIN STATE BANK—WEST MC HENRY
STATE BANK—SPRING GROVE STATE BANK—CARY STATE BANK—STATE
BANK OF RICHMOND—VICTORY LOAN SUBSCRIPTIONS—PATRIOTIC SERV-
ICE ACKNOWLEDGMENT—WAR WORK EXECUTIVE COMMITTEE—BANK
SUMMARY.

A bank is an indispensable adjunct to any community. The wealth-
iest men in the country have for years followed a practice now being
adopted by the majority of their fellow citizens, of carrying on their
business transactions by means of checks, drawing against their accounts
with the bank of their choice, instead of carrying large amounts of money
on their person. The banks of the country, however, play a much more
important part in the commercial and industrial life than merely to
afford accommodation for the personal needs of their customers. They
determine the stability of every undertaking; stand back of all industry
from the agriculturalist who produces the raw material to the retail
merchant who sell it direct to the consumer. Through their medium
foreign trade is stimulated and encouraged; countries, as well as individuals and corporations, are financed, and the future of a nation oftentimes lies in the hands of the capable and astute financiers. Therefore
in dealing with the banks and banking interests of any community, the

Historian is handling one of the most important subjects of his record, and too much emphasis cannot be accorded to the value to the people of all classes of the services rendered by these institutions within its confines.

FIRST UNITED STATES BANKS

The *Wall Street Journal,* N. Y., is the authority for the statement that the Bank of New York is the oldest bank in this country, its clearing house number being "1," while the Bank of Manhattan is number "2" and the Merchant's National Bank is number "3." There are now nine banks in the United States reaching back into the eighteenth century. Of these, two are in Massachusetts, two in Connecticut, one in Pennsylvania, one in Delaware, one in Maryland, and two in New York. The Bank of Manhattan was organized by Aaron Burr in 1799, and the Merchant's National Bank of New York, was organized by Alexander Hamilton in 1803.

Corporate banking in New York began with the organization of the Bank of New York by Alexander Hamilton in 1784. It obtained its first charter in 1792, and for fifteen years this bank, together with the New York branch of the First Bank of the United States, were the only banks doing business in either the city or state of New York. With General Hamilton and the Federal party in control of the New York State Assembly, new bank charters were not obtainable by outside parties, and this gave rise to contentions on the part of the Anti-Federalists, led by Aaron Burr. By 1800, however, the United States had in operation twenty-seven banks, and a decade later the number had increased to one hundred.

CHICAGO'S FIRST BANK

The city of Chicago had no regular banking facilities prior to 1835, but during December of that year, a branch of the State Bank of Illinois was located in that city. It was opened for business in a four-story building at the corner of LaSalle and Washington streets, where it was continued until 1843.

BANKS AND BANKING

Under the above caption, the late Lyman J. Gage, one of the most distinguished bankers of Chicago, wrote in part as follows for a contemporary history:

"The bank does not come to an embryo town perfectly organized and fully capitalized. It does not come on the first boat, nor build up its solid walls in a settlement of cabins and tents. There must precede it some degree of maturity in business, some considerable accumulation of wealth, and an active commerce with distant regions.

"So long as a man uses his own wealth he is a capitalist; it is only when he begins to employ money belonging to others and puts forth an organized system of credit that he becomes a banker.

"The different banking functions of deposit, discount, exchange and circulation do not arise simultaneously, but are put in operation successfully as the operations of business become diversified, and its needs pass beyond the facilities employed in ordinary transactions.

"An accumulation of money beyond the need of the present and which may be required at some unexpected moment, calls for a place of deposit where it may be kept safely and withdrawn at a moment when it can be profitably employed. A growth of manufactures calling for a temporary use of capital, or an enlargement of trade, giving occasion for the employment of money, while products are transported from point of production to that of consumption, give occasion for discount; the need to realize at one point, the avails of sales at a distant place, or the transmission of funds for the purchase of the raw-material of manufactures or the supply of trade, furnish a demand for exchange; while the requirements of daily transactions of traffic in the store, the shop, the farm, at home and abroad, call for a circulating medium less ponderous than the precious metals, and yet convertible at once into them.

"As the business of banking is the outcome of the need of its facilities, so the men who assume control of its operations are usually those not trained by a long course of apprenticeship at the counter or desk, but such as happen, by reason of natural aptitude and the circumstances surrounding them, to be drawn into the vocation. Thus, the first bankers in a community are usually drawn from other callings—successful merchants, lawyers and men of versatility and ready adaption.

"As a community passes out of its embryo, and assumes a more stable condition, when the frontier settlement becomes the metropolis of a great and productive region, these conditions change, and there arises a call for banking institutions, with large capital, carefully regulated by law; and for managers learned in the principles of monetary science, and trained in the intricate business of the bank.

"From 1843 until the enactment of the general banking law of 1851, there existed no chartered bank with full powers, in Chicago.

"During this period, a most heterogeneous mixture of paper had greater or less circulation. There were banknotes issued by Eastern and Southern banks, some good and others ranging through all degrees of depreciation to utter worthlessness. The city issued script which had local use as money, as it was receivable in payment of taxes. Canal script constituted a considerable part of the local circulation. There was also State Auditor's script, and St. Louis script, and the script issued by the small tradesmen 'good for groceries,' 'good for merchandise' and even it is reported 'good for a drink.' "

Such, then, was the condition of money affairs, not only at Chicago, but throughout the state, including McHenry County, until the enactment of the national banking system which went into effect in March, 1863, after which "greenbacks" and banknotes were circulated as a medium.

MC HENRY COUNTY BANKING.

Before 1852 this county had no regular banks in organized form. Such transactions as usually go through the local banks had to be executed in some outside city where there was a bank. Much of the trade prior to the Civil War was carried on by barter, one commodity being exchanged for another. The farmer traded his butter, eggs, meat and potatoes to the home merchant for their value in sugar, coffee, tobacco, cloth and similar commodities, for use by himself and his family. In case he needed to borrow a certain amount of money, he applied to one of the few men throughout the county, who fortunately for themselves and their neighbors, had possessed considerable ready cash when they settled in the locality. In emergencies, a good citizen could obtain from such a man what he needed by paying the prevailing rate of interest which until about 1880, amounted to from ten to fifteen percent per annum. The amount in excess of the legal state interest was known as "commission." Doubtless as late as 1876, the average of interest paid in this county on approved notes, ranged as high as twelve and one-half percent per annum.

According to statements made by several of the older residents of this county, the following conditions prevailed prior to the establishment of regular banking institutions in the county. S. R. Ward of Richmond recalls Judge William A. McConnell, commonly known as

"Squire" McConnell, and Col. C. H. Gibbs, as gentlemen so circumstanced as to be able to render service to their fellow citizens in the matter of making loans to them.

"Squire" McConnell lived in a grove a considerable distance northwest of the village of Richmond, and used to keep his money in a small iron safe, but his neighbors, including Doctor Ward, told him that he was imprudent in not providing a better repository for his wealth, and insisted that he establish a bank at Richmond. This he finally did, but whether on account of the advice proffered him so freely, or because of his own excellent business sense, is only a matter of conjecture. He was for many years a justice of the peace, and for sixteen years was an associate judge of the county. Col. C. H. Gibbs was proprietor of the Richmond House, and both of these gentlemen loaned thousands of dollars on short and longer loans, to people in the vicinity of Richmond and Hebron.

T. C. Schroeder, a general dealer at Richmond, in connection with his merchandising, also loaned money, even long after a bank had been established in the village. Many of the laboring men would leave their money with him for safe keeping, receiving from him a small rate of interest. This money he loaned to farmers in the surrounding regions.

J. C. Crumb carried on a banking business in a small way at Harvard, in the general merchandise store of A. E. Axtell, during 1866, but the following year he erected a bank on the corner still occupied by the banking institution in which the Crumb family is represented by the third generation as a stockholder. Before that date money had to be borrowed of individuals, or from some distant bank.

At Cary, the first banking was carried on by L. E. Mentch, who, in October, 1902, organized the Cary Exchange Bank. It was his practice to keep about $3,000 in his safe, which was in a small frame building. At midnight, in July, 1903, his safe was blown open and his capital stolen. The criminals were never brought to justice. While his losses amounted to $5,555, he was insured, and was able to continue his business. He erected the present brick bank building, and continued in the banking business until in April, 1914, when he sold his interest to thirty-seven stockholders, who organized the present Cary State Bank. Mr. Mentch then turned his attention to the real-estate business at Cary.

Joseph W. Christy, general merchant and postmaster at Ringwood, sometime in the seventies, began to loan money in small amounts on short time, to his neighbors and other patrons. He usually received about fifteen percent interest. A number of the laborers in his neighbor-heed, deposited their wages with him, and this money, on which he paid a small rate of interest, enabled him to enlarge his operations.

WOODSTOCK BANKING INSTITUTIONS

Dr. C. B. Durfee began the banking business at Woodstock in 1852, and carried it on for about two years, when he failed and was succeeded by the firm of Fuller & Johnson Co., at first composed of A. W. Fuller, C. B. Durfee, L. S. Church, Neill Donnelly, J. H. Johnson and W. G. Bentley. This firm of private bankers was re-organized under the national banking act, and became the First National Bank of Woodstock, but, in 1869, C. B. Durfee & Co. again commenced business and continued as bankers for several years thereafter. In May, 1875, T. D. Murphy and Richard Bishop opened a private bank, which was continued for about three years. The First National Bank of Woodstock was established in 1864, with a capital of $50,000. L. S. Church was president; C. B. Durfee, cashier, and N. Donnelly, M. F. Irwin, L. S. Church, C. B. Durfee, A. M. Fuller and J. H. Johnson, directors.

STATE BANK OF WOODSTOCK

The State Bank of Woodstock was established December 19, 1889, by E. E. Richards, E. C. Jewett, A. B. McConnell, G. K. Bunker, A. K. Bunker, M. L. Joslyn, William H. Stewart, B. S. Austin, George McConnell and F. W. Buell. The original officials were: E. E. Richards, president; W. H. Stewart, vice president, and E. C. Jewett, cashier. The original capital of $25,000 has been increased to $50,000, and there is a surplus of $50,000, with undivided profits of upwards of $8,000. A recent statement shows the following condition:

RESOURCES

Loans and Discounts	$386,154.66
Overdrafts	170.35
U. S. Government Investments	45,184.00
Other Bonds and Stocks	87,477.56
Banking House, Furniture and Fixtures	21,600.00
Other Real Estate	2,007.94
Due from Banks, Cash, Exchanges, Checks & Collections.....	114,455.81
Total Resources	$657,050.32

LIABILITIES

Capital Stock	$ 50,000.00
Surplus	50,000.00
Undivided Profits (Net)	8,307.44
Deposits	546,604.26
Reserve	2,138.62
Total Liabilities	**$657,050.32**

In 1910 this banking house purchased the Sherman business block, which has greatly increased in value, and is located on one of the finest business corners in the city, and this has been made into one of the most modern financial institutions in this part of the state.

The following men have served the bank as presidents: E. E. Richards, and E. C. Jewett, and the two cashiers have been E. C. Jewett and H. T. Cooney. The present officials are: E. C. Jewett, president, W. S. McConnell, vice president and H. T. Cooney, cashier.

AMERICAN NATIONAL BANK OF WOODSTOCK

The American National Bank of Woodstock was organized June 3, 1903. It was founded by John J. Murphy and George L. Murphy. The former was president of the First National Bank of Woodstock until 1889 when that institution was liquidated. The first officials of the American National Bank were: George L. Murphy, president; Charles H. Donnelly, vice president, and W. C. Eichelberger, cashier. The present officials are: George L. Murphy, president; Charles H. Donnelly, vice president; George F. Rushton, vice president; Charles L. Quinlan, cashier; E. F. Fuess and Byron D. Cheasbro, assistant cashiers. George L. Murphy has been president of the institution ever since it was established in 1903. Charles L. Quinlan succeeded W. C. Eichelberger as cashier in 1908.

The present capital is $50,000; the surplus is $50,000. Added to this amount are the undivided profits of over $15,000. The deposits are about $700,000. The latest statement shows the following condition:

RESOURCES

Loans, Bonds and Securities	$687,129.19
Stock in Federal Reserve Bank	3,000.00

U. S. Bonds to Secure Circulation 25,000.00
Due from United States Treasurer 1,250.00
Interest Earned but not Collected 11,223.25
Cash on hand and due from Banks 141,656.49

Total $869,258.93

LIABILITIES

Capital Stock and Surplus $100,000.00
Undivided Profits 15,697.87
Circulation 24,300.00
Reserved for Interest 11,223.25
Reserved for Taxes 2,297.97
Interest Collected but not Earned 2,165.71
DEPOSITS 713,574.13

Total $869,258.93

FARMERS EXCHANGE STATE BANK

Originally a private bank, established in 1887, the Farmers Exchange State Bank was re-organized under its present name in January, 1916. It was founded by M. D. Hoy and George H. Hoy, under the name of the Farmers Exchange Bank, M. D. Hoy & Son, proprietors. The original capital was $25,000, but this has been increased until it is today $75,000, with surplus and profits shown of $26,000. The private bank did not require officials by title, but all papers were signed M. D. Hoy & Son. Several years later Fremont Hoy, John M. Hoy and William P. Hoy were admitted into partnership under the name of M. D. Hoy & Sons. Fremont Hoy disposed of his interest in the firm of M. D. Hoy & Sons. in 1915, and retired from banking in both Woodstock and Huntley.

The present officials of the bank are: George H. Hoy, president; L. T. Hoy and Geo. F. Eckert, vice presidents; John M. Hoy, cashier, and C. W. Whiting and F. V. Gieselbrecht assistant cashiers. George H. Hoy, the present presiding official has held this position since the concern was made a state institution, and has been connected with the bank since its inception.

The business block in which this bank is operated is owned by the Hoy Brothers. The bank has a surplus of $20,000; undivided profits

Howard D. Eaton M.D.

of over $6,000. Its deposits in March, 1921, were $586,759.55; their gross assets $693,073.21.

The following condensed statement was made by this bank March 31, 1921:

RESOURCES

Loans and Discounts	$548,227.45
Overdrafts	259.33
United States Liberty Loan Bonds	9,700.00
Furniture and Fixtures	2,000.00
Due from Banks	98,245.38
Cash on hand	27,669.76
Checks and Cash items	6,971.29
Total	$693,073.21

LIABILITIES

Capital	$ 75,000.00
Surplus	20,000.00
Undivided Profits	6,284.77
Saving Deposits	218,638.67
Checking Deposits	370,120.88
Certificates, etc.	
Reserved for taxes and Bond Department	3,028.89
Total	$693,073.21

WOODSTOCK NATIONAL BANK

The McHenry County State Bank, now the Woodstock National Bank, located on Benton street, Woodstock, was organized in October, 1901, with a capital of $25,000, which has been increased to $50,000; with a surplus of $10,000, and undivided profits of $7,000. Its officials were J. D. Donovan, president; M. H. Fitzsimmons, vice president; and Walter F. Conway, cashier. The above named bank was converted and became the Woodstock National Bank in 1920, the former officials being placed in charge.

The building in which the bank is operated is owned by the institution. Mr. Donovan has been president since the inception of the bank, while the cashiers have been E. E. Bower and W. F. Conway, successively. Well-known business men of the county are members of the board of directors, they being: Theo. Hamer, E. C. Hughts, H. A. Stone, M. H. Fitzsimmons, William Zimmerman, J. D. Donovan, and J. T. Bower.

The following statement was made by this bank March 17, 1921;

RESOURCES

Loans, Discounts, Securities	$343,731.95
Banking house, Furniture and Fixtures	22,300.00
Federal Reserve Bank Stock	1,800.00
Cash and due from banks	99,276.24
Checks and cash items	2,164.37
Interest earned but not collected	7,734.04
Total	$477,006.60

LIABILITIES

Capital	$ 50,000.00
Surplus	10,000.00
Undivided Profits	7,168.03
Reserve for taxes and Interest	10,073.85
Deposits	399,638.72
Dividends unpaid	126.00
Total	$477,006.60

BANKING AT CRYSTAL LAKE

Prior to 1891 Crystal Lake, or Nunda, had no banking institutions; only being accommodated in the matter of exchanges through the mercantile establishments operating there during that period.

UNITED STATE BANK

In 1891 George E. Hallock, concerning whom very little, if anything, was known by the citizens of that community, opened a banking house which operated for about two years, and without much support from the public. No bank existed subsequent to the discontinuance of the Hallock Bank, until 1895, when George K. Bunker, Burton Wright, Emery E. Richards, Emilus C. Jewett and Charles B. Wright, all of Woodstock, recognized the necessity, and the favorable opportunity, for a bank at that place, and associating themselves in a co-partnership for that purpose, opened the Citizens Bank of Nunda, with a capital of $10,000; E. E. Richards acting as president; George K. Bunker as vice president, and E. C. Jewett as cashier. On October 29, 1901, this bank was incorporated as the Citizens State Bank of Nunda, and the capital increased to $25,000. Charles B. Wright became cashier of the re-organized bank. On November 2, 1908, the title of the bank was changed to the Citizens State Bank of Crystal Lake, and subsequently, August 12, 1910, the capital was increased to $50,000. The bank continued under practically the same management up to July, 1915, excepting that E. C. Jewett had disposed of his interest in 1908, and therefore was no longer connected with it. George K. Bunker had been deceased for a number of years.

Certain large investments having been made, which the board of directors and the majority of the stockholders believed would result in heavy losses, the bank was closed July 8, 1915, and the state auditor took charge. The bank remained closed for about a month, during which time the stockholders and directors arranged to make good the impairment claimed, taking out of the bank all paper that had been questioned. At this juncture, fearing that liquidation of the bank through a receivership was imminent, which would tie up more than $300,000 of the depositors' funds, and entail great loss and hardship through delay, Fremont Hoy and Clarence F. Hoy, his son, who had been president and vice president, respectively of the competing State Bank of Crystal Lake, acquired a majority of the stock of the Citizens State Bank, and its management was assumed by them. Clarence F. Hoy was made its president and Fremont Hoy its temporary cashier and vice president. W. H. Wilbur became cashier in September of that same year.

Through the succeeding year the State Bank of Crystal Lake and the Citizens State Bank were operated under the direction of Fremont Hoy and Clarence F. Hoy, with the able assistance of Messrs. Lynn Richards and W. H. Wilbur, as cashiers of the respective banks, with the result that the depositors of the Citizens State Bank were saved from the loss of money, and the community from shock to its honor and reputation as a banking center, and most of all the confidence of the people in banking integrity was retained. The Citizens State Bank and the State Bank of Crystal Lake were consolidated August 14, 1916, becoming the United State Bank of Crystal Lake, capitalized at $75,000; by this consolidation the bank at once took rank among the more important banks of the county. It is housed in its own fine building equipped in a modern manner. The Messrs Hoy disposed of their banking interests at Crystal Lake in January, 1919, to W. H. Wilbur and Lynn Richards, thus terminating their successful banking experience of six years at Crystal Lake.

The State Bank of Crystal Lake, now consolidated with the Citizens State Bank, under the name of the United State Bank of Crystal Lake, was founded and opened for business by James R. Jackman, October 20, 1910, with a capital of $25,000. Mr. Jackman was president; J. C Nordling, cashier, and F. L. Colby was vice president. Lynn Richards, former deputy circuit clerk, became cashier, January 1, 1911. In October, 1915, Fremont Hoy, having acquired control of the majority of the stock of the bank, became its president, and his son, Clarence F. Hoy, its vice president. Mr. Richards was continued as cashier. Under this management the bank had quite a gratifying growth, having deposits of about $210,000 at the time of its consolidation with the Citizens State Bank in August, 1916. The strength of this bank was never questioned, and was amply proven when in July, 1915, it was found necessary for it to provide for the financial requirements of the entire community. The bank and its officials proved able to cope with the situation in a capable and satisfactory manner, and without any discrimination. The following is the statement made by the bank March 31, 1921:

RESOURCES

Loans and Discounts	$490,126.24
Overdrafts	830.46
U. S. Government Investments	58,034.00
Other Bonds and Stocks	5,262.40
Banking House, Furniture and Fixtures	33,173.00
Other Real Estate	16,044.55
Due from Banks, Cash, Exchanges, Checks and Collections	73,903.91
Total Resources	$677,374.56

LIABILITIES

Capital Stock Paid In	$ 50,000.00
Surplus Fund	7,500.00
Undivided Profits (net)	5,653.62
Deposits	571,296.27

Reserve 2,824.67
Bills payable and Rediscounts 40,000.00

    Total Liabilities $677,374.56

HOME STATE BANK OF CRYSTAL LAKE

In 1915 the Home State Bank of Crystal Lake was organized with its present capital of $25,000. Its first officials were William Pinnow, president; Edward Malone, and J. H. Parks, vice presidents, and A. H. Henderson, cashier. These same gentlemen are still holding the positions of responsibility they entered when the bank was opened, except that J. W. Wingat is now second vice president, vice J. H. Parks, deceased.

The building in which the bank is operated is owned by the bank, and was erected for banking purposes, of terra cotta material, at a cost of $13,500.

On March 31, 1921, the following report was issued:

RESOURCES

Loans and Discounts $193,189.19
Overdrafts .... None
U. S. Government Investments 28,600.00
Other Bonds and Stocks 35,797.50
Banking House, Furniture and Fixtures 18,030.00
Due from Banks, Cash, Exchanges, Checks and Collections.. 95,621.37

    Total Resources $371,238.06

LIABILITIES

Capital Stock Paid In .... $ 25,000.00
Surplus Fund 5,000.00
Undivided Profits (net) 3,155.77
Deposits 338,082.29

    Total Liabilities $371,238.06

HARVARD BANKING INSTITUTIONS

What was known as the Harvard Bank (now the Harvard State Bank) was established in the store of A. E. Axtell, by J. C. Crumb. The following year he bought a building at the corner of Brainard and Ayer streets, and moved to it. He came through successfully the panic day of 1873, and kept pace with the growth and prosperity of his county, and in 1880 had deposits with the Fifth National Bank of Chicago amounting to $500,000. In 1881 his deposits with the Importers and Traders Bank of New York City amounted to $46,755. The bank has been ordered by representatives of three generations of the Crumb family, namely: Joseph C. the founder; Herbert D. his son, and Edward A. Crumb, his grandson, who is now assistant cashier. This bank occupies the largest banking room in McHenry County. The building is at the corner of Ayers and Brainard streets, and was rebuilt in 1904 to conform to modern banking ideas. It was a private institution, until converted into a state bank in 1920, and has had a very successful history. The statement of March 31, 1921, shows the following condition:

RESOURCES

Loans and Discounts	$601,675.00
Overdrafts	146.55
U. S. Government Investments	4,132.72
Other Bonds and Stocks	33,603.02
Banking House, Furniture and Fixtures	35,887.48
Due from Banks, Cash, Exchanges, Checks and Collections	94,602.33
Other Resources	434,814.16
Total Resources	$1,204,861.26

LIABILITIES

Capital Stock	$ 100,000.00
Surplus	15,000.00
Undivided Profits Net	7,120.12
Deposits	630,842.27
Reserve	5,139.01
Bills Payable	20,000.00
Other Liabilities	426,759.86
Total Liabilities	$1,204,861.26

FIRST STATE BANK OF HARVARD

In 1877 A. E. Axtell established a private bank and operated it under his own name in connection with other lines of business. In April, 1878, he commenced taking deposits and prospered so that by 1880 his deposits were $40,000. On May 20, 1909 the Axtell Bank was taken over by the First State Bank of Harvard, which had been established, and re-organized with a capital stock of $50,000, which with the surplus and undivided profits, of over $97,000, gives the bank a working fund of $147,000, and greater than that of any other bank in McHenry County. In 1921 its deposits were $1,432,549.69.

The first officers were F. F. Axtell, president; W. D. Hall, vice president; E. L. Axtell, cashier, and F. B. Phelps, assistant cashier. The present officers are: F. F. Axtell, president; W. D. Hall, vice president; E. L. Axtell, cashier, and F. B. Phelps, assistant cashier. The board of directors is composed of the following: F. F. Axtell, E. L. Axtell, W. D. Hall, C. E. Hunt, E. S. Smith and L. M. Lillibridge.

The statement issued on March 31, 1921, shows the following condition:

RESOURCES

Loans and Discounts	$1,028,787.98
Overdrafts	284.29
U. S. Government Investments	120,089.65
Other Bonds and Stock	121,823.00
Banking House Furniture and Fixtures	52,383.24
Due from Banks, Cash, Exchanges, Checks and Collections	256,009.76
Other Resources	517.08
Total Resources	$1,579,895.00

LIABILITIES

Capital Stock paid in	$ 50,000.00
Surplus Fund	50,000.00
Undivided Profits (net)	47,345.31
Deposits	1,432,549.69
Total Liabilities	$1,579,895.00

FINANCIAL REMINISCENCES OF McHENRY

James B. Perry, who came to McHenry in 1864, and is still residing here, furnishes the following interesting data relative to the banking history of McHenry

Some of the more prominent financiers of the earlier period in this vicinity were Samuel H. Walker and Freeman Whiting, who were accustomed to make loans. The firm of Owen Brothers, composed of Herman N. and Edward M. Owen, located at McHenry, to which they came prior to 1850, first being engaged in general merchandising and dealing in grain, but later branched out and built and operated a mill which they used for flouring and saw-milling. In connection with other business transactions they sold some exchange, but, as far as is known, did not accept deposits. The iron safe used by them about seventy years ago is still in McHenry and in use, only, however, for the purpose of protecting books and papers against a possible fire. The mercantile business of Owen Brothers was continued by them until 1874, when it was purchased by James B. Perry and Alfred A. Martin, and they, too, issued exchange. About 1882-3 Mr. Martin disposed of his holdings to Oliver N. Owen, and the firm of Perry and Owen was formed, and in 1888 began doing a regular banking business, under the name of the Bank of McHenry, with a capital of $15,000, and deposits in 1913 of $150,000. The bank was operated in a substantial brick bank building, erected by the firm in 1901.

This bank, with James B. Perry at its head, did a conservative and satisfactory business. Mr. Perry lived in the community for so long a period that he was intimately acquainted with all of the people, and they relied upon him for advice in financial matters. Among the substantial early bankers of this county Mr. Perry is an excellent example.

In 1913 Messrs. Perry and Owen, desiring to retire from active business, negotiated a sale to Fremont Hoy and Clarence F. Hoy, who took control of the bank, November 1, 1913.

FOX RIVER VALLEY STATE BANK

The Hoy Banking Company succeeded the Bank of McHenry, the name being changed in 1914 when the capital was increased from $15,000 to $25,000. That same year the bank building was remodeled. In October, 1920 a charter was granted to the Fox River Valley State Bank, McHenry, Illinois, for the purpose of taking over the business of the Hoy Banking Company, with a capital of $50,000. Fremont Hoy became its president; James B. Perry and Clarence F. Hoy, vice presidents, and Joseph C. Holly, cashier.

Mr. Fremont Hoy belongs to a family of bankers in McHenry County, and is well known through Illinois as an astute financier. He has been variously connected with banking in this county for many years, and

is recognized as an authority on finance. This bank has for years specialized on real-estate securities.

The following recent statement discloses the following condition:

RESOURCES

Loans and Discounts	$248,408.49
Overdrafts	184.14
U. S. Government Investments	200.00
Other Bonds and Stocks	14,600.00
Banking House, Furniture and Fixtures	21,505.47
Due from Banks, Cash, Exchanges, Checks and Collections	39,494.69
Total Resources	$324,392.79

LIABILITIES

Capital Stock	$ 50,000.00
Undivided Profits (net)	1,176.66
Deposits	253,216.13
Bills Payable and Re-discounts	20,000.00
Total Liabilities	$324,392.79

RINGWOOD STATE BANK

The Bank of Ringwood was established February 3, 1916, by Fremont Hoy and Clarence F. Hoy. The first officials were: Fremont Hoy, president; Clarence F. Hoy, manager, and Henry F. Wharton, cashier. Mr Wharton died in October, 1918, of influenza, which was then epidemic. His place was filled by George H. Johnson for several months, the other officials remaining the same.

The bank started with a capital of $10,000. In 1920 the business was taken over by the Ringwood State Bank, organized for that purpose, with a capital of $25,000. Clarence F. Hoy became president; Fremont Hoy, vice president; and Kenneth O. Hoy, cashier, all of whom, together with a board of seven directors, now manage the affairs of the bank. This bank now receives, as it always has, a good patronage, as is shown by its statement which appears herewith:

RESOURCES

Loans	.$ 82,516.54
Overdrafts	65.11
U. S. Gov. Investments	1,750.00
Bonds	33,500.00
Banking House, Furniture and Fixtures	9,500.00
Due from Banks, Cash and Cash Items	9,738.20
Totals	$137,069.85

LIABILITIES

Capital	$ 25,000.00
Undivided Profits	429.26
Deposits	101,640.59
Bills Payable and Re-Discounts	10,000.00
Totals	$137,069.85

The building used by the bank for banking purposes, was built by the Ringwood Bank in 1916 following the erection of the large milk bottling plant at Ringwood, and this is now owned by the Ringwood State Bank.

FIRST NATIONAL BANK OF MARENGO

On August 8, 1871, Richard M. Patrick and G. V. Wells organized the First National Bank of Marengo to succeed the private banking house of R. M. Patrick. G. V. Wells was the first president, and he was succeeded by the following: R. M. Patrick and E. D. Patrick; while R. M. Patrick, the original cashier, has been succeeded by N. V. Wolben, E. D. Patrick and A. C. Smith. The present assistant cashiers are R. F. Dusenberry and C. H. Wolben; C. B. Whittemore and E. C. Robb are the vice presidents.

The original capital remains at $50,000, but the surplus is $50,000, and undivided profits over $10,000. In 1921 the deposits were slightly upwards of $700,000.

On February 21, 1921, the following statement was issued:

RESOURCES

Loans	$467,208.30
Overdrafts	3,022.20
U. S. Bonds	44,000.00
Other Bonds	154,071.96
Collateral Trust Notes	22,975.00
Stock Federal Reserve Bank	3,000.00
Furniture and Fixtures	12,500.00
Due from Banks, Cash and Exchange on Hand	116,628.65
Redemption Fund with and Due from U. S. Treasury	625.00
Interest Earned but Not Collected	14,750.51
Credit Reports	76.25
Total Resources	$838,857.87

LIABILITIES

Capital Stock	$ 50,000.00
Surplus	50,000.00
Undivided Profits (Net)	10,341.60
Unearned Interest Collected	26.76
Reserved for Interest, Accrued	14,723.75
Circulating Notes Outstanding	12,200.00
Deposits—All Kinds	701,565.76
Total Liabilities	$838,857.87

DAIRYMAN'S STATE BANK OF MARENGO

In 1890 Z. E. Goodrich, Loren Woodard, William Dougherty, C. S. Robb, I. R. Curtiss I. N. Muzzy, N. Buck, A. A. Ryder, R. Dalby, O. Hopkins, G. B. Richards, A. W. Kelley, Will Pringle, C. Buchte, C. E. Kelley, P. B. Smith, L. Barber, A. S. Norton, A. J. Shurtleff, John Gray, C. B. Kimball, E. P. Sperry, A. H. Penny, George Samter and T. M. Hager organized the Dairyman's State Bank of Marengo with a capital of $25,000. This has remained the same but there are now undivided profits and a surplus of $50,244.96. The officials were: Z. E. Goodrich, president; Ira R. Curtiss, vice president; Lester Barber, cashier; and A. S. Norton, assistant cashier. The original chief executive, Mr. Goodrich, has been succeeded in turn by Ira R. Curtiss, E. E. Seward and

G. W. Redpath, while Mr. Norton and C. J. Coarson, have more recently filled the place of Mr. Barber, as cashier. J. E. Williams acted as vice president for a time; however, C. J. Coarson is now the present vice president, and Carleton S. Robb and E. J. Hintz are the assistant cashiers. The bank building occupied by this bank was erected in 1915 of brick and stone.

On March 31, 1921, the following statement was issued:

RESOURCES

Loans and Discounts	$358,863.98
Overdrafts	331.62
U. S. Government Investments	28,150.00
Other Bonds and Stocks	17,000.22
Banking House, Furniture and Fixtures	26,866.00
Other Real Estate	3,000.00
Due from Banks, Cash, Exchanges, Checks and Collections..	60,595.52
Total Resources	$494,807.34

LIABILITIES

Capital Stock Paid In	$ 25,000.00
Surplus Fund	25,000.00
Undivided Profits (Net)	25,244.96
Deposits	419,322.38
Dividends Unpaid	240.00
Total Liabilities	$494,807.34

STATE BANK OF UNION

In 1911 O. E. Schnette, H. E. Franzen and A. F. Pottratz organized the State Bank of Union with a capital of $25,000, which remains the same, to which has been added $9,819.53 in surplus and undivided profits. The resources and liabilities of the bank in March, 1921, were $301,825.14, and its deposits were $247,005.61. The building in which this bank is operating is a brick structure erected in 1911. H. A. Stoxen and W. H. Deneen have been its presidents, and O. H. Schnette has continued its cashier. George L. Torrence is the vice president, and C. M. Siems is the assistant cashier.

The banks recent statement follows:

RESOURCES

Loans and Dicounts	$169,569.18
Overdrafts	105.35
Bonds	41,619.00
Banking House and Fixtures	5,800.00
Due from Banks and Cash	84,731.61
Total Resources	$301,825.14

LIABILITIES

Capital Stock	$ 25,000.00
Surplus	9,000.00
Undivided Profits	819.53
Deposits	247,005.61
Bills Payable	20,000.00
Total Liabilities	$301,825.14

Union had a bank at a slightly earlier date which only operated for a short time. Some loss sustained through its closing.

HEBRON STATE BANK

The Bank of Hebron was established in 1897 by G. W. Conn, Sr., G. W. Conn, Jr., and F. N. Torrence, with a capital of $7,500. These gentlemen operated the bank quite successfully for a short time, when the ownership passed to a syndicate composed of W. E. Wite and four other prominent local men. Mr. Wite, who has served as county superintendent of schools of McHenry County for several terms, became cashier and A. J. Cole, president. These five gentlemen gave to the bank a prestige which was a great factor in its steady growth.

In 1920 this lucrative business passed to the present Hebron State Bank which, to conform to the present law, had been organized to take over and continue the business. The present officers are: A. J. Cole, president; F. C. Slavin, vice president; J. W. Smith, cashier; and W. R. Giddings and Lora C. Mead, assistant cashiers.

The following is the statement issued by the bank under date of March 31, 1921:

RESOURCES

Loans and Discounts	$422,087.62
Overdrafts	1,117.29
U. S. Government Investments	27,000.00
Other Bonds and Stocks	2,000.00
Banking House, Furniture and Fixtures	7,444.75
Due from Banks, Cash, Exchanges, Checks and Collections	52,805.88
Total Resources	$512,455.54

LIABILITIES

Capital Stock	$ 50,000.00
Surplus	25,000.00
Undivided Profits net	5,445.63
Deposits	407,009.91
Bills Payable and Re-discounts	25,000.00
Total Liabilities	$512,455.54

STATE BANK OF HUNTLEY

On March 12, 1913, the State Bank of Huntley was established with John M. Hoy as president; A. B. Brinkerhoff, vice president; William P. Hoy, cashier; and W. F. Bartlett, assistant cashier. The present officials are: John M. Hoy, president; John T. Kelley, vice president; William P. Hoy cashier, and W. F. Bartlett and C. H. Marsh, assistant cashiers.

This bank is the outgrowth of the Bank of Huntley, founded May 1, 1901 by M. D. Hoy & Sons, successors to a banking business conducted for a few years as the Farmers Exchange Bank, by Charles E. Cook, and E. H. Cook, who sold to M. D. Hoy & Sons.

The original capital of the State Bank of Huntley $50,000, is unchanged, but there is a surplus of $30,000, and undivided profits of $5,600. The resources and liabilities are $518,558.60, deposits are $390,670.68. It stands for all that represents the highest banking standards. This bank was equipped with modern new fixtures a few years since.

The following is their showing on March 31, 1921.

RESOURCES

Loans and Discounts	$379,579.01
Overdrafts	180.22
U. S. Government Investments	51,550.00
Other Bonds and Stock	21,100.00
Banking House, Furniture and Fixtures	2,700.00
Other Real Estate	5,000.00
Due from Banks, Cash, Exchanges, Checks and Collections	58,449.37
Total Resources	$518,558.60

LIABILITIES

Capital Stock	$ 50,000.00
Surplus	30,000.00
Undivided Profits (net)	5,602.51
Deposits	390,670.68
Dividends unpaid	150.00
Reserve	2,135.41
Bills Payable and Re-discounts	40,000.00
Total Liabilities	$518,558.60

ALGONQUIN STATE BANK

In June, 1913 B. C. Getzelman established the Algonquin State Bank, and has always been its president. E. C. Peter is vice president. This bank succeeded the Bank of Algonquin. The present cashier. George D. Keyes has always held his present position since the bank became a state bank. The capital is $25,000, surplus and undivided profits $16,625.70.

In March 1921 the following statement was issued:

RESOURCES

Loans and Discounts	$167,738.97
Overdrafts	13.79
U. S. Government Investments	7,136.50
Other Bonds and Stock	33,610.97
Banking House, Furniture and Fixtures	2,289.20
Due from Banks, Cash, Exchanges, Checks and Collections	48,201.95
Total Resources	$258,991.38

LIABILITIES

Capital Stock Paid In ....$ 25,000.00
Surplus Fund 10,000.00
Undivided Profits (net) 6,625.70
Deposits 214,238.67
Reserve 3,127.01

Total Liabilities $258,991.38

WEST MC HENRY STATE BANK

On September 10, 1906, the West McHenry State Bank was established by P. S. Webster with a capital of $25,000, which has since been increased to $50,000. This thoroughly modern banking institution is the first bank of West McHenry, and its only one. E. L. Wagner and C. H. Fegers have served in turn as its presidents, and Carl W. Stenger has always been its cashier. The present vice president of the bank is Parker S. Webster and the second vice president is Simon Stoffel.

A statement made on March 31, 1921, shows the following condition:

RESOURCES

Loans and Discounts $336,270.33
Overdrafts 75.92
U. S. Government Investments........................ 63,538.00
Other Bonds and Stocks............................. 22,050.44
Banking House, Furniture and Fixtures.............. 18,645.00
Due from Banks, Cash, Exchanges, Checks and Collections... 43,752.01

Total Resources $484,331.70

LIABILITIES

Capital Stock ....$ 50,000.00
Surplus Fund 10,000.00
Undivided Profits (net) 9,873.12
Deposits 414,241.70
Contingent Fund 216.88

Total Liabilities $484,331.70

Harry L. Ehorn

SPRING GROVE STATE BANK

On December 3, 1914, the Spring Grove Bank was organized by J. E. Meredith, J. H. Gerbracht and Anton Sahaefer. The present officials are: Anton Sahaefer, president and cashier; and M. A. Sahaefer, assistant cashier.

This bank was started with a capital of $3,000, and in 1919 had resources amounting to $53,153. Its deposits amounted to $48,946 in the same year, and it carried a surplus fund of $1,207. It was located in a small village, and, in the past has had ample facilities for transacting all necessary business in its line for the surrounding neighborhood, and its management have had the good will of the people of this vicinity.

About the commencement of 1920 an organization was brought into existence under the Illinois Banking Act, with a capital of $25,000, having for its title the Spring Grove State Bank. This organization purchased the business, assets and good will of the Spring Grove Bank, and since that time has conducted a banking business at that place, with considerable success. Joseph G. Wagner is the president; John C. Furlong, vice president; and Arthur H. Franzen, cashier. Mr. H. H. Franzen of Du Page County, Illinois, a banker of considerable experience in several localities, is financially interested and is a director of this bank.

The most recent available statement, of March 31, 1921, shows the condition of the bank to be as follows:

RESOURCES

Loans and Discounts	$ 81,882.75
Other Bonds and Stocks	7,055.00
Banking House, Furniture and Fixtures	1,786.26
Other Real Estate	1,250.00
Due from Banks, Cash Exchanges, Checks and Collections	18,222.26
Total Resources	$110,196.27

LIABILITIES

Capital Stock	$ 25,000.00
Undivided Profits (net)	4,452.21
Deposits	80,544.06
Other Liabilities	200.00
Total Liabilities	$110,196.27

CARY STATE BANK

The Cary State Bank is located in the village of Cary and was organized April 3, 1914, with T. H. Wulff as president; C. W. Stenger, vice president; and Joseph J. Sutton, cashier. Its original capital of $25,000 has not been increased, but it has surplus and undivided profits of $12,430.26. In March, 1921, its deposits were $193,001.62. The Cary State Bank owns its own banking building erected at a cost of $6,000. This bank has transacted its affairs from the start in an honorable and upright manner, and its officials have the confidence of the surrounding country.

According to a statement made under date of March 31, 1921, the condition of the bank is as follows:

RESOURCES

Loans and Discounts	$150,627.75
Bonds and Stocks	38,337.50
Cash on Hand	8,248.76
Banking House, Furniture and Fixtures	8,532.00
War Savings Stamps	840.80
Overdrafts	7.37
Total Resources	$230,441.88

LIABILITIES

Capital Stock	$ 25,000.00
Surplus	7,500.00
Undivided Profits (net)	4,930.26
Individual Deposits	75,712.66
Other Deposits	10,350.80
Time Deposits	28,254.35
Savings Deposits	78,683.81
Unpaid Dividends	10.00
Total Liabilities	$230,441.88

The present officers are: T. H. Wulff, president; C. W. Stenger, vice president; and Joseph A. Stenger, cashier. The board of directors is composed of: T. H. Wulff, C. W. Stenger, H. Newbold, E. L. Wagner and N. B. Kern.

A banking business was formerly conducted by L. E. Mentch under the title of the Cary Exchange Bank, but after several years went out of existence.

STATE BANK OF RICHMOND

The Bank of Richmond was organized in 1890 by George and John McConnell, who associated with them John W. Haythorn. The original officials were: George McConnell, president; John McConnell, vice president; and John W. Haythorn, cashier. The officials immediately prior to its organization as a state bank in 1920, were: Susan McConnell, president; Cora H. Covell, vice president; May L. Parsons, vice president; Frank B. McConnell, cashier; and William A. McConnell, assistant cashier. The present officials are: Frank B. McConnell, president; Charles Kruse, first vice president; M. R. Cole, second vice president; and W. A. McConnell, cashier.

The original capital of $10,000 had not been increased up to 1920, but the bank had a surplus of $45,053.76. On March 31, 1921, shortly after re-organizing, its resources and liabilities were $399,280.76, and at the same date its deposits were $349,280.76. In September, 1890, the present substantial bank building was erected at a cost of $5,000, by George and John McConnell. It is our understanding that the present State Bank of Richmond will occupy the building under lease.

The newly-incorporated state bank has a large number of the most influential and substantial citizens for stockholders, together with the former owners, and it is our belief that the institution will continue to enjoy, to the fullest extent, the confidence of the community. The present capital is $50,000.

The official statement of March 31, 1921, follows:

RESOURCES

Loans and Discounts	$251,157.13
Overdrafts	122.44
U. S. Government Investments	12,768.47
Other Bonds and Stocks	53,758.68
Banking House, Furniture and Fixtures	1,633.57
Due from Banks, Cash, Exchanges and Collections	79,840.47
Total Resources	$399,280.76

LIABILITIES

Capital Stock .... $ 50,000.00
Deposits 349,280.76
                                                         _____
    Total Liabilities $399,280.76

VICTORY LOAN SUBSCRIPTIONS

The following is a complete list of the subscriptions received from each bank in McHenry County for the Victory Loan issued by the government, which drive was on during April, 1919. These subscriptions foot up to 110.25 per cent of the county's quota. This list is given in full to prove that no section of the county failed in doing its full patriotic duty at a time when the country had need of real Americanism.

Bank	Subscribers	Amount
Algonquin State, Algonquin................	282	$ 68,000
Cary State, Cary Station..................	174	36,300
Home State, Crystal Lake.................	144	40,300
United State, Crystal Lake................	378	61,750
First State, Harvard	846	160,600
Harvard State, Harvard...................	377	63,450
Bank of Hebron, Hebron..................	300	89,900
State Bank, Huntley	350	72,250
Dairyman's State, Marengo	298	79,300
First National, Marengo	234	54,550
Hoy Banking Co., McHenry................	154	27,600
Bank of Richmond, Richmond..............	191	74,200
Bank of Ringwood, Ringwood..............	139	29,150
Spring Grove Bank, Spring Grove..........	120	22,400
State Bank, Union	186	56,350
West McHenry State, West McHenry........	306	74,250
American National, Woodstock	520	95,000
Farmers' Exchange State, Woodstock........	629	82,000
McHenry Co. State, Woodstock.............	376	63,050
State Bank, Woodstock	675	97,350
Total	6,679	$1,347,850

It has been carefully estimated that the total amount subscribed in this county during the several drives of the World War amounted to over $5,000,000.

PATRIOTIC SERVICE ACKNOWLEDGMENT

"Woodstock, Ill., May 24, 1919.

"We, the undersigned banks of Woodstock, desire to take this means of extending our thanks to the committee, which handled the drives of the Third, Fourth and Fifth Liberty Loans, of which Charles F. Renich was chairman, for the manner in which they conducted the solicitations for subscriptions. The entire amounts were taken by the patriotic people of this community, thus relieving the banks from subscribing and carrying the bonds.

"We believe that this was only made possible through the efforts of Chairman Renich and his committee, who worked continuously in the interest of the loans, many times at the expense of their own private business.

"Woodstock and vicinity has 'gone over the top' on every Liberty Loan, and this 100-per-cent-record was made by the hearty co-operation extended to the banks by the above-mentioned committee. We feel that public acknowledgment of all due credit to these loyal workers should be made, now that the war is over and the government has announced the Victory Loan to be the last issue of Liberty Bonds.

"Signed,
"The State Bank of Woodstock, E. C. Jewett, president.
"The American National Bank, G. L. Murphy, president.
"McHenry County State Bank, J. D. Donovan, president,
"Farmers' Exchange State Bank, G. H. Hoy, president."

WAR WORK EXECUTIVE COMMITTEE

The executive committee which had charge of these various campaigns in Woodstock, working always under the direction, leadership and inspiration of national, state and county direction, were Charles F. Renich, chairman, D. R. Joslyn, O. G. Mead, F. J. Green, F. A. Walters, F. B. Bennett, A. J. Mullen, G. E. Still, C. Percy Barnes, F. E. Howe and F. W. Hartman. Carl W. Stenger, of West McHenry, was county chairman of the four campaigns, while D. R. Joslyn was chairman of the Fifth or Victory campaign.

All the subscriptions were made cheerfully by the people, even when the making of them entailed heavy personal sacrifices and the assuming of obligations through the borrowing of money to meet the payments.

BANK SUMMARY

The following summary of the banking interests as shown below gives a very creditable report on the financial conditions in McHenry County. From statements of March 31, 1921.

Name	Established	Capital, Surplus & Undivided Profits	Deposits
State Bank of Woodstock......	1889	$ 108,307.44	$ 546,604.26
Farmers' Exchange State Bank.	1887	101,284.77	586,759.55
American National Bank.......	1903	115,697.87	713,574.13
Woodstock National Banak.....	1901	67,168.02	399,638.72
First State Bank of Harvard...	1877	147,345.31	1,432,549.69
Harvard State Bank...........	1866	122,120.12	630,842.27
Home State Bk. of Crystal Lake.	1915	33,155.77	338,082.29
U. S. State Bank of Crystal Lake	1895	63,153.62	571,296.27
First National Bk. of Marengo..	1871	110,341.60	701,565.76
Dairyman's State Bank........	1890	75,244.96	419,322.38
State Bank of Huntley........	1901	85,602.51	390,670.68
Algonquin State Bank.........	1913	41,625.70	214,238.67
West McHenry State Bank.....	1906	69,873.12	414,241.70
Sp. Grove State Bank.........	....	29,452.21	80,544.06
Cary State Bank..............	1914	37,430.26	193,001.62
Hebron State Bank...........	1897	80,445.63	407,009.91
Ringwood State Bank.........	1916	25,429.26	101,640.59
State Bank of Union..........	1911	34,819.53	247,005.61
Fox River Valley State Bank...	1888	51,176.66	253,216.13
State Bank of Richmond.......	1890	50,000.00	249,280.76
Total		$1,449,674.36	$8,991,085.05

Total Capital, Surplus and Undivided Profits............$ 1,449,674.36
Total of All Deposits................................. 8,991,085.05

Total of All Banking Assets Employed.............$10,440,759.41

CHAPTER XIII

AGRICULTURE AND COUNTY FAIRS

By George A. Hunt

IMPORTANCE OF AGRICULTURE

When the pioneer settlers who came to McHenry County during the years 1834 to 1838, inclusive, secured their original farms, they were able to obtain the land from the government for the entry fee of $1.25 per acre. The settlers who followed a little later bought many acres of fertile land at prices but a little in advance of the government fee. Oftentimes they were able to purchase farms upon which considerable improvements had been made for sums so small as to seem incredible in these days of high prices. While they were engaged in tilling the soil, the importance and dignity of agricultural labor had not been recognized, and the farmer operated his farm to obtain a living, not as a business proposition. For this reason, and the facts that land was plenty and transportation poor, the best acreage sold at low figures, and there was no special inducement to anyone who had the inclination to go into farming on an extensive scale.

With the building of the great railroad systems, thus bringing the farmer into closer touch with the centers of demand; the installation of cars built upon the cold storage plan; the invention of labor-saving machinery, and the appliance of motor power, a complete revolution occurred, and the man who owned farm land began to realize that he had a plant which, if properly conducted, would yield him a handsome

197

income, and give him a prominent place among the producers of the country.

Many men who had been born and reared on farms, but later left them, lured to the cities by ambition and hope of riches easily obtained without the strenuous labor of the rural districts, returned to the soil, and put to practical use the lessons they had learned many years before. Those who had been sensible enough to remain on the farm expanded in every way, buying more land, put in modern equipment, and took advantage of the opportunities offered by federal and state government experimental stations. In fact, although somewhat late, the agriculturist came into his own.

With this expansion came an appreciable advance in land values. Twenty years ago the prophecy that Illinois farm land would sell for at least $200 per acre, was laughed at. Now many McHenry County farmers are refusing $250 per acre and over for their holdings.

Within the past few years new conditions have arisen which will make the agriculturist still more important, for upon his shoulders rests the burden of feeding the world. It will be many years before the war-devastated area can be brought back to its former productiveness and it is to the United States that the rest of the world is looking, and will have to look for some years to come, for its very subsistence.

No manufacturer, banker, merchant, or professional man is today of more actual value to his generation than is the farmer who understands his work and takes an interest in it, and in rendering to humanity the service that lies in his power. Organization of the agricultural forces of the state and nation have, during the past few years, exerted a very marked and powerful influence upon the country's development. Granges, Farmers' Institutes, Agricultural Fairs, Farm Bureaus, Farmers' Elevators, Shipping Associations and other farmer organizations have all had much to do in placing agriculture in the higher position which it now holds in relation to the other industries.

MC HENRY COUNTY FARMERS' INSTITUTE

The Farmers' Institute of McHenry County is a potent factor in progressive agriculture in the county. It holds one or more successful meetings each winter. The speakers engaged to address these meetings are men and women of recognized authority on the subjects they present and much good has been accomplished through the inspiration and enthusiasm engendered. In arranging excursions to the agricultural

Allan G. Fleming

Isabella Fleming.

colleges, securing agricultural scholarships for the boys and girls, in encouraging improved methods and in many other ways the Farmers' Institute has been an influence for good to the agricultural interests of the county.

The Officers of the McHenry County Farmers' Institute since 1896 were as follows:

1896-1897—President, M. Zimpelman, Marengo; vice-president, O. M. Hale, Nunda; secretary, Frank T. Barnes, Woodstock; treasurer, Thomas Ocock, Union.

1897-1898—President, M. Zimpelman, Marengo; vice-president, George A. Hunt, Greenwood; secretary, F. T. Barnes, Woodstock; treasurer, E. H. Cook, Huntley.

1898-1899—President, George A. Hunt, Greenwood; vice-president, William A. Saylor, West McHenry; secretary, George L. Murphy, Woodstock; treasurer, E. H. Cook, Huntley.

1899-1900—President, George A. Hunt, Greenwood; secretary, M. Zimpelman, Marengo; treasurer, H. T. Thompson, Huntley.

1900-1901—President, George A. Hunt, Greenwood; secretary, M. Zimpelman, Marengo; treasurer, H. T. Thompson, Huntley.

1901-1902—President, H. T. Thompson, Marengo; secretary, J. H. Turner, Hebron; treasurer, F. C. Wells, Harvard.

1902-1903—President, H. T. Thompson, Marengo; secretary, J. H. Turner, Hebron; treasurer, F. C. Wells, Harvard.

1903-1904—President, H. T. Thompson, Marengo; secretary, J. H. Turner, Hebron; treasurer, F. C. Wells, Harvard.

1904-1905—President, M. Zimpelman, Marengo; secretary, J. H. Turner, Hebron; treasurer, F. C. Wells, Harvard.

1905-1906—President, M. Zimpelman, Marengo; secretary, J. H. Turner, Hebron; treasurer, F. C. Wells, Harvard.

1906-1907—President, M. Long, Woodstock; secretary, F. E. Thayer, Woodstock; treasurer, F. C. Wells, Harvard.

1907-1908—President, F. E. Thayer, Woodstock; secretary, J. F. Westphall, Alden; treasurer, F. C. Wells, Harvard.

1908-1909—President, F. E. Thayer, Woodstock; secretary, J. F. Westphall, Alden; treasurer, F. C. Wells, Harvard.

1909-1910—President, F. E. Thayer, Woodstock; secretary-treasurer, F. C. Wells, Harvard.

1910-1911—President, George A. Hunt, Woodstock; secretary, E. F. Booth, Woodstock; treasurer, F. C. Wells, Harvard.

1911-1912—President, George A. Hunt, Woodstock; secretary, E. F. Booth, Woodstock; treasurer, F. C. Wells, Harvard.

1912-1913—President, M. J. Wright, Woodstock; secretary, Elmer Standish, Marengo; treasurer, F. C. Wells, Harvard.

1913-1914—President, M. J. Wright, Woodstock; secretary, Elmer Standish, Marengo; treasurer, F. C. Wells, Harvard.

1914-1915—President, M. J. Wright, Woodstock; secretary-treasurer, C. W. Colton, Woodstock.

1915-1916—President, M. J. Wright, Woodstock; secretary-treasurer, C. W. Colton, Woodstock.

1916-1917—President, M. J. Wright, Woodstock; secretary-treasurer, C. W. Colton, Woodstock.

1917-1918—President, M. J. Wright, Woodstock; secretary-treasurer, H. E. Whipple, Harvard.

1918-1919—President, B. L. Thomas, Ringwood; secretary-treasurer, H. F. Echternach, Marengo.

1919-1920—President, B. L. Thomas, Ringwood; secretary-treasurer, H. F. Echternach, Marengo.

1920-1921—President, B. L. Thomas, Ringwood; secretary-treasurer, H. F. Echternach, Marengo.

1921-1922—President, B. L. Thomas, Ringwood; secretary-treasurer, Clarence H. Ocock, Union.

MC HENRY COUNTY FARM BUREAU

McHenry County was the third county in Illinois and among the first twenty in the United States to organize a Soil Improvement Association, or Farm Bureau, as it is called in many of the counties. This organization in McHenry County, which is a unit of the state and national associations, has had a very important part in the agricultural development of the state. A great many marked changes have taken place in the agricultural conditions in this county during the time which has intervened since the organization of the McHenry County Soil Improvement Association. This association was organized in February, 1913. Several members of the County Farmers Institute were instrumental in perfecting this organization. Among those most active in promoting this movement may be mentioned M. J. Wright and C. W. Hart of Woodstock, J. H. Turner of Hebron, H. E. Whipple, F. C. Wells, R. F. Marshall and T. H. Murray of Harvard, and Bert Thomas of Ringwood. Funds for the support of this organization have been received from the following sources:

For the year

1913 U. S. Dept. of Agriculture................$ 400.00
      County Board of Supervisors 2,000.00   2,400.00

1914—U. S. Dept. of Agriculture................$ 400.00
      Board of Supervisors 2,000.00
      County Bankers Association 2,000.00   4,400.00

1915—Smith-Lever Fund ....$ 400.00
      Board of Supervisors 1,500.00   1,900.00

1916—Smith-Lever Fund $1,200.00
      Board of Supervisors 2,000.00   3,200.00

1917—Smith-Lever Fund $1,200.00
      Board of Supervisors 2,200.00   3,400.00

1918—Smith-Lever Fund $1,200.00
      Board of Supervisors 2,200.00   3,400.00

1919—Smith-Lever Fund $1,150.00
      State Appropriation 872.86
      Board of Supervisors 2,200.00   4,222.86

1920—Smith-Lever Fund ....$ 975.00
      State Appropriation 1,187.00
      Board of Supervisors 1,666.66   3,828.66

Total of appropriations above sources $26,751.52

For the year 1920 the supervisors appropriated $5,000 to be divided equally between the Soil Improvement Association, the Home Bureau and the Boys' and Girls' Club work. Additional funds for the work of the association are received from the membership fees. This fee was first placed at $5 per year, and afterward increased to $10 per year, one-half of the fee being paid for membership in the Illinois Agricultural Association. The membership fee was again increased at the beginning of the special drive for members in July, 1919, to $15. This fee of $15 also included membership in the state association, and in the American

Farm Bureau Federation. During this drive a membership of 1,350 was obtained.

Soon after the organization was formed, Delos L. James, a resident of the county and a graduate of the Illinois College of Agriculture, was employed as advisor for the association. He served in this capacity for three years. At the beginning of 1916 he left to accept the position of superintendent on ex-Gov. Frank O. Lowden's Sinnissippi Farm at Oregon, Ill. He was succeeded by Arthur J. Gafke, of Crow Wing County, Minnesota. Mr. Gafke is a graduate of the Wisconsin College of Agriculture, 1910, and was agricultural advisor in Crow Wing County, Minnesota, several years. He came to McHenry County in 1916 and is still advisor for the county at the present writing.

Before this organization was formed not over five percent of the grain sown in the county was treated for smut. At the present time probably not five percent is untreated. This treatment has resulted in a gain of approximately 500,000 bushels of grain per year for the past two or three years, showing a good gain each year. The number of pure-bred sires used in the county is four times as great as were used five years ago. In one cow testing association only fifty percent of the members were using pure-bred sires at the beginning of the work. At the close of the year's work in 1917 all but one of the members had pure-bred sires.

The census of 1910 showed an acreage in the county of ten times as much timothy as alfalfa. The assessor's book for 1920 showed more than 5,000 acres seeded to alfalfa, the wonder crop, in McHenry County. More than 1,000 acres of this acreage being reported from McHenry Township. The wisdom of this is very apparent this season of 1921 when the first cutting of alfalfa is yielding one and one-half tons or more to the acre, while clover right beside in the same fields is yielding not over half a ton to the acre. This first cutting on some farms is being sold standing at prices ranging from $15 to $25 per acre. Along with alfalfa culture was begun the use of limestone.

In 1917 between 30 and 40 cars of limestone were used to correct the acidity of the soil and to permit the growth of bacteria on the roots of the legumes, the function of which is to draw nitrogen from the air and make it available for the use of the plants. Excellent results have also been obtained by the judicious use of rock phosphate, of which nearly three thousand tons have been used in the county during the past five years.

During the same period nearly 5,000 tons of limestone have been applied to McHenry County soils. As a result of the use of lime and phosphate a much better quality of small grain, clover and corn has been produced. The yields have also been greatly increased. In some instances the yields have nearly doubled those of five and six years ago. Herbert Kiltz just doubled the yield of alfalfa on his farm south of Woodstock by the use of lime and rock phosphate. Good results have also been brought about by the proper spraying of orchards. Where it has been done thoroughly the codling moth, curculio and apple scab have been practically destroyed. This is particularly true in the orchards of Henry Street, Homer Whipple, Jacob Olbrich, R. E. Corlett, Bert Thomas, Wm. George, Frank Gustafson, E. G. Turner, and others.

Two standard varieties of corn adapted to the soil and climate have been established in the county, namely Murdock (yellow) and Wisconsin No. 7 (white), known also as Silver King. This is the outgrowth of the Boys' and Girls' Club work which was started in 1917 with 190 plats. The boys and girls sold 800 bushels of seed corn from these plats. The yield, even in 1917, a very poor corn year, were as high as forty bushels per acre of dry corn. This corn was acknowledged to be the best corn raised in the county that year. In the spring of 1918, when good seed was very scarce, the Farm Bureau distributed 2,800 bushels of seed corn among the farmers of the county at cost plus the actual expense of handling the corn. This project was financed by the American National Bank of Woodstock, the corn being selected from sections where it would be best adapted to McHenry County conditions. Much improvement has been made in the general yield of farm crops by the increased use of improved seed.

BOYS' AND GIRLS' CLUB WORK

Much interest was manifested in the Boys' and Girls' Club work. In 1917 135 girls canned between 8,000 and 9,000 quarts mostly vegetables, a large part of which would otherwise have been wasted. The girls did this work themselves. The Boys' and Girls' Club work increased to such an extent that it became necessary to have a special man to take charge of it. T. H. Murray, of Harvard, Illinois, was selected for the club work in which he has been very successful. In 1918 there were 210 boys and girls growing Murdock corn; 350 boys and girls in canning clubs; 125 boys and girls raising pigs, most of them being pure-breds and being raised for breeding purposes. In 1918 an exhibit of the McHenry County Club work was made at the Illinois State Fair. This exhibit won a number of the best prizes, including first on Corn Club Demonstration work by Chemung Township Team. Second, on canning demonstration work by the Ringwood team; fourth place by the McHenry County Club in the pageant representing the different phases of the work; first on canned fruit, exhibit by the Chemung club; fourth on canned vegetables by the Ringwood team. In 1920 more than 700 boys and girls were enrolled in the club work which included Calf Club, Pig Club, Tractor Club, Corn Club, Potato Club, Cow Testing and Judging Club, and Garment and Canning Club. The major work with the boys consisted of the dairy problems, the object being to teach them how to select, judge, buy, feed and care for the cows. There were thirty-eight entrants in the judging contest at the county fair. Then prizes were awarded. A later contest was held at Walcowis Farms, Lake Geneva, Wisconsin. Five of the best in this contest were sent to the University of Illinois for three days' training. Four of these were selected to represent the state at the National Dairy Show against nineteen other states. The boys in this team were from ten to fifteen years of age. This team won first on judging Holsteins; second on all breeds; third on Guernseys. One of the boys, Edward Schutt, of Harvard, won sixth on Holsteins; Carl Anderson, McHenry, third on Holsteins; Clarence Doran, Harvard, won first on Holsteins; second on Ayrshires, third on all breeds. The team representing McHenry County won more places than any other team at the show. Clarence Doran won more places than any other boy in the contest. The major work with the girls was sewing. The Corn Club raised over 2,000 bushels of corn and sold 387 bushels for seed. The Pig Club produced 5,000 pounds of pork. The Potato Club raised 760 bushels of potatoes. The Canning Club canned 6,103 quarts of fruits and vegetables. The Garment Club made 631 garments. The Dairy Club kept records on feed and milk production on 437 cows. The club work of McHenry County ranks first in Illinois. This has been splendid training for the boys and girls and Mr. Murray is entitled to great credit for the success of the club work.

McHenry County now has a Farm Bureau, a Home Bureau, a County Holstein Breeders Association, and nine subsidiary organizations as follows: A Federal Farm Loan Association; A Cow Testing Association; A Farmer's Co-operative Association, and six Livestock Shipping Associations. Twenty-one farmers have availed themselves of the privilege of the Federal Farm Loan to date. $150,000 was loaned to farmers of the county during the first eight months. Application for over $100,000 more was refused pending the recent court decision.

The managers of the Livestock Shipping Associations at the various points are as follows: Marengo, Max Wilson; Harvard, Adam Weaver; Woodstock, Fern Rogers; Hebron, Henry Mickle; Spring Grove, John Kattner; Pleasant Valley, F. J. Sleezer.

Mr. E. A. Carncross, graduate of the Wisconsin College of Agriculture, 1912, and later agricultural advisor at Green Bay, Wis., was employed as Assistant Advisor in October, 1919. He had charge of the cow testing, shipping associations and other livestock work which he handled in a satisfactory manner. Mr. Carncross resigned early in 1921 to accept the position of agricultural advisor in Du Page County, Ill. The officers of the McHenry County Farm Bureau since its organization are as follows: 1913, H. E. Whipple, Pres.; T. H. Murray, Vice Pres.; A. M. Shelton, Secy.; Fremont Hoy, Treas. 1914, H. E. Whipple, Pres.; T. H. Murray, Vice Pres.; A. M. Shelton, Secy.; Fremont Hoy, Treas. 1915, H. E. Whipple, Pres.; T. H. Murray, Vice Pres.; A. M. Shelton, Secy.; Fremont Hoy, Treas. 1916, H. E. Whipple, Pres.; T. H. Murray, Vice Pres.; A. M. Shelton, Secy.; Fremont Hoy, Treas. 1917, H. E. Whipple, Pres.; Wm. Bonslett, Vice Pres.; A. M. Shelton, Secy.; Fremont Hoy, Treas. 1918, H. E. Whipple, Pres.; John R. Wells, Vice Pres.; D. T. Smiley, Secy.; Fremont Hoy, Treas. 1919, H. E. Whipple, Pres.; John R. Wells, Vice Pres.; D. T. Smiley, Secy.; John M. Hoy, Treas. 1920, H. E. Whipple, Pres.; John R. Wells, Vice Pres.; C. W. Gibbs, Secy.; Jacob Olbrich, Treas. 1921, John R. Wells, Pres.; H. C. Gilkerson, Vice Pres.; C. W. Gibbs, Secy.; Jacob Olbrich, Treas.

THE MC HENRY COUNTY HOLSTEIN BREEDERS ASSOCIATION

A county Holstein Breeders Association was formed about ten years ago, and in 1914 this association put out an advertising booklet that was not surpassed by any other at that time, and the association had a good start but for some reason it was allowed to go down. However, in the spring of 1919 through the efforts of Advisor Gafke the association was reorganized and as a result of the work fifteen or more of the members have placed their herds under Federal supervision. It is the determination of the members to have their herds placed on the accredited list as being free from tuberculosis. Among the herds so tested may be mentioned F. M. Barber, B. L. Thomas, J. O. Tupper and Henry Eppel, Woodstock; W. H. Gardner, Solon Mills; R. W. Stewart and A. D.

Cornue, Hebron; H. C. LaBree and R. E. Corlett, Harvard; and C. W. Gibbs, West McHenry. The officers of the Association are as follows: President, C. W. Gibbs, West McHenry; Vice President, Don Geyer, Crystal Lake; Second Vice President, R. E. Corlett, Harvard; Secretary, R. W. Stewart, Hebron; Treasurer, B. L. Thomas, Ringwood.

MC HENRY COUNTY HOME BUREAU

After a short preliminary organization work the Home Bureau of McHenry County was organized in June, 1918, for the purpose of putting homemaking on a sounder basis. The officers elected the first year were, President, Mrs. E. E. Seward, Marengo; Vice President, Mrs. G. A. Miller, Woodstock; Secretary, Mrs. Fred B. McConnell, Woodstock; Treasurer, Mrs. Will Hoy, Huntley. Executive Committee: Mrs. D. T. Smiley, Woodstock; Mrs. E. G. Turner, Richmond; Mrs. Jack Walsh, McHenry; Mrs. J. C. Furlong, Spring Grove; Mrs. A. J. Gafke, Woodstock, and Mrs. W. E. Doyle, Harvard. Miss Eva Blair, of Sullivan, Ill., was employed July 1, 1918, as Home Advisor. She gave lectures and demonstrations in the organized townships on such subjects as canning, household equipment, gardening and poultry raising. Under her direction special schools in poultry raising and clothing conservation were carried on with the help of specialists from the university of Illinois. During the war the problems of the Home Bureau were mostly those of conservation of food and clothing. After the war its activities were broadened to assist in the development of all sides of home life and to cooperate with all organizations intended to benefit the community. In July, 1919, Miss Blair left to become Assistant State Leader in Extension Work in West Virginia, and Mrs. Mary B. Dalbey was employed as Home Advisor. Special effort has since been put upon beautifying home grounds, home management, and child welfare. As a result of the child welfare work hundreds of children have been weighed and measured, and the hot school lunch has been established in many of the rural and town schools. The Home Bureau office was combined with the Woman's Club Rest Room in the courthouse at Woodstock, making a convenient place to come for help in Home Economics. The officers for the year beginning July, 1920, are as follows: President, Mrs. Henry Echternach, Marengo; Vice President, Mrs. G. A. Miller, Woodstock; Secretary, Mrs. L. A. Stockwell, Marengo; Treasurer, Mrs. E. G. Turner, Richmond; The Executive Committee, Mrs. Jack Walsh, McHenry; Mrs. B. C. Bottum, Woodstock; Mrs. M. G. Shipton, Woodstock; Miss Mary Stevens, Marengo; Mrs. Frank Silliman, Woodstock.

Wm. M. Freeman M.D.

The McHenry County Agricultural Society was organized in 1852. Capt. William H. Stewart and Colonel J. M. Strode were appointed on the organizing committee, but most of the work devolved on Captain Stewart, who drafted the constitution and by-laws and was the prime mover in a laudable enterprise. He became the society's first secretary and treasurer. William Jackson was elected the first president. This organization remained as an agricultural society until 1874, when it availed itself of the offer made by the State, and then was under the name of the "Agricultural Board of McHenry County." For several years after organizing the society held its fairs in the streets of various villages of the county. Rail pens were built to hold the live stock, and rooms were rented in which to exhibit the "fine arts." By 1859 the society with the county had grown materially so that this society purchased ten acres of land, which formed a part of the later fair grounds so much appreciated by the county—just to the east of the city of Woodstock. There they built better shedding for the stock and held their annual fairs until 1866, when they organized a life membership, with an admittance fee of $20. Over one hundred names were added to this list, and this allowed the society to afford better accommodations, to enlarge its grounds which was carried out by purchasing five acres to the south of the first tract. They also then erected an agricultural hall, observatory, ticket office, etc. In about 1868 the society bought seven acres more to the north, making twenty-two acres in all. Here one finds a good half-mile track and here have been held some of the largest fairs in Illinois. Other improvements have been made with the passing years and much interest has been manifested and doubtless much of the present high standard of farm-life in the "Kingdom of McHenry" has been due to the efforts of those who have kept the county fairs alive, until the younger generation has caught the spirit of the age, and are not satisfied with less than the best in everything pertaining to county fairs.

Under the first society, the last executive board was composed of the following: D. E. Peck, Thomas McD. Richards, J. A. Wood, E. H. Seward, Robert Stewart, Richard Wray, E. Buck and J. E. Beckley. This was in 1872 when the old society changed to the new order of things and was thereafter known as the McHenry County Agricultural Board.

The amounts paid in premiums in the early years of the fair were very liberal considering the fact that very little encouragement was given county fairs through state appropriation. Prior to 1907 $200 was the largest appropriation any county or district fair could receive from the state and all received the same amount regardless of merit. In 1907 McHenry County started the organization known as The Illinois Association of Agricultural Fairs. This organization secured a state appropriation for each fair of a sum equal to forty percent of the amount paid in premiums. This was afterward increased to sixty percent on the first $1,000; fifty percent on the second $1,000; forty percent on the third $1,000; and thirty percent on the fourth $1,000 paid out in premiums. In 1867 the amount paid for premiums at the McHenry County Fair was $866.50; in 1868 it was $637.39; in 1875 it was $1,180.79; in the period from 1895 to 1901 from $1,400 to $1,600 was paid out for premiums not counting the money expended for speed. From 1903 to 1910, George A. Hunt, Secretary, the premiums were increased from $1,800 to $3,100 per year. In 1911, 1912, 1913 and 1914, Theodore Hamer, Secretary, the premiums were $3,014, $3,028, $3,746 and $3,654. In 1915, P. R. Forman, Secretary, $3,019 was paid in premiums; in 1916, W. C. Bartelt, Secretary, $1,948 was the amount paid. In 1917, P. R. Forman, Secretary, $1,696.50 was paid in premiums. In 1918, Guy E. Still, Secretary, $1,110.70 was paid in premiums. In the years 1919 and 1920, Hoyt E. Morris, Secretary, $2,255 and $3,427.75 were the amounts paid.

During the years 1903 to 1910, inclusive, improvements to the value of over $10,000 were placed on the grounds of the society. The names of the presidents and secretaries of the McHenry County Fair since 1867, are as follows:

1867, William M. Jackson, Pres.; C. H. Russell, Secy. 1868, James Crow, Pres.; E. E. Richards, Secy. 1869, James Crow, Pres.; E. E. Richards, Secy. 1870, James Crow, Pres.; E. E. Richards, Secy. 1871, James Crow, Pres.; E. E. Richards, Secy. 1872, James Crow, Pres.; W. H. Stewart, Secy. 1873, James Crow, Pres.; W. H. Stewart, Secy. 1874, James Crow, Pres.; Asa W. Smith, Secy. 1875, James Crow, Pres.; Asa W. Smith, Secy. 1876, L. Woodard, Pres.; E. E. Richards, Secy. 1877, James Crow, Pres.; Andrew Bourne, Secy. 1878, James Crow, Pres.; Andrew Bourne, Secy. 1879, J. S. Wheat, Pres.; L. J. Gates, Secy. 1880, Thos. McD. Richards, Pres.; W. H. Stewart, Secy. 1881, Thos. McD. Richards, Pres.; A. S. Wright, Secy. 1882, Thos. McD. Richards, Pres.; A. S. Wright, Sec. 1883, Thos. McD. Richards, Pres.; A. S. Wright, Secy. 1884, Thos. McD. Richards, Pres.; A. S. Wright, Secy. 1885, James Crow, Pres.; A. S. Wright, Secy. 1886, Thos. McD. Richards, Pres.; A. S. Wright, Secy. 1887, Thos. McD. Richards, Pres.; A. S. Wright, Secy. 1888, Thos. McD. Richards, Pres.; A. S.

Wright, Secy. 1889, Fred Hatch, Pres.; A. S. Wright, Secy. 1890, Fred Hatch, Pres.; A. F. Field, Secy. 1891, Fred Hatch, Pres.; A. F. Field, Secy. 1892, Fred Hatch, Pres.; A. F. Field, Secy. 1893, Andrew Bourne, Pres.; T. D. McRichards, Secy. 1894, R. J. Beck, Pres.; G. B. Richards, Secy. 1895, R. J. Beck, Pres.; G. B. Richards, Secy. 1896, R. J. Beck, Pres.; G. B. Richards, Secy. 1897, R. J. Beck. Pres.; D. T. Smiley, Secy. 1898, M. Zimpelmann, Pres.; A. S. Wright, Secy. 1899, M. Zimpelmann, Pres.; A. S. Wright, Secy. 1900, M. Zimpelmann, Pres.; A. S. Wright, Secy. 1901, Fred Hatch, Pres.; F. G. Arnold, Secy. 1902, Fred Hatch, Pres.; F. G. Arnold, Secy. 1903, Fred Hatch, Pres.; Geo. A. Hunt, Secy. 1904, William Desmond, Pres.; Geo. A. Hunt, Secy. 1905, William Desmond, Pres.; Geo. A. Hunt, Secy. 1906, William Desmond, Pres.; Geo. A. Hunt, Secy. 1907, William Desmond, Pres.; Geo. A. Hunt, Secy. 1908, William Desmond, Pres.; Geo. A. Hunt, Secy. 1909, William Desmond, Pres.; Geo. A. Hunt, Secy. 1910, William Desmond, Pres.; Geo. A. Hunt, Secy. 1911, Ben Throop, Pres.; Theo. Hamer, Secy. 1912, Ben Throop, Pres.; Theo. Hamer, Secy. 1913, Ben Throop, Pres.; Theo. Hamer, Secy. 1914, Ben Throop, Pres.; Theo. Hamer, Secy. 1915, D. L. James, Pres.; P. R. Forman, Secy. 1916, Frank J. Green, Pres.; W. C. Bartelt, Secy. 1917, Frank J. Green, Pres.; P. R. Forman, Secy. 1918, Frank J. Green, Pres.; Guy E. Still, Secy. 1919, C. W. Harrison, Pres.; Hoyt E. Morris, Secy. 1920, F. A. Walters, Pres.; Hoyt E. Morris, Secy. 1921, F. A. Walters, Pres.; Hoyt E. Morris, Secy.

To A. S. Wright belongs the distinction of having served the society as secretary longer than any other incumbent of the office. He was first elected in 1880 and served for the years 1881 to 1889 inclusive, making nine consecutive years, and again in 1898, 1899 and 1900, making twelve years of service for the association. Mr. Wright made an ideal secretary and was a persistent advertiser. During the years in which he officiated as secretary, and by his invitation the association had the honor of entertaining many noted men. In 1882 General Oglesby, General Black, Gen. J. C. Smith, General Raum, General Chetlain, General Beem, and the French Consul, Edmond Bruevaert, were guests of the fair. In 1883 General Longstreet, Governor Hamilton, Hon. David Littler, Gen. Clark E. Carr, and ex-minister Washburn were the association's guests. In 1884 Gen. John A. Logan, General Black, General Torrance, General Beem and Governor Fairchild were the guests of honor. In 1886 Hon. A. J. Hopkins, and in 1887 Hon. Samuel Randall of Pennsylvania, Hon. A. E. Stevenson, Vice President of the United States from 1893 to 1897, Congressman William Springer, Congressman Joseph G. Cannon, and

Hon. Joseph Fifer were the county's guests. In 1889 Gen. Russel A. Alger, and Lt. Gov. Lyman Ray visited the fair. Senator Shelby M. Cullom, of Illinois, and Senator "Long" Jones of Wisconsin, visited the fair in 1899 and gave addresses to the old settlers of whom more than 300 registered their names at the Secretary's office. Gov. Frank O. Lowden visited the fair in 1917. Gov. John M. Palmer of Illinois, Governor St. John of Kansas, Gov. Richard Yates and many other noted men have visited McHenry County at various times as guests of the county fair.

There is a strong probability that the Fair Association will be incorporated as a stock company in the near future. If this is done it will undoubtedly result in a better business organization and with the strong movement under way for road improvement, and the increasing use of automobiles the future success of the fair should be assured.

McHENRY COUNTY MEN WHO HAVE SERVED AS OFFICERS AT STATE AND OTHER FAIRS

M. Zimpelman of Marengo was Vice President of the Illinois State Fair from the Eleventh District and Superintendent of Machinery for the years 1889 and 1900. He was succeeded the following year by C. F. Dike of Crystal Lake who served as Vice President from this District and served as Superintendent of Machinery for sixteen consecutive years, or until his death which occurred March 6, 1916. Charles Gilkerson, of Marengo was Assistant Superintendent of Dairy Products at the Illinois State Fair for the years 1908, 1909, 1910 and 1911. He was also Superintendent of Dairy Products at the National Dairy Show at Chicago for several years, also at Springfield, Massachusetts and Columbus, Ohio. George A. Hunt, of Woodstock, made exhibits of agricultural products for McHenry County at the Illinois State Fair in 1901 and 1902, winning first premium for the county both years. The exhibit for 1902 consisted of six tons of products. A reproduction of this exhibit was made at the McHenry County Fair in 1903. The grains and grasses and the samples of wood from this exhibit were selected by the Illinois Commission to show at the World's Fair at St. Louis, 1904. Mr. Hunt was appointed Superintendent of Illinois Dairy Products for the World's Fair at St. Louis, 1904. The spectacular feature of this exhibit was the bust statues of President Grant and President Lincoln, made with pure creamery butter. Mr. Hunt secured the services of the well known sculptor, Leonard Crunelle, for this work.

MARENGO AGRICULTURAL BOARD

In 1872 a Driving Park Association was formed in the village of Marengo, consisting of J. M. Anderson, R. M. Patrick, T. H. St. John, L. W. Sheldon, A. H. Vail, Calvin Gilbert, S. K. Bartholomew, W. A. Boice, Calvin Spencer and a few others. The association leased of Calvin Spencer for a term of years; also went to considerable expense in grading the track and erecting an amphitheatre, but after holding two exhibitions found it to be a financial failure. The association dissolved, and the property and lease fell into the hands of a few of the former members, who tried to run it for a time, hoping that foreign horsemen might come in and take it off their hands. Failing in this they turned the property over to an Agricultural Board which was soon formed at Marengo, consisting of A. Jones, R. M. Patrick, E. H. Seward and Calvin Spencer. These gentleman ran the grounds three seasons longer, when a state charter was secured and 220 shares of stock were issued at $10 per share. Under this plan Marengo held several excellent annual fairs, but between 1885 and 1890 the enterprise was discontinued. Their mile track was the wonder of horsemen everywhere. They had an amphitheatre holding 1,000 people, and ninety box stalls.

KISHWAUKEE FARMERS' CLUB

This was the name given to a club formed in March, 1875, in Marengo Township, through the efforts of Messrs. Israel Boice, T. McD. Richards and Patterson Pringle, who met at the house of Mr. Richards early that spring, and after discussing the feasibility of the matter among themselves, selected fifteen of the best neighboring farmers to join them. Their plans were heartily accepted by all, and it was not long before the club had a membership of more than fifty farmers. They held their meetings once a month, at the residence of some of their members, where they discussed in a friendly manner various modes of farming, in all branches of agriculture, horticulture, stockraising, dairy business, etc.

Some member was appointed at a previous date to prepare or secure a lecture on some given topic and this was read at the next meeting. The wives and daughters of the members had a part in the work, as well as the men, for they, it was supposed, would furnish the "eats" for as many as might be present, and this they did with cheerfulness. The first one to act as president of this early farmers' club was Thomas McD. Richards, and he held the position for six years, and was succeeded by

R. M. Patrick. Great good among the farmers of southwestern McHenry County was the result of this early club.

George A. Hunt, who had charge of the county agricultural exhibits at the Illinois State Fair in 1901 and 1902, and Director of Farm Institutes for the Eleventh Congressional District, published a neat booklet which accompanied the exhibit from McHenry County, and that publication contained many facts, including the following:

"The area of McHenry County is 612 square miles. Its population is about 30,000. (The present population of McHenry County, as shown by the Federal Census of 1920, is 33,164.) The chief industries are agriculture, dairying and stockraising, nevertheless there are a large number of manufacturing establishments in this county, where many persons are employed. The soil over a large portion of the county is a deep dark loam with clay sub-soil admirably adapted to retain moisture. There is very little untillable land and a crop failure has never been known."

In speaking of crops, Mr. Hunt remarks that "Corn is the staple one, 100,000 acres being devoted to it; average per acre from forty to fifty bushels, making a total of from four to five million bushels per year. The oats crop is second in importance, the acreage being 50,000 acres with an average yield of from thirty-five to forty-five bushels per acre. The total crop is usually about 2,000,000 bushels of oats."

"About 2,000 acres are devoted to Irish potatoes which go as high as 300 bushels per acre and sell at an average price of from forty to eighty cents per bushel" (remember, this was written in 1901).

At the time this booklet was written there were more creameries in McHenry County than in any other county in the United States. At the present writing there is not a creamery in active operation in the county.

The wages paid farm hands are twenty per cent higher than in central Illinois and thirty-five per cent higher than in southern Illinois.

McHenry County has about 75,000 head of cattle; 10,000 head of sheep; 17,000 horses; 100,000 hogs; poultry and eggs sold to fully $100,000 besides all that are consumed in the farmers' homes.

This county is in the center of the dairy region of the world. The county has over 50,000 cows, from which comes 200,000,000 pounds of milk annually, bringing a revenue to the farmers of between $3,500,000 and $4,000,000 annually for this product alone.

Again in 1914, in a book prepared for the Holstein Breeders' Association, he states: "McHenry County, Illinois, is in the center of the greatest dairy region of the world. This county contains more than 50,000 cows, producing over 200,000 tons of milk annually, a large portion of which finds its way to the Chicago market."

"REGISTERED" FARM NAMES

Under a recent-time legislative provision any farmer who pays a recording fee of $1 is entitled to have his landed estate given a select name—no two to be alike in the same county—and the same property recorded in the book made on purpose and kept in the county recorder's office. Also he is entitled to a printed certificate of the same, showing name, name of farm, and location of same. Many of the landowners here have taken out such certificates and had them neatly framed and hung upon their home walls. Up to this date (1921) the following is a list of such registered farms, the numerals refer to section, township and range of such tracts of land:

Hill Crest—20-44-6—Ben LeRoy Andrews.
Oak Lawn—20-44-6—Philip W. Andrews.
Spring Brook—32-43-9—Charles W. Albright.
Meadow Park—9-45-7—O. H. Aavang.
Twin Oak Farm—13-46-8—W. J. Aylward.
Hillside—27-46-8—Carl Anderson.
Maple View—9-45-8—Herbert W. Allen.
Arbor Lodge—10-45-8—Herbert W. Allen.
Walnut Knoll Stock Farm—22-44-5—George D. Beldin.
Silver Spring Farm—6-43-9—Darwin E. Brown.
Spring Lake Dairy Farm—23-43-9—C. L. Bratzler.
Spring Hill Farm- -11-45-7—Frank M. Barber.
Evergreen Farm—31-44-6—P. R. Boies.
Maple Shade Farm—6 and 7-43-6—W. A. Boies.
Olenburg Farm—13-44-7—Alfred Bergquist.
Theoforda—27-45-5—Raymond Brickley.
Hill Crest Poultry Farm—25-44-9—C. E. Behan.
Woodlands Dairy Farm—6-44-8—J. F. Claxton.
Nippersink Farm—30-46-9—Estate of Franklin M. Cole.
Highwood—7-44-8—M. Conley.

Maplehurst—11-45-5 Minnie E. Carmack.
Near Brook Farm 15 45-5 Minnie E. Carmack.
Elmhurst 4-44-9 H. E. Clemens.
Maywood Farm 1 46-6 Arthur D. Cornue.
The Four Oaks 35-45-8 R. G. Chamberlain.
Lakewood Farm 22-45 8 Fred J. Colby.
Meadowmere 2-45-5 Russell and Blanche Diggins.
Greenwood Farm 10-45-7 Guy Dygert.
Kishwaukee Stock Farm—26-44-5 Ethel M. Echternach.
Crystal Springs Farm 32-45-8 Elmer J. Fellows.
Lake View Farm 21-45-8 E. P. Flanders.
Oak Glen Farm 16-44-8 Turner Flanders.
Riverside Dairy Farm— 26-45-8 Stephen H. Freund.
Twin Pine Farm—23-46-6 Roy R. Fink.
Bur Oak 30-44-7—John Ferguson.
The Gardner Farm—27-46-8—Willis H. Gardner.
Silver Crest—24-44-8—George J. Garrison.
Pleasant View—7-44-7—Christian Gasser.
Gayland Farm—22-45-5—G. A. Gay.
Pleasant Grove Farm—6-43-6 Charles Gilkerson.
Oak Ridge—17-45-8 George H. Harrison.
Oak Mound—5-45-8—George H. Harrison.
Meadow Lawn—5-45-8—Charles N. Harrison.
Three Oaks—9-45-8 Ora D. Harrison.
West View—35-45-6—Emery J. Heaton.
Hermonson Dairy Farm—9-45-5—Andrew A. Hermonson.
Riverside Farm—33-44-5—G. W. Hamlin.
Inter Prairie Farm—27-43-7.
Griswold Lake Farm—27-43-7—A. H. Hale.
Cloverland Farm—33-44-8—Mary L. Hale.
The Pines—20-44-8 G. H. Hillebrand.
Oak Grove Farm—36-46-7—C. C. Hunt.
Crystal Brook Farm—20-43-8—Edwin Hall Estate.
Shadow Lawn—1-45-5—D. 1. Hine.
Emerald Court—36-46-5 Mrs. A. J. Hoban.
Cozy Nook—29-46-8—Charles F. Krohm.
Cloverdale—22-44-7—James B. Loomis.
Sunny View Poultry Place- Wilber H. Levey. (In Ridgefield.)
Grand View—22-46-8—Earl E. Monear.
Cold Springs—12-44-7—Cora L. Mason.

O Garrison

Ardmore—24-44-8—George L. Murphy.
Bellevue—14-45-6—George L. Murphy.
Rosedale—15-45-6—George L. Murphy.
Sorek—29-45-7—George L. Murphy.
Lismore—19-45-7—George L. Murphy.
Carmel—32-45-7—George L. Murphy.
Brookfield—7-45-7—George L. Murphy.
Oakwood Farm—21-45-8—Clinton E. Martin.
Walnut Grove Dairy Farm—25-43-6—J. M. Marsh.
The Lindens—2-43-5—Dr. C. C. Miller.
Hillside View Farm—12-44-5—John L. Madison.
The Maples—31-45-6—Robert F. Marshall.
Oakside Farm—17-44-7—Charles E. Marks.
Elm Lawn—20-43-8—Mrs. F. E. Martin.
Frary Dale—township 43, range 8—Laura E. Munshaw.
Merrilldale—23-45-5—F. S. Merrill.
Windham Farm—25-46-5—James H. Moore.
Sunny Crest—8-45-8—Burton McCannon.
Fairview—4-45-8—Grace McCannon.
North View—24-44-8—James W. McNish.
Walnut Hill Stock Farm—10-45-7—M. W. Newman.
Highland Park Dairy Farm—28-46-8—C. L. Osborn.
Lilac Hill—9-46-5—Jacob Olbrich.
Silver Spring Dairy Farm—14-43-5—S. P. Olesen.
Sunnyside—34-45-8—Chas. L. Page.
Shady Lawn Farm—31-46-5—Mrs. M. J. Paul.
Cozy Dale Farm—33-45-7—Frank Piska.
Evergreen Acres—31-44-5—Frederick Pulse.
Lakeside—22-45-8—Caroline M. Petersen.
Clover Brook Farm—24-46-8—H. G. Reading.
Meadow Brook Farm—24-46-8—H. G. Reading.
Menoken Stock Farm—16-46-6—John C. Ross.
Crystal Brook Farm—20-43-8—David Reid.
Hickory Grove—14-43-6—Charles W. Rugh.
Meadow Brook Dairy Farm—13-43-6—The Riley Est.
Prairie View—5-45-8—Lucella A. Stephenson.
Seebert's Caryview Dairy Farm—13-43-8—Mrs. Georgia C. Seebert.
Oak Hill Farm—13-46-5—Fred N. Smith.
Mayflower Farm—20-44-6—E. B. Standish.
Garden of Eden—17-46-9—J. W. Sanborn.

West Lawn Farm—25-45-5—Alice B. Stevenson.
Waveland Farm 6 45-5 Ole A. Stalheim.
Florintine—18-46-7- —J. N. Turner.
Ingleside 2-45-7 - B. L. Thomas.
Glen View Farm 27-46-8 Reuben R. Turner.
Maple Dale 36-46-7— Charles H. Thompson.
Hazel Ridge 24-46-8—E. G. Turner.
Clover Hill Farm —30-45-8—F. B. Thompson.
Waverly Stock Farm -22-46-6- W. D. Thompson.
Maple Lawn 32-46-6 Milo M. Wakeley.
Groveland Stock Farm—10-44-7—Frank White & Son.
Hill Crest Stock Farm—4-44-8—W. E. Whiting.
Willobrook Farm—12-45-8—William Walkington.
Highland Stock Farm- 2-44-8—Walter J. Walsh.
Fairholme Farm—11-45-5—Flora E. Whipple.
Overlook— 13-45-5 H. E. Whipple.
The Spring- 16-46-6—J. F. Westphall.
Improvement -23-43-5- -W. H. Weaver.
Oakland Farm -33-44-8--John M. Walkup.
Orchard Knob-- 13-46-8—Walter E. Winn.
East Acres- 36-46-6 Randall D. Weitzel.
Level Acres 33-45-6- -John C. Widmayer.

CHAPTER XIV

DAIRY AND LIVE STOCK INTERESTS

By W. J. Kittle

LEADING INDUSTRY—DIFFERENCE IN METHODS—EARLY AND LATER DAY IN-
TERESTS—FORMER CHEESE AND BUTTER ACTIVITIES—RADICAL CHANGE—
PIONEER SHIPPERS—INTELLIGENT DAIRYING—DAIRY INTERESTS—IMPOR-
TANCE OF DAIRY COW.

LEADING INDUSTRY

The leading industry of this county is dairying, which gives it a
commanding position. Dairying is carried on so extensively that the
county is said to have more cows per acre than any other county in the
United States. While since its early days the farmers of the county
have been engaged in dairying, and marketed their product direct, at
present they are disposing of their milk to the large city dealers and
condensaries. The city dealers have many bottling and receiving plants
located throughout the county. These, with two condensing plants,
furnish the points at which the dairymen deliver their milk daily, and
at these plants the milk is prepared for the city consumers, or is manufactured into condensed and evaporated products.

DIFFERENCES IN METHODS

There is a great difference between modern methods of handling milk,
and those which prevailed many years ago, owing in part to state regulations, and also to the education of the farmer who has learned how to
care for his stock and milk according to sanitary ideas. Some of the
finest equipped dairy farms in the country are in McHenry County, and
several of them are rated as model agricultural plants. As long ago
as 1885 the attention of the public was called to the dairy interests of
this county, and from then on to the present day, they have been the
subject of many articles in different journals, extracts from several of
which being given below.

217

EARLY AND LATER DAY INTERESTS

From an old publication issued in 1885 the subjoined is quoted:

"The stock and dairy business of this county are fast assuming an importance which bids fair to transcend all others. The very best of pasturage and excellent water supplies abound every where in the county. The famous blue grass, so common in the South, is here indigenous and thrives luxuriantly. These facts have led the farmers to turn their attention largely to stock raising and dairying, while at the same time they continue to give a good share of their time to the production of hay, cereals, fruit and vegetables. The dairy interests are discussed more in detail, but in this connection it may be added that the importance of improving our stock of late years has become almost universal, until now choice herds of Holsteins, Alderneys and Herefords can be seen in all parts of this county. The combining of stock and dairy interests has been attended with the most satisfactory results.

"Until within the last quarter of the century 1860 cheese making in Illinois was a small industry. No cheese was made for export, except in the larger dairies. Factories were unknown, and the markets of the state were supplied with Eastern cheese products. The Western farmer had the best farming and grazing land in the country, as well as every facility for raising stock at less expense than the Eastern farmers; still dairying received little or no attention. Cattle were kept in great numbers, but they were driven or shipped East for beef purposes. Butter was made and shipped to a small extent, but so little care and skill were displayed in the manufacture of butter that Western butter acquired an unenviable reputation in the world's markets. Most of the farmers were in debt and gave their attention to stock, considering that the speediest means of raising funds. As in all new-settled countries, grains and stock received almost exclusive attention and manufacturers were discouraged. As to cheese, it was urged that only an inferior quality could be made in the West; that the milk did not contain the necessary ingredients; that the grass, soil and climate were not suitable. But all these false theories have been long since exploded, since the farmers went to work in an intelligent manner and understanding, and gave the dairy industry the attention its importance demanded.

"Before 1866 there was not a cheese factory in McHenry County. In 1866 and 1867 there were eight in operation, and the number continually increased. At first the business met with considerable opposition. There was a lack of confidence among stockholders as to profits.

There was also great difficulty in obtaining employes possessing qualifications of experience and adaptation to the work. The cheese were generally made for those furnishing the milk, at a stipulated price per pound, either two and a half or three cents. The factory proprietors furnished all other materia's, making and storing for a specified time. At the expiration of the time agreed upon the owners of the cheese either took it away or allowed the manufacturer to sell for them on commission. In 1867 the cheese factories in operation in this county were:

"The Hebron factory, built in the spring of 1866 by R. W. Stewart and W. H. Stewart; a two-story frame building, 30x55 feet, enlarged the second year.

"The Huntley factory, started in 1866 by A. A. Blanchard and A. Woodworth.

"The Marengo factory, started in 1867 by Anson Sperry and R. M. Patrick.

"The Greenwood factory, in 1867; A. C. Thompson and George Abbott, proprietors.

"The Union factory, 1867; Hunderford & Durkee, proprietors.

"The Woodstock factory, 1867; C. De Cleroq, proprietor.

"The Riley factory, built in 1867 by P. B. Merrill, E. Graves and Leonard Parker."

The amount of milk used and the number of pounds of cheese produced by the above mentioned factories during 1867 is thus given in the Woodstock Sentinel:

Name of Factory	Pounds Milk	Pounds Cheese
Richmond (six months run)	1,830,423	134,471
Hebron (five months run)	1,000,000	112,000
Huntley (four and three-fourths)	597,905	64,078
Marengo (four months run)	———	———
Greenwood (four months run)	542,365	54,236
Union (four months run)	429,000	43,000
Woodstock (four months run)	243,000	22,223
Riley (four months run)	———	40,000

"In addition to the above," says the same authority "there were a great many farmers in the county in 1867 who had dairies of from twenty to fifty cows and made cheese at home.

"The dairy interests have grown rapidly from the beginning. The county now (1885) contains fifty-three cheese factories and creameries.

Also large dairies. The shipping of milk to Chicago is carried on extensively and with great profit to the dairyman. This branch of the dairy business is also comparatively new, but its growth has been very rapid, and it is now one of the chief industries of McHenry County. Every railroad station in the county sends its quota of milk to feed the great city.

"At the Philadelphia Centennial Exposition in 1876, J. S. Watrous of the town of Nunda, placed on exhibition samples of butter made at his factory, the Edgefield Crystal Springs Factory. This exhibit was awarded a gold medal for its superior quality, a result particularly gratifying to McHenry County dairymen, when it is considered that not only the old states of the East were competitors for the honor, but also of sections in this country and Canada.

"The dairy statistics of 1877 together with those of 1883, are given below, and fully illustrate the rapid growth of this industry in this county:

	1877	1883
"Number of cows kept	18,378	28,179
"Pounds of butter sold	805,832	757,935
"Pounds cheese sold	969,229	2,213,002
"Gallons milk sold	2,331,007	7,917,321

A RADICAL CHANGE

The radical change from butter and cheese making in this county to the present plan of bottling and shipping the milk produce of the farmers of the county was brought about in 1889-90, since which time little butter and cheese have been made here and sent to the markets of the world. The milk has been daily bottled, or sent in large cans to Chicago where it supplies that great and constantly growing city, less than fifty miles distant.

In the days when cheese making was one of the leading industries of the county, the product was of excellent quality, but because of the making of what was known as "filled cheese," really a skim-milk cheese filled with lard, and the throwing of it on the market, the good name of all McHenry County cheese was damaged, and all of Illinois suffered.

Cyrus L. Mead, one of the pioneers of the county, when in his ninety-third year, then being a resident of Hebron, stated that the first cheese factory in the vicinity of Hebron was built by William and Robert

Stewart in 1865. He says that in 1868 Harry W. Mead built a factory just north of the townsite of Hebron, it being on his farm.

The earliest bottling plant in the county was that established at Crystal Lake.

Several large corporations have established themselves in the milk-bottling business within this county, including the Borden and Bowman concerns. The present condensed milk plants in the county are located at Union and Chemung.

There are the following bottling plants: those of the Borden Company at McHenry, Algonquin, Richmond, Hebron, Alden, Chemung, Woodstock, Ridgefield and Marengo; those of the Bowman Company at Crystal Lake, Cary, Hartlend, Harvard, Greenwood and Ringwood; a country plant near Crystal Lake and at Greenwood; the John F. Jelke plant at Huntley; the plant of Victor Mey at Huntley; that of the American Milk Company at Union; The Western Dairy Company plant at Belden; and that of the Weiland Company at Spring Grove.

PIONEER SHIPPERS

Among the early shippers of milk to the Chicago market was L. W. Walkup who milked fifty cows, and finding that the commissions paid in Chicago left him but little profit, he, together with his brother, who later died as a missionary in a foreign land, undertook to peddle milk in Chicago, but after two months' trial became convinced that this plan was not practical, and so abandoned their project. Mr. Walkup is still a resident of Crystal Lake, states that while he was able to dispose of his milk as above stated because he was accessible to the railroad, others less fortunately situated, including the elder James Kittle, who had forty cows in his herd, were forced to make their milk up into butter or cheese and ship the same. The butter was usually packed in sixty pound ash or spruce tubs.

INTELLIGENT DAIRYING, 1921

Perhaps no better exposition of present-day dairy conditions can be given than that taken from the Harvard Independent, as follows:

"John C. Olbrich, one of the well-known Marengo farmers, was a business caller in Harvard Monday evening, and told us a few interesting things in regard to his work. He is working 600 acres of land, there are four cement silos on his place, and he is milking about fifty cows.

His milk is delivered to the Borden plant at Marengo, and at present it is averaging about 1,400 pounds daily, his monthly milk check being in the neighborhood of $1,400. Mr. Olbrich is a great worker and uses his brains as well as his hands. In conversation with us he told us that he experienced more difficulty in securing help for the house than the ordinary male help on the farm. His practice in farming is to raise the necessary feed for the stock on his own farm, for there is no money to be made if one pays it all out for expensive feed. By making use of the four silos on his farm, Mr. Olbrich can get along if there is a failure of the corn crop. There's the secret of the whole thing. Some men make a lot of milk and pull in big milk checks, but they spend so much for feed that they are very little ahead at the end of the year. The successful farmers, the men who make the money, are those who raise their own feed and are prepared for the emergency when the crop failure comes along."

DAIRY INTERESTS

Capital invested nearly $1,500,000
Men employed in different plants throughout the
    county 500
Herds 2,500
Total milk production, pounds daily........... 655,000
Milk bottled, quarts daily.................... 267,500
Milk condensed, pounds daily................. 120,000

IMPORTANCE OF DAIRY COW

The dairy cow has been the redeemer and builder of McHenry County. Under the present reconstruction period she has kept the bank accounts of McHenry County farmers on the right side of the ledger.

Richard Gault

CHAPTER XV

RAILROADS AND INDUSTRIAL ENTERPRISES

SOURCE OF PRESENT PROSPERITY

This county owes much of its present prosperity to the railroads whose network traverse its entire area. These railroads were among the first to be built in Northern Illinois, which today has one of the finest railroad systems in the world. Every village in McHenry County has its railroad station, thus being afforded excellent shipping facilities. Each township, with the exception of Riley in the extreme southwestern portion of the county, has a railroad crossing some portion of its territory. By these roads the dairyman and farmer are brought into close touch with Chicago and other industrial centers. Milk is shipped every morning from practically every station in the county to Chicago, and milk trains are as common on the roads passing through McHenry County, as are the fruit trains on those of the Pacific Coast.

FIRST STEAM RAILROADS

The first railroad which was constructed through McHenry County was the old Galena division of the present Northwestern system, then known as the Galena & Chicago Union Railway. Completed in 1854. it had stations at Huntley, Union and Marengo, which are still maintained.

In June, 1855, the Chicago, St. Paul & Fond du Lac Railroad reached Woodstock. the following year was extended as far as Harvard, and was then rapidly pushed on to its terminus. This road is now the Wisconsin division of the Chicago & Northwestern Railroad, and maintains stations

223

at Cary, Crystal Lake, Ridgefield, Woodstock, Hartland, Harvard and Lawrence, all in this county.

About 1855 the construction work on the Fox River Valley Railroad was begun in the eastern part of the county, crossing it from north to south. This road was subsequently purchased by the Chicago & North western system, and is operated under the name of the Elgin & State Line Division of the Northwestern. It has stations in this county at Algonquin, Crystal Lake, McHenry, Terra Cotta, Ringwood and Richmond.

In 1861-62 The Kenosha & Rockford Railroad was built in the northern part, and this is now also a part of the Northwestern system with stations at Hebron, Alden, Harvard and Chemung, with "sidings" at other places in the county.

The last railroad to be built in McHenry County was the Chicago, Milwaukee & St. Paul, which enters the county in the southeastern part of Burton Township and runs in a northwesterly direction through Richmond and Hebron townships, with stations at Spring Grove, Solon Mills, and at a junction point where this road crosses Kenosha & Rockford division on section 11, Hebron Township. The Chicago, Milwaukee & St. Paul Railroad was built through this county in 1900 and furnishes an additional outlet for the freight of the county. Through the merging of the several railroads into one or more of the great systems, the people of McHenry County are now afforded the best of train service and the finest of accommodations, and all of the traffic is handled by the two great systems, the Chicago & Northwestern and the Chicago, Milwaukee & St. Paul.

ELECTRIC RAILWAYS

In addition to the many miles of steam railroads in the county, there are also two electric roads, one of which in the southwestern part, with stations at Union and Marengo, is operated as the Elgin and Belvidere; and one between Harvard and Lake Geneva, Wisconsin, is operated as the Chicago, Harvard & Lake Geneva. These two lines afford much satisfaction and accommodation to the people adjacent to them, for they can board a car for distant trading points at almost any hour of the day or night, and return within a few hours. The one between Harvard and Lake Geneva carries many passengers to the great summer resort in Wisconsin. Other lines have been projected, and one company graded a road between Marengo and Harvard over twenty years ago, but none of these enterprises reached fruition.

RAILROAD MILEAGE

The steam railroads have the following mileage: the Chicago, Milwaukee & St. Paul, twelve and one-third miles, and the Chicago & Northwestern, 118½ miles.

The electric lines have the following mileage: the Chicago, Harvard & Lake Geneva, five and one-half miles; and the Elgin & Belvidere, twenty-one and three-tenths miles, making a total of 173¹₁₀ miles of steam and electric roads in the county.

LOCAL SHOPS

When the Chicago & Northwestern Railroad was built to Harvard, a roundhouse and repair shop were erected there, but in the latter part of the last century were removed to Janesville. Woodstock also had a two-stall roundhouse for many years to house a special Chicago passenger train which ran as an accommodation, but when that was discontinued, the roundhouse was abandoned.

INDUSTRIAL ACTIVITIES

While there are a number of flourishing industrial concerns in the county whose products are shipped to far-distant points and some all over the world, the staple industry is of course dairying. However, it is with interest that the historian records the achievements in an industrial line during the past and present in the different communities of McHenry County.

WOODSTOCK

Prior to 1854 several mills were operated at Woodstock and produced much of the flour and rough lumber required by the community. The first saw-mill was constructed in 1852, although a flax-mill had been built in 1846, and this was subsequently converted into a planing mill in the early fifties.

In 1854 Roswell Enos opened his small but excellent tannery, but not long thereafter it was burned, and he did not replace it.

In 1856 Gilbert B. Drake and Cornelius Quinlan built a grist-mill at Woodstock, which they operated by steam power. After several years of operation it was abandoned.

J. C. Teeple and Henry Eckert established a machine shop, which was of great value to the early settlers of this part of the county, and also carried on a foundry and made many castings. This plant was finally owned by L. H. S. Barrows.

In 1868 Dr. C. B. Durfee began the manufacture of drain tile. This plant later became the property of the Woodstock Brick, Drain, Tile and Peat Company, which used native peat for the fuel needed. This business closed in 1873.

The pickle factory of Squire Dingee & Company was first established by a stock company, formed in 1873, with a capital stock of $50,000. The building was erected in 1874, and E. T. Hopkins was placed in charge. The business after a time was leased to Heintz, Noble & Company for five years, and this concern packed in large quantities, but after a long trial went out of existence as a producer of vinegar, although pickles were still packed. In 1880, under the ownership of Squire Dingee, the annual output was 55,000 bushels of cucumbers. The plant had fifty-five large salting vats, and employment was given to about twenty men. During the shipping season from eight to ten carloads were usually shipped per week.

Another early pickle factory was that operated by Norman Frame & Company, and it was undoubtedly the largest one in the county at that time. Norman Frame and Judge T. D. Murphy entered into partnership in 1881, under the above name, and carried on an extensive pickle and vinegar plant at Woodstock until they leased their plant to Squire Dingee, and the business was by him carried on until he went out of this line, a number of years thereafter.

The Pickle Growers' Union was formed in 1881, and had 100 members, at whose head was Edward Short. Associated with him were other representative pickle growers, whose object was to store the pickles produced by the members of the union so as to be able to take advantage of the better prices later in the season. During 1883, 1884 and 1885 this organization did a business of $40,000 annually in salted pickles. Their building was located near the depot, and had a capacity of 25,000. In 1884 the association had increased its membership, and had for its officers the following: T. McD. Richards, president; Mark Hicock, treasurer; and Edward Short, secretary. As the years went on, however, the farmers changed their crops, and, no longer raising pickles, the business was discontinued.

In 1858 a brewery was established a mile and one-half west of Woodstock by John Bertehey. It was a small plant making common beer

Later it was owned by Arnold, Zimmer & Company, which purchased the founder's rights in 1868. The new firm was continued many years and operated a large plant, the original one having been expanded, until the mammoth brewing companies at Chicago, Milwaukee and other cities monopolized the brewing industry. A never-failing spring supplied the water used by the Woodstock brewery, and ice was produced in an artificial pond nearby. In 1885 the brewery was using 25,000 bushels of malt; had three immense icehouses, fermenting rooms, cooling rooms, bottling rooms, stables and sheds for the large number of horses and wagons used in carrying on what was the largest brewing plant in this part of Illinois. Twenty-five men were employed for twelve hours a day, and 800 barrels of beer were produced monthly, including standard brands of Bohemian and export beer. This beer was sold at Woodstock, Harvard, Janesville, Rockford, Clinton, Elgin and Dundee. The brewing company also owned and farmed 180 acres of land on which they fed cattle for the markets. This brewery was destroyed by fire in 1902.

In 1897 Mrs. Edith Kingman Poyer established what was known as the "Northwestern Rabbitry" for the production of rabbits for their meat and skins, and was principally managed by Mrs. Poyer's brother, C. F. Kingman. It was expanded and in 1901 was said to be the largest plant of its kind in America, and yielded good returns. The plant was located at the end of Washington street, and in the frame building there were 275 cages, usually filled with fine specimens of imported hares and rabbits. One animal, "Fiery Fox," took prizes all over the country, and his owner was offered $2,000 for him. The Belgian hares were especially valuable, and thousands of pounds of these animals were shipped in refrigerator cars to Eastern markets, where fancy prices were received. A fire destroyed the plant and it was never rebuilt.

It is as a center for the manufacture of typewriters that Woodstock has become known all over the civilized world, the plants of two of the leading machines being located in this city. They form the chief industrial factor of Woodstock, and are of great importance to the people here and throughout the county.

The Oliver Typewriter Company, the pioneer in this industry, has its plant near the railroad station, and it manufactures the Oliver typewriter. This machine is the direct materialization of a dream held for years by Rev. Thomas Oliver, a clergyman of the Methodist Episcopal Church. A natural mechanic, with a genius for inventing, he long worked over his ideas for improving the primitive "writing" machines. Probably because of his interest in them, he pursued his idea in his dreams, and one night had what he felt was a vision, and the following day put his recollection of it on paper. From this he worked out through days of experimenting what was the first Oliver typewriter. He constructed several models before he was able to reach the fundamental principle of the now famous machine that bears his name. His was the first visible typewriter known. He made his experimental type-bars of two strips of common tin, but his model worked well, and he typed his sermons with it.

Doctor Oliver commenced making his typewriters while living at Epsworth, Iowa, a short distance west of Dubuque. His first shop was on the second floor of a wooden building, the lower floor of which was used for a restaurant. Here he made twelve experimental machines, placed them on trial, thereby gaining a full dozen recommendations, and he was then able to organize a stock company with a paid-up capital of $20,000, or its equivalent. His fellow-townsmen so appreciated the value of Doctor Oliver's invention and its importance to their community that they built him a brick shop, and employment was given to sixteen employes including Charles Fay, who accompanied him to Woodstock. The business so increased that it was deemed expedient to look for a permanent location near Chicago, and in December, 1896, the business was moved to Woodstock and the plant established in the quarters formerly occupied by the Wheeler and Tappan Pump Company. With the understanding that the plant was to remain at Woodstock for a period of five years, the city donated the buildings above referred to. Many years have elapsed since then, and the plant is still at Woodstock, and employment is now given to about 1,400 persons, the output being 325 machines daily. This contrasts vividly with the 100 machines which were the sole output of the first eight months' work of the company after coming to Woodstock. Six of the original employes came from Iowa to Woodstock with the company, namely: A. C. Peavey, Irving Greenlee, Robert Edwards, S. Horr, Charles Fay and Lester Carr. The Oliver Building at No. 159 North Dearborn street is the Chicago headquarters of the company.

The present officers are: Henry K. Gilbert, president; Delevan Smith, vice president; William B. Stewart, Jr., vice president; John Whitcomb, vice president, who is in charge of sales; E. H. Smith, secretary and treasurer, who is in charge of production; and Frank M. Farnsworth, auditor.

The Woodstock Typewriter Company was organized under the laws of Illinois, under the name of the Emerson Typewriter Company, September 14, 1909, and its plant was at Momence, Ill., and the Emerson typewriter was manufactured. Until the plant was moved to Woodstock in 1910, George M. A. Fecke was president of the company.

In December, 1910, the company was reorganized, and in June, 1911, discontinued manufacturing the Emerson typewriter, scrapping the tools, and commenced the production of the Woodstock typewriter according to the designs of Alvah C. Roebuck, the inventor. This machine was first placed on the market in 1915 and has proved to be very popular. The company erected a spacious brick building in the eastern part of Woodstock, which contains 44,270 square feet of floor space, and additional space will soon be afforded. About 350 persons are employed and the output is about fifty-five machines per day. Approximately fifty percent of these machines are sold in the United States, the remainder being shipped to foreign countries.

The present officers of this company are as follows: L. W. Meckstroth, president; Arnold J. Lethen, treasurer; N. W. Keating, secretary; J. F. Swahlstedt, assistant treasurer; O. Hokanson, chief engineer; N. W. Marsilius, superintendent; Mack Marsilius, assistant superintendent; and E. Lowe, purchasing agent.

MARENGO

In 1861 a flour-mill was built at Marengo by Butsford, Howe & Spencer at a cost of $10,000. It was operated by steam, and an excellent custom business was carried on. In the eighties it was still operated, being then owned by S. K. Partholomew, who, however, only produced feed. With changes in methods of production and the growth of the great flour and feed corporations, this mill, with similar ones, went out of existence.

A foundry and machine shop was established at Marengo in 1868, by Henry Deitz, but it later became the property of C. E. Kelley who enlarged the plant, added much modern machinery, including small engines and a line of pumps. About fifteen men were usually employed.

A cheese-box factory at Marengo was the outgrowth of a sash and blind factory which was started about 1878. It did not pay and so was converted into a coopering shop. After two years this coopering business was purchased by Wood & Sherwin, of Elgin, who began manufacturing cheese boxes. When butter and cheese were no longer produced by the farmers who found it more profitable to sell their milk, this factory ceased making butter tubs and cheese boxes for which there was no longer a local market.

A canning factory was established at Marengo in 1875 by E. F. and F. L. McKinney. It was started in a small way, but was expanded as the volume of business warranted, and here for years were manufactured jellies and jams; all kinds of vegetables and fruits were canned, and several changes were made in location. All of the products were sold to Chicago grocers at excellent prices. From twenty to sixty persons were employed according to the season. At one time the output was sold direct to the United States government for use in the army. This factory has not been in operation for many years.

The L. Woodard Pickle Company was founded in 1882 by Loren Woodard, uncle of W. C. Woodard, the present executive head. This company is incorporated, and the present officials are: W. C. Woodard, president; M. R. Woodard, secretary; and A. B. Woodard, treasurer. The L. Woodard Company are packers of salt pickles and fancy dill pickles, and in addition to the plant at Marengo, have plants at Harvard, Ill., and Covert, Hartford, Kingsley and Beulah, Mich.

HARVARD

In 1872 Burbank & Law erected at Harvard a malthouse which stood about twenty rods north of the depot, and its capacity was about 100 bushels per day. The product was sold at Chicago, Milwaukee and in Pennsylvania. On only a $5,000 capital the firm did an excellent business, exceeding 45,000 bushels of malt in their sales, but after three years closed down, and the building was converted into a grain warehouse.

Another malthouse was established about the same date by the Harvard Malting Company, and it had a capacity of 250 bushels daily, and the business was under the management of E. E. Ayer. Three years later the malthouse was closed, but was soon afterwards sold to a Kenosha firm who made a number of improvements on the plant, erecting buildings costing $25,000. At one time this firm had on hand 60,000 bushels of malt.

A pickle factory was started at Harvard in the spring of 1883, which had a capacity of 30,000 bushels of pickles. That same season Clark & Brainard built a factory of about the same size as the Sawyer factory, and for some years both concerns did a large business.

The Harvard Flouring Mills were erected in 1857, by Jonathan Wells, and in 1860 the building was sold to Colonel Blandin, and in 1870 he sold to G. H. Wood, A. S. Gournee and P. C. Farnum who enlarged it

and converted it into a flouring mill of the old millstone type. Early in the eighties it was changed to a modern roller process mill where "patent" flour was made.

The Hunt, Helm & Ferris Company was established in 1883 and incorporated in 1902. The original founders were C. E. Hunt and N. B. Helm, and H. L. Harris was the inventor and designor. The company manufactures barn equipment and builders' hardware of the "Star Line" brand. During busy seasons employment is given to about 300 men. Shipments are made all over the United States and to South America and Europe. The present officials are: C. E. Hunt, president; H. L. Ferris, vice president; H. J. Ferris, vice president; B. B. Bell, secretary and treasurer; H. B. Megran, assistant secretary; and W. J. Heatley, assistant treasurer. The company has a branch at Albany, N. Y.

The Church Hay Barrier Manufacturing Company manufactured a hay carrier, invented by E. L. Church, and patented in 1874. He was then living in Wisconsin, and was not much more than a lad, but was a born inventor. His first carriers were manufactured at Rockford, Ill., but in 1880 he came to Harvard, bought a building at the corner of Ayer and Church streets, enlarged it, and increased his production to about 4,000 carriers annually. He had traveling men in all parts of the country and he did a big business, his sales extending even as far west as California. Subsequently this business was merged with the Hunt, Helm & Ferris Company.

In 1914 H. C. Beardsley founded what is now the Beardsley Candy Company, manufacturers and jobbers of the "Fern-Bee" confections, the latter name having been assumed in 1919. In the busy season employment is given to thirty people. Sales are made to jobbers and retailers. The present officials are: H. C. Beardsley, president, and E. G. Fernholz, secretary and treasurer.

The Harvard Garment Company was established in 1920 by F. W. Lanning. This concern manufactures dolls and doll dresses, and sells to jobbers and retailers over the United States and Canada. About 200 dozen dolls are produced weekly, and employment is given to about thirty-four people.

ALGONQUIN

Benjamin Douglas and Colonel Hoffman built the first saw-mill in Algonquin Township in 1839, and it was located on Crystal Lake. In 1842 A. Dawson built a mill in the village of Algonquin. Another mill was also built on Chann Creek in 1840 by Chann & Toles. These men, with Mr. Northrop, erected a grist mill on the same creek in 1862. Burgess & Cornish built a mill, on the Cornish farm, in 1848, which was propelled by the water from the outlet of Crystal Lake. The grist-mill on the east side of the river at Algonquin was commenced by A. Dawson, and completed by Henry Petrie, in 1849. In 1850 Doctor Plumleigh built a brick grist-mill at Algonquin village on the lake outlet, and it carried on an excellent business way into the eighties.

The American Ironing Machine Company was founded in 1906, and they manufacture ironing machines, skirt boards, safety tapping attachments, abrasion metal cutters and clothes extractors. When running full capacity they employ about 250 men, and make about 200 ironing machines a day. They have branch offices in New York; Chicago; Pittsburgh; Minneapolis; Omaha; Denver; San Francisco; St. Louis; Rochester, N. Y.; Woodstock, Ontario; and have dealers in nearly every state in the United States. The present officers are: Herman G. Groose, president; Edward C. Peter, vice president; Joseph W. Taft, secretary and treasurer; and the board of directors is composed of the following: Herman G. Groose, Edward C. Peter, Joseph W. Taft, Willis T. Peter, and W. W. Armstrong. The trade mark of this company is "Simplex."

ALDEN

As late as 1885 the butter and cheese industry was active at Alden, and there were four factories for the production of butter and cheese in Alden Township. The first one was built at Alden Station in 1869, and during its most flourishing period it used as much as 15,000 pounds of milk daily. The second of these factories was built in 1877, and was subsequently consolidated with the first. In 1879 F. Ferris & Company built a factory several miles beyond the town limits, and it had a daily consumption, in 1885, of 8,000 pounds of milk. When a change came in the milk industry, these factories went out of existence, the milk now being shipped to Chicago through the several milk companies operating in the county.

McHENRY

The first saw-mill was built in the village of McHenry in 1837, by a Mr. Barnum, who later sold it to James Salisbury and several associates. James Salisbury was instantly killed, while beneath the mill looking after the machinery, at which time the water was accidentally turned on, and this was said to be the first death in the county of a person to whom a regular Christian burial was given. Rev. Joel Wheeler was the officiating clergyman.

The first grist-mill in McHenry was erected in 1851, by Owen Brothers, and they operated it until 1858. At that time E. M. Owen bought his brother's share. Changes were made until in 1885 it was a first-class, roller-process mill, with a capacity of fifty barrels daily, employment being given to twenty-five men.

In 1882 Richard Bishop established a pickle factory at McHenry. Its capacity was 30,000 bushels, and employment was given twenty persons during the season. Richard Bishop also established, and for many years operated, a wagon factory, but his plant was totally destroyed by fire July 31, 1874. His loss was $30,000, and he had no insurance. In 1878, however, this plant was rebuilt upon a much larger scale, and for many years thereafter Mr. Bishop carried on an excellent business in making wagons.

George Gribbler built a brewery at McHenry, but did not long remain the owner, and after several changes, G. Boley bought the plant for $1,400, and at once rebuilt it to a capacity of 1,200 barrels annually. He also had a malthouse in which he made his own malt. Until within recent years this business was a large and profitable one.

WEST MC HENRY

West McHenry, formerly known as Georgetown, had several factories in the past, and also a grist-mill, the latter having been erected in 1872 by William Hanley. For years it was operated as a custom mill, and frequently took in 500 bushels of wheat a day.

A butter and cheese factory was started in 1881 by Oatman & Sons, at a cost of $5,000, being when completed the finest plant of its kind in McHenry County. Its location, near Hanley Mills, was a convenient one for the farmers, and 12,000 pounds of milk were used a day in the making of butter and cheese.

The brick-making industry had its commencement at West McHenry in 1882 when 900,000 brick were made. The following year 1,800,000 brick were burned and sold, and employment was given to twenty-five hands.

In 1874 a large pickle factory was established at West McHenry by a union company composed of farmers. For years it was operated under the name of Cristy, Walker & Company. The plant made its own vinegar, and the total value of it was placed at $40,000.

CRYSTAL LAKE

At present the importance of the ice industry at Crystal Lake does not compare with what it was in former years, when an immense business was carried on, "Crystal Lake Ice" being then a household term with Chicago and McHenry County people. For many years Crystal Lake was the great natural source of the ice supply for this portion of the state. In 1855 the Crystal Lake Ice Company was organized and its members comprised Messrs. Joy and Frisbie and several others. During that year the company stored about 8,000 tons of ice which Mr. Joy sold at Chicago. The ensuing year Joy & Frisbie became the sole proprietors and from then on they shipped annually to Chicago about 10,000 tons of ice, until 1860, when their warehouses were destroyed by fire. These gentlemen then organized another ice company, and for six years more carried on extensive operations, and then again were burned out.

From 1869 to 1873 there were no ice companies operating at Crystal Lake, with the exception of one small, private concern, whose total annual output did not exceed 2,000 tons shipped to Chicago. About 1873-4 C. S. and J. H. Dole put up and filled six mammoth icehouses, each having a capacity of about 1,250 tons, or a total capacity of 7,500 tons. In addition they shipped out 3,000 tons. The next year the capacity was increased to eight icehouses with a total capacity of 19,000 tons. During the winter of 1875-6 the partners filled their icehouses and shipped 1,200 carloads, a total output of 24,400 tons. In 1877 they erected a number of large icehouses, and placed in operation a twenty-five horse-power steam engine for use in the various branches of the ice industry. These great icehouses were located on the south end of Crystal Lake, in a beautiful grove near the outlet, and were fenced in with a tight board fence, eight feet high. Employment was given to many men who were occupied in the winter with putting up the ice, and in the summer, with shipping it to outside points.

There came a time, however, when the question arose as to the legal title to the waters of the lake, and court proceedings were instituted. Thereafter smaller, more shallow and marshy lakes, or ponds in the vicinity of Crystal Lake, were utilized for ice-getting purposes, and the product was sold in Chicago for a number of years, but as soon as it became generally known that the ice was not from Crystal Lake, the consumers in Chicago and elsewhere sought and easily found places from which pure ice could be obtained.

Much enthusiasm was shown in 1879-80 over the proposed manufacture of sugar from sorghum. The government commission of agriculture came to Crystal Lake from Washington City, and encouraged the enterprise. A sugar refinery was erected at Nunda, now Crystal Lake, and was owned by F. A. Waidner & Company, under the supervision of J. B. Thomas, of Baltimore, Md. The first year's results were indeed encouraging. A barrel of this sugar was sent to President Hayes, and after he had tested it, and given some of it to his friends, he wrote a very flattering letter to the company. For some unknown reason this project was discontinued.

A clover and fruit dryer was another project of the earlier history, but like the ones above mentioned, is not represented in the business life of Crystal Lake today.

In 1916 the Express Body Corporation started business at Crystal Lake. They make commercial bodies for automobiles, porch swings and pergolas, and sell in the United States and Europe. During the busy season employment is given to from fifty to sixty men. The present officers are: O. C. George, president; M. B. George, vice president; and J. K. Seifert, secretary and treasurer.

SPRING GROVE

Large amounts of washed sand and pebbles are produced at an extensive plant at Spring Grove, on the Milwaukee Railroad. This product is used in ornamenting walks, lawns and residences in the larger cities. All foreign matter, dirt, grass, moss and roots, is washed out by a process requiring skill. The product is shipped in trainloads over a wide area.

TERRA COTTA

The American Terra Cotta & Ceramic Company was founded by William D. Gates about 1885, and incorporated in 1887, and manufactures architectural Terra Cotta and Teco pottery. The product is shipped throughout the United States and Canada, the greater portion within the Middle West. The number of employes of these works is from 200 to 400, with an average of about 300. This is the largest plant of its kind in the United States. The company has another factory at

Indianapolis, Ind. The present officials are: William D. Gates, president; M. E. Gates, assistant general manager; Neil H. Gates, treasurer; A. H. Sheffield, secretary; and Frit Wagner, Jr., sales manager.

RICHMOND

The first cheese factory in the county was started at Richmond, in 1866, by Dr. R. R. Stone and Hon. William A. McConnell.

The Nippersink Valley Creamery and Cheese Factory was built in 1880, at a cost of $1,800, and conducted by J. S. Overton & Son. In 1885, its capacity having in the meanwhile been greatly enlarged, this factory was producing 15,000 pounds of butter and 60,000 pounds of cheese.

The Wheeler Cheese Factory was opened in June, 1884. It was built at a cost of $3,500, and its capacity was 15,000 pounds of milk daily.

G. W. Eldridge and John McConnell established a pickle factory at Richmond in 1872, erecting their plant at a cost of $5,000. Its capacity was 25,000 bushels. This plant, or a similar one, is still in operation, and its product of many cars of salted encumbers is shipped to large pickle factories at different points.

The Richmond Flour Mills were the outgrowth of a mill built in 1844 by Cotting & Purdy, and subsequently acquired by W. K. Bacon, who, in 1871 sold to Cole, Cooley & Company. At that time the property was valued at $15,000, having been enlarged and improved. For a number of years this was the principal industry of the village.

THE FARMERS NEW ERA TELEPHONE COMPANY

By George A. Hunt

On the evening of April 23, 1904, a small company of farmers met at the home of J. H. Turner in Hebron Township and organized a telephone company. This company was christened The Farmers New Era Telephone Company, and was incorporated under the laws of Illinois May 25, 1904. This company had a very small beginning in everything except its name which covered quite a territory and proved to be in keeping with the later developments of its lines.

The first directors of the company were as follows: H. R. Hatch, J. J. Stewart, J. H. Turner, F. N. Torrance, C. C. Hunt, P. J. Weter, George A. Hunt, D. M. Weter, H. F. Jones. At the first annual meeting J. T. Bower, Richmond, S. C. Johnston and J. H. Turner were elected, the first two succeeding H. R. Hatch and J. J. Stewart. At the second annual meeting F. N. Torrance, C. C. Hunt, Hebron, and Charles Kruse, Richmond, were elected, the latter taking the place of P. J. Weter. At the third annual meeting George A. Hunt, H. F. Jones and Gustav Miller of Richmond were elected, D. M. Weter retiring. The fourth year J. H. McVey of Silver Lake took the place of S. C. Johnston, J. T. Bower and J. H. Turner being reelected. The fifth year M. R. Cole of Richmond took the place of F. N. Torrance and C. C. Hunt and Charles Kruse were reelected. The sixth year George A. Hunt, F. N. Torrance and F. E. Holmes of Dundee were elected on the board, Gustav Miller and H. F. Jones retiring. Since that time no changes were made on the board until the annual meeting in February, 1921, when Dr. C. W. Bailey was elected to fill the vacancy caused by the resignation of F. N. Torrance.

Since the company was incorporated George A. Hunt, now of Woodstock, has been the president and C. C. Hunt, general manager of the company. The first vice president, D. M. Weter of Hebron, served three years or until 1907 when he was succeeded by J. T. Bower of Richmond who has served continuously since that time. P. J. Weter was elected secretary of the company at the first meeting and served in that capacity two years. He was succeeded by W. D. Cornue who served four years, and he in turn was succeeded by F. N. Torrance who served as secretary and treasurer from February, 1910, to July, 1920, when he resigned and moved with his family to Minnesota. E. H. Lines, who succeeded Mr. Torrance, entered upon his duties as secretary August 1, 1920, and is the present incumbent of the office.

The original capital stock of the company was only $5,000, distributed among forty stockholders. This capital was increased, December 20 of the same year to $15,000. May 5 of the following year it was again increased to $30,000; again July 10, 1906, to $50,000, and since February 6, 1907, the company has had an authorized capital stock of $100,000.

Among the first activities of the company was the purchase, July 7, 1904, from The Citizens Telephone Company, of the Hebron Telephone Exchange with seventeen subscribers and the farmer lines extending from Greenwood to Hebron and Bissel. A second purchase from The Citizens Company March 1, 1905, included the toll lines extending from Hebron to Alden, Harvard, Woodstock, McHenry, Richmond, Solon Mills and Spring Grove.

A temporary agreement for the interchange of business was made with The Chicago Telephone Company, August 19, 1904. A more complete agreement was concluded with the Chicago Company (now The

Illinois Bell) July 19, 1905. A similar agreement was made with the Wisconsin Company September 26, 1905. These agreements, in addition to other considerations, provided an opportunity for long distance connection between New Era subscribers and all outside points.

The initial directory of the company issued November 23, 1904, contained the names of seventy-three subscribers. In September, 1906, there were 380 subscribers. In February, 1907, the number of subscribers had increased to 480 in the two exchanges, 200 at Richmond and 280 at Hebron, and the number of stockholders had increased from forty to 129.

The territory around Wilmot, Wisconsin, was acquired during the spring of 1907, and an exchange established at that point. During the same year the company erected a brick building at Richmond at a cost of $8,200. The local office was established on the second floor, the main floor bringing in a good revenue from rentals. A building lot was purchased in Hebron Jan. 15, 1916, on which it is proposed to some day build a home office for the company. The central office being now located in the building used for the local exchange. The number of subscribers have increased since July 7, 1904, from seventeen to 1,117. These subscribers are now being served through the exchanges at Hebron, Richmond and Wilmot.

The Farmers New Era Telephone Company has been beset by many storms and difficulties. Especially during its early history was its horizon clouded with dire forebodings and prophesies of misfortune and ultimate disaster. The clouds have blown away however after every storm leaving no sign of calamity or of reverses excepting losses of several thousands of dollars occasioned by sleet storms, and the company has continued to grow and prosper during the seventeen years of its existence until it now owns, in addition to the lot in Hebron and the building in Richmond, 325 miles of poles, 1,500 miles of wire, 35,000 feet of cable and 1,132 telephones. Service is being furnished subscribers of the company through these telephones and over lines of the company extending from the Hebron Exchange four miles to the north, eight miles to the south, six miles to the west and eighteen miles to the east and reaching patrons of the company in and adjacent to the following towns: Alden, Hebron, Greenwood, Richmond, Ringwood, Solon Mills and Spring Grove, Ill., and Basset, Camp Lake, Wilmot, Silver Lake, Twin Lakes, Trevor and Zenda, Wis.

Harry C. Gile

Hattie May Gile.

CHAPTER XVI

MILITARY

PATRIOTISM

In 1917 the people of the United States awoke from the deep lethargy years of prosperity had brought upon them and began to define in their hearts and actions the real meaning of patriotism. They soon began to realize that the time had passed when standing at the playing of the national anthem or cheering the passing troops through the streets, constituted the full measure of true Americanism. In the hard, dark days to follow they were to come through the bitterest sacrifices to appreciate what our forefathers won for us in their struggles to secure freedom, and bring about an era of peace and prosperity. Thus awakening, it was natural that all should take a renewed interest in the exploits of the heroes of past wars, and to demand that some account of them be included together with those of the present-day soldiers and sailors. Thus the latest History of McHenry County would in no sense be complete without showing what the people of the county performed in a military line, beginning with the Indian warfare, the Mexican war, the

239

Civil war, the Spanish American war, as well as to give all that can be obtained at this date concerning "our own boys," who, animated by the same spirit as prompted their forefathers and grandsires, leaving their homes and business associations to engage in the same kind of a war as has always interested this country—one for the oppressed against the oppressor. The part taken in the Indian war was necessarily small in this county. But this chapter will treat especially on the deeds of Mexican, Civil war, Spanish-American and World war soldiery. All are given with due respect and reverence as well as the tenderest of feelings—the tear falls from the young life sacrificed, whether it was terminated in the sixties, the nineties or in the World war just closed, victorious for Liberty and Democracy, practically the world over.

WAR WITH MEXICO

Only the aged men of these times will recall the excitement that prevailed in this country when war was declared against Mexico in 1846. The volunteers from Illinois performed such an aggressive, conspicuous part in the war with Mexico that it is necessary to give an epitome of the war, to be able to understand and appreciate the nature and value of their services, and render them due credit which their importance demands. The records in the State Adjutant General's office give the following information:

"On the 11th day of May, 1846, Congress passed an act, declaring that 'By the act of the Republic of Mexico, a state of war exists between that Government and the United States.' At the same time that body made an appropriation of $10,000,000 to carry on the war, and authorized the President to accept 50,000 volunteers.

"This force, for convenience sake, to save transportation, and because of their already well-known ability and familiarity with firearms, was drawn principally from the Southern and Western States. Illinois was called upon for three regiments of infantry or riflemen, and the pay, with all allowances, placed at $15.50 per month to the private soldier. The militia of the state being then in an unorganized condition, Governor Ford issued a call for thirty full companies of volunteers of a maximum of eighty men, to serve for twelve months, and with the privilege of electing their own officers for their regiment."

The response to this call was indeed enthusiastic. Within ten days thirty-five full companies had organized and reported. By the time the place of rendezvous had been selected (Alton), there had been seventy-five companies recruited—each furious to get to the front, and from this number Governor Ford was compelled to select thirty companies. Of these thirty companies, were organized the First Regiment, Col. John J. Hardin; the Second Regiment, Col. William H. Bissell; and the Third Regiment, Col. Ferris Foreman, which were recruited during the months of April, May and June, and mustered into service of the United States at Alton, Illinois, July 2, 1846.

Hon. E. D. Baker, then in Congress from Illinois, induced the President to let him recruit the Fourth Regiment, which was mustered in July 18, 1846. These four Illinois regiments served through the war and were mustered out together.

On account of the many failures upon the part of Illinois, at Washington, to get an accurate list of Mexican War soldiers' names, even as far back as when Robert T. Lincoln was Secretary of War, it will be impossible to give a roster of such soldiers as served from this county. While it is true that McHenry County was thinly settled at that date, yet there were pioneers of this county who served in that war and it is to be regretted that such lists cannot be compiled and given to the department at Springfield. Suffice to say the men who went from here were men who feared not the yell of the Mexican.

QUOTA IN CIVIL WAR

McHenry's men have always been loyal, there is no question about that. It furnished 2,533 men during the Civil war, within three of its quota, and there was no need of any draft there. It must be remembered that the drafted service had another meaning during the Civil war than it has today. Owing to the much smaller army raised, until the latter part of the war there were plenty of volunteers, and the draft was not made until a community showed that its men were actively disloyal. With the opening up of our participation as a country, in the greatest war the world has ever known, it was necessary to follow entirely new methods, and after due consideration of the subject, Congress decided to place under a universal draft all men between the ages of twenty-one and thirty-one years at the very outset of the formation of the new army, and from that draft thus secured 10,000,000 men in the very prime of manhood, from which has been developed an army that commands the enthusiastic respect and admiration of the seasoned troops of countries which have always kept large standing armies, and inculcated military training of all classes.

FIFTEENTH ILLINOIS

Companies A, D and F, of the Fifteenth Illinois Volunteer Infantry, during the Civil war, were composed chiefly of McHenry County men, and these were the first companies raised in McHenry County for this war. Captain Lewis D. Kelly, of Company A, was from Woodstock; First Lieutenants Daniel C. Joslyn, Lawrence H. Jones, Frederick W. Smith and William H. Sherman, were all from Woodstock. Second Lieutenants Mark Hathaway, Frederick W. Smith, William H. Sherman and George A. Austin, were also from Woodstock. Company D had as its captain, Harley Wayne, of Union, while its first lieutenants were Frank S. Curtis, Marengo; Frederick A. Smith of Genoa; Calvin H. Shapely of Harmony; John Waldock of Marengo; and its second lieutenants were Fred A. Smith of Genoa; Peter J. Labaugh, Marengo; John Waldock, Marengo; and Michael Schoonmaker, Marengo. In Company F, the captain was John Paddock, who resigned, and he was followed by William Henry of Algonquin, and Frank D. Patterson of Nunda. McHenry County was represented in this company by first lieutenants as follows: William Henry of Algonquin; John J. Sears of Algonquin; and Frank D. Patterson of Nunda; and Simeon L. Eells of Algonquin; while all of the second lieutenants at the time of organization were McHenry County men, promoted to a first lieutenancy as given above. The regiment was mustered into service May 21, 1861; re-enlisted veterans in 1864; re-organized in March, 1865, and mustered out September 20, 1865.

TWENTY-THIRD CONSOLIDATED

The Twenty-third Illinois Volunteer Infantry, known as the "Irish Brigade," was mustered into the service, June 15, 1861; re-enlisted men in August, 1864, and was mustered out at Richmond, Va., July 24, 1865. McHenry County had men in Companies F, G, H and K. The captain of Company F, Hiram C. Edison, was from Chemung; the captain of Company H, Edwin R. Cross, was from Chemung; the captain of Company K, Henry Seigel, was from Chemung; and its first lieutenant, Daniel Morgan, was from Nunda.

THIRTY-SIXTH

About thirty-six of Company A, and nearly all of Company H of the Thirty-sixth Illinois Volunteer Infantry were from McHenry County,

Children of Harry D Gile + Wife

among the officers being George L. Lyon, chaplain, from Woodstock; William Mitchell, captain of Company A, from Crystal Lake; Franklin J. Thwing, first lieutenant, from Crystal Lake; George L. Peeler, first lieutenant, from Crystal Lake; Merritt L. Joslyn, captain of Company H, from Woodstock; Theodore L. Griffin, captain, from Woodstock; Horace N. Crittenden, captain, from Crystal Lake; Alfred H. Sellers, first lieutenant, from Woodstock; Charles F. Dyle, first lieutenant, from Crystal Lake; Morris Briggs, first lieutenant, from Algonquin. This regiment was mustered into the service September 23, 1861, and mustered out at New Orleans, La., October 8, 1865.

NINETY-FIFTH

The Ninety-fifth Illinois Volunteer Infantry had in it 673 men from this county. In Company A, commanded by Capt. William Avery, there were ninety-nine men; in Company C, commanded by Capt. John B. Manzer, there were 100 men; in Company D, commanded by Capt. Edward J. Cook, there were eighty-four men; in Company E, commanded by Capt. John Eddy, there were ninety-six men; in Company F, commanded by Capt. William H. Stewart, there were ninety-nine men; in Company H, commanded by Capt. Charles H. Tryon, there were ninety-nine men; and in Company I, commanded by Capt. James Nish, there were ninety-six men, making the total from McHenry County of 673 in these seven companies. This regiment was mustered into the service September 4, 1862; recruited in August, 1864; and mustered out August 8, 1865.

ONE HUNDRED FORTY-FIRST

Among the commissioned officers of the One Hundred and Forty-first Illinois Volunteer Infantry, a 100-day regiment, were Jacob D. Lansing, Marengo, lieutenant-colonel; Harmon A. Buck, Marengo, surgeon; F. W. Watson, Marengo, second assistant surgeon; Charles W. Ingersol, Marengo, first lieutenant, Company F. Company A contained one McHenry County man; Company F, twenty-six; and Company K, twenty-one.

ONE HUNDRED FORTY-SEVENTH

In Company I of the One Hundred and Forty-seventh Illinois Volunteer Infantry (one year's service), there were twenty-five men from this county. This regiment was mustered into service February 18, 1864, and was mustered out January 20, 1866.

ONE HUNDRED FORTY-SECOND

About twenty McHenry County men served in Company C, One Hundred and Forty-second Illinois Volunteer Infantry, which was a 100-day regiment, mustered in June 18, 1864, and mustered out October 26, 1864.

ONE HUNDRED FIFTY-THIRD

The One Hundred and Fifty-third Illinois Volunteer Infantry had the following men in it from this county: Company A, seventeen; Company B, thirty-three; Company C, twenty-one; Company F, two; Company K, eighty-five. The commissioned officers of this regiment from McHenry County were as follows: Capt. Charles H. Hickcock, Hartland; First Lieutenants John H. Payne, Hartland, and William R. Colburn, Richmond. This company was mustered into the service February 18, 1865, for one year, and was mustered out September 15, 1865.

ONE HUNDRED FIFTY-SIXTH

There were no privates from this county in the One Hundred and Fifty-sixth Illinois Volunteer Infantry, but the following commissioned officers were from this county: Erwin B. Messer, Chemung, lieutenant-colonel; Mortimor P. Bundy, Hebron, captain, Company C; Chester M. Stewart, Hebron, second lieutenant, Company C; Emanuel Engelsted, first lieutenant, Company C; Thomas S. Sexton, Chemung, captain, Company E; David G. Hudson, first lieutenant, Company E; Martin Dalwy, Chemung, second lieutenant, Company E; Nelson W. Clark, Hebron, captain, Company K; John W. S. Bergman, Hebron, second lieutenant, Company K. This regiment was mustered into the service March 9, 1865, and mustered out September 20, 1865.

EIGHTH CAVALRY

The Eighth Illinois Volunteer Cavalry had several companies recruited from McHenry County, Company II being composed almost entirely of men from here. In Company G there were twenty-six men from McHenry County; in Company H, about 150; in Company I, about thirty-three, and there were about thirty more scattered throughout the regiment. This regiment was mustered into the service September 18, 1861, and was mustered out July 17, 1865. Its commissioned officers from McHenry County were as follows: Edward D. Dowd, captain, Company H; first lieutenants, Company H, Isaac F. Russell, Crystal Lake, and Isaac M. Brooks, McHenry.

SEVENTEENTH CAVALRY

About twenty men from McHenry County served in Company B of the above regiment. Company G was made up almost entirely of them. Its commissioned officers were as follows: Louis D. Kelly, Dorr, and Cyrus Hutchinson, Benton, captains; Christopher D. Kelly, Dorr, and Albert A. Amet, Evanston, first lieutenants; and Ebenezer Knapp, Richmond, and William H. Austin, Richmond, second lieutenants. This regiment was mustered in January 22, 1864, and was mustered out in November and December of 1865.

MISCELLANEOUS

Thirty-two men from McHenry County served in Company I, Fifty-second Illinois Volunteer Infantry, and about twelve in Company G of that regiment. Twenty-six from McHenry County served in Company E, Eighty-fourth Illinois Volunteer Infantry. In the Sixteenth Cavalry about twenty-five of the McHenry County men served, principally in Company H. Among its officers were Captain Hiram M. Planchett, Woodstock, Company M; and First Lieutenant Henry D. Stocker, of McHenry, Company M.

RETROSPECT

Many years have passed since the "boys in blue" came marching home. The majority of them settled down into private life, and were spared to round out a long and useful life.

In looking over the records at the McHenry County courthouse, it is discovered that this county issued bounty orders amounting to $260,000, of which $90,000 were outstanding in 1876. These orders drew eight and ten per cent interest, but were about that date made uniformly eight per cent interest. This debt has long since been wiped out.

The old camp-ground is silent now,
　All hushed the martial tread;
The night winds cannot soothe their brow,
　They slumber with the dead.
"Tenting tonight" they will not sing:
　Ah, boys, the camps are still;
The battle's and the cannons' ring
　Is silent on the hill.

You will not march again;
　God bless your rest tonight.
Your suffering and pain
　Have clothed your soul in white.
The battle-call is ended,
　The bugle notes are still,
'Tis silent on the hill.

(The last line refers to the National Cemetery on Arlington Heights, near Washington, D. C.)

SPANISH-AMERICAN WAR

Not since 1846 and 1848 had the United States been forced to measure strength with a foreign foe. Not since the Mexican War had it been necessary to pit the courage and military ability of the United States soldier and sailor against those of a foreign power. It remained for Spain to rouse the ire and just resentment of "Uncle Sam" and bring on a conflict which, for short, sharp, and incisive action cannot be paralleled in the history of nations.

The tragedy of the "Maine" in the friendly harbor of Havana, Cuba, electrified the people of the globe with horror and indignation. In the United States amidst the cries for just revenge could be heard the sobs of anguish and distress from the lips of the bereaved parents, wives and sweethearts. The thunders of a nation's resentment filled the air while millions demanded that full punishment should be meted out to those guilty of this wholesale murder.

On February 17, 1898, while the General Assembly of Illinois was convened in an extra session, one foresaw the conflict that was to come and sent to the House of Representatives the following message:

"To the Honorable House of Representatives:

"The news of the calamity which has overtaken the United States battleship 'Maine' and its ill-fated crew, fills me with grief and horror and I assume that the General Assembly will by joint-resolution express the sympathy of the people of this State for the gallant dead and wounded of our Navy and their surviving relatives.

"I am unwilling to believe that the loss of the 'Maine' was the result of intention, and trust that the official investigation ordered by our government may demonstrate that it was due to accidental causes. In view of the uncertainty which exists, as to this point, it would seem that before the Legislature adjourns *sine die* it would authorize the executive to tender to the President of the United States, on behalf of the State of Illinois, whatever moral and material support may be necessary in this emergency to maintain the honor of the American flag and prevent or punish any attempt at hostile invasion of our common country.

JOHN R. TANNER, Governor."

All that was requested by the governor was granted by the Illinois Legislature.

In this war with Spain in 1898, and the subsequent campaign in the Philippines, McHenry County did her part loyally, promptly and well. The most of the men from this county were members of the Third Regiment of Illinois Infantry Volunteers. The regiment was enrolled April 26, 1898, and mustered into the service for two years, May 7, 1898, at Camp Tanner, Springfield, Ill. The regiment left Camp Tanner, and arrived at Chickamauga Park May 16, 1898; arrived at Newport News, July 24, 1898; sailed on the "St. Louis" for Porto Rico, July 25, 1898; arrived Ponce, P. R., July 31, 1898; landed at Arroyo, August 2, 1898, under slight resistance of Spanish. They participated in engagements at Guayama, August 5, 1898, north of Guayama, August 8 and 13, 1898; did outpost duty north of Guayama till October 1, 1898; were in camp east of Guayama until November 2, 1898; embarked on "Roumania" for New York, November 2, 1898, and sailed November 3, 1898, arriving, November 9, 1898. The men were ordered to home stations via railroad, arriving November 11, 1898. The regiment was finally mustered out at Joliet, Ill., January 24, 1899.

The soldiers from McHenry County were mostly members of Company G, Third Regiment, and their names, according to the adjutant's report for Illinois are as follows:

Captain—William C. Eichelberger, Woodstock. First lieutenant Horatio W. Wright, Woodstock. Second lieutenant—Frank C. Hanaford, Woodstock. First sergeant—Joseph S. Kline, Woodstock. Sergeants—James Sullivan, Woodstock; Conute Lee, Woodstock, promoted to first sergeant; William T. Charles, Woodstock, discharged for disability, July 18, 1898. Corporals—Thomas O. Cowlin, Woodstock, promoted sergeant May 7, 1898, and mustered out, January, 1899; John M. Burbank, Woodstock, promoted sergeant, May, 1898; Augustus W. Wagner, Woodstock; Alex G. Darrall, Woodstock. Artificer—George H. Wood, Woodstock. Musician—John W. Metzger, Woodstock, promoted corporal June 24, 1898. Privates—Aspholm, Herman, Woodstock; Anderson, Charles, Woodstock; Bachman, Emil, Woodstock; Brown, Henry, Woodstock; Brass, Ernest F., Woodstock; Charles, Clayton, Woodstock, transferred to general hospital corps, June 13, 1898; Vonover, Howard L., Huntley; Carr, Owen, Woodstock; Durenberger, A. H., Woodstock, promoted to corporal; Fay, Charles S., Woodstock; Fleming, Jesse L., Woodstock, promoted sergeant; Fritz, William F., Woodstock; Frazier, William H., Woodstock; Gilbert, Noah L., Harvard; Hanson, Louis F., Woodstock; Hanver, Louis L., Woodstock; Hanson, Walter, Woodstock; Houdson, Isaac W., Woodstock; Hohn, John, Woodstock; Jensen, Nels, Woodstock; Jensen, Christian, Woodstock, died, November 11, 1898; Jensen, Anders P., Woodstock; Keating, Michael G., Huntley; Larson, Peter, Woodstock; Merwin, Thomas P., Woodstock, promoted musician, June, 1898; Mortenson, Jens P., Huntley; Matterson, Win L., Harvard; Mountain, Henry E., Woodstock, promoted corporal, June, 1898; Miner, Clyde C., Woodstock, promoted corporal, July, 1898; McCarthy, Charles E., Woodstock; McCauley, Simon B., Woodstock; Peterson, Frank, Woodstock; Peterson, Michael M., Woodstock; Parsons, William L., Woodstock; Pierson, James W., Woodstock; Rouning, Charles A., Woodstock; Roach, Arthur B., Harvard, discharged, June, 1898; Siebel, August F. W., Woodstock; Smith, Paul, Woodstock; Smith, E. D. J., Woodstock; Smith, Charles M., Woodstock; Stevens, Oliver L., Harvard, died in Porto Rico, his remains being brought back for burial; Stratton, William L., Woodstock; Sullivan, Alva A., Woodstock; Snitkey, William A., Harvard; Tranto, Charles, Woodstock; Tweed, Robert G., Woodstock; Wurtzinger, John J., Woodstock, promoted to corporal, June, 1898; Woodward, A., Woodstock, died, November 22, 1898; Windt, Herman J., Woodstock; Windt, Carl F.,

Woodstock; Walton, Frank, Woodstock; Woodard, Arthur E., Harvard; Williams, Charles E., Hartland, discharged, May 22, 1898; Allworden, William C., Woodstock; Averill, Fred H., Hebron; Bennett, Frank W., McHenry; Bennett, Herbert L., McHenry; Brown, Thomas L., Marengo: Colby, Nye W., McHenry; Corrigan, Joseph J., Woodstock; Delaunty, Richard F., Woodstock; Deitz, Frank A., Woodstock; Engeln, George, McHenry; Grace, Thomas R., Woodstock, died, October 1, 1898, on board ship hospital, "Missouri"; Hall, Guy C., Ringwood; Holly, Albert, McHenry; Murphy, Burt R., Greenwood; Nichel, Charles, Marengo; Rothermel, William, McHenry; Selby, Alex C., Marengo; Smith, Edward, Woodstock; Stoddard, William P., Hebron; Swadish, Charles, McHenry; Theln, Martin, McHenry; Theln, Michael J., McHenry; VanSlyke, Jesse M., McHenry.

MEXICAN BORDER WARFARE

During 1916 trouble fomented, as is well recognized now, by the enemies abroad and at home of this country, the republic across the Rio Grande began to question the integrity of the good faith of the government of the United States. The various disturbances which had arisen from time to time along the border, had been handled with the same open-handed and generous policy which has always characterized this nation, but with the internal troubles the recognized government were having with Villa, decided this government to send into Mexico an expedition to assist the Mexican government in capturing the rebel. When the Mexican government signified that it was able to resume full control, our troops were withdrawn as they were at no time regarded, nor were they meant to be regarded, as an invading force sent into Mexico to interfere with that country's home government. The National Guards were mobilized from all over the country, and sent into Texas, where those who did not participate in the trip into the interior of Mexico had the benefit of some months of training on the border, which prepared them for the more strenuous life in the training camps after the United States had declared war upon Germany. Never before in the history of any country was so large a force of men assembled, with so peaceful a purpose, under the name of war, and the President of the United States reiterated his assertions as to the good faith of this government to the Mexican representatives when they met with him in the spring of 1918. At that time the rebel Villa was still at large, the Mexican government having not been able as yet to that date, to capture him in spite of declining the help of the United States to do so.

DEPARTING FOR MEXICAN BORDER

When the Mexican Border War commenced in the spring of 1916, the National Guards were at once called to the colors, and on the evening of June 22, Company G, of Woodstock, left for Springfield, Illinois, at the command of the Governor. This company saw service in the hot sands of a far southern clime—real soldier hardships they endured, and in a year from that time they were sworn in as soldiers to "go over seas." It is befitting in this chapter that a roster of these men be given in this, a History of their home county:

THIRD REGIMENT STAFF

Colonel—Charles Greene, Aurora. Lieutenant Colonel—Frank Bacon, Aurora. Adjutant Captain—W. H. Brogunier, Rockford. Quartermaster Captain—Richard Boyer, Rockford. Commissary Captain—Wilbur Thornton, Pontiac. Chaplain—Captain A. R. Clinch, Rockford. Medical Department—Major Robert Bourland, Rockford; Captain J. A. McCaughey, Hoopeston; Captain A. E. Lord, Plano; Major Sergeant Emil Rhutishauser, Aurora. Battalion Majors —C. C. Miner, Woodstock; Edward Leonard, Rockford; L. F. Strawn, Pontiac. Battalion Adjutant—James Sanders, Aurora. Battalion Quartermaster—Second Lieutenant Paul Ritt, Woodstock. Companies—A, DeKalb, Captain H. Goodeson; B, Hoopeston, Captain Earl Thornton; C, Ottawa, Captain Ralph C. Woodard; D, Aurora, Captain Charles Harkison; E, Elgin, Captain William Peck; F, Pontiac, Captain Fred Dewey; G, Woodstock, Captain O. H. Corr; H, Rockford, Captain A. R. Tetlow; I, Aurora, Captain John H. Newman; K, Rockford, Captain Charles Sowel; L, Kankakee. Being organized and new officers elected—M, Belvidere, Captain Harry Haskins.

COMPANY G

Officers: Captain—O. H. Corr. First Lieutenant—William Thompson. Second Lieutenant—Lester Edinger. First Sergeant—C. Haldeman. Sergeants—William Donnelly, Ralph Thayer, Earl Clement, Fred Brewer, Harry Francisco, Henry Schmitt. Corporals—George

Robert E. Haeger.

Brahy, John Long, Louis Thayer, Charles Woodard, William Stewart, Alderson Dove. Cook—Martin Olson. Musicians—Leo Schryver, Andrew Grafmueller.

Privates—Anderson, Theodore; Bartlett, Porter; Bennett, Bert; Bennett, James; Bergthal, Joseph; Berners, John; Berry, William; Bill, Ransom; Boone, Lester; Botts, Charles; Bowman, Herbert; Brahy, Harry; Brown, Henry; Burbridge, Richard; Buxton, Bernard; Carlson, Henry; Carvey, Harley; Churchill, Ralph; Clark, Leo; Clark, Everett; Clark, LeRoy; Clyde, Teddy; Dunker, Herman; Emanuel, Fred; Fairmount, William; Feffer, Albert; Fish, Isaac; Fish, Warren; Fitzek, Joseph; Floyd, Dale; Foss, Merle; Fredendall, Elmer; Garrison, George; Geske, Charles; Geske, Walter; Gruidl, Joseph; Haase, William; Hausmann, Clarence; Hayward, Ed.; Hildebrandt, Ralph; Hinderlider, Ernest; Hoffmeyer, Walter; Hoke, William; Howell, John; Howell, Ogle; Jessen, Chris; Kilburne, William; Knapp, Grey; Kohls, William; Kramer, Rudolph; Kretchmer, Lloyd; Larson, Eugene; Leighty, Wedge; Long, Ray; McCarthy, Bruce; Mackey, Leo; McGee, Raymond; McLaughlin, Lester; Miller, William; Nohr, William; O'Brien, Jesse; Ogden, Glenn; Paepke, Rudolph; Rasmussen, Edmund; Redman, Mark; Reese, Roy; Richards, Clifton; Risting, John; Roderick, Chester; Roderick, Ray; Sandford, Cyrus; Schneider, Harry; Schmulle, William; Schutt, Albert; Sheehy, Frank; Sponholtz, William; Sommers, Adolph; Stephenson, Frank; Stott, James; Strubbe, Roy; Tennyson, Joyce; Terwilliger, Everett; Tuite, John C.; Umathum, Michael; Umathum, Peter; Walker, Benjamin; Warner, Edward; Wendt, Fred; Williams, Burns; Winegar, Ralph; Woods, Raymond; Wright, Armour.

TRUE SPIRIT OF AMERICANISM

On the same day that this company left for Mexico, the *Sentinel*, of Woodstock, had the following call which was freely responded to, and the same is entitled to a place in the history of the community which has always been "over the top" in such matters, even from away back in Civil war days.

Will you do your duty?

Company G is called to the colors.

Eighteen years ago the call to arms rang out over this free land, and Company G responded, just as Company G is responding today. Down in Chickamauga Park and in Porto Rico our boys from home learned the meaning of need, of sickness, of suffering. There were many things necessary—emergencies arose demanding immediate attention, quick action.

Somebody back in Woodstock, with the love of Christ and humanity in his heart, had foreseen all this and started a relief fund for Company G. That relief fund brought comforts and necessities for the Woodstock boy who lay ill under the hot Porto Rican sun. Had it not been for that fund he might now be lying in a narrow green bed, which you and I would strew with flowers on every thirtieth of May. Or the wasted form might have found its last resting place under the tropic skies, or in the still waters to the far South.

*   *   *   *   *   *   *   *   *

Again Company G is called to the colors.

Perhaps our boys will go to the border or into Mexico. There is an arid region, a burning sun, water unfit to drink.

There may be battles, weary marches—there may be fever and pestilence. All of these things the boys of Company G bravely risk, and in most cases they are giving up remunerative employment to shoulder the responsibility of your community and my community, for the magnificent return of fifty cents per day.

Not all of us can go to war. But all of us can be patriotic. Each one of us can do his share in one way or another.

Who is there among us who cannot donate something toward a fund for Company G?

*   *   *   *   *   *   *   *   *

The Sentinel is starting a movement to establish a relief fund to be used for the boys of Company G in case of need, of sickness, of suffering. Such a fund may prove the saving of one life, or of many lives—if but one of our boys from home is rescued out of the shadow of death because you and I had forethought for his comfort, will it not all have been worth while?

We devoutly pray that none of the hardships cited may befall our lads, but all are possibilities for which it is our duty to be prepared. Will you do your share to alleviate suffering, should suffering come?

Subscription blanks are being prepared and will be placed in all of the stores and business houses about town. These provide that all money donated in the cause shall be placed in any of the banks of Woodstock to the credit of Company G, to be used for the company as its commanding officer may deem best.

Will you help?

A number of the business men of Woodstock are holding a meeting in the association rooms this afternoon for the purpose of raising a purse to send with the boys tonight. This is to be only a starter, and the appeal is to be general. Residents, not only of Woodstock, but of McHenry County, and any others who may be interested in Company G, are invited to make contributions to the fund. A list of all contributions will be kept and acknowledgment made through the newspapers of Woodstock. Donations can be sent to The Sentinel if desired.

The road of the soldier is not strewn with flowers. Veterans of the Civil and Spanish wars can tell you what the camp, the march, the battle bring. If your boy, or that neighbor's boy whom you have known since childhood, goes out of Woodstock, tonight into unknown dangers, into the strife of battle, into the weary, painful monotony of the field hospital, wouldn't you like to feel that YOU are helping to ease his pain, comfort his loneliness and nourish his body?

What will you give to Company G?

THE WORLD WAR

At the beginning this was a war between numerous European countries, the cause of which will not here be discussed. From August, 1914, to April 6, 1917, it was fought without the aid of America, but on that date the United States declared war against the German Empire. The war terminated in the signal defeat and overthrow of the Germans and their long boasted military power.

DECLARATION OF WAR

Although the people had foreseen that war was inevitable, the actual declaration of it on April 6, 1917, brought a realization home to the country that now would the mettle of the populace be tried as in a fiery furnace. Aside from chronic objectors, and uninformed pacifieists, no one not in active sympathy with Germany had any criticism to offer, and the majority were fired with wild enthusiasm. Many schemes were put forth, ideas were exchanged, and advice offered, but acting deliberately and systematically, studying the question from all angles, and in the light of the experience of our allies, the President and his advisors laid out a plan of conduct for war which placed practically a million trained men in France before July 4, 1918, and had American soldiers fighting long before that date.

VOLUNTEERS

This country has always called for volunteers when making war against another country, or a section of this one, and so following this old custom, the Government first issued the call. And McHenry County responded with about 530 enlisted men, in various departments, at various recruiting stations, from Maine to California, hence no accurate record of these men will be had until an adjutant-general's report is published some years hence. The same is true concerning the drafted men, no complete roster is now obtainable, as no true record was retained by the local board, but all records were sent to either the state or national capital. It is known, however, from memoranda kept, that there was between 1,450 and 1,500 men served in all departments of the service, who went from, and in the end will be credited to McHenry County. Of this number 760 were accepted under the drafts; 153 in Company G National Guards from Woodstock, while the remainder were enlisted in the army and navy and in other branches of the service, making in round numbers about 1,475 men, of whom fifty-seven lost their lives.

SELECTIVE DRAFT

No better explanation for passing of the legislation and the levying of the selective draft can be given than by publishing the following letter written by President Wilson in reply to one written to him by Representative Guy T. Helvering of Kansas, a Democrat, which Mr. Wilson made public April 19, 1917.

"I welcome the inquiry of your letter of April 19, because I have realized the truth of what you say from my own observations—namely, that what is meant to be understood by the selective draft is not generally understood throughout the country.

"The process of the draft is, I think, very clearly set forth in the bill drafted by the war department and which I so earnestly hope the congress will adopt, but it is worth while to state the idea which underlies the bill a little more fully.

"I took occasion the other day in an address to the people of the country to point out the many forms of patriotic service that were open to them and to emphasize the fact that the military part of the service was by no means the only part, and perhaps, all things considered, not the most vital part.

"Our object is a mobilization of all the productive and active forces

of the nation, and their development to the highest point of co-operation and efficiency, and the idea of the selective draft is that those
should be chosen for service in the army who can be most readily spared
from the prosecution of the other activities the country must engage
in and to which it must devote a great deal of its best energy and
capacity.

"The volunteer system does not do this. When men choose themselves they sometimes choose without due regard to their other responsibilities. Men may come from the farms or the mines or from the factories or centers of business who ought not to come, but ought to stand
back of the armies in the field and see that they get everything that
they need and that the people of the country are sustained in the meanwhile."

There was great opposition to the passing of this selective draft
bill, but the Emergency War Bill, which had, among its provisions the
selective draft measure, was passed April 18, 1917, and immediately
signed by the President.

By this bill all male citizens between the ages of twenty-one and
thirty-one years were required to register, June 5 later being set aside
for this purpose. McHenry County men within these ages obeyed the
call, and to their credit, be it said, that they did so cheerfully and
promptly, and those appointed to look after the slackers had little or
nothing to do, for this county has never shirked its duty, or failed to
respond to all the calls the country has made upon its people.

REGISTRATIONS

At the first registration there were 3,016 men between the ages
of twenty-one and thirty-one, who registered in McHenry County in
the first draft. The quota for this county was then easily filled. Company G National Guard at Woodstock, belonging to the Third Illinois
Regiment, was increased on registration day by enlistment of twenty-
three men, making a total in the company of 153, and the required
number was only 150.

WORLD WAR REGISTRARS

The following is a list of those who were appointed and served
as registrars during the late World war, in and for McHenry County,
and it was under these persons that the several registers of the county

were made to determine the number of available able bodied men in the county. These registrars were appointed by the sheriff and were from the several townships:

Riley Township—R. W. Metcalf; Marengo, 1st, F. W. Benjamin, A. D. Allison; 2nd, D. M. Wright, Charles Scofield; Dunham—Homer E. Whipple; Chemung—1st, Charles J. Vierck, Eugene Saunders; 2nd, Frank E. Beck, Hugh Houston Megran; 3rd, Edwin J. Barr; Alden—E. L. Kingsley; Hartland—W. H. Forrest; Seneca—E. F. Kuecker; Coral—Charles H. Ackman, Jr., and Clarence Siems; Grafton—John Hawley, F. R. Ferris; Dorr—1st, Charles F. Renich, G. W. Lemmers; 2nd, Fred A. Walters, L. J. Young; 3rd, N. A. Sunderlin, A. E. Schroeder; 4th, Fred W. Hartman; Greenwood—M. Dassaw; Hebron—Henry W. Turner, Clifton H. Merry; Richmond—J. T. Bower, G. W. Eldridge; McHenry—1st, J. C. Ladd, R. B. Bradley; 2nd, Ed. L. Hayes, Albert H. Pause; Nunda—1st, James A. Nish; 2nd, Harry H. McCollum, L. W. Cobb; Algonquin—1st, Henry Keyes, John Peter; 2nd, Thomas F. Leonard, John Buehler; 3rd, T. H. Wulff; Burton—V. S. Esh, W. F. Pierce.

ADMINISTERING THE OATH OF CITIZENSHIP

Many years hence the following item will be read with much interest, no doubt, throwing light on what was considered by the courts of today "good citizenship." Judge Donnelly, before administering the oath to many foreign-born, seeking citizenship here, during the first part of the World war, spoke to the subjects as follows:

"You are about to become citizens of the United States. In taking this step you are assuming certain duties and obligations in return for which you will receive certain rights and privileges from this government with which you are affiliating yourself. Our country is now at war and it may be that you will be called upon to sacrifice your lives if need be. If you are so called upon, I trust that you will not hesitate to respond willingly.

"We have the best government on the face of the earth. That flag before you (pointing to the flag hanging in the courtroom), is the emblem of freedom. Ever respect it and be ready to defend it. If there is any reason why you cannot from now on fight for that flag, do not take the solemn oath of allegiance which you are about to take. There is nothing in your obligation to this government which requires you to forget the tender feelings you have for your Fatherland.

"It is human for a man to have reverence and high regard for his Fatherland, and if you did not have that reverence in your breast, we could not expect that you would have a high regard for our country. But from now on you will be citizens of the United States and it will devolve upon you to place the interests of this country above all others. Your country's welfare means your own welfare, and if need be, you must sacrifice your property or your life in its defense.

"The oath of allegiance you are about to take is full of significance; listen attentively to every word of it and let its meaning make upon you a deep impression."

EXEMPTION BOARDS

The Exemption Board for McHenry County during this great conflict was as follows: Dr. E. V. Anderson, Woodstock; William Desmond, Woodstock; and F. F. Axtell, of Harvard. These men faithfully performed their duty which was no small task. It took men of sound judgment, decision of character, knowledge of human nature and withal men of undoubted integrity and loyalty to from week to week and month to month pass on the hundreds of individual cases that came before them for adjustment.

WAR WORK

While men eligible for military service were preparing to do a man's part in the world, those who were left behind, of both sexes, were not idle. Active co-operation was immediately accorded the Government in all of the suggestions relative to food conservation, and later fuel conservation, as well as the further extension of cultivated lands then vacant. When the first Liberty Loan was floated, McHenry County people subscribed until "over the top," and kept on doing so with each of the successive loans till the last loan was asked for in the spring of 1919. This was true in each of all of the war measures, the Red Cross, the War Savings Stamps, the Young Men's Christian Association and Knights of Columbus calls, each and all "went over the top," signifying of course, that this county went beyond her allotment or quota in these war calls for funds and supplies. In round numbers the amount of War Bonds subscribed and paid for by the people of McHenry County was $5,180,000.

By interviewing the various treasurers and secretaries who had to do with the collection of funds for the various societies, the following statement has been compiled:

Amount raised by the Red Cross Chapters..................$	76,000
Amount raised for the Young Men's Christian Association...	17,431
Amount raised by the Knights of Columbus................	7,757
Amount raised for Salvation Army purposes................	4,500
Amount raised in United Victory "Drive".................	63,730
Grand total raised during war........................$	169,424

First Liberty Loan Bonds (About).......................$	200,000
Second Liberty Loan Bonds.............................	938,760
Third Liberty Loan Bonds.............................	1,042,950
Fourth Liberty Loan Bonds.............................	1,665,100
Fifth or "Victory" Bonds.............................	1,333,200
Total amount sold in county........................	$5,180,010

The county over-subscribed in this "drive" fifty per cent of her quota as first designated and this was accomplished without fuss or excitement. All seemed to realize the emergency was great and buckled on the full armor and went forth to supply the demands of the men at the fighting front.

The total amount subscribed in McHenry County was $63,079.57, according to Treasurer Charles F. Renich, and Chairman Hon. E. D. Shurtleff. At first it seemed that such an amount could not be raised after all that had been subscribed in way of Government War Bonds, but taking the Illinois slogan: "Salute and go to it," all ended well.

Not all of the towns in this county did equally well, although only two out of the seventeen, Coral and Grafton, failed to subscribe the minimum quota assigned to them. Richmond Township led with more than 200 per cent, Hartland, Dorr and Dunham exceeded 150 per cent, while Seneca, Algonquin, Burton, Riley, Cary, Hebron, Chemung, Greenwood, Alden and Nunda exceeded their original quotas, some of these precincts approaching well toward the 150 per cent mark.

By townships the reports showed:

STANDING: DANIEL BURTON, FRANK E. HANAFORD, ANDREW LAS CELLA

	Quota	Subscribed
Hartland	$ 1,200	$ 1,820.75
Seneca	1,000	1,262.00
Algonquin	2,100	2,471.50
Burton	600	698.50
Dorr	8,500	13,555.85
Greenwood	1,000	1,044.25
McHenry	3,700	7,295.95
Coral	2,100	1,697.35
Riley	1,000	1,129.00
Grafton	2,100	1,936.00
Marengo	4,500	6,440.40
Cary	1,500	1,539.00
Chemung	6,200	7,848.50
Dunham	1,000	1,502.50
Hebron	2,100	2,423.75
Richmond	2,100	4,357.00
Alden	1,200	1,204.25
Nunda and Crystal Lake...	4,200	4,948.02
Total	$46,000	$63,079.57

The Woodstock *Sentinel* in speaking of this great "drive" said: "Of interest is the fact that of the $63,000 subscribed, over $42,000 was paid in spot cash. In some towns almost the entire subscription was made in cash, notably Cary, turning in $1,514 in cash, leaving only $25 unpaid, while Burton Township had only $8.00 remaining unpaid. At Algonquin only $225 remained outstanding, and in Coral the chairman turned in all in cash except $133. Huntley turned in all cash but $150. In Dorr, including Woodstock, the amount of cash turned in at first was about one-half of the large sum of $13,555.85, but daily thereafter the outstanding amounts kept coming into the various banks of the city."

Treasurer Renich's report shows that the "Victory Boys and Girls" in McHenry County subscribed $8,305.95—a remarkable contribution from such a source as that.

CASUALTIES

If the heartfelt wish of all the loyal people of the county could materialize, there would be no names written beneath this caption by the most relentless of all historians, Time, but as no really great reform was ever effected without heavy sacrifice, so do the people of McHenry County have to pay their quota for patriotism, and in recording the names of the heroes who lived up to the highest conception of American manhood, in the midst of their tears, they must also rejoice that when the need arose, there was no lack of brave young soldiers to carry the American flag and principles to victory. The GOLD STARS in McHenry County's "service flag" are set in the subjoined Roll of Honor:

ROLL OF HONOR

The subjoined is a list of the honored dead from McHenry County, who made the "supreme sacrifice" in the late World War, while marching and fighting in the trenches, midst shot, shell and deadly gas:

Alexander P. C. Rassmussen, Arthur Dollman, Ernst Kalbow, Walter Lind, Arthur Dunker, Fred Boyle, W. J. Henshaw, Arthur J. Shultz, Horace Bratzman, Herman Steinke, William J. Metzen, Claude Mc-Comb, Geo. F. Raltzlaff, August Klaman, Ray A. Howard, John Janowski, Maurice Blake, Ed Killeen, Paul Gehrke, Carl J. Dittman, Clark Hall, Henry F. Miller, Frank Helwig, A. C. Graupner, Eugene P. Griebel, Ralph P. Wells, Peter Umathum, Carl H. Bartelt, William Ward, William C. Peterson, Victor E. Peterson, Harold Beebe, John Farrell, Richard Japp, Eugene Drill, Frank Wien, Paul C. Hoffman, Henry Stevenson, Edward Tonyan, George Schreiner, Jack Mitchell, Charles Geske, Joseph Meyers, Robert Martin, Ernest W. Blank, Harry G. Fulton, Albert Moritz, Bert Randau, Walter W. Pederson, Harry L. Carlson, David Brown, Chas. Bartumis, Gus Swanson, Burdett A. Briggs, Roy H. Randel, Phil J. Anderson, Charles Knutson.

SOLDIER'S HOME-COMING WEEK

While the Armistice was signed in November, 1918, the McHenry County soldiers did not return to their homes until the first week in June, 1919, and a public "Welcome" or reception was tendered them in Woodstock for the whole county, at first, and later Harvard, Marengo and Algonquin received the men who went from their precincts. The big celebration, however, was naturally the first one, as it was held at the county seat from which the men had enlisted or been called to service. The day, June 10, 1919, will long be a red-letter day in the minds of those residing in McHenry County at that time, whether soldier or civilian. The glad and alas the sad scenes at the home-coming of the men from Camp Grant, at Rockford, from which point the McHenry County men were transported by from fifty to sixty automobiles, just at the close of a hot day. Upon arriving at the city park thousands of "fathers and mothers, lovers and friends" were waiting there to meet them for the first time since going "overseas." An hour was passed in smiles and tears and tears and smiles. Joy reigned supreme about the park that June evening, save for the relatives and friends of the fifty-seven men who in the prime of their young manhood had died in France.

Between 15,000 and 20,000 people gathered in and around the park in Woodstock that perfect day in June to welcome the soldiers home. The city had spent many thousands of dollars during the two weeks preparation made in decorating every business place in the city and hundreds of residences were displaying the colors. A triumphal Arch spanned the street at the north entrance of the park, enroute from the depot, with the words "Welcome Home" in brilliant colors across the face of the archway. At night, it was lighted by electric bulbs, presenting a most beautiful sight.

The soldiers, to the number of about 700, marched in uniforms to band music to various parts of the city where lodges and societies galore were there to welcome them. The soldiers had the keys to Woodstock, as they did later at Harvard and other places in McHenry County. They all acquitted themselves manfully. Each one was provided with a carnation at the Armory in the morning as they marched. The various churches and societies furnished the soldiers with all they could eat and smoke that day and night. A street dance was on during the evening. The brick pavement had been nicely coated with paraffine and hundreds danced in front of the city building till a late hour.

A solemn service was held at the southeast corner of the park where there had been constructed a miniature "Flanders Field," with fifty-seven white crosses in rows and between them were poppies. The number fifty-seven indicated the gold stars on the Roll of Honor which stood near by.

In Flanders fields, the poppies grow
Between the crosses, row on row.
That mark our place; and in the sky
The larks, still bravely singing, fly,
Since heard amid the guns below.

We are the dead. Short days ago
We lived, felt dawn, saw sunset glow,
Loved and were loved; but now we lie
    In Flanders fields.

Take up our quarrel with the foe!
To you, from failing hands, we throw
The torch—Be yours to bear it high!
If ye break faith with us who die
We shall not sleep, though poppies blow
    In Flanders field.

Eloquent remarks were made by both Father Conway of the Catholic church of Woodstock and a returned Y. M. C. A. worker, Rev. Kilbourne. Few if any more impressive scenes were ever noted in any community than those of that Home-Coming Day.

The seventeen remaining members of the Grand Army Post of Woodstock with many Spanish-American soldiers, were present at the reviewing stand. These represented three great conflicts, all wars waged for right and justice, and in defense of the country's honor.

Not only did McHenry County and Woodstock "go over the top" in all of its Liberty and Victory Loan undertakings, but in this Home-Coming affair the subscriptions amounted to about $1,100 more than was expended for giving the returning soldiers a hearty welcome. This additional amount was used to "Welcome" home the remainder of the men later on.

CHAIRMEN OF "HOME-COMING" COMMITTEES

No event in the county ever had the large number of committeemen and all were active factors in bringing about the complete success which crowned this long-to-be-remembered event. In all there were thirty committees and in this connection it is only practical to give the names of their chairmen.

Executive Committee—F. J. Green; Finance Committee, F. A. Walters; Memorial Committee—G. E. Still; Publicity Committee—A. H. Mosher; Pavement Dance Committee—Lester Fish and Howard Conn, supervisors; Decoration Committee—O. G. Mead, to erect Victory Arch—A. M. Clark; Armory Decorations—T. B. Owens; Decorating Residences—D. G. Olmstead; To Welcome Soldiers—George Eckert; Woman's Relief Corps—Mrs. H. L. Eddy; To Welcome Soldiers at Camp Grant—B. C. Young; To Welcome Soldiers in New York City—W. T. Charles; Registration Committee—Henry G. Fisher; Employment Committee—John Whitworth; Reception Committee—Judge Donnelly; Parade Review Committee—F. J. Green; Receiving Visitors —G. W. Lemmers; Inviting Neighboring Cities—J. P. Alt; For Widowed Mothers—A. J. Deitz; Community War Service—Mrs. Mary Shipton; Parade Committee—R. W. Bardwell; To Build Review Stand —G. F. Knaack; First Aid Red Cross—Dr. W. Freeman; Music Committee—W. F. Weldon; Booths Committee—E. F. Meyer; Cafeteria Lunch—E. A. Judd; Ladies' Aid Executive—Mrs. George W. Field; Committee Dinner Arrangements—Mrs. E. C. Thomas; Assistant Women's Committee—J. C. Miller.

These various chairmen had under them 371 persons, all fitting in where they were most efficient in the matter of properly "Welcoming Home" the returned soldiery of McHenry County, June 10, 1919.

WOODSTOCK NATIONAL GUARDS

Woodstock has been the headquarters of a company of National Guards since early in 1880, when so many of the Illinois National Guard companies were organized under the State Military Department. Company G, Third Infantry, was organized at that date. Fifty-three young men were mustered into service in the courthouse, on February 24, 1880, by Lieutenant-Colonel Frank Noble, who had been detailed for that purpose. The company commenced drilling at old Phoenix Hall and used the same for an armory for about one year. March 1, 1888, they moved into the old Universalist Church. They were provided with old muzzle-loading Springfield muskets, caliber fifty, which they used until the summer of 1882, when they were furnished with the new breech-loading Springfield rifles, caliber forty-five, direct from the United States Arsenal at Rock Island, Illinois, at the expense of the state with new accoutrements to correspond. A small supply of metallic cartridges was furnished by the State and kept constantly on hand. Fatigue uniforms were also soon furnished for non-commissioned officers and privates. Commissioned officers furnished their own uniforms. The members of the company were each furnished with a full-dress uniform at their own expense. The citizens of Woodstock presented the company with a fine silk flag in 1882. They attended the encampment at Rockford in 1880; at Aurora in 1882; at Lake

Geneva, Wis., in 1883; at Rockford in 1884, and many later encampments. They were called to do duty at various times and places within Illinois as the years went by, aiding in putting down strikes and riots.

They entered many contests, the first being in a prize drill at the McHenry County Fair in the autumn of 1883, taking third money.

When the Spanish-American war broke out the National Guards were called to arms, and gladly tendered their services, and went wherever ordered, as is shown in the "Military History of the State." They were mustered in May 7, 1898, and mustered out at Joliet, November 3, 1898. From that time on until the late World War this company of Guards kept intact until President Wilson, through Act of Congress declared a state of war existed between this country and Germany, when the full strength of the National Guard system was thrust into that terrible conflict. Other parts of this chapter tell the later story of how well and nobly this company and regiment performed their duty.

It should be stated in passing, that the original guard company here was organized through the efforts of Prof. A. E. Bourne, then principal in the High Schools of Woodstock. He was elected its first captain, served several years and was succeeded by George Eckert, Charles H. Donnelly, and John H. Higgins. The latter resigned, and in 1893, W. C. Eicherberger was elected captain in his place. In 1901, he resigned when George W. Field was made captain of the company. They served in the Spanish-American war under Gen. Fred Grant, in Porto Rico.

For many years a frame armory which stood on the south side of Calhoun street, near Jefferson street was leased by the State for the use of this company, but it was finally burned and for a few years the Guard was without a home, but in about 1913 a brick Armory building was built by the State, in the eastern part of the city, and so planned that additions could easily be made to the original structure which was effected in 1915-16.

GRAND ARMY OF THE REPUBLIC

Not long after the close of the Civil War, Dr. B. F. Stephenson, who had been a surgeon in a volunteer regiment, suggested an organization of Union veterans into a national association for mutual assistance. Through his efforts the first post was established at Decatur, Ill., April 6, 1866, and it was not long before the national organization was completed, Gen. John A. Logan being one of the most enthusiastic advocates of it. The first commander-in-chief was Stephen A. Hurlburt, elected in 1866, and General Logan was elected in 1868. The commander-in-chief for 1921-22 is Lewis S. Pilcher, of Brooklyn, N. Y.

The history of the Grand Army of the Republic in McHenry County is as follows:

Harley Wayne Post, No. 169 at Marengo was organized December 29, 1882, by T. G. Lawler, Department Commander. Its charter members were: I. W. Green, R. Miller, C. L. Strickland, C. A. White, J. Casley, W. H. Sanders, B. Parker, J. B. Babcock, J. Q. Adams, D. A. Stedman, S. Rowland, A. J. Boyington, A. London, W. A. Mallory, C. W. Mallory, Henry Fillmore, John Kennedy, W. C. Sullivan. This post was named in honor of Capt. Harley Wayne, killed at the battle of Shiloh.

At one time the Marengo Post had 150 names enrolled, but it has now decreased to eighteen of those who once were the loyal blue and fought to preserve the Union of States. The first officers of this post were: Ira S. Curtiss, Commander; John Kennedy, Senior Vice Commander; E. S. Parker, Junior Vice Commander; W. H. Sanders, Quartermaster; I. W. Green, Surgeon; I. B. Babcock, Chaplain; D. A. Stedman, Officer of the Day; A. J. Boyington, Officer of the Guard; and G. L. Strickland, Adjutant.

The present officers are: F. S. Loomis, Commander; G. C. Clark, Senior Vice Commander; A. Sehwager, Junior Vice Commander; F. J. Pray, Chaplain; W. C. Sullivan, Adjutant; W. H. Havens, Officer of the Day; John Backes, Officer of the Guard.

The following is a list of the past Commanders and adjutants: Commanders: Ira R. Curtiss, J. B. Babcock, A. J. Boyington, E. R. Morris, J. W. Green, W. C. Sullivan, Joseph Schneider, John Kennedy, W. W. Ocock, F. S. Loomis. The Adjutants have been: C. L. Strickland, A. J. Boyington, W. C. Sullivan, A. L. London, C. G. Teeple, John Kennedy, Ira S. Curtiss.

J. B. Manzer Post No. 215, was organized at Harvard, April 7, 1883, with the following charter members: Joseph La Bree, John Forby, Edwin Rector, J. W. Groesbeck, C. W. Onthank, James White, R. J. Whittleson, R. Wheeler, Samuel Cole, H. W. Grovenstein, Wm. Hollister, J. W. Seaverns, N. B. Burteh, Edward Hancock, Burt Adderman, W. H. Gillis, Thomas Welch, D. E. Pixley, W. T. Hill, George King, Willard J. Scott, H. H. Paynter and H. T. Woodruff. The last named was selected Commander of the original post.

The present membership of this post is twenty-five. A very successful

Woman's Relief Corps of 118 members is a valuable aid to this post.

The present officers of this post include these: S. M. Butts, Commander; E. V. Phelps, Senior Vice-commander; S. Cole, Junior Vice-commander; W. J. Fox, Adjutant; J. L. Anderson, Quartermaster; J. W. Groesbeck, Surgeon; W. Ferrell, Officer of Day; and H. W. Butts, Officer of the Guard.

Woodstock Post No. 108, was organized August 24, 1881, with the following list of members, all being honored and honorably discharged Civil-War veterans: E. E. Richards, A. F. McGee, I. R. Curtiss, Allen Giles, L. H. Jones, W. H. Cowlin, G. S. Southworth, E. W. Blossom, George Eckert, A. W. Anderson, M. L. Joslyn, James Dufield, L. D. Kelly, Asbad Udell, William Avery, J. Q. Adams, F. W. Smith, D. A. Stedman, W. H. Sanders, M. M. Clothier, W. H. Sherman, Joseph Hill, James Nish, W. V. Walker, J. W. Green, Amos Boyington, L. P. Carver, John Kennedy, W. H. Stewart, S. Van Curan, L. H. S. Barrows. The first commander was William Avery; Senior Vice-Commander—L. D. Kelly; E. E. Richards, Adjutant. During the year of organization this post had more than one hundred names enrolled. Now there are but fifteen members.

George Eckert is the present Commander; and A. S. Wright is the present Adjutant.

Nunda Post No. 226, was organized at the old village of Nunda, now Crystal Lake, April 21, 1883, with charter members as follows: John E. Beckley, William H. Huffman, J. J. Adams, L. E. Warner, D. B. Warner, N. M. Paine, William St. Clair, William Shales, M. F. Ellsworth, H. W. Beardsley, I. N. Powell, M. Battershall, Charles Wilson, C. C. Pettibone, J. H. Cox, Frank Grimes, L. McGee, J. M. Mallory, Henry Keys, John H. Paddock, L. Beckley, M. F. Richards, W. P. Morse, William Butler.

The first Commander was W. H. Huffman; first Adjutant, J. M. Mallory. In 1884 this Post had a membership of fifty and at one date, it was still larger. Today there are only eight enrolled members, and J. H. Shuler, Quartermaster, is the only one now residing at Crystal Lake.

WOMAN'S RELIEF CORPS

Harley Wayne Relief Corps No. 52, auxiliary to Grand Army Post No. 169 at Marengo, was organized June 19, 1886, by Julie G. Sine. The subjoined is a list of charter members: Louisa Green, Emily Sted-

Homer. M. Hastings

man, Minnie Dietz, Bertha Robbins, L. R. Tyler, Margaret Galloway, Nancy Scougall, Mary Ward, Jennie Strickland, Mary Henry, Mary Belden, Elmira Griffin, Jennie Chandler, Polly Tyler, Mary Ford, Hattie Southern, Minerva Ryder, Sarah Morris, Lou London, Nancy Betts, Ursula Hewitt, Josephine Curtiss, Hulda Lewis, Maggie Ford, Harriet Hart, Caroline Spragg, L. Colwell, Jane Metcalf, Delia Buck, Emma Miller, Sylvia Lewis, Lenora Nickerson, Lucy Carver, Amy Hendrickson, Hattie Loomis, Harriet Bailey, Jane Swager, Mabel Griffin, Richard Harris, Louisa Randall, Emma Patrick, Hannah Miller, Sadie Dimon, Carrie Broughton, Anna Kennedy, Maria McIntyre.

The first officers were as follows: Louisa Green, President; Minervia Ryder, Senior Vice President; Emily Stedman, Jr. Vice President; Sarah Morris, Secretary; Lucy Carver, Treasurer; Minnie Dietz, Chaplain; Lou London, Conductor; Amy Hendrickson, Assistant Conductor; Bertha Robbins, Guard; Nancy Betts, Assistant Guard. The following have served as presidents of the Corps: Louisa Green, Minervia Ryder, Sarah Morris, Anna Patrick, Mary Belden, Hattie Bailey, Hattie Loomis, Anna Bushaw, Ella Rowland, Lillie Pringle, Ada Wegite, Mary Johnson, Hattie Read, Kate Wilson. The membership is fifty-two. Its officers are: Kate Wilson, President; Martha Rose, Senior Vice President; Jessie Jobe, Junior Vice President; Emma Worf, Secretary; Gertrude Kennedy, Treasurer.

AMERICAN LEGION

The American Legion was organized during a convention at St. Louis, Missouri, May 8-10, 1919, and a regular convention was held at Minneapolis, Minn., November 10-12, 1919, when national officers were elected and the organization completed. All who were in the military, naval or marine service during the World War, between April 6, 1917, and November 11, 1918, are eligible to membership. The Legion was incorporated by an Act of Congress approved September 16, 1919.

The Legion is represented in McHenry County by the following posts:

Peter Umathum Post No. 412, Woodstock, was organized in August, 1919, and has a membership of 207. The commander for 1921 is D. R. Joslyn, Junior, and the other officers are: Warren Fish, vice commander; Glenn Shales, adjutant; Raymond Woods, chaplain; Cy Sanford, sergeant-at-arms; Walter Conway, finance officer; and George More, historian. In March, 1921, this post won the second prize of $90 offered by the Chicago Evening Journal in the membership campaign, and was given a banquet at the Hotel La Salle, Chicago. The money was used in purchasing the post "colors." The post has lost by death Simon Febber and Adelbert Sullivan.

The post at Algonquin was organized July 27, 1920, and has a membership of thirty-five. The officers for 1921 are as follows: John R. Heidinger, commander; Benjamin Pflaum, vice commander; Joseph J. Fitzeek, adjutant; Clarence Ehel, chaplain; Edward Janak, sergeant-at-arms; Arnold Duensing, finance officer; and William J. O'Connor, historian.

The Crystal Lake Post was organized in December, 1919, and has a membership of sixty-six. The present officers are: Harry D. Hull, commander; Walter McCollum, adjutant; Warren Swenson, chaplain; Fred Morgan, sergeant-at-arms; and Elton Huffman, finance officer.

The William J. Metzen Post No. 265, of Harvard, was organized in September, 1919, with a membership of 130. The officers for 1921 are: James J. McCauley, commander; Thomas King, vice commander; George Brown, adjutant; Reverend Newham, chaplain; Lester Peacock, sergeant-at-arms; James Davidson, finance officer. The following members have died: Clev Thompson, Daniel Hayden and Ernest Kelljstrom. This post has held military funerals for the following returned overseas bodies: Edward Kileen, George Ratzloff and Raymond Howard.

The post at Hebron was organized August 1, 1920, and has a membership of thirty-three. The officers for 1921 are: Clarence Judson, commander; Herman Peterson, vice commander; Miles Koblentz, adjutant; Charles Bailey, chaplain; Clarence Grabbert, sergeant-at-arms; and Clyde Arp, finance officer.

The Huntley Post No. 673 was organized in August, 1920, with a membership of thirty-five. The officers for 1921 are as follows: Dr. Oliver I. Statler, commander; William Amos, vice commander; Clyde Clanton, adjutant; Edwin Hener, sergeant-at-arms; and William Bartlett, finance officer.

Paul C. Hoffman Post No. 253, of Richmond, made application for a charter in November, 1919. It has a membership of fifty-three. The officers for 1921 are: Richard G. Richardson, commander; Ernest Snyder, vice commander; Charles Golden, adjutant; Dr. Foster, chaplain; Floyd Perkins, sergeant-at-arms; Hugh Howden, historian; Dr. John Ducey, finance officer.

McHenry Post No. 491, was organized January 22, 1920. It now has a membership of seventy. The officers for 1921 include Alfred H.

Pouse, commander; Charles J. Reihausperger, adjutant; and Gerald J. Casey, finance officer.

Kiswaukee Post No. 192, at Marengo, was organized September 24. 1919. It now has a membership of seventy-nine. The officers for 1921 include Harry C. Patrick, commander; Carlton S. Robb, adjutant; and B. F. Duzenberry, finance officer.

CHAPTER XVII

DAYS OF MOURNING

DEATH OF ABRAHAM LINCOLN—DEATH OF JAMES ABRAM GARFIELD—DEATH OF U. S. GRANT—DEATH OF PRESIDENT WILLIAM MC KINLEY.

Every country has its days of bereavement and deep sorrow over the death of some great ruler, friend or benefactor. In a kingdom, when the king dies, great is the mourning. In a republic, when a president dies, even greater is the sorrow, for being of a democratic government, the feeling is much closer between the head of the government and the common people, who have chosen such person to rule for them.

The United States has been called upon to mourn at the fall of three of their greatest presidents, Lincoln, Garfield and McKinley. On the occasion of each one of these sad blows the loyal men and women of every section of the land have congregated at a set time and place, to publicly show their deep sorrow for their departed dead.

THE DEATH OF ABRAHAM LINCOLN

President Lincoln had just guided the ship of State through an awful civil conflict, when he was suddenly shot down by the hand of an assassin. As most of the able-bodied men from McHenry County were at that time in the Union army, the war having just ended the week in which Mr. Lincoln was killed, there was no large turnout at a set day of mourning. The churches did, however, all have memorial sermons. The editor of the Woodstock Sentinel, Abraham E. Smith, in his issue of April 26, 1865, the week after the assassination, wrote an editorial which has never been heralded abroad like other gems of oratory and eloquence, because of its appearance in so small a town and a paper, but indeed those who have read it, see new beauty in it as the years roll by. It shall, therefore, find a place in the annals of this county.

"Abler pens than ours have written eulogies and touching tributes to the worth of the dead statesman whose loss the nation now deplores. We shall not attempt it. The genial kindness of his nature, the marvelous acuteness of his intellect, his plain, simple, and yet apt manner of addressing himself to the people, his wonderful sagacity and practical common sense, the versatility of his genius—and above all, the never failing amiability of the man; are all written on memory's page, seared in by the fearful death he died, and will never be erased from the hearts of American citizens while liberty is enjoyed.

"Personally, Abraham Lincoln had no enemies. He died through no personal malice. He fell because he represented his country, as no other man ever did. He died a martyr on the altar of liberty—of his country's unity and glory! Let us then do honor to his name. In honoring him, we honor ourselves. In him were the virtues of the American Nation combined. Peace to his ashes! Honor to his memory. With him life's fitful fever is over; and what an eventful life he lived. Thousands upon thousands yet unborn will hail him as their Father and Liberator. Fare-well, noble Lincoln. Good Night to thy form, but Good Morn to thy Fame!"

It should be remembered that this was penned on the spur of the moment, "press-day" in Woodstock fifty-four years ago. And still the name LINCOLN stands out among the untarnished stars of the American Republic.

In common with other parts of the country, houses were draped in appropriate emblems of mourning in Woodstock and other towns of this county. All places surrounding the public square were tastily draped and decorated by tender and skilful hands.

The local paper had a notice inviting all who could to join the committee appointed to attend the great funeral gathering which was held in Chicago, where but little more than five years before, he had been nominated in the "Wigwam" as the standard-bearer of the then new Republican party. Many responded to this call. This was McHenry County's first public mourning day.

DEATH OF JAMES ABRAM GARFIELD

In sixteen years after Lincoln fell, the people of this county wore the emblems of mourning again, this time, for President Garfield, who was elected in the autumn of 1880. In July, 1881, he was shot in the back, while walking arm-in-arm with James G. Blaine, in the Potomac depot at Washington, while waiting for a train. The beloved president lingered on, a great sufferer, until in September of that year, when he passed from earth's shining circle, and this was another stinging blow to the loyal hearts of all American people. President Lincoln had been killed in heat of war days, but President Garfield was cut down in the days of supreme national peace.

Upon the news being flashed that "Garfield was dead," Mayor Joslyn, of Woodstock, made a proclamation which was, in common with all cities and hamlets from ocean to ocean, obeyed to the letter. On the day of the great soldier-statesman's burial at Cleveland, Ohio, memorial services were held in the Woodstock Park at the afternoon hours—two to four. All business houses were closed from noon for the remainder of that day. There had been appropriate staging, platform and seats placed in the center of the park. At the four entrances to the enclosure of the park were seen arches mounted by drapery and a portrait of the dead executive. Long before the hour for the exercises, the park was filled with sorrowing people from town and country, to pay homage to the great departed one. Shortly after two o'clock the Guards appeared at the square, marching to muffled drum and reversed arms, the left arm of each soldier bearing the badge of mourning. The Grand Army of the Republic soon left their hall and when these military organizations passed to the stand, Mayor Joslyn called the meeting to order and quickly introduced Hon. Neill Donnelly as president. The first number on the program was singing of "Nearer, My God, to Thee" rendered by a choir, followed by scripture reading by Rev. J. Adams and prayer by Rev. J. D. Wells. Then came the address by Rev. J. D. McLean, of the Presbyterian Church. Fully 3,000 people were packed in the park grounds that day, and all listened with marked attention. The speaker dwelt on the noble traits of General Garfield's manhood, as soldier, scholar and president; this took him from the humble log cabin to the White House.

Another address was made by Rev. Father Leydon of the Catholic Church, who also paid a glowing tribute to the departed. It is said by those who still survive, that Woodstock had never listened to such periods of true eloquence before.

At Marengo, on Sunday, the churches were befittingly draped and memorial services were had. Rockford furnished their chief speaker. For many days the half-mast flags and drapery were seen fluttering in the breeze along Main street in Marengo. The colors used were black and white.

At Algonquin, on the day and hour which Garfield's body was being lowered into the tomb in Cleveland, services truly befitting were being held. All business was suspended for the day. Services were held in St. John's Episcopal Church at 11 A. M. At 2 P. M. a large congregation assembled in the German Lutheran and also one at the Free Methodist churches. The bells of the church and schools tolled mournfully and slow, striking forty-nine times, representing Garfield's age.

At Richmond, this county, all business was closed for the day. The Garfield Guards from Grand Junction marched through the streets in funeral step.

Thus it will be seen that all McHenry County mourned for him whom they had cause to respect and love.

DEATH OF U. S. GRANT

While not a tragic death, that of the great Civil War commander, and ex-president, U. S. Grant, which took place in July, 1885, caused an almost world-wide sorrow. He died of a cancer in his throat, after being a patient sufferer for many weary months, and it is recorded that no murmur of complaint fell from his lips during all that period.

The Woodstock Sentinel on July 30, that year, devoted six and one-half columns to his obituary notes and a review of his wonderful career. At the memorial services in Woodstock, the order of exercises was about as follows: The line formed at 1:30 p. m. and marched around the public square to the east entrance, the order being, the marshal, Col. William Avery; the McHenry military band; Company "G" of the National Guards, Capt. A. E. Bourne; Woodstock Legion Select Knights, George Eckert, commander; and others including the Grand Army of the Republic, Judge B. N. Smith, commander, followed by citizens. Over 2,000 people attended this memorial for the "Silent Soldier." The services were under the auspices of the Grand Army Post. Mayor Bunker was president of the day. Adjutant Wright read the orders; scriptures were read by Rev. D. S. McEwan of Kansas City; Rev. Hoover offered prayer. The music was in charge of E. E. Richards. Hon. Frank Crosby delivered a beautiful and truly appropriate address and reviewed in detail the deeds of the great hero. Rev. S. C. Hoy pronounced the benediction. The decorations and emblems of military and civic mourning were never more impressive than those furnished at the park on that occasion. Each of the four corners of the park entrances were draped and each had a portrait of the deceased soldier-president, he who succeeded in bringing a great rebellion to its close where many others had failed, and he who was twice elected to the presidential chair of his country. About the portrait thus suspended were the simple words:

"The Nation's Loss." On the reverse of these words were the names of the many battles in which General Grant had fought.

All business of the county seat and other places in McHenry County were closed for that solemn day. Nunda Grand Army Post was up to Woodstock and took part in the exercises. The ladies, unaided by the men, furnished the entire decoration and drapery of the grounds at the park.

The exercises included music by the McHenry band, reading of the orders, music by the band, prayer, music by the choir, the address, music by the choir, music by the band, short address by Rev. Hoover and others. The vice presidents of the day were: T. M. Cook, Seneca Township; Burton Wright, Greenwood; William Walkup, Ridgefield; Wm. G. Conklin, Hartford; H. M. Mead, Hebron; R. Bishop, McHenry.

It should be stated that all preparations had been made to hold these exercises on Saturday but on account of a rain storm on that date it was postponed until Sunday afternoon.

DEATH OF PRESIDENT WILLIAM M'KINLEY

Again the hand of an assassin cut down a dearly-beloved president, causing universal sorrow to prevail throughout the land, when William McKinley was shot by Louis Czolgosz, while attending the Pan-American Exposition at Buffalo, N. Y., September 6, 1909, and from such wounds, died on the 14th of that month and year. He had just commenced his second term as president.

Thirty minutes after the telephone message to Woodstock from Chicago that "McKinley is dead," the Sentinel had out extras, nine by twelve inches, and was scattering them broadcast throughout the city. This was 5:35 P. M. and it was 8 o'clock that night before the Chicago papers reached McHenry County. The following Thursday an immense audience gathered at the city hall at 2 P. M. to pay a fitting homage to the third president killed by an assassin within thirty-six years. The hall was not large enough to hold one-half of the people who wanted entrance. All business was suspended and evidences of great sorrow were seen on every face and in all places. Men of strong wills and sturdy frame would meet and glancing at one another, pass without speaking for fear that they would break down and cry. Every flag in the city was flying at half-mast and the pictures of the dead president were to be seen everywhere, at the city building and at the near-by park. At the corner entrances of the public square might have been seen draped arches

Charles C. Higbee

and portraits of McKinley whom all had honored in life, and truly mourned in death. No Sunday was ever more quiet in Woodstock than this week-day of mourning. The decorations at the hall were never so fine and bore mute testimony to the skillful hands who had tenderly fashioned them. The Oliver Typewriter band headed the procession made up of the local Grand Army Post and Women's Relief Corps, with members of Company "G," Illinois National Guard. They marched once around the park and then entered the city hall auditorium, which was almost filled before this procession reached the building. At the rear of the stage were seated fifty of the older citizens of the county and just in front of them were twenty-four singers and at the front of the platform were the ministers and speakers, members of the McHenry County bar, etc. Mayor E. C. Jewett presided in a most dignified manner. The band played Handel's "Dead March in Saul," and Rev. S. H. Hay of the Presbyterian church read the scripture lesson, after which the quartette sang "Soldier Rest in Peace." At just 2:30 P. M. (the exact hour that the body of the lamented president was being lowered to the tomb at Canton, Ohio), the chairman requested the entire audience to rise and stand five minutes with heads bowed. In silence of death this was carried out and at the close, the band broke the long silence by striking up "Nearer, My God, to Thee," and all who could control their feelings joined in the singing of that hymn now made immortal as Major McKinley's favorite.

The address was made by Attorney Lumley, and after him a personal friend of the deceased president, Rev. Sunderlin of the Methodist Episcopal Church, spoke feelingly.

At the Methodist Episcopal Church in the evening of the same memorial occasion, A. S. Wright spoke of his several meetings with Major McKinley, as governor and president.

More was printed in the secular and religious press concerning Major McKinley than of any other deceased president. After the memorial services were over and the addresses made, all in which the Woodstock and McHenry County people participated, were printed in a neat booklet and sold at five cents each, and 1,000 were thus disposed of, and many are yet in existence throughout the county. The addresses are given in full in this booklet.

CHAPTER XVIII

PERSONAL REMINISCENCES

By E. E. Richards

PREAMBLE

Having assumed the position of historian of my personal reminiscences, I enter upon my task with some misgivings as to whether I shall
make my story of sufficient interest to pay for a perusal thereof. If
there be any criticism that my own personality be unduly in evidence,
I ask you to remember that this is my story of what has happened to
myself and others during the years from 1852 to 1918, and that I must
necessarily be present, either as an auditor, a participant, or a looker
on. It has been the custom of some writers to introduce their subject with
a long erudite disquisition of the philosophical aspects of the subjects,
and with tedious elaboration, allow their pen to run away from their
subject, thereby inducing but little further interest in the story. I shall
take the more modern plan of giving this short prelude and then at once
start on my "Story."

FIRST MEMORIES

My birthplace was Sharon, Massachusetts, the date of my birth being
February 12, 1838. On June 10, 1852, we arrived in the village of
Woodstock, father, mother and six children. Our trip was from Boston
to Buffalo, New York, by rail, thence by steamboat by way of Lake Erie
to Monroe, Michigan, and from that place to Chicago, by the railroad.
We stopped at the City Hotel on Lake street one night. The next day
we extracted ourselves from the mud of Chicago streets and via Chicago
& Galena Railroad arrived at Marengo, and from there by stage to

Woodstock. One of the passengers on the stage was a young lawyer, Theodore D. Murphy, afterwards Judge of the Circuit Court, and also of the Appellate Court. He was very pleasant and was enthusiastic about the country and its possibilities in the future, possibilities that became actualities.

Our home was on the farm of my uncle Joel H. Johnson, opposite the residence of the Rev. R. K. Todd, now the site of the Todd Seminary.

I remember that I thought Mr. Todd was the finest gentleman I had ever seen and that Mrs. Todd was his fitting mate. Mr. and Mrs. Todd were exceedingly kind to us and during the years that soon passed, we became greatly attached to them. Mr. and Mrs. Todd had musical evenings, frequently, at which my brothers and sisters and I assisted. In the year 1864 the students at the seminary, under the direction of Mr. and Mrs. Todd, gave a spectacular representation of the great Rebellion, which was ably gotten up. I had charge of the music. I afterward led the Presbyterian choir for several years. Mrs. Fidelia Belcher Hamilton was organist.

The question of water supply was one of a serious nature, as the wells were, most of them, only from fourteen to twenty feet deep and became dry if the seasons were dry ones. I remember of going to the well in front of the courthouse for a pail of water after nine o'clock in the evening many a time. If the season was a wet one, many cattle got mired and men would have to get them out, or the cattle would have perished as they were helpless.

There were many rattlesnakes (Massaugers) around the sloughs. We killed eleven in one summer during haying time. While threshing on the Olson farm, as now known, some hunters over near the Fair grounds set fire to the slough grass, and we barely saved the grain stacks and threshing machine, by fighting the fire with brush and plowing furrows between the fire and the stacks. The roads were poorly built. In low places logs from the woods were laid and brush cut, and laid on the logs, and then earth laid on the brush. After driving over these roads a few times and after a good hard rain the earth was sifted and washed into and through the brush, leaving but little but logs to ride on. This caused cramps and bruises as well as blasphemy. But to be truthful, some of our roads at the present time are as bad as they were sixty years ago, and the torrents of profanity are let loose with more justice and reason than in the olden time, because machinery and methods are greatly improved and only need to be put to use intelligently to have good roads.

IN EARLY YEARS

The only brick buildings on the public square were the store now owned by Mr. Lyman T. Hoy, and then used by himself as a drug store, and the old Rat Hole building, wood being the usual material for buildings until later years. In after years these old wooden buildings were destroyed by fires and replaced by brick structures. These fires will doubtless be written up in this work, hence are only referred to here. The burning of the old courthouse in the square on the evening of July 4, 1858, was an event of much importance. The bank had purchased the old building and for a long time had neglected to remove it, which had caused some feeling as it was not pleasant to look at. After one attempt to burn the building a young attorney, whose libations pouring at the shrine of Bacchus were frequent and copious, told a friend during the day that, although he had made a previous attempt to burn the old courthouse, there would be no failure this time, as he had hired a first class incendiary from Chicago. He would make no mistake! The bank being suspicious of the attempt to thus summarily remove the old courthouse, a watchman to foil any attempt of the kind was engaged. A friend of the watchman, desiring, no doubt, somewhat to relieve the tedious lonely hours of the night, asked the watchman across the street to quench his thirst, and during the absence of this guardian of the building the first class incendiary got in his work!

An alarm of fire was heard and the watchman, rushing back to assist in quenching the fire, saw what he supposed was a pail of water (it really was a lot of camphene, a most inflammable fluid), caught up the pail and threw the contents upon the flames, which act with the preliminary work of the first class incendiary, made a complete and successful conflagration.

FREE PASTURES

In those early days the pastures were the commons, the forest extending from the village to the prairie. The cows would stray away through the woods and usually come home at night to be milked and fed. Sometimes our bossy would not come up. A hunt would ensue, an extended one sometimes, and end by finding the recreant cow feeding demurely, near a thicket, greeting us with an assumption of surprise at our presence. However, when we began to explore that thicket of bushes, bossy at once became intensely interested and also our close companion in our exploration, which would end in the discovery of a calf (her baby). We would drive the cow and calf home. The mother of the calf did not stray far from home for a number of days, she being duly impressed with the importance of her duties as a good mother.

I remember one thicket where we found a newly-born calf, and where there were several wild plum trees loaded with yellow, dead ripe plums which were delicious indeed.

THE COURTS

My experience in the courts of this county began when I was about nineteen years of age. Many amusing and interesting episodes occurred during the years that followed. I was deputy circuit clerk under my uncle Joel H. Johnson. Then followed many years as deputy county clerk under Elam M. Lamb, William H. Stewart, M. D. Hoy, all grand, good men who honored the position they held. November, 1876, I was elected clerk of the Circuit Court and held that office for three terms, twelve years. I met men of fine abilities. The judges were Isaac G. Wilson, a distinguished, dignified, scholarly man; Allen C. Fuller, Charles Fuller and Robert Wright, of Belvidere; Charles Kellum, of Sycamore; Clark W. Upton, of Waukegan; Theo. D. Murphy, of Woodstock; Charles H. Donnelly, also of Woodstock.

Among the attorneys who practiced in the courts were: Lawrence S. Church, William Kerr, Charles M. Willard, A. B. Coon, Merritt L. Joslyn, James H. Slavin, John B. Lyer, T. B. Workman, Frank Crosby, and many more.

The famous Jim Dacy murder trial was heard. Dacy was convicted and hung in the courtyard.

There were many lively verbal passages between attorneys; sometimes approaching physical encounters. One day there was a tilt between A. B. Coon and Frank Crosby, which showed great quickness of retort. Mr. Crosby had accused Mr. Coon of conduct that was not strictly in accord with the ethics that should obtain within the sacred precincts of the courtroom. Mr. Coon replied: "Well, Mr. Crosby, I never get drunk and roll in the mud and gutter and made a d—— fool of myself as you did." The retort came from Mr. Crosby instantly: "No, Mr. Coon, you did not make a d—— fool of yourself, nature anticipated you."

At one time a decree of divorce had been granted to the wife. As certain real estate was involved, it was deemed necessary to formally default the defendant (the husband). He was hustled into a side room adjoining the courtroom and told to stay there. The sheriff therefore began calling the defendant's name. Richard Roe, Richard Roe, whereupon defendant opened the door and came into the courtroom, saying: "I'm here." The attorneys began shouting to him in whispers: "Go back, go back! Go back, you darned fool, you!" A bailiff caught the defendant by the collar and yanked him back into the room. The judge was busy writing the order for default of the defendant.

COUNTY FAIRS

The county fairs held a half century ago, were primitive, unsatisfactory and discouraging. The cattle, sheep and swine were exhibited along the streets. Store rooms were rented and exhibits were placed there. Later on the grounds now in use were secured.

Col. Horace Capren of Alden exhibited his herd of Devons. No finer animals were ever shown. E. A. Seward of Marengo had a fine herd of Durhams. Elsworth was on hand with Poland-Chinas and David Crinklaw, of Riley, with his Berkshires. The Morgan and Black Hawk horses were the favorite breeds at that time. Charles S. Dole, of Crystal Lake, had a stable of fine-bred horses. "Lakeland," a direct son of "Hamilton 10." "Brigand," the sire of Maud S.; "Patchen" and many others were on exhibition. Dan Duffy, with his grinning Old Barney, was always a favorite in the races. It is a discouraging thing to make a county fair a success financially.

MUSICAL EVENTS

In the years from 1858 and afterwards, musical conventions were held. William B. Bradbury of New York, George F. Root, Everitt L. Baker of Buffalo, Prof. Fargo, Dr. Palmer, Prof. Wheeler of Boston were engaged to instruct and conduct. As many as 200 persons would attend. Our Woodstock people opened their homes to them and after a week's instruction, a grand concert would close the convention. Great enthusiasm prevailed. In 1861, Prof. Wheeler was drilling a large children's chorus. A telegram came, stating that Ft. Sumter had been fired on by rebels. I took the telegram to Prof. Wheeler. He read it and then turned to the children and said: "The rebels have fired on Ft. Sumter, on the flag, our flag, and I want you to sing the 'Star Spangled Banner' as you never sang it before." They sang it at him, they just screamed at him as he stood before them with the tears running down his face. I never knew the National Hymn sung as those children sang it. As it ought to be sung now with every fibre of our being vibrating with love and devotion for our flag, for our country.

These musical conventions were productive of a great interest in music. Among the persons who contributed their time and their talents for the promoting of further interest in music in the early years I would name Harvey Denfee, Mrs. Fidelia B. Hamilton, Mrs. Ball McEwan, Mrs. Olive Wright, Miss Agnes Quinlan, Mrs. Sadie Murphy, Mr. Alvois Dryer, Charles D. Lemmon, A. R. Murphy and others. The cantata of Esther, the Oratoria of Daniel and other cantatas were given. My operetta of "The Reception" was given and was accorded a kind reception by the audience filling the city hall and netting $210 for the public library. The Oliver Typewriter Band was an organization of which we were justly proud.

FISHING

Fishing, like hunting, "is not what it used to be." Duffield's Lake, near Woodstock, Fox Lake, Pistaqua Lake, Crystal Lake, Fox River, all furnished good fishing. Pickerel, pike, black bass, river bass, rock bass, silver bass and muskalonge were abundant in those days. I saw a forty-two-pound muskalonge that was caught in Pistakee Bay thirty years ago. And this reminds me of a letter and a Christmas present received from a cousin of ours, a conductor on the Northern Pacific Railroad, residing at St. Paul, Minn., a splendid good fellow, albeit he is given to the perpetrating of practical jokes upon his friends. Last Christmas he sent me a Christmas present. It was in a red box, marked "Fishing Twine," and a two-pound fish would break that twine the first lunge after being hooked. It was an insinuation that that fishing twine was good enough for any fish I would catch down here. To show proper resentment, I wrote him a letter, as follows:

"Dear Dock—
I give you my thanks for the fishing twine
You send to me for the fishing line
You use for the minnows and such up there,
Which, with pride in your skill, you safely snare.

But say, Dock, up in Pistaqua Bay,
When the shout goes up: "Give the right away!"
When the boat starts with a surge and a plunge,
You know you have hooked a Muskalonge—
He is at least a forty-pounder;
You've a fight on hand for an hour or more,
And to land this whale, you steer for the shore.
When the beast you've landed the fight is o'er,
You've had fight enough—don't want any more.

But say, Dock, when you're making such a race,
With a forty-pound muskie to make the pace;
When through the water, with a rush and a roar,
The boat sends waves rushing from shore to shore,
And everything's going nice and fine,
Say, Dock: What would happen to that fishing twine!
                    Yours thankfully and sincerely,
Dec. 27, 1916.   E. E. RICHARDS.

Among my earliest recollections was a fishing party consisting of nine persons, among whom were Charles Crawford, James Tappan, John M. Harper, myself and a few others whose names I have forgotten. The place was Fox River, near Burton's Bridge. We had a seine sixteen rods long. My share was a two-bushel grain sack full. The number of fishes taken was great. It is a crime to draw a seine now, and should have been then or at any time.

Spearing fish in Fox River was an exciting sport. With a torch attached to the bow of the boat, the spearman with his spear poised, awaited the swiftly darting red horse and other fish. When the fish was near enough a sudden lunge impaled the fish and it was lifted struggling into the boat. Red horse usually weighed from six to twelve pounds.

Trolling with a spoon-hook was one way to capture fish and many were taken in that manner. The stocking the waters of the State with German carp was a mistake. They destroy the breeding places of the game fish and are a nuisance.

HUNTING

The game found in the years from 1852 to 1870 was abundant as compared with the present time. Jack snipe, sandpiper, yellow legs, plover,

Riley Holmes

Dora Holmes.

woodcock, quail, prairie chickens in clouds, rabbits, squirrels, raccoons, woodchucks, gophers, to say nothing of the tens of thousands of ducks, wild geese, wild pigeons, etc. Hunters lived on the fat of the land. The slaughter of wild pigeons was as bad as seining fish, and consequently these pigeons are extinct. I will relate one instance to show the possibilities in hunting in the early days. An uncle of mine, living near Boston, paid us a visit. He had never been west of New York City. So one morning we called the liver-colored pointer dog and said to him: "we propose to hunt prairie chickens." The dog manifested his delight by rolling over and over. We hunted over the farms of the Hartlets and others of Greenwood Township for about three hours and bagged eleven prairie chickens, which gave my uncle great pleasure, not only the shooting, but the wonderful intelligence of the dog. The broiled prairie chicken for breakfast next morning furnished a fitting climax to the hunting trip. The spring and fall gave the hunters fine sport in hunting ducks and geese. Burney Sherman was our guide and advisor in the hunting field in the early days, and is still with us hale and hearty.

ORIGINAL CHARACTERS

In every small town and village there are persons, men and women, who have peculiar characteristics and are denominated "characters." One man in Woodstock whose name was John Metcalf was supposed to be possessed of Indian lore, and who was perfectly willing to be considered such. He had the shuffle or walk peculiar to the Indian (assumed I think). He claimed to be able to locate bee trees, and to be familiar with the habits of the birds of the woods and fields, the wolves, the foxes, wildcats and the fishes whose habitat was the river and lake. He could and did make excellent fish lines of horse hair, and of course was by the youngsters considered a wonderful man.

Col. James M. Strode, a tall Kentuckian, who had seen service in the Black Hawk war, and was for one term Judge of this county, was a man of some peculiar characteristics. After the old courthouse was burned, courts were held in the halls of the brick blocks on the public square. One morning soon after opening court, Judge Strode, who doubtless felt the need of a stimulant to fit him for the arduous duties of the day, said to Mr. M. L. Joslyn, then a young lawyer, "Mr. Joslyn I wish to step down stairs for a few moments, will you preside in my absence until I return?" Thereupon Judge Strode retired and Mr. Joslyn assumed the position of County Judge pro tem. for a span of about two minutes, when he said, "Mr. Sheriff adjourn this court until nine o'clock tomorrow morning." Whereupon the sheriff: "Hear ye, hear ye, hear ye, this honorable court is now adjourned until tomorrow morning." The judge pro tem. then confirmed the proclamation of the sheriff. Judge Joslyn put on his hat, and proceeded down stairs from the court room, at the head of a hilarious crowd. Meeting Judge Strode at the foot of the stairs descending the stairs, he said, "Mr. Joslyn, what does this mean? I left you to preside during my absence." Joslyn replied—"You did Judge Strode and I adjourned court until tomorrow morning at nine o'clock." Of course Judge Strode was furious. His wrath was appeased upon an invitation to come and have "something" and he came! Judge Strode was an orator and indeed eloquent and pleasing. He repeated himself in his perorations, and frequently concluded his remarks thus: "But ladies and gentlemen I will not elaborate further. The few remarks I have made have been entirely without premeditation, and thanking you for your kind attention I will conclude."

Capt. Charles G. Tryon was the owner of a large farm in the south-west corner of Richland Township. The Tryon home was a hospitable one and a social center. The captain relates an incident showing the lawless condition of the country at that time (about 1840). One day as the family and some neighbors were in the front yard, Henry M. Wait the sheriff of McHenry County, rode in on horseback. A horse saddled was standing in the yard. "One of you men get onto that horse and follow me," was the sheriff's order, which was obeyed and they rode out to the highway, where a short distance ahead was a man on horseback riding towards the Wisconsin line. They galloped up to the man and Mr. Wait, the sheriff caught him by the collar, turning him around and headed for Woodstock. This man was a horse thief, caught with the goods!

Captain Tryon had one old Irishman working for him named Pat Dooley. One day in returning from the village of Richmond five or six miles distant, he was met by Pat who said: "Mr. Tryon there were siveral gintlemin from Woodstock here to see you." "Oh, probably a lot of politicians," said the captain. "No sir, they were not," said Pat, "they were perfect gintlemin."

In the year 1852, Mr. George Gage of West McHenry was a candidate for state senator and was duly elected to that honorable position. During his canvass, in company with Hank McLean, he held a meeting at the village of Alden. At the conclusion of their speeches they were invited to spend the night with a wealthy farmer, Mr. Asahel Disbrow, which invitation was accepted. The wife of the farmer provided a good luncheon. An hour was engaged in pleasant conversation. Their host then said: "Gentlemen, we usually retire at this hour, after having prayers and reading a portion of the scriptures. You may retire now if you wish to, or we would be happy to have you join us in our devotions." An invitation which they were glad to accept. There was a son in the family who was not quite right mentally. However he certainly had a brain of some use as will presently be observed. The good farmer knelt down in prayer and among his requests prayed the Lord to remember the strangers who sojourned within their gates, temporarily for a season, and especially him who would soon represent us in the Legislature and make laws for our government. "And O Lord, we pray that thou will give him wisdom, make him honest, Amen." "Dad, that's what he needs, make him honest, make him honest," shouted the young man who was supposed to be mentally deficient.

Dan Sweeney was a good hearted Irishman, who never in his life harmed anyone. He unfortunately was addicted and wedded to the use of the "ardent," and didn't believe in divorces. He evidently adhered to the advice given by Timothy (I-5-23) "Drink no longer water, but use a little wine for thy stomach's sake and thine often infirmities." Dan was taking care of an old hermit who lived in a little hut in Hartland and was very ill. Doctor Windmuller was sent for. Answering the call he went to the hut and going in saw at once that the man was dying. He sat down and in a few minutes the old hermit died. At that moment a woman opened the door, looked in and said, "Dan Sweeney, how's the mons?" "Well, Madame by the grace of God and the help of Doctor Windmuller, he's dead," was Dan's reply.

MUSICAL REMINISCENCES OF HALF A CENTURY

No better index of the musical talent that has been displayed in McHenry County can be given here than to insert portions of a lengthy, and highly interesting "paper" read before the Woman's Club in Woodstock, in the winter of 1918-19, the same being by pioneer E. E. Richards, the gifted composer, director and tenor singer, who has been at the head of music as leader since the days of the Civil War:

"Mrs. Kathryn M. Fields, Chairman of Committee of Music and Art of the Woodstock Woman's Club—

"My Dear Mrs. Fields: I must thank you for the compliment paid me in this assignment. It is a task worthy of one more competent than myself. Therefore I have called to my aid some musical friends to wit: Miss Agnes Quinlan, Mrs. Olive Wright, Mrs. Jessie Charles, Mrs. Mary Buck, Mrs. Fidelia B. Hamilton would, I know, have joined me as a collaborator in this work had her bodily health permitted.

"If this write-up reads like an autobiography and if the personal pronoun, I, obtrudes itself too persistently, please remember that I am writing of what I have seen and what I have heard and many times have had a part in the performances of the years long ago.

"In this history, we begin at the years 1853-4-5, when the only Protestant church here was a small wood building where Dacy's lumber yard now is. The Presbyterian Church, and I remember the Catholic Church nearly on the site of the present splendid edifice now owned by that society. Other societies held their services in halls.

"In 1852-3-4-5 musical instruments were not numerous. Churches did not have organs. I remember that Fidelia Belcher (now Hamilton) had a melodion that was played in the lap of the performer. The Baptist Church at a later date secured a bass viol, presented to them by the Baptist Church of Sharon, Massachusetts, where my father played it.

"When I was fifteen or sixteen years old, I began playing the violin in the choir of the Baptist Church. One old lady, a member, objected, saying, if she saw a fiddle in church, she didn't know but she would want to dance. My mother, also a member of the Baptist Church, and a worthy one, said to this disciple of terpsichore, that if her thoughts were on sacred things, she would not be thinking of dancing.

"It was not many years before the church organ was introduced, then the pipe organs.

"Professor Tower of Greenwood was the singing teacher, and taught us rurals to sing do, re, me, fa, sol, etc. and then hymns and anthems and choruses. A revival of old fashioned singing schools would be of value to many who now become members of church choirs, knowing little or nothing of pitch, rhythm, the value of notes, whole, half, quarter, etc., but gifted by dynamics especially in the fortissimos, and who demoralize choirs, and suggest bad language to the leader of the choir.

"Mrs. Martha Clover Todd, wife of Rev. Richard K. Todd, was a gifted woman and did much for the advancement of music in those early days. Dr. C. B. Durfee and Harvey Durfee were prominent in musical affairs. Harvey Durfee was a gifted musician and had a voice of great sweetness and power. He did much for church music. Mrs. Fidelia B. Hamilton and the writer of this paper were in charge of the Presbyterian choir at this period, and labored early and late in the attempt to furnish acceptable music, sometimes with very poor material, but usually with satisfactory results.

"In those days of fifty and sixty years ago, the choir of the Catholic Church was composed of singers, most of whom have since joined the heavenly choir above. Among those singers were Mary Quinlan, now deceased, Mrs. Elizabeth Murphy, and a tenor, a brother of Mrs. Quinlan. The daughters of these noble women have since that time taken the places of their mothers in the musical services of the church and it has been wonderfully blessed by the talents and ability of their daughters, given willingly and with sincerity and fidelity.

"Miss Agnes Quinlan for many years had charge of the music of her church and was an able and faithful director of the musical services. Miss Eveline Murphy, a daughter of Mrs. Elizabeth Murphy, was a lovely young woman. Her musical education was thorough. Her compositions for the piano were of great merit and were portrayals of the fineness and loveliness of her character.

"It was the custom in the years prior to the Civil War to hold musical conventions, singers coming to Woodstock from all parts of the county, sometimes to the number of 200 and hold their conventions for a whole week, the citizens of Woodstock taking the singers into their homes willingly.

"Eminent musicians were engaged to conduct the meetings. Such men as William B. Bradbury, George F. Root, Everett L. Baker, Mr. Wheeler of Boston, Dr. Fargo and Dr. Palmer came and under the direction and instruction we sang the musical compositions of Mozart, Beethoven, Franz Abt. Also those of William Bradbury, George F. Root, Lowell Mason and many others, thereby becoming familiar with better music than we had known and being greatly benefitted thereby.

"The cantata of Esther, composed by Mr. Bradbury was sung under his direction and instruction, my sister Mrs. Harper, taking the part of Esther. George F. Root was with us at Marengo, and a most interesting meeting was held. At Marengo a quartette composed of Mrs. Fidelia B. Hamilton, Mrs. Lorietta Harper (my sister), John Harper, her husband, and myself sang for George F. Root, he playing our accompaniments. In the midst of one of our pieces Mr. Root stopped playing, stood up and said: 'Young ladies and gentlemen you sing splendidly.' Of course we were proud of such a compliment from such a man.

"Professor Fargo and Dr. H. L. Palmer were here, also Professor Wheeler of Boston. Everett L. Baker of Buffalo, a fine pianist and singer was also here. Professor Tower of Greenwood was here and acted as master of ceremonies. As was his usual custom he called on some of the lawyers to make remarks, knowing that they would say something complimentary about our singing. Among those called was Rev. Adoni som Joslyn, brother of M. L. Joslyn, who referred to the chorus we sang. 'Hail, Hail, This Happy Day,' and said that he didn't quite understand the allusion to happy and sappy days. Mr. Baker was always ready at repartee, quickly replied that the reverend gentleman must admit there was some sap and some snap in the singing of the chorus, that no one would go to sleep while the chorus was sung, and that he was very well satisfied with the singing.

"The cantata of Queen Esther was given here several times, including one when A. R. Murphy acted as king, Mrs. Belle McEwen as Queen Esther, Mrs. Chollar as Zeresh, James R. Reynolds as Haman, E. E. Richards as Mordecai the Jew, and with other officers personated and with a fine chorus we gave three representations of the cantata, which netted us $400. After paying our expenses, however, we had the princely sum of $75 left. We rented costumes in Chicago which were valued at $700.

"The Oratorio of Belshazzar's Feast was sung at Greenwood, under the direction of Professor Tower. Mrs. Mary Buck and Mrs. George Hunt took solo parts.

"The brothers Frank and Jule Lumbard were heard in concerts here. The celebrated Baker family, with George Baker as lion bass, often gave concerts in Woodstock, and these were great musical events."

Among the musicians of this place Mr. Richards mentioned in detail, in his paper above quoted from, the following:

"Mrs. Bell McEwen and her daughter Mrs. Winnie Curtis; Mrs. Olive Wright, for years organizer in the Congregational Church; Mrs. Fidelia B. Hamilton, organist in the Presbyterian Church for many years; Mrs. Sadie Murphy, pianist and organist; Mrs. Ethel Greenleaf, pianist has studied under eminent instructors; Mrs. Florence Sherwood once prominent here was a fine pianist and harpist. Alois Dryer, leader of the choir at the Presbyterian Church many years, had a beautiful tenor voice. Charles W. Lammers, basso, was always public spirited and ready to do his part in music. Walter T. Wheeler and his wife Fanny, have at all times contributed of their talent. Mrs. Bessie Allen and Mrs. Jessie Charles, and Anderson Murphy have all been faithful workers in the interest of good music. A. Dwight Hoy is a fine pianist as well as organist. Mrs. Rollo Andrews Southworth has on more than one occasion delighted Woodstock audiences."

On April 25, 1895, the Operetta, "The Reception," the libretto and music being composed by E. E. Richards of Woodstock, was given before a large audience in the opera house, under direction of the composer. This was a musical success with all home talent and was greatly appreciated.

The Oliver Typewriter band organized by E. E. Richards, we believe, has always been one of musical features of Woodstock. Mr. Richards retired from active part in musicals several years ago hence he leaves the history of music in this county at the point where he quit, but certain it is, he has had wonderful experiences in McHenry County along the line of voice culture, and instrumental music, both as composer and performer. But few communicants can point to so great a number of excellent musicians, some of whom are still living while many of the earlier ones have gone beyond.

CHAPTER XIX

FRATERNAL SOCIETIES AND ORGANIZATIONS

FREEMASONRY—ORDER OF THE EASTERN STAR—INDEPENDENT ORDER OF ODD FELLOWS—DAUGHTERS OF REBEKAH—KNIGHTS OF PYTHIAS—MODERN WOODMEN OF AMERICA—ROYAL NEIGHBORS OF AMERICA—MYSTIC WORKERS OF THE WORLD—KNIGHTS OF COLUMBUS—BENEVOLENT AND PROTECTIVE ORDER OF ELKS.

TEMPERANCE UNION

During the early days of this county's history, only two fraternities flourished, and they have come down to us today, the Masons and the Odd Fellows. Several others came into existence but were in existence for only a brief period and were not worthy of a permanent place in the community. New secret and semi-secret societies have been organized, generally along the lines of temperance workers or mutual beneficiary societies or lodges. These have found many supporters and are doing excellent work today.

FREEMASONRY

Saint Mark's Lodge at Woodstock was organized under dispensation September 20, 1847, by John F. Gray, Worshipful Master; with Luke Coon senior warden; Calvin Serl, junior warden, as appointed by the Grand Master. This lodge was instituted under charter by R. W. Carding Jackson, D.D. G.M., November 23, 1848. The charter members were as follows: John F. Gray, A. Reynolds, Jonathan Kimball, Benjamin B. Brown, Sidney Condit, D. W. P. Tower, Joseph F. Blevin, Derrick C. Bush, Patrick T. McMahon, Enos W. Smith, Edward I. Peckham, Andrew J. Haywood, Henry M. Wait, E. I. Smith, Alexander H. Nixon, Elias E. Wightman, Alex S. Lansing, C. Eggleston, Z. W. Burnham, James R. Mock, Levi Sherwood, James McCanna, Thomas M. White, Parker H. Pierson, Calvin Searl, Luke Coon, J. Bliss, Henry Petrie, and Geo. W. Dana. The first officers were: John F. Gray, worshipful master;

Luke Coon, senior warden; Calvin Serl, junior warden; Elzaphan I. Smith, treasurer; D. C. Bush, secretary. The present officers are: Edwin F. Meyer, worshipful master; Elmer E. Carlson, senior warden; Henry F. Bennewies, junior warden; Edward A. Rogers, treasurer; and Walter T. Wheeler, secretary. The membership of this lodge is 110.

Among the past masters of this lodge may be mentioned the following: John F. Gray, 1848; Derrick C. Bush, 1849-51; Enos W. Smith, 1852; Z. W. Burnham, 1853; H. T. Rice, 1854-55-57; C. M. Willard, 1856; H. M. Wait, 1858-62; Leander Church, 1859-60-63-64-71-72-73; John S. Pierce, 1861; W. N. Willis, 1865; B. F. Church, 1866-67-69-74; E. E. Thomas, 1868-75-76; E. E. Richards, 1870; George L. Sherwood, 1877-78-79; Alex L. Salisbury, 1880-81; Asa W. Smith, 1882-88-89; C. N. Kendall, 1883-84; W. E. Hughes, 1885-86; E. C. Jewett, 1887-90; L. T. Hoy, 1891-92-93; L. C. Waters, 1894; J. S. Andrews, 1895; D. T. Smiley, 1896; George B. Richards, 1897-98-99; F. W. Buell, 1900; H. J. Dygert, 1901-02-03-04; Theo. Hamer, 1905-06; C. F. Renich, 1907; E. J. Heimerdinger, 1908-09; L. W. Richards, 1910-11; J. R. Kingsley, 1912-13; H. R. Buckley, 1914-15; C. H. Buckley, 1916; W. S. Blanchard, 1917; F. D. Wynkoop, 1918.

WOODSTOCK CHAPTER No. 36 was chartered October 6, 1856, with charter members as follows: John D. Pence, Ephraim I. Smith, Benjamin Carter, G. W. Pooler, L. S. Church, R. G. Schryver, E. W. Smith, and G. A. Austin. The first officers were: John D. Pence, high priest; Ephraim I. Smith, king; Benjamin Carter, scribe; G. W. Pooler, L. S.

The present officers are: Guy E. Still, high priest; Elmer E. Carlson, king; Byron D. Chesbro, scribe; Emilus C. Jewett, treasurer, and Walter T. Wheeler, secretary.

CAVALRY COMMANDERY No. 25 was organized October 27, 1867, and adopted in November. The charter members were: Enos Smith, John J. Murphy, Holbert Nickerson, John S. Wheat, Benj. F. Church, Edwin E. Thomas, James Northrup, J. S. Miller, Alex. L. Salisbury, Leander Church. The present membership is 189, and its officers are: Chester I. Nelson, commander; Henry T. Bennewies, generalissimo; William Hyde West, captain general; Edward Albert Rogers, senior warden; B. D. Chesbro, junior warden; James S. Andrews, prelate; Erastus E. Richards, treasurer; Guy E. Still, recorder.

The past commanders have been as follows: Sir Knights, Erastus Emery Richards, Luman Thomas Hoy, Emilus Clark Jewett, Ed. Vernon

Anderson, David Templeton Smiley, Hiram Judson Dygert, James Stephenson Andrews, Fred Burt Bennett, George Albert Cutteridge, Augustus Wilbur Wagner, G. William Lenners, Hugh Heaston Megran, James Hecht.

HARVARD LODGE No. 309 was allowed to work under dispensation from March 15, 1859 to October 5, 1859, when it was granted a charter. The following were the charter members: Henry T. Rice, Elbridge G. Ayer, Alonzo E. Axtell, Benj. Lowell Thaddeus B. Wakeman, Henry B. Minier, Hiram Jackson, Enos Kellogg, Lyman Backus and a few others. The first officers were master, Henry T. Rice; senior warden, Elbridge G. Ayer, junior warden, Alonzo E. Axtell. The present membership of this lodge is 277. Its present officers include W. H. Coburn, worshipful master; Ray E. Lush, senior warden, Raymond G. Orcutt junior warden; Thomas P. Marshall, treasurer; Hugh H. Megran, secretary; John C. Diener, chaplain George B. Lake senior deacon; Frederick L. Fisher, junior deacon.; Albert Whaples, senior steward; Edward D. Fuller, junior steward, James D. Clark, marshal; John P. Lang, tyler.

The following is a list of all presiding officers—worshipful masters: Henry T Rice, Thaddeus B. Wakeman, Abraham Carmack, James M. Nichols, Alonzo E. Axtell, Horatio B. Coe, J. B. Rosenkrantz, Herbert S. Williams, Lot P. Smith, Remus Coventry, Albert W. Young, Wallace C. Wellington, Hugh H. Megran, Silas H. Callender, Herbert D. Crumb, David Davidson, Austin L. Darling, John H. Crawford, John C. Diener, Ploney E. Whittleton, Judson E. Hancock, Frank E. Beck, William R. Ferrier, William A. Mueller, John C. Harris.

The Masonic Order at Harvard recently erected a Masonic Temple costing about $50,000.

HARVARD CHAPTER No. 91 was organized at Harvard October 5, 1866. The first officers were as follows: J. G. Callender, high priest; H. B. Minier, king; Holland Norton scribe. During all these years since the close of the Civil War, this degree of Masonry has flourished at Harvard and is today in an excellent condition. Many of the Masons at Harvard and immediate vicinity hold membership in the Commandery at Woodstock.

The present membership is 230 and the officials are: R. E. Lush, high priest; W. H. Coburn, king; G. B. Lake, scribe; G. A. Burney, captain of the host; H W. Lanning, principal sojourner; H. E. Olson, royal arch captain; S. M. Kirshner, master of the third vail; R. G.

Orcutt, master of the second vail; W. R. Diener, master of the first vail; W. H. Ward, sentinel; J. H. Diener, chaplain; J. C. Diener, secretary; C. F. Barker, steward.

HEBRON LODGE No. 604 was organized October 6, 1868, by Jerome R. Gorian and had the following as its charter members: James P. Eranbrack, M. S. Goodsell, P. Eranbrack, C. Branson, Crandall F. Thayer, William T. Eranbrack, David Rowe, Henry Rowe, D. A. Clary, W. H. Groesbeck, C. H. Prouth, G. W. DeGraw, R. Regan and George Colborn.

The present membership of the lodge is 110. Its present officers are: G. M. Housholder, worshipful master; M. B. Spooner, senior warden; James Anderson, junior warden; J. W. Smith, treasurer; W. M. Millar, secretary; Chet Button, senior deacon; H. P. Padske, junior deacon; John Sumner, tyler. The order leases its hall.

MARENGO LODGE No. 138 was organized at the village of Marengo October 5, 1853, by John W. Green, Clinton D. Connor and Amos B. Coon. There is now a total membership of 135. Among the present officers are: J. C. Tanner, worshipful master; E. C. Robb, treasurer; C. H. Woleben, secretary.

RICHMOND LODGE No. 143 was organized by the Grand Lodge of Illinois October 2, 1854, and was the second Masonic lodge instituted within this county. The records from 1854 to 1862 were destroyed by fire, and all that is known locally of this lodge is that among the first officers and charter members were the following: Charles G. Cotting, Robert F. Bennett, George M. Leach and a few others. The lodge now has a membership of eighty. The Order leases its hall. The past presiding officers were: Masters Charles G. Cotting, 1854-56; R. F. Bennett, 1857 and 1873; Alonzo Ransom, 1858-1870; George P. Wadell, 1871-72; and 1877 to 1880; William Smaites, 1874; G. B. Carpenter, 1875-76 and in 1883; Josiah R. Hyde, 1881-82; James V. Aldrich, 1884-86; and in 1888, 1902, 1904; Henry J. Christian, 1887; William McGaw, 1889-91; G. W. Eldridge, 1892-96; R. W. Overton, 1897-98; J. T. Bower, 1899-90; also in 1903 and 1906 to 1908; F. E. Holmes, 1901; G. E. Miller, 1905; A. M. Gibbs, 1909-12; F. W. Sanford, 1913-14; Fred Arp, 1915-16; J. B. Richardson, 1917-18; L. E. Sweet, 1919. The secretaries have been: A. F. Bennett, 1854-62; Charles G. Cotting 1863-70; and 1872 to 1883; J. G. Darling, 1871; A. R. Alexander, 1884-85; and in 1892; L. B. Rice, 1889; J. T. Bower, 1890-91; also 1896 and 1910 to 1919; F. E. Holmes,

1893 to 1895; P. K Wright, 1899-1901; G. E. Miller, 1902-3-9; S. A. Ward, 1904 to 1908.

The present membership is eighty-nine, and the officers are: W. G. Sandgren, worshipful master; R. G. Richardson, senior warden; F. G. Buchert, junior warden; W. P. Stevens, treasurer; J. T. Bower, secretary; Fred Ark, senior deacon; W. A. Austin, junior deacon; William Elfers, tyler.

ALGONQUIN LODGE No. 256 was organized and a charter granted in October, 1858. The first officers were: Samuel A. French, worshipful master; William Henry, senior warden; Thomas Plumleigh, junior warden; A. S. Thomas, treasurer; S. D. Pease, secretary; James Philip, senior deacon; J. J. Sears, junior deacon; R. R. Sherwood, tyler. This lodge has a membership of seventy-three. Among the present officers are: Peter Serres, worshipful master; Z. A. Susted, senior warden; E. W. Pedersen, junior warden; George E. Bailey, secretary.

McHENRY LODGE No. 158 was organized in 1854, with officers as follows: Z. W. Burnham, worshipful master; J. R. Mack, senior warden; H. N. Owen, junior warden; George Gage, treasurer; Horace Burton, secretary; A. H. Nixon, senior deacon; G. W. Burnham, junior deacon; Abner Mack, tyler. With the passing years this lodge has been active in the work of Masonry and now enjoys a fair membership.

FULL MOON LODGE No. 341 was organized in the fall of 1858, with charter members as follows: A. J. Rodman, Asa Northway, William S. Rabb, Charles Jones, James Ferguson, John Wales, William Renwick, John Cole, S. C. Rowell, William Tyson, Homer Whitney and William Wright. The first worshipful master was William Wright.

The present membership of Full Moon Lodge is ninety-eight, and its officers are as follows: E. H. Calhoun, worshipful master; R. S. Meysenburg, senior warden; Rosco Baxter, junior warden; J. W. Newland, treasurer; G. H. Larsen, secretary; Fred Spatz, senior deacon; Clinton Cape, junior deacon; L. Foster, tyler.

ORION LODGE No. 358, at Union, was organized by a charter granted October 1, 1861, with a membership as follows: Samuel A. Randall, William M. Jackson, W. Tompkins, P. M. Frisbie, H. W. Belden, N. C. Gardner, Harley Wayne, Cyrus Ladd, John Eddy, Philip B. Smith, George Gorlis, E. W. Fillmore.

The officers of Orion Lodge are as follows: W. P. Groth, worshipful master; W. D. Force, senior warden; E. Bush, junior warden; W. C. Nulle, senior deacon; W. H. Johansen, junior deacon; Glen Noble, senior steward; Henry Poppe, junior steward; Charles Ackman, treasurer; Eugene Shaw, secretary; Frank Ballard, chaplain; G. W. Shaw, tyler.

EASTERN STAR

RICHMOND CHAPTER No. 267 was instituted March 26, 1894, by Mrs. Lydia Eldredge, and was composed of the following charter members: Mrs. E. J. Rose, Rev. E. J. Rose, Mrs. Mary E. Rehorst, Mr. H. E. Boutelle, Mrs. Kate Boutelle, Mrs. L. B. Rice, Mrs. Fannie Overton, Mr. Richard Overton, Mrs. Sylvia Vogel, Mrs. Mary Ransom, Mrs. F. E. Holmes, Mrs. J. V. Aldrich, Mrs. Susan McConnell, Mrs. Bertha Mathers, Mrs. P. K. Allen, Miss Hannah Cotting, Mrs. M. C. Haught, G. W. Eldredge, Robert Hunter, Albert Wright, L. B. Rice, F. E. Holmes and P. K. Allen.

The present officers are: Mrs. May Parsons, worthy matron; William Westmont, worthy patron; Mrs. Ivy Marzahl, secretary. The lodge now has a membership of 145.

HAVEN CHAPTER No. 727, at Marengo, was organized January 29, 1913, by Cassie Gregory Orr, worthy grand matron; Samuel W. Fitch, worthy grand patron; Vivian Scott, grand secretary; and other Grand Lodge officers. The charter members were as follows: Harriet Barber Keeling, Lester Barber, Mrs. Mary Barber, Mrs. Nora Bright, Miss Gertrude Smith, Mrs. Minnie Hartman, Mrs. Anna Fry, Mrs. Emma Hoof, Mrs. Leora Dunbar, John B. Hoof, Miss Emma Lanning, Mrs. Nellie Loomis, Glenne Haugens, Mrs. Blanche Scofield, Charles Scofield, William C. Woodard, Mrs. Mary Woodard, Clarence J. Coarson and Harry H. Dunbar.

The first officers were: Harriet E. Barber, worthy matron; William C. Woodard, worthy patron; Anna D. Fry, associate matron; Nora Bright, secretary; Clarence Coarson, treasurer; Mary ——, conductress; Nellie Tanner, assistant conductress. The present officers are: Mrs. Mabel Johnson, worthy matron; William C. Woodard, worthy patron; Mrs. Florence Miller, associate matron; Mrs. Minnie Heath, secretary; Mrs. Maude Olesen, treasurer; Mrs. Vina Poyer, conductress; Mrs. Ella Mead, assistant conductress. The chapter has a membership of 126.

ALGONQUIN CHAPTER No. 752 was organized at the village of Algonquin, April 6, 1914, by Florence Lowell, worthy matron; Fred Lowell, worthy patron; Anna Van Dyne, associate matron; Charles Van Dyne, secretary; Louis Lehky, treasurer; Amelia Lehky, conductress; Nettie Van Dyne, assistant conductress. This chapter now has a membership of sixty-eight. Its past presiding officers have been as follows: Anna Van Dyne, worthy matron, Charles Van Dyne, worthy patron, in 1915; Amelia Lehky, worthy matron, Louis Lehky, worthy patron, 1916; Nettie Vanderane, worthy matron, Michael Griffin, worthy patron, 1917; Florence Hunter, worthy matron, George Hunter, worthy patron, 1918.

The present officers are as follows: Mrs. Alma Bond, worthy matron; Stewart W. Bond, worthy patron; Amelia Lehky, secretary.

HARVARD CHAPTER No. 362 was organized February 4, 1897, and had for its charter members the following persons: Adelvia V. Clark, Grace Harris, Augusta Rogers, Christina Ward, Mary E. Blake, Addie Stuart, L. B. Jordon, Ella M. Hogan, Jennie Astrup, Fanny Wellington, Grace Carpenter, Jennie Wakely, Addie Beardsley, W. H. Ward, F. H. Wheelwright, Julia Miles, Glenn Wheelwright, Emma Lake, Rosa E. Marshall, Robert J. Marshall, Lucy G. Young, Daisy Goodsell, Harriet Towne, Mabel H. Manley, Belle Purington. The present membership is about 275. The following are the past worthy matrons: Adelvia V. Clark, Belle Purington, Catherine Brewer, Delia Diener, Agnes Andrews, May Cortney, Fannie Lillibridge, Carrie North, Besse Heatley, Julia L. Peck, Anna Bushnell and Olive K. Ford. The worthy past patrons have been: F. S. Brainard, F. H. Wheelwright, W. A. Hosehild, C. A. Stone, J. H. Vickers, W. C. Wellington, J. H. Crawford, H. H. Megran, S. E. Betzer and Harold S. Cash.

McHENRY CHAPTER No. 547 was organized April 1, 1905, by William H. Bridger, and had a charter membership as follows: Mrs. Maude Cormack, Miss Eolia Boyer, Mrs. Julia Gallaher, Mrs. Ethel Fisher, Miss Kate F. Howe, Mrs. Ella Eranson, Mrs. Violet Petesch, Miss Elsie Howe, Miss Florence Howe, Miss Mildred Stevens, Miss Viletta Stevens, Mrs. Petra Grot, Mrs. Luella Lodtz, Mrs. Fannie Chamberlin, Nettie Parks, Miss Alice Waite, J. M. Carmack, F. A. Holly and E. C. Fisher. The membership is now about eighty-five. The past presiding officers have been: Maude Cormack, worthy matron, Eolia Boyer, Julia Gallaher, Dora Price, Florence Wray, Alice Waite, Flora Ott, Clara Starrit, Martha Page and Fannie Chamberlain, and Martha Page.

ODD FELLOWS

MARENGO LODGE No. 175 was organized at Marengo, August 21, 1886, with charter members as follows: H. W. Richardson, C. P. Corbey, A. P. Marquis, A. P. Sison and F. W. Hovey. The first elective officers were: H. W. Richardson, noble grand; C. P. Corby, vice grand; A. P. Sison, secretary, and F. W. Hovey, treasurer, taking all of the members to hold what offices were needed to receive their charter from the Grand Lodge.

The present officers are: Ben Dietzen, noble grand; Walford Carlson, vice grand; B. O. Mead, secretary. The present membership is ninety-four.

HARVARD LODGE No. 1013 was organized at Harvard, January 1, 1912, by Guardian Lodge No. 60, of Woodstock. The charter members were Charles W. Short, Peter T. Rowe, Elmer Rector, Winn L. Matteson, Charles Stein, James H. Vickers, William C. Gaye, W. A. Dilley and J. G. Maxon.

The present membership of the Lodge is 177. A hall is leased by the order at present. The following have served as noble grands since the organization took place: J. H. Vickers, Charles W. Short, Elmer Rector, P. T. Rowe, Otto Fiek, S. E. Betzer, A. N. Dullam, George R. Adams, H. B. Kline, Walter Johnson, William Olbrich, William Hinkley, C. E. Wittmus and F. A. Clark. The present officers are: J. O. McClure, noble grand; William Halliday, vice grand; W. A. Dilley, secretary, and William Sweatman, treasurer.

CRYSTAL LAKE LODGE No. 451 was organized June 12, 1914, by Cary Lodge No. 360, R. H. Grantham acting as special deputy grand. The petition for a charter was signed by George Joseph Garrison, Eugene Cox, J. A. Gilbert, E. J. King, Eugene Mathews, and Jacob Horwitz. The first officers were as follows: E. J. King, noble grand; George J. Garrison, vice grand; J. A. Gilbert, secretary, and Eugene Mathews, treasurer. The present officers are: Eugene Cox, noble grand; Eugene Matthews, vice grand, J. M. Walkup, recording secretary. There is a membership at present of 163.

The noble grands of Crystal Lodge, according to their seniority, are as follows: E. J. King, George J. Garrison, John McWhorter, H. F. Gray, P. R. Frederich, Phil Huffman, E. T. Bryant, Herman Steinbach, and J. A. Peterson. This lodge owns its own hall; it is located on

Railroad street, near the depot, and is expressly fitted up for lodge uses. The building contains a spacious lodge hall, reception room, outer room, stage, dressing rooms, two toilets, a banquet room, kitchen, furnace room, property room and regalia and paraphernalia closets.

The deceased members of the lodge are: John Miller, William Ferguson and Thomas Miller. During the recent World war this lodge was represented in the army as follows: Charles Jolly, Nels Greer, Otto Kammin, Bert Randau, William Eickhoff, Arthur Adamack, Walter Heidel, James Howell, Herald Mathews, George Johnston, Mark Redman, Arthur Nelson, Rev. Theo. Kellogg, S. Pearson, Paul Rosell, E. Huffman, Martin Ekeland, Arthur F. Hamden, H. M. Warner. One brother Odd Fellow, Bert Randau, made the "supreme sacrifice" and another was severely wounded during the World war.

HUNTLEY LODGE was organized November 18, 1897, with the following charter members: E. H. Cook, C. W. Rugh, John Torry, B. F. Ellis and W. S. Cummings. The lodge now has a membership of fifty-one with officers as follows: Noble grand, O. H. Schmaltz; vice grand, Clay Marsh; secretary, Theo. Frederick.

HEBRON LODGE No. 767 was organized October 15, 1889, with charter members as follows: Hurley B. Begun, George A. Finch, D. McKenzie, John Galis, E. E. Taylor, M. B. Manor, Beal Finch, L. Z. Peirce, W. E. Wire, D. A. Clary, Peter Robertson, A. J. Cole, H. D. Walling and Fred Barragon. There are now about eighty members. They lease a hall for a meeting place.

The present elective officers are as follows: John Peterson, noble grand; Andy Judson, vice grand; Will Clark, secretary; Frank Holmes, treasurer; Clyde Frow, conductor, and Fred Buchte, chaplain.

Among the past noble grands are: Charles Smith, A. J. Cole, Arthur Alexander, Harry Alexander, L. Z. Peirce, Will Clark, E. F. Hewes, H. F. Jones, E. L. Phillips, Frank Rowe, M. A. Chandler, Frank Holmes, Guy C. Lemmers, S. Holder, John Cairns, W. S. Stewart, H. B. Begun and W. I. Torbess.

GUARDIAN LODGE No. 60 was organized at Woodstock in 1849, during the month of December, by Grand Master Isaac J. Wilson. The charter members were as follows: J. H. Johnson, Alonzo Platt, John B. Platt, Phineas W. Platt, and Hiram Hathaway. J. H. Johnson was the first noble grand and Alonzo Platt, secretary. The first meetings were held

Martin H. Hubrig, M.D.

in a hall over Donnelly's store. As early as 1852 this lodge had as many as 100 active members. But interest, for some reason was lost, and in 1857 the lodge gave up its charter, which was, however, renewed by the present lodge in 1872. Noble Grand J. C. Choate re-organized the lodge, with only five members. In 1884 the lodge room, records, regalia and other property was lost by fire February 22, involving a heavy loss to both lodge and encampment. The latter was organized in 1883.

The present membership of this lodge is 303, and its home since 1907 has been in Odd Fellows Hall, a large three-story brick block in which the post office is now located, the same costing $30,000 including the lot. Prior to that date it had been in Joslyn building until burned out. This made the third disastrous fire to visit the Odd Fellows' lodge rooms in Woodstock, each time it lost most of the valuable records. The present officers are: G. F. Burnstedt, noble grand; W. B. Brown, vice grand; A. E. Erickson, recording secretary; E. A. Gregory, financial secretary.

ENCAMPMENT

Besides the Subordinate lodge the Order of Odd Fellows here have an Encampment and the only Canton within McHenry County, has a membership of about 151. The Canton, organized January 19, 1916, has a membership of forty-two. Its officers at first were: T. B. Merwin, captain; Charles P. Caldwell, lieutenant; A. H. Hill, ensign.

REBEKAHS

CRYSTAL LAKE LODGE NO. 784 was organized October 15, 1914, and was instituted by Elgin Rebekah Lodge, and when one year old had a membership of one hundred. The first officers were as follows: Gertrude Barber, noble grand; Anna Gray, vice grand; Etta Convers, recording secretary; Alice Cole, treasurer; and Isabella King, chaplain.

The list of past noble grands is as follows: Gertrude Barber, Anna Gray, Ella Bryant, Alice Cole, Lillian Cox, Dora Messenger, Grace Howell, Gertrude Bryant, Hattie Mair. The present officers are as follows: Ada Walkuk, noble grand; Addie Bohl, vice grand; Jane Cannon, recording secretary; Josephine Nelson, financial secretary; Emma Peterson, conductress. The present membership is fifty-seven.

The order has its hall accommodation with the brother Odd Fellows. There is also a degree staff for putting on their own work and an installing team.

Crystal Lake Lodge No. 793 was instituted March 29, 1916, by Flora Smythe of Elgin, Ill., Fox River Lodge putting on the degree work for the seventy two charter members namely: E. J. King, P. F Hunt, G. J. Garrison, E. G. Mathews, A. W. Mink, C. H. Paine, Avery Holmes, R. H. Grantham, J. Horwitz, H. Steinback, J. D. Howell, Claude Mathews, Louis Pinnow, Frank Mathews, Ethel Rowley, Mayme Huffman, Minnie Nelson, Rose Sturbans, Vera Shales, G. H. Dike, Mae Dike, Lena Peterson, Luna Mentch, Lila Mentch, Martha Osgood, Julius Brown, Barbara Smith, W. D. Marshall, Ella Wilson, Fannie Pederson, Mabel Gray, Mary Wingate, Frank Dye, E. M. Dye, Clara Wilson, E. Pinnow, Louis Pinnow, Jr., Caroline Henk, John Smith, J. A. Peterson, Harry Mathews, Phillip Huffman, Theressa Huffman, Perdetta Mink, Anna Shuman, Mary Hanson, Minnie Steinback, Lena Holmes, Nellie Grantham, E. Pinnow, Sr., Hildah Pinnow, Clara Frederik, Carrie Miller, Anna Mathews, Margaret Hanson, J. R. McWhorten, E. O. Rowley, Dan Brandt, R. F. Gray, Isabelle King, Ella Hunt, Emma Gerlack, Elsie McWhorter, Anna Gray, Flora Paine and Minnie Burton.

The elective officers were: Sadie Garrison, Noble Grand; Perdetta Mink, vice grand; Carrie Miller, recording secretary; Minnie Nelson, financial secretary; and Ella Hunt, treasurer.

The past noble grands have been: Sadie Garrison, Perdetta Mink, Minnie Nelson, Minnie Steinback and Ethel Rowley.

The principal duty of Crystal Lake Lodge is to help the brothers and sisters when in trouble and need, and to extend sympathy to the bereaved. Each year the lodge sends goodly amounts of money to the Old Folk's Home at Mattoon, as well as to the Children's Home at Lincoln, Ill. During the recent World War, the lodge gave an entertainment and social, the proceeds of which were equally divided between the Rebekah Ambulance Fund and the local Red Cross. The total proceeds of this social was $90. The Rebekah Sisters met each alternate Friday and sewed for the Belgian Relief, and knitted for the soldiers. A large number of hospital shirts were also made. Crystal Lake Lodge had eight brothers in the service. They were; Paul Roeselle, served with the famous Black Hawk division in France; Mark Redmond, enlisted at the outbreak of the war and became a member of the 129th Infantry, serving near Luxemburg with the Army of Occupation; Harry Mathews, James Howell; Arthur Harnden, served in Siberia; Rev. Kellogg, Chaplain, was in France; Sture Pierson was in France; J. C. Jolly was also in France.

The lodge thinks very highly of their patriotic brothers, and a record of their comings and goings was kept.

The present officers are as follows: Mildred Babcock, noble grand; Christena Grantham, vice grand; Alta Nish, recording secretary.

On January 11th, 1919, the lodge moved into its hall in the new Odd Fellows building, located on Railroad street. It is thoroughly modern and a great credit to the fraternity of "three links." The present membership is 157.

HARVARD LODGE No. 795 was organized May 19, 1916, by Special Deputy Grand Master Ida E. G. Sherman of Chicago, assisted by Degree Team from Woodstock Rebekah Lodge No. 205. The charter members were: George B. Adams, Bert R. Cone, Otto Fick, H. B. Kline, H. W. Eastman, William Sweatman, H. J. Kolls, A. M. Dullam, Fred R. Goddard, F. A. Clark, Peter T. Rowe, Walter Johnson, Carl E. Wittmus, William J. Vierck, Walter F. Searle, Frank A. Scott, Abner McWithey, Leslie Douglas, Herman Frederich, William A. Dilley, Nellie Cone, Bertha Fick, May Kline, Abbie Price, Bessie Searle, Alice Kieskowski, Ida L. Kolls, Olga O. Kieskowski, Kate Huckstadt, Jessie Sweatman, Gertrude Dullam, Emma Adams, Lula Clark, Etta E. Rowe, Alice Johnson.

The membership is 117. The Past Noble Grands have been: Mary Kline, Gertrude Dullam, Jessie Sweatman, Emma Adams, Jessie Shepard, Lydia Talone. The present officials are: Ida Kolls, noble grand; Grace Rodd, vice grand; Jessie Sweatman, recording secretary; Gertrude Dullam, financial secretary; Nellie Betzer, treasurer. The lodge leases its hall rights of the Odd Fellows Order.

KNIGHTS OF PYTHIAS

KISHWAUKEE LODGE at Marengo, was organized October 14, 1909, by Walter Hays. It now has a membership of eighteen. The present officers are: Herman Abraham, chancellor commander; Charles Higbee, vice chancellor; D. E. Erbaugh, prelate; B. O. Mead, keeper of records and seals.

THE MODERN WOODMEN OF AMERICA

PISKASAW CAMP No. 865 was organized at the village of Chemung, March 13, 1889, and had as its charter members: F. A. Bosworth, W

J. Barth, J. Chilson, William Dawson, O. A. Hill, J. W. Lampart, Robert Myrick, J. J. Marvin, G. J. Sinderson, J. W. King and H. H. Ladd. The present membership is fifty-two. The present elective officers are: J. R. Dawson, Consul; John Haire, advisor; Ray Bosworth, banker; John R. Beck, clerk; Henry Jones, escort; Ernest Palmer, watchman; Don Shufeldt, sentinel.

When this camp was first instituted, a part of the officers were: J. J. Marvin, consul; Clerk, J. W. Lampart; escort, G. J. Sinderson, and J. W. King, banker. The camp was unfortunate in having its hall with all its valuable records burned. This fire occurred in 1914. The property of the order at this point is now in charge of the following trustees: William Douglas, J. J. Kennedy and H. M. Esmond.

RIDGEFIELD CAMP No. 779 was organized at the village of Ridgefield, November 6, 1888, by J. H. Fulton. The charter members were: G. R. Truax, P. D. Castle, E. Roderick, William H. Jones, Ben Throop, Delmer Duffield, L. T. Wade, S. M. Simmons, C. E. Lockwood, J. M. Barden and Clark Jacobs. The present membership is fifty-three. They assemble in Hartman's Hall. The present officers are: Ira Burdick, venerable consul; Frank Wilkus, worthy advisor; A. H. Skinner, banker; R. D. Kinlans, clerk; S. A. Merchant, escort; Erland Burman, watchman; S. Reed, sentry.

RICHMOND CAMP No. 268 was organized, November 26, 1886, with charter members as follows: L. B. Rice, L. W. Howe, C. S. Miller, E. R. Bennett, E. W. Weeks, William Besteder, C. N. Culver, W. W. Bogart, J. H. Alexander, C. F. Smith, Robert Hunter, H. J. Christian.

This camp now enjoys a membership of seventy-eight. They assemble in Osmond's Hall. The present officers are: J. T. Bower, venerable consul; George A. Osmond, banker; R. F. Parsons, worthy advisor; H. L. Chevillon, clerk; Fred Arp, escort; C. H. Heck, watchman; H. H. Reed, sentry; and W. E. Foster, physician.

RINGWOOD CAMP No. 597 was organized May 9, 1888, with charter members as follows: James M. Carr, E. J. Hopper, C. N. Thompson, Ed. Dates, John Pint, C. H. Stephenson, J. W. Grinoldby, R. D. Carr. The first officers were as follows: E. J. Hopper, venerable consul; J. W. Grinoldby, worthy advisor; Ed. Dates, clerk; C. N. Thompson, banker; C. H. Stephenson, escort; E. J. Hopper, watchman; John Pint, sentry. The present membership of this camp is seventy-three. They assemble at the Modern Woodmen Hall in Ringwood. For the past ten years the following have been in office: E. J. Hopper, venerable consul; J. V. Buckland, banker; C. W. Harrison, clerk.

The presiding officers have been: James M. Carr, 1888-93; C. W. Harrison, 1893-1908; J. L. Conway, 1908-09; E. J. Hopper, 1909-1921.

LONE TREE CAMP No. 195 was organized at the village of Hebron, May 7, 1886, with charter members as follows: Henry Earle, E. L. Herrick, Herman Houson, N. B. Manor, E. E. Taylor, John Reynolds, F. N. Torrance. The membership is seventy-one.

W. E. Wire is venerable consul and E. A. Mead, clerk.

VALLEY CAMP No. 97 was organized at West McHenry, December 31, 1885, with charter members as follows: A. S. Childs, John Evanson, H. H. King, F. A. Parker, Freeman Petley, I. N. Mead, H. E. Colby, C. A. Hutson, H. C. Mead, Will H. Mead, Jacob Hetzel, E. J. Handy. The camp has a membership of 121.

The past presiding officers are as follows: H. C. Mead, J. Van Slyke, C. C. Colby, Robert Howard, W. P. Stevens, T. P. Walsh, J. H. Kimball, Charles L. Page, W. D. Wentworth, E. E. Bassett, Joseph C. Holly, John Stoffel, A. M. Brown, Alford H. Pouse, James N. Sayler. The following are the present officials: W. J. Welch, vice consul; James N. Sayler, past consul; Frank Thurhoell, Sr., advisor; P. M. Joslen, banker; E. E. Bassett, clerk; R. Gehamberlin, escort; M. A. Conway, watchman; Walter Warner, sentry; Drs. D. G. Wells, A. F. Mueller, and A. l. Froehlick, physicians; John W. Schaffer, A. M. Brown and John Stoffel, trustees.

BOXWOOD CAMP No. 86 was organized at Harvard March 27, 1885, by S. L. Lincoln. The charter members were as follows: L. J. Camron, Francis M. Drake, John Foley, Charles Goddard, H. Gray, T. Hallisey, S. L. Lincoln, A. Parlet, F. M. Martin, George W. Parmely, R. E. Tooker, M. M. McMahon, J. C. Sorenson, O. Carpenter, T. Condon, H. Senger, J. B. Stevens, O. Powers, W. L. Collins, E. C. Hammond, M. Howard, M. A. F. Ottman, Dr. Cole and C. H. Adams. The lodge now has a membership of 209. Its first officers were: S. L. Lincoln, consul; H. Gray, advisor; Dr. Goddard, banker; Geroge Parmely, clerk. The officers now serving are: Charles Kath, vice consul; William Watson, worthy advisor; W. A. Dilley, clerk; and F. H. Dobson, banker.

The presiding officers have been: S. L. Lincoln, W. H. Conway, F. H. Dobson, J. C. Diever, E. C. Hammond, Ed Smith, J. H. Diener.

BAY TREE CAMP No. 574 was organized a few years ago at Alden, and now enjoys a membership of sixty two. This camp lost all records in a fire and was re-organized in 1918. The present officers are: W. P. Thompson, consul; E. C. Hammond, advisor, N. B. Clawson, banker; T. O. Bungard, clerk.

ROYAL NEIGHBORS OF AMERICA

This order is the Woman's Auxiliary of the Modern Woodmen of America, and has several Camps in this county.

BOXWOOD CAMP No. 298, at Harvard, was organized in 1896 by Mary A. Scott. The first officers were: Hattie Hancock, oracle; Mary A. Scott, vice oracle; Clara Stedge, recorder; and Mary Powers, receiver.

The present membership is 289. The following have served as Oracles at this point: Hattie Hancock, three years; Mary Scott Lanning, eighteen years; Mabel A. Bordwell for four years and is still in office. Mattie E. Stafford is the recorder. This order has lodges in nearly every place the Woodmen have lodges in this county.

FOX RIVER VALLEY CAMP was organized at West McHenry in April, 1906, with charter members as follows: Eli B. Brink, Alfred M. Brown, Dr. Harry Beebe, Anna Byrd, Polly Brink, Bernice Kimball, Henry C. Mead, Anna Mollohan, Amy L. Mead, Laura Nellis, Martha Page, Alice Simpson, Nina Sherman, Benson Sherman, Etta E. Wattles, D. Wentworth, D. G. Nellis, A. Matthews, Calla Loomis. It now has a membership of 94. The past presiding officers are: Anna Byrd, Agnes Wentworth, Etta E. Wattles, Cora Bassett, Laura Nellis, Etta E. Wattles.

MINERVA SPRING CAMP was organized at Cary, February 4, 1896. It was formed by Mrs. B. Prickett of Summit Camp. The charter members consisted of twenty-two ladies and eleven Woodmen brothers. There are nineteen beneficial members and one social member. The present members are: Nellie Grantham, oracle; Julia Brown, recorder; Lila Mentch, receiver; Nettie Trout, chancellor; Martha Osgood, marshal; Sophronia Lindsey and Amy Rowsen, sentinels.

PROGRESSIVE CAMP No. 5,300 was organized at Woodstock April 1, 1908, by District Deputy Minnie Dillon. The charter members were as follows: Lawrence Gillispie, Rachael Gillispie, C. A. Lammers, Alice Lemmers, Ellen Jacobs, Emma Joorfritz, William Rushton, Ella Hakes,

Anna Lichty, William M. Lichty, Blanche Dietz, Beatrice Dewey, Harry Dewey, Mary Gaulke, Clara Wicks, Lillian Rose, Lewis Dean, H. T. Brown, Rosa Brown, E. E. Stevens, Lon Stevens, Lizzie Walson, Clyde Miner, May Miner, Frank Heine and Reka Waller.

The first officers were: Past oracle, William Lichty; oracle, Ellen Jacobs; vice oracle, Rosa Brown; chancellor, Ella Hakes; recorder, Alice Lemmers; receiver, Anna Lichty; marshal, Emma Joorfritz; inner sentinel, Lewis Dean; and outer sentinel, William Rushton. The past presiding officers have been: Ellen Jacobs, Niobe Griffiths, Dora Johnston, William Lichty. The present officers are: Past oracle, Deborah Haldeman; oracle, Brookie Fosdick; vice oracle, Elsie Smith; chancellor, Lovina Thomas; recorder, Jennie Ellsworth; receiver, Mary Baker.

The membership of this prosperous camp of Royal Neighbors is 213.

MYSTIC WORKERS OF THE WORLD

HARVARD LODGE No. 21 was organized April 4, 1899 by Joanna E. Downes and commenced with charter members as follows: William Bombard, Pearl Bombard, Edwin Brickley, Sarah Brickley, William Brickley, Cora Butts, Edgar Butts, Mary Burk, Patrick Burk, James Burk, Walter Bowman, Albert Brown, Michael Breen, William Budde, Charles Cramer, Celia Donovan, George Diggins, Ernest Diggins, Carrie Diggins, Judson Davis, Catherine Donovan, Herbert Emerson, Frank Ellis, Otto Fick, Bertha Fick, Julia Gleason, August Hochrath, Albert Hammerstead, William Jenkins, Mary Jenkins, Joseph Jones, Henrietta Kiskoski, Henry Lembsky, Lewis Leverenz, Mathew McRoberts, Margaret McCabe, Rose McGee, William Maguire, Emma Ottman, Edward O'Brien, James Phinney, Jennie Phinney, August Rogers, Melvin Smith, John Sweeney, Kate Sullivan, Nellie Sullivan, Herman Stroede, John Waters, Daniel Waters, Kate Waters and Riley Whitmarsh. There are now 471 adult and thirteen juvenile members in this flourishing beneficiary lodge. They meet in Odd Fellows' Hall.

Their elective officers included these: Joanna E. Downes, prefect; Earl Dowens, moderator; John A. Sweeney, banker; Ernest Downes, secretary. The officers now serving are: John Dacy, prefect; Robert Kolls, monitor; Agnes Sweeney, secretary; Margaret Hayden, banker; Cora Goodwish, marshal; George Jones, warder; Mary Hubble, sentinel; Charles Helmke and Anna Beherns, supervisors. The past presiding officers have been: Joanna E. Downes, Catherine Nihan, Catherine Lyons, Frances Powers.

Nunda Lodge 382 was instituted at Crystal Lake, December 20, 1900, by Worthy Downes of Harvard. The charter members were as follows: J. P. Sughrua, Mary Sughrua, Charles Kliber, Herman Freye, Hattie Freye, Mary Kliber. Dr. H. D. Hull, Harrison Sargeant, Nellie Sargeant. Charles Vermilya, Louisa Vermilya, Amelia Schultz, Fred Schultz, Cora E. Dickinson. Charles L. Curphey, Anna Curphey, Gillard Frost, Josehena Westphal, Mary Buford, Edwin Bissell, Floyd Terwilliger, and Lena Frost.

The present officers are as follows: J. D. Blackman, prefect; Esther Allen, monitor; Alice Cole, secretary; Lunn Richards, banker; Lenore Schneider. marshal; J. P. Sughrua, warder; George Bryant, sentinel. ·

The lodge now has a membership of 190. They assemble at Woodman Hall at Crystal Lake. The presiding officers have been inclusive of these to date: J. P. Sughrua, who was prefect for thirteen years without a break, and is known as "Old Stand-by," Earl Bryant. E. M. Bissell, Dr. H. D. Hull, and John Mair.

The Juvenile Department is rapidly growing in numbers. Dancing and refreshments frequently occur at their meetings which are held the first Thursday in every month.

Prosperity Lodge No. 1030 was organized April 15, 1911, with charter members as follows: Prefect, Carlton D. Ross; monitor, Helena M. Stoffel; secretary, Adah A. Casey; banker, John I. Sutton; physician, Dr. Wells; marshal, Florence Howe; warder, Phillip Aylwood; sentinel, Glenn Barker; supervisors, Katheryn Heiner, Frank E. Cobb and Rose Justen.

The present membership is 438. A. W. Hill is the prefect, and Nino Conn is secretary.

KNIGHTS OF COLUMBUS

Mc Henry Council No. 1288 was organized in 1908, at the village of McHenry and now enjoys a membership of 320. The present officers include: Grand knight, E. R. McGee; deputy grand knight, J. H. Miller; secretary, M. P. Freund.

The following have served as presiding officers: Joseph W. Freund, C. W. Stenger, M. J. Walsh, Thomas Bolger, Walter J. Walsh, Casper Biekler, Ed. L. Hayes and A. E. Nye, Casper M. Biekler.

Harvard Council No. 1204 was organized February 24, 1907, with charter members as follows: Thomas C. Carey, R. J. Starr, A. C.

Harry D. Hull

Strain, P. T. Brickley, B. F. Brickley, J. P. Burke, Frank Clarke, Bert Clarke, F. J. Condon, J. W. Conway, J. J. Crowley, E. J. Field, J. J. Flannery, J. Googley, B. J. Gregory, C. S. Hanson, W. J. Hereley, P. H. Howard, J. M. Iserman, C. P. Regan, F. J. Shepard, W. J. Sheahan, F. Sheahan, R. V. Sloey, E. C. Strain, W. T. Strain, J. H. Vrooman, W. H. Ashley, F. Behringer, E. M. Brickley, W. H. Boyle, R. P. Boodle, W. H. Sweeney, D. B. Waters, John Clarke, Thomas Burke, W. C. Crowley, W. H. Daly, E. J. Dolan, W. E. Doyle, E. N. Fernholz, G. Fitzgerald, M. F. Haley, P. J. Hayes, F. Hereley, M. Hereley, C. A. Madden, G. F. Massey, J. J. McGuire, A. J. McCarthy, C. E. McCarthy, H. E. Munger, T. J. Murphy, M. J. Nolan, John T. O'Brien, William H. Phillips, Richard Phalen, J. P. O'Connor, M. B. O'Connor, Joseph D. O'Brien, John W. Phalen, W. H. Powers, T. G. Ruffie, M. P. Sullivan, Dan Sullivan, J. A. Sweeney, M. J. Breen, D. T. Phalen. The present total number of members is about 206. The total amount raised for the war fund by Harvard Council of K. of C. was $2,757.

The following have served as presiding officers since the organization of the council in 1907: A. C. Strain, 1907-08; Thomas C. Carey, 1908-13; John P. O'Connor, 1913-15; James P. Burke, 1915-17; John T. O'Brien, 1917-20.

ELKS

Woodstock Lodge No. 1043 was organized October 24, 1906, with forty-three charter members. At present the lodge has a membership of 400. The original officers were as follows: John C. Donnelly, exalted ruler; John J. Cooney, esteemed leading knight; J. P. Alt, esteemed loyal knight; V. E. Brown, esteemed lecturing knight; George W. Lemmers, secretary; R. A. Pratt, treasurer; Fred Derrenberger, tyler; Garry R. Austin, trustee (one year); D. J. Omstead, trustee (two years); George A. Darmer, trustee (three years).

The order first met in Waverly Hall on Main street and from there moved to its present home in Odd Fellows' Building.

The chief presiding officers have been: John C. Donnelly, E. C. Jewett, George A. Cutteridge, Dell J. Omstead, E. D. Hannaford, C. C. Harting, J. E. Guy, D. J. Omstead, J. C. Rowe, J. L. Brown, George W. Lemmers, C. F. Baccus. T. L. Griffing is the present exalted ruler; and Edwin M. Kemerling is the present secretary.

CHAPTER XX

PUBLIC LIBRARIES

By Ida L. Gehrig

WOODSTOCK LIBRARY—MARENGO LIBRARY—DELOS F. DIGGINS LIBRARY.

In a number of the school districts in McHenry County, there have been for many years, small school libraries, some even with quite a goodly number of valuable books. The county has a fair law library for the use of practicing attorneys, and the high schools of the county have excellent collections of books, but the three real public libraries, well established, and now supported by a tax or endowment fund, are those located at Woodstock, Harvard and Marengo. To the ladies of these communities must be given chief praise for the hard work they performed during former years, trying to get together a suitable collection of library books. Year after year this work went forward, until finally the public generally took an interest, and as a result these public libraries were established.

WOODSTOCK PUBLIC LIBRARY

The Woodstock library had its origin some time in 1856, when through the efforts of a number of citizens in and near Woodstock contributions of books were made, and money secured from Judge Church, Doctor Perry, W. Murphy, C. H. Russell, Elmer Lamb, E. E. Richards, R. G. Shryver, M. F. Irving, J. A. Parrish and others, and in this way was started a library. This library was not free to the public, but was kept up by subscription for many years. When the Woodstock Literary and Library Association was formed, December 10, 1877, it had as one of its aims the accumulation and maintenance of a library and the books left in the old library collection were put with the new ones. These books were sometimes kept in stores, but were free only to members of the club or association; others paid $1 a year, or ten cents a book, for their use.

On March 5, 1880, a new by-law was added providing for the election of a librarian and A. R. Murphy was the first one to hold that office. In a report made by him in 1881, he gave the number of books on hand as 148. In May, 1882, the books owned by the Young Men's Association were purchased for $20. In 1886 A. S. Wright, the druggist, was made Mr. Murphy's successor and the library was removed to the Wright drug store on the south side of the square, where a room was provided. For the year 1887 he reported the number of volumes to be 678. Verne Wright succeeded his father as librarian in 1888, and he in turn was followed in 1890 by C. D. Parsons. Through these years the Woodstock Library Association gradually gathered together a library of standard books and the present library is greatly indebted to those progressive and intellectual members who had the forethought and energy to build as they did. Mrs. Mary Joslyn and J. C. Choate were especially untiring and inspiring leaders.

At a meeting of the association, held June 23, 1890, it was voted to move the books to a room in the city hall and January 26, 1891, it was decided to transfer the library to the City of Woodstock, to be the nucleus of the Woodstock Public Library. The books were now made free to all the people residing within the corporate city. The mayor and council appointed the first directors: J. C. Choate, L. T. Hoy, C. A. Lemmers, A. Dreyer, Mrs. Mary R. Joslyn, Mrs. Frank Spitzer, V. S. Lumley, Dr. W. C. Cook, and Miss Mary F. Murphy. The librarian appointed was Erastus Richards, who was followed in turn by H. B. Rogers and Miss Winifred Hall (now Mrs. C. Curtis) from 1893 to July 10, 1911, when the present librarian, Lura Wandrack was chosen. On the evening of March 12, 1814, there was a fire in the city hall which caused the total loss of 1,906 books and necessitated the removal of the library to the Rest Room in the courthouse until the latter part of May.

The library reports show number of books on shelves to be 6,912. The present directors are: R. C. Kaufman, J. S. Andrews, Miss Pauline McMannis, Mrs. J. R. Kellogg, Mrs. J. J. Stafford, Mrs. W. H. Shipton, C. R. Belcher, N. A. Sunderlin, and V. S. Lumley.

MARENGO PUBLIC LIBRARY

A collection of books were left to the city of Marengo by a former resident, Mrs. M. J. Harrington, for the purpose of starting a public library. A number of members of the Woman's Club formed a Library Carnival Aid Society to finance the library until taken over as a city library on June 19, 1907. A room was rented in the old Green homestead, but later the books were removed to Doctor Nutt's office building where the library remained until May 1, 1917, when two suites of rooms in the Community Club Building became the home of the library. Miss Mabel Fay was the first librarian and she was succeeded by Miss Anna Blair. The present librarian is Nellie Fillmore.

This library has 38,000 volumes, seventeen magazines and papers on the reading tables, which are accessible to any one in Marengo or vicinity. The library is supported by a tax levied by the city. The present trustees are: Mrs. C. B. Whittemore, N. V. Woleben, Mrs. A. W. Kelley, Mrs. A. A. Crissey, Miss Mildred Burke, J. V. Patterson, E. D. Patrick and C. H. Bremer.

DELOS F. DIGGINS LIBRARY OF HARVARD

What is known as The Delos F. Diggins Library in the city of Harvard, was first established through the generosity of Mr. Delos F. Diggins, a man born and reared in this community. During his later years, Mr. Diggins resided in Cadillac, Michigan, but wishing to be remembered by his home townspeople he gave a fund sufficient to build the present beautiful structure situated near the central part of the city; also placing an endowment fund in the care of library trustees whom he appointed .to fill that position for their lifetime or residence in Harvard. In case of death or removal from the city of any of the trustees the vacancy thus formed was to be filled by the remaining trustees. Mr. Diggins' idea in 'having one continuous board of trustees was principally to keep the' library affairs strictly free from politics.

The following named gentlemen comprised the first board of trustees of the library: A. B. Diggins, president; R. A. Nugent, vice president; M. F. Walsh, secretary; F. F. Axtell, treasurer; and H. D. Crumb, W. D. Hall, and James Lake.

On May 7th, 1909, the library, which is a perfect structure with all modern appointments and conveniences and as near fireproof as a building can well be constructed, was dedicated to the public with appropriate exercises. W. H. Ward, of Harvard, Ill., was the contractor; Mr. Watterman, of Chicago, was the architect.

Miss Elizabeth E. Wilson was the first librarian appointed, and on the second day of August, 1909, the library was open to the public for the issue of books for home use. The collection consisted of 1,794 volumes on the shelves ready for use. The first annual report shows a book circulation for home use, 11,627. Subsequent librarians were as follows: Miss B. Hamilton, Miss Cleo Lichtenberger, Miss V. K. Gher. In September, 1917, Miss I. L. Gehrig was appointed librarian, and she was succeeded by the present librarian, Mrs. I. L. G. Dickson.

One of the notable events of the year 1917-18 was the reorganization of the library according to more modern methods. In October, 1917, through the efforts of Miss Anna May Price, secretary of The Illinois Library Extension Commission, Miss Marie Hammond and the librarian began the work of reclassifying and cataloguing the books according to the decimal classification and completed the work in February, 1918, and the valuable dictionary card catalogue for public use was placed in the delivery room. In this card catalogue are entered all books contained in the library arranged according to author, title and subject.

In the spring of 1919, at a Roosevelt Memorial, the Womans Club of Harvard presented the library with a fine etching of the late ex-president, Theodore Roosevelt; Father Lepper of the Episcopal Church, Harvard, Ill., making the presentation speech.

The present board of trustees are as follows: R. C. Uecke, president; H. D. Crumb, M. F. Walsh, F. F. Axtell, B. B. Bell, W. D. Hall, James Lake.

The first tax levy appropriating money for the public library of Harvard was passed September 21, 1916, when the sum of $900 was given for the further maintenance of the library. For the year 1917 the same amount was received and since then the appropriation has been $1,000. This annual income, together with the interest from the endowment fund, maintains the library in a fitting manner.

Following board of directors was appointed by the mayor to govern the expenditures of the city's annual appropriation; six of the board being library trustees: B. B. Bell, president; Mrs. A. C. McCarty, Mrs. Robert Hall, F. F. Axtell, H. D. Crumb, W. D. Hall, James Lake, Mrs. H. A. Towne, M. F. Walsh.

For a small library, there is a strong reference collection, which has been recently strengthened through many purchases and some gifts. The collection of bound magazines is especially valuable, suitable shelves having been built for them in the main reading and reference room.

The reference use made of the library by the high school pupils and general public has been wholly satisfactory, though there is room for still greater use of the library in the future. The juvenile department has been materially strengthened by the purchase of many books and subscriptions to the popular and scientific magazines. The library has the permanent loan of the valuable and most attractive collection of butterflies owned by Mrs. H. A. Towne.

There has always been a hearty cooperation and assistance of the prominent clubs of Harvard and the community and for several years of "The Library Carnival Association." There are 6,900 volumes on the shelves.

CHAPTER XXI

WOMAN'S CLUBS

By Mrs. W. H. Doolittle

ALGONQUIN—CRYSTAL LAKE—HARVARD CIVIC ASSOCIATION—HARVARD FORT-
NIGHTLY—HARVARD WOMEN'S CLUB—HUNTLEY—LOTUS COUNTRY — MA-
RENGO—M'HENRY COUNTY FEDERATION—RICHMOND—RUSH CREEK—
SCHUMANN-SENECA ASSOCIATION OF DOMESTIC SCIENCE—WOODSTOCK.

Until recent years the women of the country had little opportunity to give expression to their individuality outside their home and church circles. Any public appearance of a woman, unless she were an actress or singer, was discouraged, and the present desirable freedom of the sex with relation to their mental development, has been brought about through the untiring zeal and hard work of the pioneers in the movement. Today, small is the community that does not have one or more clubs of earnest, sincere women, whose efforts are concentrated upon not only expanding their own horizons, but the education of others to bring them to a similar condition; the betterment of civic conditions; and the inauguration of much needed reforms of all kinds. The original prejudice harbored by the narrow-minded against these clubs, has passed, being wiped out by the record made by these organizations, and the time is not far distant when every woman of any intelligence will realize that it is her duty to herself, her family and her community, to avail herself of the privilege of club membership.

ALGONQUIN WOMAN'S CLUB

The Algonquin Woman's Club was organized in June, 1915, with forty members, Mrs. Whittemore of Marengo aiding in the organization. Mrs. B. C. Getzelman, who was also very active in securing these forty charter members and organizing them into a club, was elected the club's first president. During the first year the club affiliated with the county, district and state organizations. There is a present membership of fifty.

The club motto is: "Who stays in the valley never gets over the hill."

From October, 1915, to April, 1916, the Algonquin Woman's Club was instrumental in securing a park for the town. The members of the club prepared a petition asking the town board to purchase a park site. An entertainment course given by the International Entertainment Bureau was sponsored by the club. The McHenry County Federation meeting was held at the Congregational Church, Algonquin, May 6, 1916.

During the summer of 1916 the club had the mineral spring at the park cemented, and also had a cement bench made at the park. In the fall of 1917, the club gave a children's course of special moving pictures.

During the period of the World War, the Algonquin Woman's Club was active in the Thrift Stamp campaigns, the Liberty Loan drives, Red Cross work and the sale of Red Cross Seals.

Flower seeds were distributed to school children by the club in May, 1918.

Work done by the Home Improvement Club was under the supervision of the Woman's Club. On February 11, 1918, the Woman's Club gave a cafeteria supper. It sent several boxes of old clothing, toys, canned fruit and apples to the Home for Destitute Children, to Erie Chapel Institute, Samaritan House Settlement and the Daily News Sanitarium. The club also sent contributions to the Illinois Cottage at Park Ridge, the Library Extension Fund, Country War Fund, Benefit Fund for Soldiers and Sailors stationed in Illinois, and to the district work of the state federation.

The Philanthropy and Reform department in April, 1918, turned over to the club $25 to start a library fund.

The president of the club is Miss Ella Kee.

MRS. GEORGE KEYES

CRYSTAL LAKE WOMAN'S CLUB

The first Woman's Club at Crystal Lake was organized May 26, 1914, although previous to that date the women of the town had banded themselves together, choosing Mrs. C. L. Teckler as president of the organization which was known as the Woman's Voting Club. Their chief aim at that time was to become familiar with the voting system, to post themselves on parliamentary law, and matters pertaining to town, county and state work.

Early in the spring of 1914, the club held a mock election at the town hall and nearly every woman in the town went to the polls and

voted correctly. This paved the way for the spring election at which time women were to vote on the question of local option. The votes polled by the women placed Crystal Lake in the dry section of the map. After this victory was gained, it was suggested, by the president of the voting club, that the organization merge into a Woman's Club for improvement, and broaden their lines of work, which met with the approval of all, and a committee was appointed to draft a constitution and by-laws.

Sixty-eight charter members were enrolled, and the following officers were elected: Mrs. Bertha Dolle, president; Mrs. Ella Freeman, vice president; Mrs. Mae Dike, recording secretary; Miss Edythe Leach, corresponding secretary; and Mrs. Carrie Teckler, treasurer. During 1914 and 1915 meetings were held every second and fourth Tuesday in the month, the usual summer vacations being omitted. Great interest continued to be manifested, and at the end of the year 1915, the club had an enrollment of ninety-four members.

The lines of work taken up by the club have been various, and as many similar organizations, the members have worked for the improvement of their town, taking up the cleaning of the streets and alleys, disposing of rubbish and garbage, placing of flowers and shrubs in the park and on high school grounds, making annual donations to the public library, establishing a charity fund, looking after those in need, visiting the Chicago Tribune Camp at Algonquin and donating to same, sending barrels of clothing and groceries to the Children's Home at Woodstock, contributing $20 to the Girls' Home at Park Ridge, observing National Baby Week, giving showers to the Domestic Science room at the high school, and sending delegates to the county, district and state conventions.

During 1917 and 1918 the club members gave a large portion of their time to the Red Cross and Council of Defense work, beside selling Liberty Bonds and War Savings Stamps. During the past five years the club has been giving fine entertainments, engaging many speakers and artists of rare ability. Believing that education and thrift go hand in hand and that in community work there is strength, the club has been working to establish a community center at the high school.

The graduating class of 1919 of the high school has given the school a Motiograph De Luxe, which has been installed in the gymnasium by Superintendent H. A. Dean, of the Crystal Lake schools, and a coworker with the Woman's Improvement Club, helping to build a solid foundation on which the rising generation may stand high above all that is worthless and unstable.

The club is looking forward to many community gatherings for the purpose of enjoying the educational and government films which are already being shown.

Dr. Mary King has been engaged by the club to examine the teeth of the grade pupils, and send a chart of same to the parents for inspection. This movement in connection with the health crusade that is awakening so much interest among pupils and parents, will be another step forward in teaching the children to care for their bodies and preserve their health.

The Woman's Improvement Club is always ready to take up new lines of work that will be beneficial or improve the town and build up the country, so that we may all be called true American citizens.

Mrs. Carrie D. Teckler.
Crystal Lake, Ill.

HARVARD CIVIC ASSOCIATION

The Harvard Civic Association was organized April 4, 1906, with the following officers: Mrs. J. W. Groesbeck, president; Mrs. C. W. Goddard, secretary; and Mrs. H. B. Minier, treasurer. Several vice presidents were appointed, and later an advisory board drew into line many energetic workers from all sections of the city.

The aim of the organization was to do its utmost along all lines beneficial to the city; to co-operate with the mayor and city council, and the then recently formed Business Men's Association, and to assist in every possible way to promote the welfare of Harvard.

The first objective of the club was "the city beautiful;" special cleanliness of the home and home surroundings was advocated; the anti-spitting ordinance was to be enforced; a general paintup, cleanup and keep clean policy was to be undertaken, and always Harvard was to be "boosted."

Every woman resident above the age of sixteen was personally invited to join the club and take an active interest in its efforts. No membership fee was imposed. Funds were secured as needs arose by various methods, such as tag days, card games, food sales, which latter proved wonderfully successful, considerable sums being secured by the sales of homemade bread, pies, doughnuts, cakes and other homemade bakery goods. Also, later, movie benefit picture shows were extremely profitable.

For our first cleanup day we planned a grand roundup of workers with rakes and hoes and other necessary tools, who were to start promptly at nine A. M., when all bells would ring and whistles blow. And such a scurrying and cleaning of corners was never before seen and such a merry army of men and women, boys and girls, responded as made a clean Harvard a surety. Papers and tin cans and all rubbish in the streets were raked into convenient piles and later teams were sent to gather up and cart away the refuse. The alleys presented a problem by themselves, and as we had no laws to enforce clean alleys, we hired a man with a team to go certain days through the alleys back of the stores and cart away all collections ready. The result was immediate improvement in the looks of the alleys, and the cleaning out of spaces that had been for years untouched, besides the hauling away of immense wagon loads every week. Later this work led to the city garbage collection system which has been very successfully carried on under the supervision of the city health officer for several years, and incidentally, has removed to a remarkable extent that deadly pest, the house fly, thus proving a wonderful gain in sanitation.

As early as 1908 we originated a plan for districting our city, and appointed chairmen of streets, each chairman to appoint assistants, who would have not to exceed two blocks or squares under her supervision. In this simple way, every house could be quickly reached with the least effort of time or labor. The plan commended itself in many ways. It fostered neighborhood pride and spurred to individual effort and brought about splendid results.

At the early meetings considerable study and discussion were carried on relative to the ornamental planting of gardens and home grounds, and resulted in an enthusiastic planting of flowers, shrubs and vines, that changed the city as if by magic. Special care was urged in the cutting of parkings or spaces outside the sidewalks, with the result that a wonderful improvement was soon seen, the grass being cut way to the wheel tracks in the center of the streets, which were then unpaved, producing a park effect which was extremely effective even in the humblest neighborhoods, no unsightly fringe of tall grasses and unsightly weeds being left to mar the beauty of the smooth, green lawn. The last plan of street cutting was quickly acted upon by the up-to-date farmers in the vicinity, and their homes have attracted universal attention and praise, being singled out as models of the progressive farm home.

Much credit is due to the officers and members of the advisory boards in which lists, in addition to those already mentioned, will be found the following dependable members: Mrs. John King, Mrs. A. J. McCarthy, Mrs. W. H. Cobb, Mrs. K. B. Titcomb, Mrs. W. D. Hall, Mrs. James Shehan, Mrs. M. F. Walsh, Mrs. J. B. Lyon, Mrs. Lucy Young, Mrs. Mart Stafford, Mrs. W. C. Wellington, Mrs. Fannie Webster, Mrs. O. L. Putnam, Mrs. John Boodle, Mrs. L. A. Gardner, Mrs. F. C. Peters, Mrs. H. L. Ferris, Mrs. Rev. Giesel, Mrs. Carrie North, Mrs. Aubrey Cook, Mrs. Asad Udell, Mrs. J. M. Harris, Mrs. Harry Beardsley, Mrs. Harriet Eastman, Mrs. M. J. Emerson, Mrs. R. G. Jones, Mrs. Gilbert Wagar, Mrs. J. H. Vickers, Mrs. E. Carpenter, Mrs. Frank Bordwell, Mrs. Alex. Diggins, Mrs. Robert Minshull, Mrs. M. M. Towne, Mrs. Robert Nihan, Mrs. C. J. Hendricks, Mrs. Bert Ford, Mrs. Frank Phelps, Mrs. Albert Whaples, Mrs. James Lake, Mrs. A. C. Manley, Mrs. F. H. Dobson, Mrs. George Martin, Mrs. Helen Johnson, Mrs. George Walker, Mrs. Ora Stewart, Mrs. Richard Engle, Mrs. Robert Hall, Mrs. William Doyle, Mrs. A. C. Strain, Mrs. J. Keeler, Mrs. Eugene Ferris, Mrs. Howard Ferris, Mrs. Anna Fountain, Miss Florence Crumb, Miss Carrie Wyant, Miss Minnie Breitenfeldt, Miss Alda Wilbur, Miss Ella Miller, Miss Nell Richardson and Miss Fannie Powers. Every enterprise entered upon for the good of the city has been splendidly upheld and all possible assistance has been given. Cemetery sidewalk building, as well as other cement sidewalk construction demanded by city standards, received full support, as well as the oiling of streets and the planting of vines and shrubs on school grounds and in numbers of vacant spaces.

Community clubrooms have been continued through the support and efforts of the Civic Club. In fact every movement for the city's benefit or improvement has been actively sustained and furthered by this association and through all these years the interest and work has grown until Harvard stands today, largely through the work of this club, in the front ranks of attractively planted and beautifully cared for small towns of northern Illinois, if not of the entire state.

MRS. C. W. GODDARD, Pres.

The following letter belongs to the above article:

'Dear Mrs. Doolittle:—

"I have heard the history of the Harvard Civic Association read, and find it pleasing in every way save one. The writer has given herself no credit for all the good work she has done for our organization, and I feel that it is unjust.

"I was president for three years through the hard work of establishing a permanent association, and know that it was her persistent efforts that brought success to us, for although she had good help, she was, and is, the backbone of the Harvard Civic Association.

"I have written the above from my own sense of right, and hope it will be kindly considered by the party credited.

"One of the presidents of the

"Harvard Civic Association."

In 1919 this organization was merged with the civic department of the Harvard Woman's Club with Mrs. Charles W. Goddard as chairman.

HARVARD FORTNIGHTLY CLUB

In the summer of 1898 the Up-To-Date Club and the Honor Club united to become the present Harvard Fortnightly Club.

The Up-To-Date kept posted on the Spanish-American War; also general current events. The Honor represented Hope, Faith, Charity and Progression.

The new organization was named the Harvard Fortnightly Club by unanimous vote, forty members being the maximum, though the membership has since been increased to fifty.

Mrs. J. W. Groesbeck was chosen president and held the office from October, 1898, to October, 1904. Mrs. Harriet Eastman, Mrs. Fannie Wellington, Mrs. A. C. Manley, Mrs. H. W. Blodgett and Mrs. J. H. Deaner have each served three years. The present president is Mrs. Daisy Goodsell.

The club federated with the state in 1906, and with the county the same year; in 1913, with the eleventh district.

For several years the work was for higher social and moral conditions but as interest increased local educational work was taken up and the public library, the schools and the Red Cross received benefits from the organization. For a number of years a lecture course has been sponsored and food sales and the movies have played their part toward charitable earnings. A Chautauqua, beginning August 1, was added to the list of 1919 work.

All moneys gained by club effort are used to help the needy or for local improvement, so in April, 1919, fifty trees were set out along the cemetery road in honor of our Harvard soldier boys. A Parent-Teacher Association was formulated in January, 1919, with a membership of ninety-six. Last, but not least, the French and Belgian orphans have received a portion of the H. F. C.'s earnings.

Since organization seven members have died, eight moved from Harvard and eleven resigned, but the waiting list was large enough to fill these vacancies without delay.

The names of charter members are: Mrs. J. C. Blake, Miss Daisy Blake, Mrs. J. S. Brasier, Miss Florence Bowman, Miss Edna Blanchard, Mrs. H. D. Crumb, Mrs. Elmer Carpenter, Mrs. E. L. Church, Miss G. Carlson, Mrs. D. Davidson, Mrs. J. C. Diener, Miss W. Diener, Mrs. H. Eastman, Mrs. G. T. Griswold, Mrs. J. W. Groesbeck, Miss Mayme Groesbeck, Mrs. J. M. Harris, Mrs. R. W. Hall, Mrs. W. D. Hall, Mrs. F. J. Hubbell, Mrs. E. Krotzer, Mrs. James Lake, Mrs. M. W. Lake, Miss Genevieve Lake, Mrs. Frank Mason, Mrs. H. B. Minier, Mrs. V. McKinstry, Miss J. Marshall, Mrs. J. J. Rountain, Mrs. P. E. Saunders, Mrs. Stewart Saunders, Mrs. M. A. Stafford, Mrs. W. C. Wellington, Mrs. P. E. Whittleton, Mrs. Fannie Webster, Mrs. Freeman Wilson, Miss Hattie Wilson, Mrs. H. S. Williams, Miss Nellie Williams, Mrs. H. T. Woodruff and Mrs. A. W. Young.—By President's Committee.

HARVARD WOMAN'S CLUB

The Harvard Woman's Club was the outgrowth of an idea. Many years ago a number of Harvard ladies were invited for a social afternoon when a fine lecture or a good story was read by the hostess or one of the guests. The time was so happily and profitably spent, the plan of entertainment met with enthusiastic appreciation and other ladies followed with like entertainment. It is from the influence of these afternoons that our club undoubtedly received its origin, being organized October 19, 1891. Mrs. W. C. Wellington and Mrs. R. W. Hall, having it in mind for some time, had carefully worked out a plan for a club beginning. That the selection of members was most satisfactory, although in several instances those brought together were mere acquaintances, the years have proved by uniting all into a wonderfully intimate friendship which has greatly enriched and blessed our lives.

The following is the list of charter members: Mrs. Fannie Kinnie Wellington, Mrs. Anna Bagley Hall, Mrs. Harriet Nims Binnie, Mrs. Julia Ayer Minier, Mrs. Harriet Watson, Mrs. Lucelia Hunt, Mrs. Harriet Miles Eastman, Mrs. Mary Crumb, Mrs. Clara Curts, and Mrs. Caroline Blake Goddard.

The rules and by-laws first formulated have practically remained unchanged. The club is not a study club, but a reading and social club. The season opens in October. Meetings are held every Monday afternoon, reading from 2:30 to 4:30, followed by refreshments at five o'clock, closing with post prandial.

Reading entertainment and post prandial are furnished by members in turn, the reader selecting any subject or matter she chooses. Each member invites one guest so that each week a company of twenty enjoys the reading and very informal discussions in which both guests and members are urged to participate, in addition to the dinner and the delightful post prandial which latter has always seemed especially helpful and inspiring.

No change in membership has occurred in the past twenty-three years until our loss, by death, of our youngest member, Mrs. Crumb. Several removals from Harvard and one withdrawal, added the names of Mrs. Mary Bagley Nims, who also moved away after one year, Mrs. Harriet Ayer Towne, Mrs. Lucy Gardner Young, Mrs. Mary Young Williams, and Mrs. Leretha Austin Axtell.

The officers being elected annually by ballot, it has necessarily somewhat of a rotation from vice president to president, most of the members serving many seasons. The office of secretary and treasurer, however, has not been so changeable, the present incumbent, Mrs. Goddard, having held the office since the close of the first year.

The club has secured for Harvard several noted lecturers including Prof. David Swing, Newel Dwight Hillis, Rev. Frank Gunsaulus, and Jenkin Lloyd Jones. Also one season a lecture course of several numbers was held, the proceeds of $95.00 being given to the library. The club has held many delightful receptions for out-of-town guests, some for teachers of our public schools, one colonial reception when the members were dressed to represent historic dames, and a large number for the husbands of the members at which other guests were included. Several receptions were also held in celebration of important club events, such as the one hundredth meeting when one hundred guests were served with special refreshments, a program, toasts and a general good time. The 400th meeting was celebrated as a New Year's-day book reception at the public library. This added 400 books to our new library collection.

To the Harvard Woman's Club the library is deeply indebted in that through its efforts, under the leadership of the library committee of the club, Mrs. Hall, watchful supervision has been maintained and invaluable assistance given. It is also largely due to this club that the constant stream of new books, necessary to carry on, has been supplied. One of the club's "library memorials" was our "Pay Shelf Fund" started in the fall of 1913 by our gift of $10.00, this to launch a perpetual fund for the purchase of the latest fiction, which should be on a special shelf, and all books drawn from it were to be paid for by a small charge per week, all money so received to be re-invested in more "new books."

Our 500th celebration, November 2, 1915, consisted in a trip to the library in a body, where our president, Mrs. Hunt, presented our anniversary gift of an additional $20.00 to the pay shelf. During 1918 this fund has accumulated $150.00 for the purchase of new live literature for circulation, and as the years follow must roll up larger and larger sums annually. Another club gift to the library was a good, serviceable clock. Through the efforts of our club, a library tax has for some time yearly been secured, in 1918 amounting to $1,000.00. Besides Mrs. Towne's gifts of hundreds of books either purchased expressly for the library, or taken from her private library, she presented to the library her very valuable and exquisite collection of butterflies, mounted in plaster or cotton plaeques, together with the cabinet in which they are housed. This gift is of great beauty and will ever be a source of delight and education.

A fine picture of President Lincoln was given to our high school. To the activities of the Woman's Club, the Harvard Red Cross directly owes its origin. An initial membership of about fifty was secured by them after reading and discussion of the Red Cross and its work at a regular meeting of the Woman's Club, when our secretary volunteered to receive the names and dues to be forwarded to Washington. Later through the club's agitation and insistence, a leader was secured, Miss Florence Crumb, and her splendid perseverance resulted in the establishment of the Harvard branch of the Red Cross. Every member of the Woman's Club has been an active worker in the Red Cross either as head of some department, or a contributor of funds, or knitting. For two years the club has supported a French Orphan.

The Woman's Club has been an active force in assisting every movement for the benefit of Harvard and the uplift of her citizens. Over 8,000 persons have been dined and entertained by it, the largest number recorded in one year being 650. Approximately 1,500 of the choicest magazine stories and articles by the most brilliant writers of all ages have been read and freely discussed, all of which must have broadened and deepened the community thoughts and lives as surely as they have broadened and deepened ours.

Geo. A. Hunt

HUNTLEY WOMAN'S CLUB

A company of women met on the afternoon of August 11, 1911, and were addressed by Mrs. Minnie Starr Granger, then state president of the Federated Clubs of Illinois. The subject considered was the organization of a Woman's Club in Huntley. After the address discussion resulted in a vote by those present to form a club and become federated with the state at once.

Mrs. Belle Hoy was elected president, and committees were appointed to draft a constitution and prepare the work for the coming year. The name of the organization was to be The Huntley Woman's Club and the object, intellectual advancement, interchange of ideas and the promotion of the best interests of our community. The charter members were as follows: Mrs. Meda L. Smith, Mrs. Sarah Hadley, Mrs. Jennie L. Mason, Miss Catherine Donahue, Mrs. Myrtle S. Cook, Mrs. Claribel Hoy, Mrs. Beatrice Hoy, Miss Etta Sheehan, Mrs. Minnie C. Devine, Miss Georgiana Hadley, Mrs. R. Donahue, Mrs. Neva Hawley Van Ness, Mrs. Bessie Cook Butler, Miss Elizabeth Keating, Mrs. Harriet Crowley, Mrs. Rose Safford, Mrs. Abigail Richardson, Mrs. Ella Hart, Mrs. Theodore Fredericks, Mrs. Minnie Keating, Mrs. Anna Hadley, Mrs. Hester Disbrow, Mrs. Catherine Ober, Mrs. J. A. Sinnett, Miss Helen Grace Randall, Miss Lida Eleanor Randall, Mrs. Mae Statler, Miss Edith Hooker, Miss Gertrude Mason, Miss Alma Pabst, Mrs. Mabel Cruikshank, Mrs. Rene Marks, Mrs. Arletta Yarwood, Mrs Lora Harvey.

The first year the club had but two departments, a study class which met in the afternoon, and evening meetings once a month. The next year four departments were created, as follows: home and education, history and travel, civics, and literature and music.

The presidents of the clubs have been as follows: Mrs. Belle Hoy, Mrs. Beatrice Hoy, Miss Gertrude Mason, Miss Lida Randall, Mrs. Arletta Yarwood, Mrs. Neva Hawley Van Ness, Mrs. Mary Bartholomew, Mrs. Arletta Yarwood, Mrs. O. W. Mason, Mrs. J. W. Burns, and Mrs. F. R. Liddil.

The charter members of the club of Huntley should feel proud of the record of their work. There have been mistakes without doubt, but it has always been the purpose of the club to keep their object in view, even if at times it might seem far off. It has been the purpose of the club to bring all the good things into the community within its power and as we look back we can feel that the efforts have not been fruitless. There is a present membership of forty-five.

In February, 1915, a public library was started by the members of the club, and has been in active operation ever since. When our country became involved in the Great War, the club set aside its routine work as all other loyal clubs did, and gave preference to the Council of Defense and Red Cross. Our active club members took up this broader work as capably and intelligently as they had previously done the regular club work, thus proving the value of their training, and their loyalty to their country.

The Huntley Woman's Club affiliated with the District Federation in 1911, the State Federation in 1911, and the County Federation in 1917.

GERTRUDE MASON.

LOTUS COUNTRY WOMAN'S CLUB

The Lotus Country Woman's Club of Spring Grove was organized December 9, 1911, at the home of Mrs. Fred H. Hatch. Nine women met to discuss the possibilities of a study club. Those present were as follows: Mrs. Fred L. Hatch, Mrs. F. W. Hatch, Mrs. B. A. Steven, Mrs. T. D. Cole, Mrs. G. E. Wieland, Mrs. J. P. Vidward, Miss Julia Vidward, Mrs. Robert Currier, and Mrs. G. B. Hardy. It was decided to form a club and the following officers were elected: Mrs. Fred L. Hatch, president; Mrs. B. A. Stevens, vice president; Mrs. F. W. Hatch, corresponding secretary; Mrs. G. E. Wieland, recording secretary; and Miss Julia Vidward, treasurer. The directors were as follows: Mrs. W. E. Colby, Mrs. T. D. Cole, and Mrs. G. B. Hardy. The chairman of the constitution and by-laws committee was Mrs. G. B. Hardy. The program committee was as follows: Mrs. G. B. Hardy, Mrs. G. C. Wieland, and the chairman of social committee was T. D. Cole. It was decided the club was to be a literary and social organization, with meetings on the first and third Saturdays in the month at two, p. m., at the homes of the members, refreshments to be limited to tea or coffee and wafers or cookies.

The club was named after the beautiful Lotus beds in Grass Lake. A few years later the word "Country" was added, making it the Lotus Country Woman's Club. The club affiliated with the State federation, the District federation, and the Federation for Country Life.

The progress of the club in 1912 was as follows:

Flower, Lotus. Colors, yellow and green. Motto, "Not for ourselves alone."

The following women have acted as presidents: Mrs. F. L. Hatch.

Mrs. B. A. Stevens, Mrs. J. C. Furlong, Mrs. G. C. Wieland, Mrs. J. C. Furlong.

At the sixth meeting of the club, held at the home of Mrs. F. W. Hatch, March 2, 1912, it was suggested that as the old officers were the originators of the club, it would be proper and fair that they be re-elected to their respective offices the ensuing year, thus giving an officer the privilege of holding office for two years. With a little change the following were elected: Mrs. F. L. Hatch, president; Mrs. B. A. Stevens, first vice president; Mrs. Lynn Overton, second vice president; Mrs. G. C. Wieland, secretary and treasurer; Mrs. F. L. Hatch, corresponding secretary; directors, Mrs. E. G. Turner and Mrs. J. C. Furlong.

At this time the club had about twenty members, but it grew until at the present time there are forty members, not including the Music Club of fifteen girls which is an auxiliary to our club.

A farm festival and children's flower and vegetable show was held September 15 to 20, 1913. Among the speakers were Joseph E. Wing, Mrs. H. M. Dunlap and Dr. Cyril G. Hopkins.

During 1918-19, it was voted to hold the meetings in Schramm's Hall, which the club had just rented. All of the members belong to the Red Cross, and the club has given generously toward its support.

There is a library connected with this club, which was started by the donation by each member of a book to be read by the members. Now there are over 100 volumes in the library, besides the use of a traveling library from Springfield.

A French orphan was adopted through our club, by the four schools representing members in our club, Spring Grove, Creek, English Prairie, and Solon Mills schools.

It has been the aim of the club to provide entertainment for the young people of the community, and many are the good times they have had. A study course was decided upon for 1919 and 1920. Mrs. J. C. Furlong is the present president; G. Turner, recording secretary; Mrs. R. R. Turner, corresponding secretary; Miss Mary Swenson, treasurer; Mrs. Reed Carr, auditor; directors, Mrs. F. W. Hatch and Mrs. G. J. Richardson.

We have had two deaths in the club, Mrs. Elizabeth Pinney of Solon Mills, dying May 14, 1917; and Mrs. Catherine Westlake of Spring Grove, dying January 6, 1919.

MRS. E. G. TURNER.

MARENGO WOMAN'S CLUB

In 1894 eight ladies met at the home of Miss Nellie Fillmore to form a conversation club, so unpretentious as to have no rules or regulations. The object of the club was for the members to become easy and proficient conversationalists. At each meeting on Monday afternoon, every member was obliged to relate a short and select story. It was such a success that by the end of the first year the most retiring and unassuming member gave a review of J. M. Barrie's "Little Minister" like a gifted reader.

The charter members of this club were as follows: Mrs. Helen Husted, Mrs. Caroline Coon, Mrs. Harris G. Otis, Mrs. M. G. Hackley, Mrs. Elizabeth Shurtleff, Miss Jean Stanford, Miss Elizabeth Sperry, and Miss Nellie Filmore. It was thought best for us to broaden out and enlarge the membership of our club to twenty-five members, who appointed Mrs. John Parkhurst, Mrs. Caroline Coon and Mrs. Harris G. Otis, assisted by a most able lawyer, Mr. A. B. Coon, to draw up a constitution and some by-laws. Mrs. Gertrude Dorman gave instruction in parliamentary law. The object of the club was to study art and literature for mutual benefit. We reviewed the art and literature of Italy, France, England, Germany, Japan, Egypt and the United States, oftentimes spending months and even a year on one country. We met in private homes, but after the Community Hall was completed in 1916, we again changed our plan, increasing our membership to nearly one hundred, and began meeting in the new hall. The club now meets in the hall the first and third Friday from October to May 1. There are five departments of the club: civics, philanthropy, reform, science and education, literature and art and music. The club now has a membership of ninety-eight.

Before the war, each department held meetings outside the club for study. At the regular meetings we have had outside talent, being addressed by ministers, lawyers, physicians, philanthropists and educators, and otherwise entertained by opera singers, bands, cartoonists, clay modelers and artists. Ross Crane brought a fine exhibit from the Art Institute and give us several lectures. Bonnie Snow brought a wonderful collection of art and crafts from public schools all over the United States, and gave us two or more lectures on the subject.

The club cared for the public library for fifteen years, and its demands from that day to this keep growing, and now through the aid of C. B. Whittemore, we have a two mill tax and the library now requires no further aid from the club. Mrs. C. B. Whittemore, one of our members, is president of the library board. At different times the club has given teas, luncheons, banquets and garden parties, for great social features.

Among those who have served the club as president, are the following: Mrs. Harris G. Otis, Marengo; Mrs. Gertrude Dorman, Colorado; Mrs. James Ingersoll, New Haven, Conn.; Mrs. C. W. Hart, Seattle, Ore.; Mrs. Henry Rehbock, Fort Worth, Tex.; Mrs. Ellsworth Seward, Marengo; Mrs. Caroline Coon, Marengo; Mrs. C. L. Lundgren, Ann Harbor, Mich.; Mrs. C. B. Whittemore, Marengo; Miss Nellie Fillmore, 5918 W. Erie Street, Chicago, Ill.; Mrs. A. A. Crissey, Marengo; Miss Kate Bloodgood, Marengo; Mrs. Frank Hackley, Marengo; Mrs. Charles Talbott, Duluth, Minn.; Mrs. Jarvis Heath, Marengo; Mrs. J. M. Patterson, Marengo; Mrs. C. Dyke, Crystal Lake, and Mrs. A. W. Kelley, the present incumbent.   Mrs. H. G. Otis.

MC HENRY COUNTY FEDERATION OF WOMAN'S CLUBS

An invitation was extended to the different woman's clubs of McHenry County, by the Woman's Club of Woodstock, to meet on their regular day, February 6, 1906, to discuss the forming of a county federation. Other county federations were explained by Mrs. A. S. Wright of Woodstock, and after careful consideration, the president of each club retired and formulated the resolution, on which to federate.

"Resolved to federate as a county federation; our aims being a higher social, moral and intellectual influence in the county."

Signed by the Marengo, Harvard, Hebron and Woodstock clubs.

The first officers elected were as follows: Mrs. King of Hebron, president; Mrs. McEwan of Woodstock, vice president; Mrs. Wellington of Harvard, recording secretary; Miss Groesbeck of Hebron, corresponding secretary; and Mrs. Whittemore of Marengo, treasurer.

On May 12, 1906, the constitution was adopted. The federation meets every June in the city which invites it.

After the business of the meeting is transacted, a literary program is given. We have heard the following speakers: Mrs. Harriet Vittum, "Civics;" Clifford Roe, "White Slave;" Miss Brooks of the Illinois University, "Home Care of the Sick;" Carl Wentz, president of the Academy of Fine Arts, "Line and Color in Dress;" Minnie Starr Granger, state president, and Jessie Spafford, Illinois president, federated clubs and Christine Tomlin, "War Work."

The clubs now belonging to the federation are: Harvard Woman's Club, Harvard Fortnightly Club, Harvard Civic Club, Woodstock Woman's Club, Marengo Woman's Club, Hebron Woman's Club, Rush Creek Woman's Club, Crystal Lake Woman's Club, Algonquin Woman's Club, Huntley Woman's Club, and the Seneca Domestic Science Club.

The officers are: Mrs. Frank Tanner of Harvard, president; Mrs. Watkins of Marengo, vice president; Mrs. Cameron of Hebron, recording secretary; Mrs. Sedlye of Harvard, corresponding secretary; Mrs. Flora Richards of Woodstock, treasurer.   MRS. E. C. ROBB.

RICHMOND WOMAN'S CLUB

In the fall of 1911 a group of the Richmond women organized, in order to study domestic science. The following year they voted to become a woman's club, at the same time increasing the membership of the original organization. The charter members were as follows: Mrs. M. R. Cole, Mrs. J. U. Benton, Mrs. F. H. McAssey, Mrs. F. B. McConnell, Mrs. E. M. Stewart, Mrs. W. C. Heck, Mrs. C. Otto, Mrs. Nellie Phillips, Mrs. Ella Lang, Misses Nellie Rehorat, Clare Hobart, Elizabeth Ward. There are now twenty members. The following have held the office of president: Mrs. M. R. Cole, 1912-1914; Mrs. Gertrude Burgerzei, 1914-1916; and Mrs. F. B. McConnell, 1916-1919. Elizabeth C. Ward is now serving as president.

The Richmond woman's club has always taken an active part in promoting progressive movements along civic, educational and patriotic lines. Among other things, the club has co-operated with the University of Illinois in two public demonstrations, the first a five day domestic science school, with two instructors; the second, a wheel of lectures on household science illustrated by practical demonstrations in the state demonstration car.

The most enterprising undertaking was the exhibition of paintings by the Chicago Water Color Club and curious local collections, which lasted for five days, with entertainments each evening. The proceeds, amounting to $400.00, were expended for pictures and books for the schools.

Two civic tag days have been held at Richmond, the ultimate result being a keener interest in bird protection and shrub planting around the town hall. One winter a successful lecture course was directed by the club. During 1918-1919, the club activities have centered upon the work of the Woman's National Council of Defense.

From the first it has been the policy of the club to hold several open meetings each year, on various subjects of interest to the community.

Miss Elizabeth Ward.

RUSH CREEK WOMAN'S CLUB

On October 24, 1901, the ladies of the Rush Creek neighborhood met at the home of Mrs. Horace Porter and organized the Rush Creek Aid Society to promote charity and sociability, realizing that by united effort a great deal of good could be accomplished. The first officers were as follows: Mrs. T. Graves, president; Mrs. Fred Tanner, vice president; and Mrs. Clark Porter, secretary and treasurer. The charter membership was fifty, and great enthusiasm was aroused.

Many changes have taken place since the organization of that first society. Eight of the charter members have passed on, and only six now remain active in the club work.

The day of October 26, 1911, marked the beginning of a new epoch for the Rush Creek ladies, when the Rush Creek Aid Society was reorganized into a full-fledged Woman's Club, under the guidance of Mrs. Charles Talbot of Marengo, as the Rush Creek Woman's Club, and federated with the state, district and county Woman's clubs, in November, 1911.

The following are among those who have served as presidents of the club: Mrs. Ira Puls, Mrs. C. A. Porter, Mrs. F. C. Curtis, Mrs. F. J. Miller, Mrs. Earl Swan and Mrs. Fred Watkins, and they have kept the various activities of the club very much alive. During 1917 and 1918, with a membership of thirty-two, the departments of the club united in doing war work. The sum of $500.00 was raised and expended for urgent calls for money. The club's war orphans have been cared for. The club sent to France 599 articles of clothing for the use of refugees. Seven barrels of clothing and food were sent to Chicago. Individual members bought generously of Liberty bonds and thrift stamps, and all in every way assisted in the war work.

At the beginning of a new year and a new era of peace, the members of the club realize the many blessings God has bestowed upon them, and pledge themselves to be in the future, as in the past, worthy of the trust reposed in them.

Mrs. F. J. Miller, Historian.

On February 12, 1906, six music lovers of Harvard, Ill., met to organize a club "to promote interest in the study of and cultivate a taste for the better class of music." These six ladies, who named their organization The Schumann Club, were Mesdames Aubrey Cook, Lawrence Norton, Robert Minshull, James Keeler and Misses Nella Williams and Lora Waters.

The Schumann Club has grown in numbers and power until it has won for itself a distinctive place in the city's life and has become federated with both the state and national Federations of Music Clubs. The club now has twenty active members. It meets fortnightly and the afternoon is divided into study and choral practice.

This club has given numerous musicales and has furnished music for many of the other clubs' programs. It has also brought to the community many musicians of note in lectures and concerts, among whom were the following: William L. Tomlins, Maude Fenlon Bolman, Mabel Corlew Schmid, Day Williams, Helen Brown Read, Jessie Daggett, Helena Bingham and Alberto Salvi.

During the two years when the members have been devoting themselves to war activities of various kinds, the outside work of the club was largely the sponsoring of many community sings, which have been such a potent factor at Harvard, as elsewhere, in winning the war.

The latest activity of the club has been the collections of victrola records, nearly one hundred of which have been sent to the military hospital at Ft. Bayard, N. M.

During the years of the club's life, the following members have served in the capacity of president: Mrs. Aubrey Cook, Miss Adeline Brainard, Mrs. Howard Ferris, Mrs. F. A. Barter, Mrs. Robert Minshull, Miss Frances Kees, Mrs. Howard Eaton and Mrs. H. B. Megran.

KATHERINE I. EATON.

The Seneca Association of Domestic Science was organized in the fall of 1908. The first president was Mrs. Kate Andrews, and the first secretary was Mrs. Frances Greene. The charter members were as follows: Mrs. Kate Andrews, Mrs. R. M. Bean, Mrs. Charles Broek, Miss Ella Bockman, Mrs. Delos Diggins, Mrs. Henry Echternach, Mrs. Frances Greene, Miss Mabel Greene, Mrs. L. Hand, Mrs. Fred Hill, Miss Mary Purvis, Miss Aggie Purvis, Miss Grace Redpath, Mrs. Elizabeth Standish,

Mrs. Charles Standish, Mrs. G. Stewart, Mrs. Henry Torman, Mrs. A. G. Waterman and Mrs. Charles Weiss.

The club was first a social organization, and as such it always met the needs of the community. Among the customs was that of holding monthly an all day meeting at the homes of the members. A dinner, to which all contributed, was served at noon. The families of the members were entertained formally four times a year, and visitors were always welcome. Picnics, socials, suppers, etc., contributed to the neighborhood enjoyment.

The motto of the club is that of the State Household Association, "For Better Health, Better Homes and Better Schools." The work of the club is expressed in the motto, and might be classified as social, educational and charitable. The social activities are outlined above. Under the head of educational, may be mentioned the frequent public meetings, addressed by speakers and demonstrators from both the University at Urbana, and the State Institute, and also by local speakers, including doctors, lawyers, teachers and other professional people who have a message for the club members. The organization has always encouraged all work in the schools which comes under the aims of the society. Among them may be mentioned school gardens, hot lunches for rural school children, sewing in the school, and special attention to health study. The election of at least one woman on the board of directors for country schools has been urged.

The charitable work of the club consists of contributing both money and supplies to needy persons or causes, and sewing for those in need. During the war the members have worked collectively and individually in the Red Cross and also for the Woman's Committee of National Defense. Money has been contributed to war work and two French orphans have been adopted.

The club has affiliated with the Household Science Department of the State Farmer's Institute, and also with the county and district federation of woman's clubs.

The present membership numbers eighteen. The officers are as follows: Mrs. Mary Witson, president; Mrs. Verna Bockman, vice president; Mrs. Helen Wright, secretary; and Mrs. Nettie Standish, treasurer.

MRS. H. F. ECHTERNACH.

WOODSTOCK WOMAN'S CLUB

Two years before the actual organization of the Woodstock Woman's Club, the idea of such a club was born in the mind of the first president,

Mrs. A. S. Wright, and it found fruition on the afternoon of the first Tuesday of October, 1905, which saw an organized club of four departments, a membership of fifty-seven and a printed calendar.

The Woodstock Woman's Club was incorporated in 1905; joined the state federation in 1906, the McHenry County federation in 1906, and the Eleventh district federation in 1909.

During the first three years the club secured the erection of a shelter at the Woodstock depot; the adoption of manual training in the public schools, and the gift of pictures and statuary to the schools; the passage of the anti-spitting ordinance; and began the agitation for the establishment of a hospital for Woodstock which paved the way for the building of the one now standing. In 1908, the club secured the installing of the rest room in the courthouse, which during the Great War was used for Red Cross headquarters for the county, but following the close of hostilities, was returned to the public for its original purpose. The club in 1910 issued a cook book, which in 1917, was revised, although the original name of The Woodstock Woman's Club Cook Book, was not changed. The establishment of a nursery in the Industrial Home, the adoption of domestic science in the public schools, and an addition to the public school library, are among the organization's recent activities.

The members of the Woodstock Woman's Club took upon themselves the work of assisting during the World War, in addition to the regular routine, beginning in 1914, with the Belgium Relief activities, and continuing as long as there was any need of their assistance. Among other things, the club assisted in securing the Soldier's rest room at Camp Grant; Furlough Home in France, and finding homes for the fatherless children of France.

The scope of the club work was broadened continuously. The membership average seventy-eight. The best to be obtained has been furnished in the programs, and other cultural opportunities have been afforded by the Shakespeare Study Class, organized at the very beginning, and later an Opera Study Class, and during one year, The Modern Drama Class. With the organization of the club, came a club chorus. Recreations and hospitality have not been neglected. Reaching out into unselfish service, the club is moving on to enlarge and better its already important function in the community, and its influence is such as cannot be ignored. Its proposed service will include the agitation for a new public library building and community house.

                                        PAULINE McMANUS.

CHAPTER XXII

MISCELLANEOUS

In this chapter will be found many items of historic interest, which in and of themselves, would scarce make a chapter, but when coupled together make one replete with interest to almost all classes of readers.

TAXABLE PROPERTY

When this county was first organized its rate of taxation was one per cent, on the following schedule: slaves or indentured or registered negro or mulatto servants, stock in trade, horses, mules, asses, and meat cattle above three years of age, swine, lumber. and one-horse wagons, clocks, watches, etc, but no revenue was raised on bank or railroad stock, pianos or silverware. The tax of 1837 realized $370.86.

EARLY RATES

Among the curiosities of ancient legislation is a tavern license of 1837, for which the fee was $8. There was a provision that the landlord should not overcharge his "dry" customer for the price asked for drinks. The license stipulated the rate he might charge, which was as follows: brandy, rum or gin, twenty-five cents a pint; wine, thirty-seven and one-half cents a pint; whisky, twelve and one-half cents per pint; beer or cider the same rate last mentioned. Meals were not to exceed thirty-seven and one-half cents each; lodging, twelve and one-half cents each; while a span of horses might chew hay all night for twenty-five cents.

But be it remembered that the shillings charged then were harder to obtain than at this date, if commodities were cheaper.

In the thirties and forties the nearest market was Chicago, and the only means of reaching there was by wading through mud in warm weather, and riding over frozen trails in winter. The wagons were for the most part drawn by oxen, the trip taking at least three full days, and the prices received for all kinds of produce was what farmers today and even for the last thirty years, would regard as not worth consider- ing. The seed, sowing, cultivating, harvesting and marketing cost more than the amount received in many cases. Thirty to forty cents a bushel for wheat, and that was the only article the farmer was certain he could sell at all for cash, after he had hauled it to the lake, camping out on his trip to and from the market place. The great yield of the early wheat crops was all that helped the pioneer out. He many years realized as high as forty-five bushels per acre for his spring wheat. Twenty teams in a line, thus going to market with their only staple product, was no uncommon sight.

Beginning with the year 1885, taken from the Republican Free- Press of Woodstock of January that year, and winding up with quo- tations from the successor of that newspaper the Sentinel of the pres- ent day, may be had the following quotations:

1855—brown sheeting, five to nine cents per yard; bleached shirt- ing, six to fifteen cents; linen pants from sixty-two cents up; linen coats, $1 to $1.50; sugar, twenty pounds for ninety-nine cents; coffee, thirteen to eighteen cents; teas, three to five shillings per pound; molasses, forty cents per gallon; salaratus, eight cents; salt, $6 per barrel.

1862—No. 1 spring wheat, eighty-eight cents; corn, thirty cents; oats, thirty-four cents; barley, seventy-eight cents; green hides, seven cents per pound; dry hides, fourteen cents; lard, seven cents; eggs, per dozen, thirteen cents; chickens, per pound, nine cents; turkey, six cents; butter, twelve cents; potatoes, fifty-five cents, per bushel; onions, sixty cents, per bushel.

April 26, 1865—spring wheat, $1.08; winter wheat, ninety-five cents to $1; oats, thirty-five cents; ear corn, fifty-five cents; shelled corn, sixty cents; clover seed, $14.50; beans, choice dull at seventy-five cents to $1; live chickens, $4 per dozen; hides, four and five cents per pound; eggs, per dozen, fourteen and fifteen cents; butter, good roll, twenty-five cents; firkin, fifteen to twenty cents.

September, 1881—cattle, extra choice, $5.90 to $6.20; butcher stock, $2.75 to $3.75; hogs, $6 to $7; sheep, $3.50 to $4.25; creamery butter, twenty to thirty-three cents; fine dairy butter, twenty-one to twenty-eight cents; eggs, twenty cents per dozen; No. 2 spring wheat, $1.31; corn, sixty-eight cents; oats, forty-one cents; barley, $1.13; lumber, (common boards) $15 to $17 per M; fencing, $13 to $15 per M.

Fall of 1885—cattle, $5; hogs, $4.50; mess pork, $9.40; lard, seven cents per pound; cheese, five to eight cents; wool, twenty-seven to thirty-six cents; creamery butter, nineteen cents; dairy butter, fifteen cents; eggs, fifteen cents; No. 2 wheat, seventy-nine cents; corn, forty-three cents; potatoes, forty cents; lumber (common boards), $12.50 to $13.00; fencing, $10.50.

1893—World's Fair Year shipping steers, $3.50 to $5.24; cows, $1.25 to $3.10; hogs, $5 to $6 per cwt.; sheep, $2 to $4; butter, creamery, eighteen cents; dairy, fifteen cents; eggs, twelve cents; lard, ten cents; wheat, sixty-seven cents; corn, forty cents; oats, twenty-eight.

In the month of July, 1919—cattle, prime steers, $16.40; medium, $14.25; prime cows for beef, $10; hogs, choice light butcher's stock, $22.50; heavy weight butchers, $22; butter, forty-four to forty-eight cents for best; eggs, thirty-six to forty-one cents per dozen; cheese, thirty-one to thirty-four cents; poultry, thirty to thirty-one cents per pound; beans, hand picked $7 to $7.50 per bushel; sugar, ten cents; wheat No. 1 Red, $2.28; No. 2 hard, $2.32; corn (Chicago), $1.80 to $1.90; oats, sixty to seventy cents; gasoline twenty-three cents per gallon (small lots); Milk, $2.13 per cwt.

A Northern Illinois local newspaper spoke of prices in June, 1919, in language as follows:

"The hog is king. Long live the hog!" Prices quoted now are $22.50 a hundred pounds and still "going strong." Bacon and eggs will soon be on the menus of millionaires only! The 1919 model hog is silver-lined and gold-plated. Who wouldn't be a farmer if he could?

VILLAGE PLATS

Since the organization of this county the following village plats have been executed, and nearly all are still in existence, though some are long since defunct.

Algonquin was surveyed by J. Brink, county surveyor, September 26, 1844, in the northwest of the northwest of section 34 and the southwest of section 27, bounded by Fox River on the east, and on the south by Crystal Lake outlet, all in township 43, range 8 east. The proprietors were Eli Henderson and Alexander Dawson. Its original name was "Osceola."

Alden was platted September, 1849, by Frances Wedgewood, in Alden Township.

Cary was platted in section 13, township 43, range 8 by John Brink county surveyor June 4 to 7 in 1856, and filed for record February 23, 1859. The proprietor was William D. Cary.

Chemung was platted in the southwest quarter of section 33, township 46, range 5, by Lorenzo D. Dana.

Coral was platted July 16, 1866, in sections 6 and 7 in township 43, range 8.

Crystal Lake was platted by Benjamin Douglas and several others, in August, 1837, but was not really recorded until March 31, 1840.

Greenwood, see Troy.

Gatesville was platted near Crystal Lake in section 13, township 43, range 8, by Simon Gates, June 16, 1855.

Harvard was platted in sections 35 and 36 of township 46, range 5, on November 25, 1856, by Amos Page, proprietor.

Hartland was platted in the southwest of section 13 and the southeast of section 14, township 45, range 6. The date was July 26, 1878.

Huntley was platted as "Huntley station" in sections 28 and 33, in township 43, range 7, by Thomas S. Huntley. The date was April 14, 1853.

Hebron was platted in May, 1860, in the northwest quarter of section 16, township 46, range 7, by Henry W. Meno.

Johnsburg was platted in section 13, township 43, range 8, by a company of men, the work of surveying being executed on June 4, 5, 6, 1868.

Lawrence was platted March 9, 1841 in section 30, township 46, range 9, by C. C. Taylor.

Marengo was platted July 21, 1846, by proprietors Amos Daman and Calvin Spencer, September 14, 1846.

McHenry was platted in section 26, township 45, range 8, in May, 1837. The platters were Messrs. White, Colby and Brown.

Nunda was platted by land speculators and filed for record August 13, 1868. It was platted in the southeast quarter of section 32, township 44, range 8.

Ridgefield was platted in section 25, township 44, range 7, January 8, 1855, by William Hartman.

Richmond was platted in the west half of the southeast quarter and the east half of the southwest quarter of section 9, township 46, range 8, by Charles G. Cotting, September 2, 1844.

Ringwood was platted in section 9, township 45, range 8, July 2, 1878, by John Huermann.

Solon was platted by Henry White, proprietor, November 13, 1840, the tract being situated in section 26, township 46, range 8.

Spring Grove was platted May 3, 1855, by John E. and Emily J. Mann. This village is located in section 30, township 46, range 9 east.

Troy was platted by Lewis Boon, September 1, 1847, in the southwest quarter of section 12, township 45, range 7. This is now Greenwood.

Woodstock was platted in the south half of the southwest quarter of section 5, township 44, range 7 east. It was at first named by the county commissioners who laid it out, "Centerville" as it was near the exact geographical center of the county. The plat was executed April 10, 1844, by County Commissioners—Messrs. Troop, Hayward and Tryan, and was received for record June 10, 1844, by Recorder William H. Beach.

Union was platted October, 1851, in the east half of the northwest quarter of section 4, township 43, range 6 east.

CEMETERIES

The burying grounds of the county are numerous, and many of them are well improved and cared for by tender hands. Of course there are several of the older ones that were used in pioneer times which have not been used of later years, and hence have run down and are not cared for as well as the others. The record for several of the cemeteries is not to be found in the county books, but the tombstones speak louder than printed record that the departed dead are within such sacred enclosures.

The principal cemeteries in the county are listed as follows:

Algonquin Township, in sections 27 and 19.

Alden Township, in the northeast quarter of section 23-46-6, and in sections 14 and 15.

Burton Township, one in section 17, one in section 18, one in section 23.

Chemung Township, Mt. Auburn Cemetery in section 1, township 45, range 5, and one in each of sections 27 and 33.

Dunham Township, Oakland Cemetery, and one in each of sections 7, 19 and 35.

Greenwood Township, Greenwood Cemetery, and one in each of sections 20, 22 and 35.

Hebron Township, Parkers Cemetery; and one in section 26.

Marengo Township, Stewart's burying ground, and Marengo Cemetery.

Nunda Township, Mosgrove Cemetery.

Riley Township, Riley Center Cemetery.

Richmond Township, one in the village of Richmond; and one in each of sections 4, 11, 20 and 26, the last being known as Cedar Vale.

Dorr Township, one at "Oakland" and the Catholic Cemetery, "Calvary."

Harvard Township, Mt. Auburn, principal one used now.

McHenry Township, those found in sections 8, 9 and 20.

Grafton Township, one in each of sections 10 and 23.

Coral Township, one in section 5 at the village of Union.

Seneca Township, one in section 24.

Hartland Township, one at the village; and one in section 6.

POPULATION

The population of this county at different periods has been as follows: in 1840, 2,578; in 1850, 14,978; in 1860, 22,089; in 1870, 23,762; in 1880, 24,908; in 1910, 32,509, and in 1920, 33,164.

By townships the population for the years 1890, 1900, 1910 and 1920 was as follows:

	1890	1900	1910	1920
Alden Township	1,026	1,015	1,014	964
Algonquin Township	3,675	3,043	2,512	3,528
Algonquin Village	....	550	642	693
Burton Township	296	400	451	441
Chemung Township	3,057	3,814	4,101	4,421
Harvard City	1,967	2,602	3,008	3,296
Coral Township	1,354	1,451	1,432	1,296
Union Village	....	322	406	399
Dorr Township	2,796	3,470	5,335	6,408
Woodstock City	1,683	2,502	4,331	5,523
Dunham Township	919	859	849	857
Grafton Township	1,437	1,484	1,589	1,475
Huntley Village	550	606	773	...

	1890	1900	1910	1920
Greenwood Township	889	901	908	858
Hartland Township	960	874	905	860
Hebron Township	1,167	1,430	1,430	1,363
Hebron Village	....	611	644	631
Marengo Township	2,255	2,859	2,702	2,442
Marengo City	1,445	2,005	1,936	1,758
McHenry Township	2,555	2,673	2,679	2,825
McHenry Village	979	1,013	1,031	1,146
Nunda Township	1,805	1,963	2,110	2,321
Crystal Lake	1,219	1,554	1,932	2,449
Richmond Township	1,212	1,498	1,472	1,448
Richmond Village	415	776	554	533
Spring Grove	....	....	203	363
Riley Township	830	915	822	717
Seneca Township	1,046	1,105	1,023	940
Union Village	....	322	432	399

SELECTED NATIVITY—1860

Native.		Foreign.	
Born in this State	10,214	British America	382
Ohio	448	England and Wales	713
New York	4,790	Ireland	1,661
Pennsylvania	560	Scotland	207
Indiana	96	Germany	1,187
Kentucky	24	France	160
		Sweden and Norway	172
Total	16,132	Switzerland	11
		Bohemia	90
		Holland	11
		Denmark	23
		Total	4,617

INTERESTING ITEMS

In 1837 McHenry County paid its assessor $2 per day; county commissioners received $2.50 per day.

In the summer of 1838 the commissioners fixed the rate of compensation for jurors, both grand and petit, at seventy-five cents per day.

In 1838 the total tax in the county, which then included what is now Lake County, was $564.41.

It cost this county in 1842 $102 for assessing the property. In 1843 the county revenue amounted to $793.14.

The first justices of the peace in Fox precinct, and consequently first in the county, were William H. Buck, and William L. Way, elected July 3, 1837.

In 1918 McHenry County had assessed 381,521, 38 100 acres of land, valued at, for assessment purposes, $18,388,027. The value of improvements on these lands was $6,762,569.

Number of automobiles in county in 1918 were..... 3,096
Carriages and wagons............................. 7,067

The automobiles were assessed at $259.06 each, while the wagons were assessed at $16.37 each.

Of diamonds and jewelry there was............$5,227.00
Horses of all ages.............................. 13,890
Cattle of all ages.............................. 56,888
Mules and asses 122
Hogs and sheep 9,675

TORNADO OF 1862

From newspaper and personal accounts the following is gleaned:

"On Monday, August 4, 1862, a tornado, which was very destructive to both life and property, passed through the southwestern part of McHenry County. The storm began at three o'clock in the afternoon, with sheets of rain, heavy thunder and extremely sharp lightning. At the Deitz school house in Seneca Township, school was in session, and about eighteen scholars and the teacher, Mary E. Goodrich, were present. The house standing directly in the track of the storm was taken from its foundation and carried several feet, turned half around and torn to pieces leaving only the front end of the building standing. Strange to say, not a single scholar was seriously injured, though all were badly frightened.

"Fences, buildings, stacks and bundles of grain—everything that stood in the way of the terrible storm—was madly seized and torn to pieces. The residence of John E. Green, in Marengo, was blown down.

Mr. Green's mother, wife and daughter were in it at the time. The old lady was so badly hurt that she died the next day, and the wife and daughter were seriously injured. Robert Smith's son, John, aged fifteen years, took shelter in a shock of wheat in the harvest field. He was struck in the side by a board, blown from a neighboring structure, and so injured that he died the next hour. The wife of G. H. Sumner, a tailor, was found among the ruins of the barn, with her neck broken. Edwin Morris was so badly wounded that he died soon afterward. This storm was closely estimated to have caused a loss of $30,000 worth of property in this county.''

CYCLONE OF 1883

McHenry County has been quite fortunate in not being located in the natural zones of periodical wind-storms, especially the ever-to-be-dreaded cyclone. However, one did pass through the townships of Chemung and Alden, Friday, May 18, 1883. Three lives were sacrificed in this terrible storm, and an immense amount of damage done to property all along its pathway. Strange to relate, its direction was from the southeast moving northwest, and every building in its pathway was removed and swept out of existence. An account given by the local press says that near the Village of Chemung the farm buildings of Henry Baker, occupied by George Conn were utterly demolished. Seven persons were in the house at the time the storm struck. They fled to the cellar for protection. Patrick Corrigan, a hired man, was killed, and Mr. Conn injured by a falling timber. Just across the way the buildings of Mr. Downs were also destroyed, the owner rendered unconscious, and several members of the family injured. A near neighbor of Mr. Downs, R. J. Williams, lost his barn and a portion of his house. Owen McGee's buildings were destroyed and large oak trees were uprooted as if but mere saplings.

The railroad depot at Lawrence, and other buildings were damaged. Patrick Kennedy lost all of his buildings, and his hired man, John McGuirk, was killed. J. W. Rogers lost all of his buildings, except his house; also his horses, sheep, fences, carriages and farming implements.

In Alden Township the barns of James Vick and Mr. Campbell were destroyed, the residence of Fred Bombard damaged and his outbuildings ruined.

The Alden *Sentinel* correspondent, at the date of the storm wrote as follows: ''A few minutes after six o'clock the storm struck the residence of Fred Bottlemy. The family consisted of himself and wife, and four small children and one hired man. Mr. Bottlemy says they did not even have time to descend into the cellar; he reached for the two children to take them below, and the next he remembers anything about, he was lying upon the ground. The building was strewn to the four winds, the house in atoms, not one stick left upon another, even the stones composing the foundation were scattered for rods around. The scene beggars description. Parts of bedding and other clothing were found in the tops of tall trees fully a quarter of a mile away. Huge oaks were torn up by the roots and carried along for many rods to be lodged against the house where were the family. The hired man, a German named Soule, thirty-two years of age, was found dead in front of the house; he seems to have been killed by being thrown violently against some sharp pointed grubs that were sticking out of the ground at that spot. His skull was pierced in several places; the body was removed to the residence of Casper Bottlemy, one mile distant.

"Mr. Bottlemy was seriously injured across the lungs and bruised about the head. The small children were unhurt. Mrs. Bottlemy was found with her back firmly planted against a tree, her left arm broken below the elbow, her right arm dislocated at the shoulder. Her case is very critical. The oldest child, a girl of twelve summers, was badly bruised about the head and shoulders. These were all taken to the residence of Fred Bombard where they were kindly cared for. Dr. Barringer, of Alden, was sent for as soon as possible and arrived on the terrible scene about 6:30 P. M. Dr. Brigham arrived about midnight. The sufferers were all properly cared for. An inquest was held Saturday on the body of the hired man, and a verdict rendered in accordance with the above facts.

"Mr. Bottlemy's sheds and barns were leveled to the earth, one horse being killed. The next building struck was the schoolhouse, a good frame structure which was actually swept from existence, not a single vistage remaining. The storm happily occurred two hours after school closed for the day, or the consequences would have been terrible indeed.

"A few rods east is the residence of C. L. Kingsley, a large square house with a cupola. The whole roof was torn off and carried away. The barn, over sixty feet long, in which twenty-five cattle were standing, was flattened to the earth, the fragments were strewn for a mile around. There were also three persons in the barn at the time it was struck, none of whom were seriously injured. That they escaped seems almost incredible. A cow and horse were killed, and one double buggy and a single carriage are entirely missing. The next place visited was that of Fred Mode, a quarter of a mile further on. The barns were all destroyed; the houses were saved, although the porch was torn off. Still further to the east, the barn belonging to Mrs. M. A. Weter was destroyed. The storm was very severe further along toward the east, and much damage was done.

"From Alden, the cyclone passed over the line into Wisconsin, and just north of Hebron station, destroyed Levi Nichol's house, barn, etc. His hired man was killed outright. His father's barn was also wrecked. At Racine, eight persons were killed, a large number injured, and one hundred and fifty buildings destroyed."

UNUSUAL AND UNFORTUNATE OCCURRENCES

These peculiar and unfortunate incidents have all taken place within this county:

A snow storm in December, 1856, blocked up roads and the new railroad so effectually that travel by any method was impossible for days at a time. On the railroad running through Woodstock several trains were snowed in between stations.

In the Fremont political campaign in 1856, this county was won by the Republicans, and in ratifying the news what was styled as the "Woodstock Cannon" was used. By some mismanagement it was prematurely discharged, thereby badly injuring Orson Bates so as to require the amputation of his right arm, and the left hand above the wrist.

Sunday, August 28, 1859, James Ashe, a prisoner confined in the jail for beating his wife, probably through remorse, hung himself and he was found dead.

In the spring of 1859 a young man named Deming, son of Jedediah Deming, of Harvard, started for Pike's Peak as a gold seeker. When near there he was taken ill and being almost overcome by hardship and exposure, he turned back; but being joined on the Missouri River by his brother John, concluded to start for California. He was sick enroute most of the trip, but upon getting through was much improved. On January 20, 1860, he went out hunting, and not returning when expected, his brother went out to search for him. Seeing tracks of

Indians he at once concluded that John had been foully dealt with, and went to the neighboring miners for aid. The body was found shot through the head. While the brother of the murdered man was absent from his cabin, the Indians raided it, carrying off whatever they fancied. They were not pursued.

On October 22, 1859, William Dalzell, while bricking up a thirty feet well, on a farm a mile or so northeast of McHenry, was buried alive by being covered by the caving in of the walls to a depth of eighteen feet. When his body was recovered it was found that his head and face had been horribly mangled and that probably he met death instantly. A man named Babcock was drowned in the Nippersink, near Spring Grove, while fishing with a seine, May 19, 1860. He was thirty-five years of age and had recently come from the East.

A. C. Wilson, twenty years old, was killed at Harvard, July 20, 1860, while attending to his duties as a railroad employe, in trying to get cars on the track that had accidentally backed off.

In July, 1861, Andrew Austin, a young farmer, of Greenwood, was killed by being thrown from a horse.

At Harvard, June 6, 1862, a man named Cutter, a railway employe, was instantly killed by the cars.

March 7, 1862, Solomon West, in Seneca, committed suicide by taking poison. He was comparatively a stranger.

On Monday, May 5, 1862, John E. Burr, of Greenwood, met his death by accidentally falling from a tree. He was twenty-three years of age.

On October, 1863, Mrs. Bridget Lee was killed while attempting to cross in front of a freight train.

Adam Schneider, a very worthy farmer, was killed near Greenwood, October, 1863, while at work in his field. His team became frightened and ran over him.

John Steffer, working near Ringwood, April, 1863, ate wild parsnips and was killed by the same.

In March, 1864, Willard Joslyn, was killed on the farm near Harvard, while trying to turn a somersault over a pole.

In April, 1865, while celebrating the fall of Richmond, an anvil which they were firing exploded, and a large piece struck H. G. Otis, who died two hours later.

On June 16, 1865, John Dolan, of Woodstock, nineteen years old, was shot and killed while trying to enter the house of Rutledge Harris, near Crystal Lake. He with a companion, both drunk, went to Harris's house to see a girl and were denied admission. While trying to force an entrance Dolan was killed.

In June, 1865, while boating at Crystal Lake, two young ladies, Addie Deitz and Lucy Adams, both of prominent families, were drowned.

In August, 1867, Michael Dwyer, of Woodstock, aged seventeen, was accidentally drowned while bathing in Crystal Lake. The next day efforts were made to recover his body and the old cannon from Woodstock was brought into use. The second time it was discharged, it exploded and so injured the drowned boy's father that it was thought he would die; it also injured several others.

In May, 1868, a boy named Ira Clason, eighteen years old, was struck by lightning, while plowing on a farm six miles south of Marengo. The team he was driving at the time were also killed.

Henry Jackson, twenty-three years of age, was drowned in Crystal Lake while fishing, August 15, 1869.

T. J. Hobart was instantly killed in October, 1869, by the falling in upon him as he was digging, a cellar under a building. This was on the McHenry road six miles east of Woodstock.

In October, 1869, a four year old girl belonging to Patrick Crowley, of Marengo, was so badly burned by her clothes catching fire, that she died ten days later.

In August, 1870, at Woodstock, while moving a building, a timber fell in such a manner, that Bela Darrell was strangled to death.

Jeremiah Halesley was killed near Harvard by a railroad train. He was riding a horse and had crossed the track, but the horse had become frightened and ran back with its rider, who was thrown in front of the oncoming train and killed.

In January, 1873, a boiler exploded in the steam mill at Huntley, killing the engineer and injuring others about the flouring mill.

In August, 1873, Watson Heath, of Dunham, had both legs and an arm cut off in a mowing machine, and died soon after. He had lived in this county sixty-four years, and was a popular man and a good citizen.

On December 7, 1872, the night watchman, Jacob Hurst, at the Woodstock brewery, met his death in a singular manner. A bin of malt above him broke through the floor, and he was buried in it and smothered to death.

On June 9, 1874, a very sweeping storm caused heavy damage in this county as well as adjoining counties. Trees, houses, barns and fences suffered severely. The damage was especially great at Harvard,

McHenry, Union and Richmond. At Harvard the new engine house of the Chicago & North Western Railroad was destroyed and much other property damaged.

On August 24, 1874, the ten months' old child of Wm. H. Howe and wife was drowned in a pail of milk.

On October 12, 1874, a ten year old son of Issac Mussey, of Seneca, went to the pasture to catch a horse. While returning home his hands got cold, and to warm them he tied the rope by which he was leading the horse, about his body. The horse, taking fright at something, ran, and the boy was dragged until killed.

On December 15, 1874, on the farm of J. E. Nourse, two miles west of McHenry. William Grant, aged twenty-four years, was buried in a well, sixty feet deep. Eleven feet of earth caved in from the top and fell upon him. It required the work of two men for a day to recover his body.

On October 30, 1875, two miles from Woodstock, on the Austin Frame farm, George Schneider was struck by lightning and instantly killed. He and his wife were sorting potatoes in the cellar at the time, and she was uninjured.

In March, 1876, a man named Sweet, at Harvard, while sawing wood with a horse-power, was caught by the coat in the machinery and killed by being drawn into the saw frame.

In August, 1878, a German named Christian Beir, six miles west of Huntley, was standing on top of a threshing machine and slipped down into the cylinder while it was at full speed. His body was horribly mangled, too shocking for description. He lived an hour, being conscious to the end.

FROZEN TO DEATH

Under the above heading the *Woodstock Sentinel* of January 18, 1877, has the following:

"On last Sabbath afternoon the lifeless form of John Burk, of the town of Greenwood, was found in McHenry Township, near the old residence of Hon. H. McLean. The circumstances connected with this sad affair are substantially as follows: Mr. Burk left his house on Friday morning for McHenry with a load of oats, and not returning that night, his mother, who lived with him, notified his brothers of the fact on Saturday afternoon, and Sunday morning they started out to find him. They went directly to McHenry and were informed

that John was there Friday afternoon and left for home in the evening. They also learned that there was a sleigh, from which the horses were detached, near the railroad track north of the village. On examination, it was soon found that on leaving McHenry Mr. Burk took the railroad track instead of the wagon road, driving over cattle-guards, etc., until he came to the outlet of Lake McCollum; and at this point it seems the horses refused to cross the bridge, left the track and undertook to cross the stream on the ice, but it gave way, precipitating horses and sleigh into the water. It appears that Mr. Burk left the sleigh and succeeded in detaching the horses therefrom, removed the fence and started to cross the slough, but ran into a soft place or spring and here the horses left him, he traveling in one direction and they in another. Mr. Burk went but a short distance from where the team left him, took shelter under some bushes on the shores of the lake, where he was found by his brothers, frozen to death. His clothes were wet nearly to his waist, which proves he had been in the water. John has been in the habit of drinking strong drink too freely for several years, and no doubt but this was the case on Friday night, causing him to lose his way and bringing about his untimely death."

AN EARLY TEMPERANCE SOCIETY MEETING

It is not the province of this work to discuss the Prohibition and liquor questions of the long ago years in this county, as doubtless it is best to cover old John Barleycorn's putrid corpse with a mantle of charity. He no longer lives here, enough mean things have been spoken and written of him in the last seventy-five years to damn him for ever and a day, and we cannot find a record of authority showing that he had any saving traits of character, so let him rest where he fell, at the hand of the people of America in 1919.

But it may not be out of place to give the reader of this volume an account of a meeting of the "Ladies Temperance Association of McHenry County," held at Marengo in 1855. We give it as written up by a delegate from Elgin, who attended it and wrote her report in the Elgin Palladium of January 18, 1855:

"First in the order of events, after leaving Elgin depot, was the demand by the conductor for our fare, and we were greatly surprised at his unwillingness to accord to our party the courtesy, which in every instance heretofore has been shown ladies of this Association, in their frequent interchange of kindly regard and sympathy by attending the meetings of the different societies; by allowing them passage at the half fare usual rate. And still more were we surprised when upon representation of these facts to the superintendent, who chanced to be on board, he also refused the customary tribute to the cause of temperance. Sorry we are to record such an ungallant act. We felt indignant at such ungentlemanly treatment, but not sufficient to disturb our equanimity, and we arrived at Marengo in good spirits—were received by the ladies of that place with great cordiality—partook of their cheer and repaired to the Presbyterian meeting house, where after the transaction of business, we listened to an entertaining address from Mrs. Randall of Belvidere; after this resolutions were discussed, one being with regard to the rightfulness of *mob force* if necessary, for the restraint of the traffic in ardent spirits. It elicited a spirited discussion from Mrs. Safford, Mrs. Lindsey, and Mrs. Misick of Marengo, Mrs. Randall of Belvidere, Mrs. Hubbard of Huntley, and Mrs. Wright, Mrs. Waldron and Mrs. Tefft of Elgin, and was put to the house and lost. A number of resolutions to the effect that the rumseller is equally guilty and alike deserving of condemnation with the rum-drinker; and that they withdraw all patronage from all those who deal in intoxicating drinks we adopted unanimously. If lived up to this cannot fail to be of great good and it should enlist the energies and zeal of all temperance people. There seems to be a great amount of talent among the ladies of Marengo, compared to their numbers, some few noble-minded women, who are willing to hazard much in the cause they have espoused, and to 'hope on and hope ever,' until they see that accomplished for which they have been swelling the number of petitions to our state legislature, a prohibitory law similar to the Maine Law."

(Signed.)   ONE OF THE LADIES.

CENTENARY DRIVE.

The Centenary Celebration, or the 100th anniversary of the sending the first church missionary from the Methodist Episcopal church, was celebrated in 1919, and among other plans in this great movement, started by the Methodist denomination, and carried out by most of the Protestant denominations, for the betterment of the world's people, was the raising of an immense fund to carry on the missionary, home and foreign, cause. The Methodist Church alone asked for subscriptions for $105,000,000, to be paid in five equal annual payments. A staggering amount, seemingly, to confront a war-ridden people who have been subscribing such large sums to support the government in time of war, and to help European countries. Yet, through the force of good financial management on the part of the leaders of the church, this amount was subscribed and considerable more, too.

McHenry County "went over the top" in this, as well as in Liberty Loans. The exact figures are not at hand, but in the single case of the local Methodist Episcopal Church at Woodstock, it may be stated that its allotment was $15,850 for the five year period, and this amount was oversubscribed by about $1,000, enough to make up all shrinkage.

Among the logical arguments used in appealing to the church-going people here was one, that Woodstock expended on an average of $20,000 a year for picture shows, and only $25,000 for all her churches. And going outside, it was shown that the United States spends $320,000,000 a year for soda and other light drinks and $1,000,000,000 for tobacco. These and like arguments, properly presented, brought the subscribers to see that it was only their Christian duty to spend, at least $105,000-000 for trying to help answer the Lord's Prayer "Thy Kingdom Come."

In this county the "drive" was on only from May 18 to May 25.

HOME BUREAU

During the late World War the women of this county organized what is styled the Home Bureau, the aim of which is to better look after the domestic and home side of life. In a meeting held in the City School building in Woodstock, July 7, 1919, the women from all parts of the county were present with reports of the work accomplished during the past year. Miss Bunch, of the University of Illinois, and Mrs. Dunlap, of Champaign, were present and made addresses. The following officers were re-elected for the ensuing year: Mrs. A. E. Seward, Marengo, president; Mrs. G. A. Miller, Pleasant Valley, vice-president; Mrs. Fred McConnell, Woodstock, secretary; Mrs. Will Hoy, Huntley, treasurer. The executive committee consisted of the following: Mrs. E. G. Turner, Richmond; Mrs. Fred Baier, Harvard; Mrs. Will Dyke, Crystal Lake; Mrs. J. C. Furlong, Spring Grove; Mrs. A. J. Gafke, Woodstock.

Work was begun by this society in July, 1918, with 272 members enrolled. During the year work was carried on to the best interests of housekeeping and home-making; how to use better methods, and adopt better equipment to save time and energy in daily household tasks.

During the year, 129 meetings were held in McHenry County; eighty-seven of which were demonstrations at which the women were taught the preparation of war foods, canning of fruits, vegetables and meats and the remodeling of old clothing, forty-two lectures were given on better kitchen arrangement, labor-saving devices, poultry-raising, gardening, planning of meals and feeding of children. The total attendance at these meetings was 11,956. Miss Blair, in charge of the work, travelled during the year 2,737 miles by rail and 1,457 by car, holding meetings in every township in the county. As a result of the work, hot lunches were installed in three country schools. Twenty four women are making a special study of the planning of meals, keeping records of the time, expense and amount of food used. Twenty-nine women are keeping records of their gardens; thirty-seven are making special study of the poultry business. Six townships are studying the care and feeding of children. A week's sewing school has been conducted. Three days' instruction in poultry raising were given by a specialist with an attendance of 153. Besides all this much food was canned and dried, especially vegetables and meats and much wool saved by the re-making of clothes. This is an excellent innovation.

CIVIL WAR RELICS

In the summer of 1919, at Woodstock, druggist A. S. Wright had on exhibition in his show-window on the south side of the public square, a collection of valuable and highly interesting Civil War relics belonging to Col. William Avery. Colonel Avery's daughter, M. Ella Avery, in disposing of her household goods, tendered these war relics of her father's as trophies to the Memorial Hall in Chicago, which offer was accepted. This consists of revolver, saber, box of bullets; the bullet which wounded the colonel; shoulder straps from the rank of captain to colonel; well preserved piece of "hard-tack" (soldier's bread) now over fifty years old, still in good condition. Colonel Avery was county clerk of McHenry County for a period of twelve years. The Grand Army men took special delight in looking at these relics which reminded them of the days of their young manhood.

INSTALLING A NEW TYPESETTING MACHINE

Editor Scott, of the Richmond local newspaper, had troubles of his own according to the following paragraphs written by him after the battle was over in the month of August, 1915. It appears he had purchased a new linotype machine and upon unpacking it found it had been smashed up badly in a railroad wreck and a new one had to be sent for:

"Anyhow the expert linotype man, who knows bushels of things about printing machines, looked with some scorn on the mashed up machine and declared the "thing" was no good at all. Another was ordered and there was indigo atmosphere which lingered in the print shop all last week. The chief editor wouldn't even go fishing!

"The news editor was going tramping over the hills; going fishing and listening to the wind-waves in the trees and watch the shadows grow long when the sun was low.

"It rained there; there was no sunshine; there was no wind; and the fish wouldn't bite. The news editor was obliged to spend part of the time in a darkened room because of a vacation head ache, which was doubtless a just penance for planning to be a genuine gypsy for a whole week."

"There are several other chapters to this vacation story, but they are of the same color as those already described, hence we decline to enter further details. What's the use? The perfect linotype has arrived and is being installed and the glint of sunshine fills the office all around and back again."

WAR WAGED ON CANADA THISTLES

The state law concerning Canada thistles and other objectionable weeds is being rigidly enforced in the county at this time. The encroachment of late of the Canada thistle is something fearful to behold. The county has its regular thistle commissioners and they in turn have been authorized to engage scores of assistants to aid in doing away with these pests. June, July and August are the three available months in which to try to annihilate the thistles. The report shows that there were 743 different strips of Canada thistles on farms in Dunham Township alone, of which twenty-four were in the highways. The commissioners are provided with an outline map which they are supposed to fill in as fast as the thistle sections are discovered. When a farmer claims his farm is not in the thistle belt, the commissioner simply pulls out his map or plat and shows him that he is mistaken and that unless he gets busy and removes the pests at once that the county will hire a person to remove the same and add the expense, which is usually from $3 to $4 per day, to his next tax bill.

In Hartland Township there is a ten-acre tract, where the pests have grown to an alarming extent. Mowing machines have been employed to cut them down.

Many of the worst tracts are on farms which are rented out and the owners live so far away that they seldom visit the place hence the thistles have grown almost beyond control of anyone.

In Chemung Township, the commissioner declared, "There is one farm in my district in this township that has sufficient Canada thistles, if permitted to ripen, to supply enough seed to cover all of the great State of Texas." One commissioner, Mr. Dacy, walks over his territory, going many days as much as twenty miles.

There is no escape from assuming the thistle obligation. If the land owner refuses to cut them down at the lawful time, the commissioner simply hires a man to do the work and reports the transaction and makes a bill which is placed against the land at the coming tax paying season.

WORLD'S FAIR CORN EXHIBITS

During the great Columbian Fair at Chicago, in 1893, McHenry County had a large and complete assortment of corn grown from her rich soil. The men who under director James Crow, of Crystal Lake, furnished such corn exhibit were worthy a record in the annals of their county, hence find the list here annexed.

Smith Brothers, Ringwood; George Lewis, Cary Station; James Stewart, Cary Station; F. B. Peck, McHenry; Dr. Warren Chase, Chemung; S. M. Wardlow, Hebron; C. Lockwood, Ridgefield; Prentice Smith, Cary Station; James Brennon, Huntley; Henry Leesberg, Algonquin; C. Techler, Algonquin; Calvin Davis, Ridgefield; James R Jackman, Crystal Lake; C. Pinnow, Crystal Lake; Nels Ackerson, Crystal Lake; Louis Cammine, Crystal Lake; William Peet, Crystal Lake; E. D. Barnard, Greenwood; O. McCollum, Nunda; O. N. Brass, Seneca; John Duggan, Hartland; A. Walkup, Nunda; George L. Bryant, Nunda; Peter Berger, Hebron; M. C. Morris, Crystal Lake, R. Rowley, Nunda; Chet Burgett, Richmond; James Burgett, Richmond; Fred Kernow, Riley; C. N. Webber, Seneca; Franklin Morris, Crystal Lake; James Whiston, Ridgefield.

SPRING GROVE FISH HATCHERY

The State has a fish-hatchery located at the village of Spring Grove in Burton Township, this county, and reports show that in May, 1916, many visitors present saw 50,000 rainbow trout, all four months old and at the same date there were 30,000,000 pike eggs just hatching out, also 25,000 brook trout two months old. Most of these young trout were to be planted in the spring-fed streams of McHenry County. In 1915, 350,000 black bass and 12,000,000 pike-perch were planted in the water courses and lakes of the county by the State Fish Commission.

CHAPTER XXIII

ALDEN TOWNSHIP

BOUNDARIES

Alden Township is bounded on the north by the State of Wisconsin; on the east by Hebron Township; on the south by Hartland Township; and on the west by Chemung Township. It comprises all of congressional township 46, range 6.

ORIGIN OF NAME

Like many other townships, Alden took its name from its first post office. Originally, the post office was named Wedgewood, but on account of another in Illinois by the same name it was changed to Alden after Alden, N. Y., from which place several early settlers to this township had emigrated.

FIRST SETTLEMENT

The very first settlers in Alden Township were Nathan and Darius Disbrow, who came here in the fall of 1836, and built cabins in the following spring. They located on section 15, which later was destined to become the site of the village of Alden. Miles Booty, a native of England, was the third to locate in Alden Township, he arriving during the summer of 1837, settling on what later became the Capron farm, east of the village. Ashael Disbrow, with his wife and eleven children, came here from Greene County, N. Y., about the same time. Another settler, John Alberty, from the same location, came in 1838, and Dennis Ryder of York State arrived about that same year.

354

FRANK KREUTZER

MRS. FRANK KREUTZER

TOPOGRAPHY

Alden Township is a prairie township, although originally some tracts of very fine timber were found growing within its borders. There are to be seen considerable artificial timber planted by the hands of the hardy pioneers, which trees have come to tower up some twenty, thirty and even forty feet, providing shade in the heated seasons and a windbreak in winter. Nippersink Creek is the principal water course, it rising from Mud Creek, and from it flow Kiswaukee Creek and Piskasaw Creek.

PIONEER EVENTS

Timothy M. Eller and Esther Disbrow were married on January 7, 1839, by Wesley Diggins, a justice of the peace, and this was the first wedding celebrated in the township, although in 1838, Darius Disbrow, who lived in Alden Township, was married in Milwaukee, to Sarah Cross, a resident of Hebron Township. Their child, Lorain J. Disbrow was the first white child born in the township, the date of his birth being in 1839. Twin daughters of Mr. and Mrs. Timothy M. Fuller, were the next white children born in the township.

BURIAL PLACES

The first burial in Alden Township took place near Mud Lake, it being that of a child who died at the home of Ashael Disbrow. This infant belonged to the family who were going on further west to settle. The first cemetery, however, was that located in 1846, and A. Broughton was the first to be buried there. This tract originally had two acres set off as a cemetery. In 1847 a graveyard was platted to the east of the village of Alden, and there repose the remains of scores of pioneers, but later this tract was abandoned, and the bodies were transferred to other cemeteries, chiefly to the one originally laid out as above noted.

FIRST SCHOOLS AND CHURCHES

Miss Clarissa Nelson of Geneva Lake taught the first school in Alden Township, in the spring of 1841, in the first schoolhouse which was built of logs.

Rev. Leander Walker held the first religious services in the township in the fall of 1838, at the home of Ashael Disbrow, and there he organized a Methodist society, which held meetings until 1845, when it was disbanded.

POST OFFICES

The first post office was established in 1843 at the home of Francis Wedgewood, and he continued as postmaster until 1847, when the office was transferred to the railroad station. In 1849, P. W. Lake was made postmaster, and he was followed by N. M. Capron in 1850. In 1858 Mr. Capron died, and he was succeeded by George B. Andrews, and in 1881, E. S. Smith was appointed. The later postmasters are generally well recalled by the present patrons of the office.

ALDEN VILLAGE

The village of Alden was laid out in 1848 by Francis Wedgewood, and John Brink of Crystal Lake made the survey. Nathan Disbrow built the first house at that point, and the first store was opened by P. W. Lake, in 1847, prior to the platting of the village. The first wagon shop was run by C. N. Jiles; J. Wood was the first blacksmith and M. D. Hoy was the first shoemaker. Other early business and professional men included these: J. C. Brewer, barber; Ferris & Son and Julian Brothers, butter and cheese factory; Copeland & Manning, operators of a creamery; John Snell, wagon maker; Edward Wright, carpenter; C. H. Bennett, harness maker; T. J. Disbrow proprietor of the hotel; Thomas Rushton, lawyer; E. S. Smith, merchant; and Dr. G. R. Barringer, physician.

The village has never grown to any considerable extent, and now there are a few stores and small shops for the accommodation of the surrounding rich farming community. Alden Township has many beautiful and valuable farms and fine herds of excellent milch cows, the milk from which is sold at the station of Alden where a large collecting station is conducted by one of the great milk companies mentioned in the chapter on dairying. In 1877 Alden had a cheese factory, built in 1870, and used the milk of 500 cows, but it has been long discontinued.

The early settlers from New York being great fruit lovers demanded fruit trees in this new country and a Mr. Easton in 1848 planted out a good sized nursery from which the farmers were soon able to get trees. The first apple seeds were planted by Sidney Disbrow, in 1838, and these trees thus started, come to be excellent bearing trees within a few years.

The Alden Mutual Fire Insurance Company was organized at the village of Alden, in 1874, but since then it has enlarged its scope and takes in the townships of Alden, Hebron, Richmond, Burton and Mc-Henry.

It now has in force 500 policies, with insurance amounting to $1,800,000. The rate for insurance is a trifle more than one per cent for a five year period.

The officers are: James H. Turner, Hebron, President; Arthur D. Cornue, of Alden, Vice-President; A. G. Dickerson, Hebron, Secretary; The board of directors are: H. E. Street, Hebron, Arthur D. Cornue, E. G. Kingsley, H. G. Durkee, Alden; E. G. Turner, Spring Grove; J. B. Richardson, Richmond.

This mutual fire insurance company has been of great benefit to the farming community of North McHenry County.

POPULATION

The population of Alden Township in 1890 was 1,026; in 1900 it was 1,015; in 1910, 1,014 and in 1920, 964.

OFFICIALS

The following are serving as the township officials of Alden Township: supervisor, H. G. Durkee; assessor, J. L. Baldock; clerk, E. M. Fink; highway commissioner, E. C. Hammond; justices of the peace, A. L. Disbrow and William W. Fleming; constable, J. H. Carbrey.

CHAPTER XXIV

ALGONQUIN TOWNSHIP

BOUNDARIES

In the southeastern part of McHenry County is found Algonquin Township; it is bounded on the north by Nunda Township; on the east by Lake County; on the south by Kane County, and on the west by Grafton Township.

ORIGIN OF NAME

Before the adoption of the township organization, this section of the county was known as Fox Township. When a name was required for this new township, Samuel Edwards, formerly of Philadelphia, suggested the name Algonquin. In his youth he had been a sailor on a boat by that name, and he desired to thus commemorate a happy period of his life. The name met with the approval of all who had charge of such naming, and it was adopted.

TOPOGRAPHY

Algonquin Township is more broken than any other township within the county, there being many bluffs and hills in the region of Algonquin village and in fact all along the Fox River. The land is about equally divided between prairie and timber. It is adapted to both small grain and pasture lands and is used for such purposes. Crystal Lake lies in section 6 of this township, and runs over into a portion of Grafton Township. From it flows the outlet of the lake that joins the Fox River at the village of Algonquin. Big Spring Creek is another water course found within the township.

EARLY SETTLERS

The first settler to locate in this county chose Algonquin Township for his new home. He was Samuel Gillian, and he located in section 23, on the west bank of Fox River, November 18, 1834. John Gillian came soon thereafter, and he settled on the east bank of Fox River. Levi Seebert arrived in 1837; Hosea Throop was a settler of 1839; and Newman Crabtree, Simon Chandler, Thomas Chunn, Beman Crandall, William King, Isaac Denney, Edwin Powell, Major Beardsley, John Kern, Isaac King, Wesley Hickox, Dr. Plumleigh, Dr. Cornish and John Brink with possibly others made up the first settlements.

PIONEER EVENTS

The first white child to be born in this township was William Beardsley, son of Abner Beardsley and wife, who came into the world in 1837. Franklin Wallace and Hannah S. Beardsley were married by Benjamin Crandall, a justice of the peace, in 1839, and theirs was the first marriage in Algonquin township. The first person to die in the township was Delia, daughter of Samuel Gillian and wife, when she was about fifteen years old, August 26, 1835.

The first saw-mill was built on Crystal Lake outlet by Benjamin Douglas and Colonel Hoffman in 1839; and the second one was built in 1842, by A. Dawson, who located at Algonquin in 1848. This last was completed in 1849 by Henry Petrie. A brick-mill was built in the village in 1850 by Dr. Plumleigh.

The schools and churches are all treated in special chapters on these topics in this volume.

POPULATION

In 1890 the population of this township was 3,675; in 1900 it was 3,043; in 1910 it was 2,512; and in 1920 it was 3,528.

ALGONQUIN VILLAGE

This is the oldest village in this county, having been first laid out in 1836 by Dawson & Powell, the platting being accepted and recorded in 1844. Prior to the laying out of the place Mr. Powell had erected a residence on the present site of the village. The first store was conducted in 1837 by Dr. Cornish. Henry Tubbs was the first wagonmaker; Henry Benthusean, was the first blacksmith; and O. Leach the first shoemaker, while William Clark was the first tailor. At one time William Powell owned all of the original site of Algonquin and he built the first hotel in 1840. It was a log structure, to which he added a frame building, in 1850. In 1858, the whole building was torn down and a new one erected by James Dixon and John Gillian, and later it became the property of Charles Pingree.

POST OFFICE

A post office was established at this point in 1836, and it was the first in the township. Dr. Cornish was the first to serve as postmaster. He was succeeded by the following: Isaac Denney, John Peter (deputy), John Sears, Charles Chunn, Eli Henderson, Peter Potter, Samuel Finch, Col. William Henry, C. C. Chunn, John Adamak, C. C. Chunn, John T. Kalahan, Nettie Threadgold (many years) with present postmaster John T. Kalahan.

This is a third-class post office and has one rural free delivery route extending to the surrounding country. To show that this is an early post office it only need be stated that the office was established under President Andrew Jackson.

PRESENT OFFICIALS

The following are the present officials of Algonquin: president, Willis T. Peter; clerk, George Dewitt Keyes; treasurer, Louis J. Lehky; magistrate, Harvey J. Weir; marshal, John Dvorak, Jr.; attorney, Charles T. Allen; trustees, Clarence Franke, Frank Dvorak, Ernest Reimer, Fred Duensing, Albert Wilbrandt and Herman Mertens.

The enterprising little city in 1907 erected a fine two-story brick city building at a cost of $10,000. This provides a home and protection for all the city property, fire department, city offices and jail. In the western portion of the village is found a nice public park. Nature has made the spot charming and a gushing spring of pure water offers an appreciated refreshment.

PUBLIC IMPROVEMENTS

In 1896 the city installed its first and really its present system of water works which consists of piping from the business part of the town

WILLIAMS STREET, LOOKING SOUTH, CRYSTAL LAKE

to a distance of seventy-three feet above the river-bed, to a point on the hillside where was discovered a strong spring of the best drinking water to be had anywhere in Illinois. For fire purposes other lines of piping extend further on up the hill to a distance of 147 feet, where was erected a basin in which sufficient water is forced to meet any demand in case of fire. This whole system is "natural direct pressure" and affords a splendid water system, such as is seldom found in prairie sections. The common pressure is about eighty pounds per square inch.

The fire company is the ordinary volunteer company of fifteen men, with Peter Serrs as present chief. The city has two hose carts, each having 800 feet of good hose; a chemical engine holding forty-five gallons; hook and ladders, and other appliances.

CITY OF CRYSTAL LAKE

What was first known as the village of Crystal Lake is now a city and governed by a board of aldermen and a mayor. This place was platted by Benjamin Douglas and others in August, 1837, but not recorded until 1840. From an old county directory it is learned that in 1877 the village then had three general stores. Hill, Fitch & Marlow and Buckholtz & Dydeman were early business firms. T. G. Ashton conducted a hotel. It will be understood that a part of present Crystal Lake city was once within the incorporation of Nunda village and its early history will be treated in the history of Nunda Township.

Aside from the above named business interests it should be stated in this connection that for many years the ice taken from the lake near Crystal Lake has been cut and shipped to Chicago, where the name sells the product, while it is said, however, that much sold under this catchy name came from some dirty pond much nearer Chicago. The land containing this beautiful lake has been the subject of much recent litigation, and the question of ownership is still in the courts.

Three miles distant from the city of Crystal Lake is located the celebrated Terra Cotta plant, where sometimes 300 men are employed, although during the World War the number was cut down materially. Where this plant stands is known on railroad maps as Terra Cotta.

The great bottling plant of the Bowman Dairy Company is located right in the town and handles all the vast amount of milk produced in the surrounding country, instead of it being shipped direct to the city. At this plant are bottled and shipped to Chicago four carloads of bottled milk daily.

POST OFFICE

An exact list of postmasters at this office cannot be now obtained
wh any degree of a accuracy The earliest postoffice
M s. H C was in charge of the his late years ago. I was
l in 1840 w the office was established. Among the post
l s Mrs. De Gras E. G.
M A. s. L. J. M W present postmast H
S P A

North Crystal Lake was originally incorporated as the village of
Nunda, January 24, 1874, under a legislative act dated April 10, 1872.
T wa incorporation was filed in the County Court of McHenry
C Josph W orders Dec 30, 1873, and January
5, 1874. C July 6, N. Sm t to La
y 24 a l as judges s O. M. P k.
E B A P M C L s. Na Be y
W H s S N y s w cast at
g V s lo g w t a O. February 17,
t C. E. W N. G a , W. S. De W , R. R v O.
M l A. A. P t w trustees a m
T V N a w North Cyst L
i

f Cryst Lake was g t form g vi
vis passed A 10, 1872. Jam s Cro T H Ash J. B.
R having been appointed by the ear of McHenry County as
j g coeffi ob b y ball w r they
w ll corpora s village un less said law an d n was ll

nine votes for such incorporation and six against the measure. The court then ordered an election of officers which resulted in the election of trustees as follows: William Miller, John Brink, Thomas Leonard, B. Carpenter, H. H. Ford, and L. D. Lowell. Hence it will be seen that two incorporated villages existed side by side for a considerable number of years. It was not until 1914 that the villages of North Crystal Lake and Crystal Lake were consolidated under the name of Crystal Lake. It was on April 21, 1914, that this was legally brought about, and in September, the same year, the place adopted a city form of government. The first officers were elected December 14, 1914, to hold office until April, 1915. The first set of officers were as follows: William Pinnow, mayor; John C. Flotow, city clerk; James B. Ford, city treasurer; Herman P. Hasse, city attorney and William M. Freeman, Henry Meyer, A. M. Shelton, W. J. Buchholz, Andrew Pierson and Henry Breudigam, aldermen.

The officers elected in the spring of 1915 were: William Pinnow, mayor; John C. Floto, city clerk; Jennie H. Ford, city treasurer; Herman P. Hasse, city attorney; and Andrew Pierson, Henry Meir, A. M. Shelton, W. J. Bruedigam, Martin Naslund, Addison M. Shelton, William M. Freeman, Henry Meier, aldermen.

February 2, 1915, the city census returns was taken showing a population of the city of Crystal Lake to be 2,364 and the city was thereupon divided into three wards, two aldermen to be elected annually for each ward. May 4, 1915, the aldermen by lot decided to hold office the following terms: First ward, Henry Bruedigam, one year; Andrew Pierson, two years; second ward, A. M. Shelton, one year; Martin Naslund, two years; third ward, Henry Meier, one year; William M. Freeman, two years.

CITY OFFICIALS

1887—J. H. Sheldon, president; I. M. Mallory, clerk.

1888—W. T. Hamilton, president; I. M. Mallory, clerk.

1889—O. C. Colby, president; C. E. Warner, clerk.

1890-91—W. T. Hamilton, president; T. Huffman, clerk.

1892—O. C. Colby, president; T. Huffman, clerk.

1893—D. L. Borney, president; A. S. Cool, clerk.

1894—D. L. Borney, president; B. W. Colby, clerk.

1895—C. C. Watson, president; I. M. Mallory, clerk.

1896—C. C. Watson, president; D. L. Borney, clerk.

1897—P. A. England, president ; D. L. Borney, clerk.
1898 P. A. England, president ; W. T. Huffman, clerk.
1899 C. C. Watson, president ; W. T. Huffman, clerk.
1900 C. C. Watson, president ; A. J. Thompson, clerk.
1901 P. A. England, president ; A. J. Thompson, clerk.
1902 Robt. Philips, president ; A. J. Thompson, clerk.
1903— Robt. Philips, president ; A. J. Thompson, clerk.
1904- Robt. Philips, president ; A. J. Thompson, clerk.
1905- Robt. Philips, president ; A. J. Thompson, clerk.
1906- Robt. Philips, president ; A. J. Thompson, clerk.
1907—Robt. Philips, president ; A. J. Thompson, clerk.
1908—Robt. Philips, president ; A. J. Thompson, clerk.

NAME CHANGED TO NORTH CRYSTAL LAKE

1909-10—H. D. Hull, president ; H. H. McCollum, clerk.
1911—F. W. Covalt, president ; H. H. McCollum, clerk.
1912—F. W. Covalt, president ; A. E. Kiest, clerk.
H. D. Hull, president ; John C. Flotow, clerk.

The village of North Crystal Lake was annexed to Crystal Lake in the spring of 1914. The subjoined is a list of officers serving in Crystal Lake from its organization to the time it was united with North Crystal Lake, as well as present consolidated incorporation officials :

1882—J. W. Marlow, president ; Thomas Ford, clerk.
1883—William Hill, president ; Thomas Ford, clerk.
1884—E. Pease, president ; L. L. Smith, clerk.
1885- E. Pease, president ; J. B. Robinson, clerk.
1886—Geo. W. Davis, president ; J. P. Smith, clerk.
1887—C. M. Pendleton, president ; J. P. Smith, clerk.
1888—W. A. Rollins, president ; J. B. Ford, clerk.
1889- F. E. Cox, president ; J. B. Ford, clerk.
1890—Thomas Whittaker, president ; J. B. Ford, clerk.
1891- Thomas Whittaker, president ; J. B. Ford, clerk.
1892- H. H. Ford, president ; J. B. Ford, clerk.
1893—H. T. Jones, president ; A. H. Hale, clerk.
1894—Thomas Whittaker, president ; J. B. Ford, clerk.
1895- J. B. Robinson, president ; J. B. Ford, clerk.
1896- C. F. Dike, president ; J. B. Ford, clerk.
1897— H. T. Jones, president ; J. B. Ford, clerk.

1898—S. M. Grimes, president; G. Peterson, clerk.
1899—J. B. Moore, president; J. B. Ford, clerk.
1900—J. B. Robinson, president; J. B. Ford, clerk.
1901—C. F. Dike, president; J. B. Ford, clerk.
1902—C. F. Dike, president; J. B. Ford, clerk.
1903—A. M. Hale, president; J. B. Ford, clerk.
1904—O. M. Hale, president; J. B. Ford, clerk.
1905-7—C. F. Dike, president; J. B. Ford, clerk.
1907-8—R. G. Smith, president; J. B. Ford, clerk.
1909-13—C. F. Dike, president; J. B. Ford, clerk.
1914—P. W. Ranhut, president; J. B. Ford, clerk.

September, 1914, the city form of government was adopted through an election and officers held over until December, 1914, when the first city officers were elected and took office. The same held only until the ensuing spring election.

1914—William Pinnow, mayor; John C. Flotow, clerk.
1915-16—Wm. Pinnow, mayor; John C. Flotow, clerk.
1917-18—W. A. Goodwin, mayor; John C. Flotow, clerk.

PRESENT OFFICIALS

The following are the present officials of the city of Crystal Lake: mayor, W. A. Goodwin; clerk, John C. Flotow; health commissioner, H. D. Hull; treasurer, Carl Ortman; magistrate, C. H. Schlottman; attorney, L. D. Lowell; aldermen, Fred Peterson, Henry Bruedigam, Henry Meier, G. D. Crabtree, Mort Ritt and J. B. Kitchen.

PUBLIC IMPROVEMENTS

In 1906-07 a city building was constructed of brick. It cost $8,000. The second floor is leased out to various lodges, while the ground floor is used by the councilmen and for other municipal purposes.

A public park comprising a full city block has been improved, trees have been planted, seats furnished, and a band-stand erected, so that it is an attractive resort for the people of this region.

The water supply was furnished in both the old village of Nunda in 1903 and in the other part of the city in 1912. Deep wells are used and water is forced from the same by electric pumps, giving a direct pressure. There are now two stand-pipes.

The city has a volunteer fire company of a dozen men and in 1913 purchased at a cost of $4,800 a fine auto-fire truck.

Light is furnished by the Public Service Company, which supplies so many small towns in this portion of Northern Illinois.

VILLAGE OF CARY

Cary in the northeast quarter of section 13 of Algonquin Township is a station point on the Chicago & Northwestern railroad and the first southeast of Crystal Lake. It was laid out June 7, 1856, by William D. Cary and became a post office in 1856, with James Nish as first postmaster. He was succeeded, when he entered the Civil War, by his brother John Nish, who served until relieved by H. M. Burton, who was postmaster for two years and was followed by Robert Burk, and he by James Nish, who had returned from war with the rank of captain, and he served until his death, when his daughter, Miss Ann J. Nish, was appointed and served until in the Democratic administration of President Wilson, Mary H. Hrdlicka was appointed, the date of her appointment being December 8, 1913. This is a fourth class post office and from it runs one rural delivery route.

Cary became an incorporated village, January 9, 1893, and the following have been among its presidents: L. E. Mentch, G. A. Ellingson, Theodore H. Wulff, J. F. Pichen, F. M. Abbott, and in 1909 L. E. Mentch was elected again, and he was followed by Ralph B. Powers. From an ordinance book kept by the trustees the following is found: At the first election for incorporation, ordered by Judge C. H. Donnelly, February 27, 1893, to be held March 4, 1893, the following were elected: L. E. Mentch, president; Ed. Kerns, Joe Dunn, Z. L. Blaisdell, E. J. King, J. C. Lemkee and S. B. McNett, trustees; H. P. Hoagland, clerk.

The village has a deep well water-works system; water is forced by electricity to a large reservoir and a stand-pipe is maintained so that plenty of water is had at all times. This plant was placed in operation about 1910, and for it the village was bonded for the sum of $20,000. The electric lighting of the place is done by a private corporation. In 1915 the village built a fine, solid village hall of brick and cement. It is two-story high and has a basement. Ample room is afforded for council room, fire department, etc.

PRESENT OFFICIALS

The following are the village officials of Cary Station: president. R. B. Powers; clerk, C. W. Meyer; treasurer, P. J. Bloner; marshal,

J. A. Parsley; attorney, Charles T. Allen; trustees, R. H. Grantham, A. E. Baheman, A. O. Hack, F. D. Smith, F. Krenz and O. J. Synek.

TOWNSHIP OFFICIALS

The following are the township officials of Algonquin Township: supervisor, R. E. Haeger; assessor, Henry Breudigam; clerk, V. N. Ford; highway commissioner, Ed Wallace; justices of the peace, L. E. Mentch, John Buehler and Henry Keyes; constable, John Purvey.

CHAPTER XXV

BURTON TOWNSHIP

BOUNDARIES

Burton Township has the least area of any township in this county. It contains one-third of congressional township 46, range 9 and lies in the extreme northeastern part of the county. It is bounded on the north by the State of Wisconsin; on the east by Lake County, Ill.; on the south by McHenry Township; and on the west by Richmond Township. It is drained by Nippersink Creek, and is well situated and by nature adapted to high-class agriculture and stockraising.

EARLY SETTLEMENT

Burton Township was among the first to be settled. It was first settled by Englishmen, and the name English Prairie was given it. The original settler was Jonathan Imeson, who came here from England in 1836 and located in section 18 of this township, and in 1885, when seventy-five years old, was still residing on this land. A year or two later Richard Wray settled on sections 17 and 18; Stephen Lawson on section 18; and Martin Hoffman, William Fowles, Richard Upston, Joseph Rice, John A. Mann, and Joseph Blivin, all located in section 30.

In an account published concerning the settlement in this township, the following appears and is too good to be lost in the annals of the county: "The English settlers, after their arrival staked out their claims and then went on further west thinking to find more eligible lands. But not succeeding in this, they returned to their first choice only to find that a Yankee named John Sanborn had arrived and was occupying their claims. They asked him to quit. He would not. Words multiplied, but with this result: Sanborn stayed and the Englishmen stayed. One day when Sanborn was mowing, a dozen or more of his

368

Paul Kreutzer

Kunigunda Kreutzer

neighbors came to him and ordered him to leave; he turned upon them with his scythe and drove the whole crowd away. In the excitement Sanborn lost his hat. One of the visitors found it and kept it. Sanborn went bareheaded for several months until he could find time to go to town and purchase another. There was a long time that an unfriendly feeling obtained against the Englishmen living upon the "English Prairie" and any other class who might come in to settle there. John Sanborn completed his days in the spot he had chosen for his home."

EARLY EVENTS

The township was first called Benton by Jackson Wray, but upon it being learned that there was already a post office and township of Benton in Illinois, the name was changed to Burton.

The first religious services within the township were held at the residence of Jonathan Imeson in 1843. The minister came from Kenosha, then called Southport, to conduct them.

Cemeteries were early located at Spring Grove, English Prairie, Stevens, Cole's, Sanborn's and Wray's.

Soon after the settlement was made William Stearns taught a term of school having fifteen pupils. The building in which it was taught was a log one on the Nippersink Creek.

The first death known among white people here was that of Mrs. Frank Richardson, who passed away in the autumn of 1837.

The first marriage was that uniting Jonathan Imeson and Mary Wray, November 30, 1837. The minister who performed the ceremony was Rev. Joel Wheeler. Their first son, Robert T. Imerson, was the first child born within the township.

The first post office was called Blivin's Mills. It was established in 1851, with Joseph Rice as postmaster. Rice held the office during his lifetime. The name was changed to Spring Grove, January 24, 1883. English Prairie post office was established about 1854. Here it is known that the postmasters were: Gideon B. Cooley, Harvey Wilson and Carl C. Mead.

SPRING GROVE VILLAGE

This little village takes its name, evidently, from the spring, and the beautiful grove that once surrounded it, which was viewed by the pioneer band who first located here. It was laid out in 1845 by Mr. Barnum.

William Fowles and Richard Robinson built a log house east of the grove, and these constituted the first cabins in the place. John E. Mann opened the first store in 1845.

A grist-mill and cheese factory were among the early industries at this point. Here Joseph Rice built and conducted a hotel in 1848, continuing it until 1868.

INCORPORATION

This place was legally incorporated October 6, 1902. The following is a list of the various presidents and clerks to the present date: William Seaver, president November, 1902, to May, 1903; William B. Johonnote, village clerk, November, 1902, to May, 1903; Charles G. Andrews, president, May 1, 1903, to May 1, 1904; D. W. Lichty, clerk, May 1, 1903, to May 1, 1904; Anton Schoefer, president, May, 1904, to May, 1905; Nick N. Weber, clerk, May, 1904, to May, 1905; Joseph Meredith, president, May, 1905, to May, 1906; Nick N. Weber, clerk, May, 1905, to May, 1906; John Wagner, president, May, 1906, to May, 1907; Nick N. Weber, clerk, May, 1906, to May, 1907; John Wagner, president from May 1, 1907, to January, 1908; Otto Hasse filled out unexpired term to May, 1909; John Karls, clerk, 1907-08; Herbert R. Peacock appointed to fill term out to May, 1909; Anton Schoefer, president, May, 1909, to 1910; Howard Westlake, clerk, 1909 to 1910; William Rauen, clerk from May, 1910 to 1912; Anton Schoefer, president, 1911 to 1913; William Rauen, clerk, May, 1912, to May, 1913, resigned, Albert Pepping appointed to fill vacancy to May 1, 1914; John Karls, president, May, 1913, to May, 1914; Glen Esh, clerk, from May, 1916, to May, 1918; John Karls, president, May, 1917, to May, 1919; Glen Esh, clerk, May, 1918, to May, 1920; Joseph Wagner, president, May, 1919, to May, 1921.

The following are the present officials of the village of Spring Grove: president, Joseph G. Wagner; clerk, Glen A. Esh; treasurer, Paul F. Siegler; trustees, John Rauen, Anton May, Frank May, Frank Wagner, Nick Freund and Henry Sweet.

POST OFFICE

The first post office in this township was known as Blivin's Mills, and was established in 1851, with Joseph Rice as postmaster. He was succeeded by R. J. Osmann, Mrs. Rice, widow of former postmaster, and Robert Tweed, who held the office until at least 1885, since which time the postmasters have been: John Hendricks, Andrew Neish, Robert Esh, Andrew Neish, J. O. McLeon, Herbert Peacock, Mrs. Sarah Freeman, who was appointed in 1915. It is a fourth class post office, with one rural free delivery route, the length of which is about twenty-eight miles; covers a ten mile square area and accommodates ninety-six families and a population of nearly 300. It was established October 7, 1905.

POPULATION

In 1890 Burton Township had a population of 296; in 1900 it had 400; in 1910 it had 451; and in 1920 it had 441.

TOWNSHIP OFFICIALS

The following are the township officials of Burton Township: Supervisor, Frank May; assessor, Henry C. Sweet; clerk, Joseph Brown; highway commissioner, Howard Siedschlag; justice of the peace, Robert Esh; constable, Michael Rauen.

CHAPTER XXVI

CHEMUNG TOWNSHIP

BOUNDARIES

Chemung Township is located in the extreme northwestern portion
of this county, and is bounded on the north by Wisconsin, on the east
by Alden Township, on the south by Dunham Township, and on the west
by Boone County. It comprises all of congressional township 45, range 5.

TOPOGRAPHY

This township originally had more low wet land than any of the
other townships, but through a course of scientific draining this land
has come to be very valuable, having as it does the richest of soil. Piskasaw Creek and its three branches, are its principal water courses.

ORIGIN OF NAME

The name Chemung was given the village of Chemung before the
township was organized, by a Mr. Steward who came from Chemung
County, N. Y., and he desired to name the place after his old home.
The township was organized in 1850, and took on the name of the
village.

EARLY SETTLERS

Between 1836 and 1838 the following came into the township for
the purpose of making permanent settlement: George Trumbull, M.

372

MASONIC TEMPLE, HARVARD

Wheeler, Wesley Diggins, Alonzo Riley, and William Hart, and these were the first to effect the settlement, although it has been claimed that the two brothers, David and Ransley Shaw lived here for a brief time. David Smith, T. B. Wakeman and Daniel and Adolphus Hutchinson came here several years later.

Between 1840 and 1845 William Sewer built a saw-mill which finally became a flour-mill, and in 1853 Mr. Myer built the stone-mill in the village of Chemung, later owned by the Sandersons. In the seventies and eighties this mill was doing a large business in grinding buckwheat flour for the Chicago markets.

The settlement of the township was about the palmy days of Jacksonian Democracy, and Whigs were not very numerous, but the five of them including W. G. Billings, who later was made internal revenue collector, Hayden Hutchinson, and C. R. Brown, just enough for a caucus, kept up the party organization till they finally carried the county.

The first church in the township was erected by the Presbyterians, at Chemung village. This original church was replaced in 1873 by a new structure.

David Baker and S. L. Puffer were the first general merchants at Chemung village.

LAWRENCE

The old village of Lawrence, sections 22 and 27, was settled in 1855, the railroad depot being built in 1856. Bixby & Conklin first offered goods for sale, but ere long three others went into trade, believing that the depot at that point would eventually kill Chemung. G. F. Kasson and G. Blakeslee next began business, but it was not long before the store was burned. This village was named for Lawrence Bixby, its first merchant. In 1857 a steam flouring mill was operated, but did not pay and was soon abandoned.

Lawrence had a post office several years, but when the railroad shops were located at Harvard all business drifted to that village and since then Lawrence has not progressed commercially.

Among the pioneer dealers in Lawrence may be recalled by the older citizens of the county, W. L. Boyd, R. Gillis, F. Beidt, E. S. Bowen, H. S. Gould, C. Palmer, S. Clark, A. Thompson and J. L. Anderson. The business of the village has long since disappeared entirely.

VILLAGE OF CHEMUNG

Chemung was laid out in 1844, but like Lawrence has suffered from being too near to Harvard, also within this township. The first house in Chemung was erected by a Mr. Lewis and was built of logs. Burge & Aisles kept the first store; Mr. Baker the second. Other business men were: Jacob A. Wood, B. F. Carey, A. J. DeGraw, Peter Fitzer, Henry Munger, Householder Brothers, J. P. Kennedy, E. D. Maxon, S. L. Puffer, J. A. Little, John Alexander, G. I. Sinderson, Warren Chase, James Potts and N. Crane. With a store and shop or two Chemung has kept its name and place on the map but has never been able to increase in commercial interest.

CITY OF HARVARD

This city is sixty-three miles northwest of Chicago, on the Chicago & Northwestern railroad, and is beautifully situated in section 35 of Chemung Township. It was platted November 25, 1856 by Amos Page, proprietor. Abraham Carmack and Jacob A. Davis were the original owners of the town site of Harvard, having obtained it from the government in 1845. They sold it to Gilbert Brainard, and after his death the land was secured by a company of railroad men, who laid out the town in 1856. E. G. Ayer, a member of the company named the place Harvard in honor of Harvard, Mass. Many additions have been made to the place with the growth of recent years.

EARLY EVENTS

In 1856 the first stock of merchandise was placed on the shelves in the new town of Harvard, the owner of these goods was Charles Crawford. His store was in reality a railroad shanty. Soon after Hull & Julius opened their store in a one-story log cabin. The first frame building was erected by J. C. Crum on the corner of the railroad right-of-way and the crossing of Ayer street; it was used for a lumber yard office. Mr. Crum was engaged in the lumber trade before the coming of the railroad. He used to purchase his stock of lumber in Kenosha, Wis., shipping it to Chicago by rail, and thence back to Woodstock by rail, and from there freighted it. The first frame store was built in the spring of 1857 by John Diggins. The earliest blacksmith was H. Norton; the first wagonmaker was J. Flemming; the first shoemaker was Daniel Carpenter.

The first hotel of note was that erected by David Smith in 1856. Its many landlords included these: J. E. Sanford, Milton Stevenson, William Parker, Lewis Thompson, Schuyler Higgins and Everton Walker who called the property the "Walker House."

The Ayer Hotel, still standing and used as a commercial traveler's stopping place, was erected by Wesley Diggins in 1859, and H. C. Blackman became proprietor. At first it backed up to the tracks and depot but later it was turned around and now faces the main street of the city; also a part of it faces the depot.

HARVARD IN 1876

From a directory of McHenry County published in 1876, the following facts concerning Harvard have been obtained, and when contrasted with the city of Harvard of today, are indeed interesting.

"Harvard is the junior town of Chemung, and, like many other juniors, it has absorbed the substance of the seniors till it almost rivals the county seat in size, containing five dry goods stores, four grocery stores, one boot and shoe store, two mixed stores, such as clothing, boots and shoes, two drug stores, two hardwares, eight saloons, two livery stables, two bakeries, three confectioneries, two clothing stores, two jewelry stores, two furniture stores, one photograph gallery, three hotels, one bank, five doctors, two lawyers, two harness shops, one flouring mill, one planing-mill, sash and blind factory, three millinery stores, one dentist, one news depot, two barber shops, two malt houses, one cheese factory, four blacksmith shops, three wagon shops, one car repair shop, three meat shops, one agricultural implement warehouse, three churches and a schoolhouse."

A steam flouring mill was built here in 1865 by Mr. Wood, and its total cost was $15,000.

The first store was that opened by Holden Julius in 1857. The first school building was erected in 1859 of brick.

The first church was the Methodist Episcopal one erected in 1859. The Presbyterian, built in 1867 and Congregationalist, in 1870.

Another description of Harvard in 1877 reads thus: "All trains of cars shipped from Minnesota or Baraboo to Milwaukee have to be made up here. In one month last year (1876) there were 9,918 cars left here to be made up into trains. Some days as many as thirty trains are received here and it is no uncommon sight to see thirty engines in town at one time. Harvard is the headquarters for all division men to Baraboo. About 125 railroad men work here constantly, the coal sheds alone employing thirty men; the engines coming here consume 1,500 tons of coal a month, and the company pays out about $8,000 here each month; no small item for so small a town.''

But the coming and going of years make changes, especially in railroad affairs. Divisions and shops are liable to be removed at anytime, as the railroad system extends on to greater distance, so it has been in Harvard, but the advantage of its early day boom has left its mark for good and other enterprises have made up for the loss of what was once supposed would be still larger railroad interests.

HARVARD IN 1885

The following is a list of business and professional men at Harvard prior to 1885 and during that year:

Eugene O'Connor, Sterns & Peters, Joseph C. Crumb, A. E. Axtell, E. J. Smith, J. H. O'Connor, W. H. Milligan, John Cullen, Thomas Collins, Albert Haffner, Edward Haffner, George Haffner, Elmer Carpenter, N. L. Jackson, Miles Munger, Haven Bros., Thompson & Hodkins, Henry Sewger, John Flemming, E. N. Blake & Son, Lewis Whitmar, Gault Bros, Dr. M. A. Adams, Samuel Richardson, Groesbeck & Wilkinson, Stafford & Gardner, Edward Rector, J. M. O'Neil, J. Sullivan, W. C. Wellington, L. Van Wie & Co., Hubbard Bros., M. J. Powers, Matthew Ottman, H. B. Miner, W. B. Walker, Hunt & Helm, Megraw & Wakley, Marshal & Saunders, E. D. Beardsley, H. Wellstein, L. R. Lines, Lake & Logne, D. C. Downs, Lake & Crumb, W. D. Hall, A. W. Young, G. R. Wager, Telcomb & Co., William Fay & Bro., George Ducker, Rupert Church, J. H. Callender, H. W. Binnie, Williams Bros., Rogers & Stevens, William George & Co., Scott & Walfrom, T. G. Spriggs, Dr. C. M. Johnson, B. H. Wade, M. D., A. C. Bingham, H. T. Woodruff, G. W. Parmley, Clark & Brainard, G. T. Barrows, Wm. I. Wooster, Elmer Simons, Simon Hill, Richard Powers, Thomas O'Brien, Wallen & Sloey, William McGee, John L. Hayes, E. U. Hayes, Henry Zyschach.

INCORPORATION

Harvard became an incorporated village February 28, 1867, and the following were the first officials: H. G. Ayer, president; William Marshall, clerk. The trustees were: J. C. Crumb, Frank Cobb, Owen McGee, B. F. Groesbeck. In 1891 Harvard became an incorporated city and its

J. P. Kroeger

affairs have usually been well administered to the best interests of its
population. The mayors and clerks have been as follows: mayors, N. B.
Helm, P. E. Saunders, M. W. Lake, L. A. Gardner, James Logue, John
A. Sweeney, W. D. Hall, Richard Phalen, J. H. Vickers, C. J. Hendricks,
F. O. Thompson.

The clerks have been few in number but very efficient. From about
the date of the city's beginning P. E. Saunders was clerk until his
death in 1913, when his son, Eugene Saunders, the present clerk, took the
office and has attended to it ever since. No finer set of city records (mostly
reduced to typewriting) can be seen in the state than those found at
Harvard.

PRESENT OFFICIALS

The following are the officials of the city of Harvard: mayor, J. G.
Maxon; clerk, Eugene Saunders; health official, Dr. C. W. Goddard;
magistrate, H. S. Williams; treasurer, E. A. Crumb; attorney, R. F.
Marshall; aldermen, Jerome Crowley, J. M. Harris, Benjamin Hagar,
H. A. Jordan, Amos G. Smith, and F. O. Thompson.

PUBLIC IMPROVEMENT

The waterworks were established at Harvard in 1891, for which the
city has been variously bonded, and for which some bonds are still unpaid. Water is obtained from two deep wells, one 900 and one 1,800
feet, and these furnish an abundant supply of pure water. A volunteer
fire company of sixteen members looks after the fire department. In 1918
a $3,000 auto-fire-truck was purchased by the city.

The city receives its electric lighting from the Illinois Northern
Utility Company and has since 1911; prior to that private concerns furnished the lights of Harvard.

A full square in the center of the city is devoted to public park purposes, however it has not been much improved.

The two story brick city hall was erected in 1895.

POST OFFICE

Harvard secured a post office in 1851. Its first postmaster was
William Randall; he was succeeded by the following persons: R. W. M.
De Lee, A. E. Axtell, J. W. Groesbeck who was appointed in 1880 and

he in turn by Messrs. J. A. Sweeney, Dr. Woodruff, J. A. Sweeney, M. F. Walsh and M. F. O'Connor.

There are numerous rural free delivery routes out from Harvard; the office in Harvard is well managed by competent help and general satisfaction is had by the patrons of the office.

INDUSTRIES

The various factory interests of Harvard include the branch of the famous "Black Cat" Hosiery Company of Kenosha, Wis., the Bowman Milk Bottling Works and the Hunt, Helm & Ferris factory which are treated in another chapter of this work.

CEMETERY

Just to the south and east of Harvard is found the beautiful, though silent city, the cemetery which was laid out about the time the village of Harvard was platted. In all northern Illinois one can find none so beautiful and well cared for. It can be seen from incoming trains, as having been originally planned, and is annually kept up to a high state of perfection. The shade trees and flowers in season are indexes to the passerby of a people of religious and cultivated tastes. This is indeed a true index of Christian civilization, proper care for the departed. The monuments erected here are in keeping with the grounds wherein repose hundreds of Harvard's deceased pioneers and later citizens.

POPULATION

The 1910 Federal census reports gave Chemung Township, including Harvard city, a population of 4,101; and in 1920 it was 4,421.

TOWNSHIP OFFICIALS

The following are the township officials of Chemung Township: supervisor, W. H. Ward; assessor, John Dean; clerk, F. O. Thompson; highway commissioner, W. D. Cornwell; justices of the peace, John T. O'Brien and Charles J. Vierck; constables, R. W. Hall, James Hagen and Fred Dean.

CHAPTER XXVII

CORAL TOWNSHIP

BOUNDARIES

In the southwestern part of the county is found the civil township of Coral, which comprises all of congressional township 43, range 6, east, hence is six miles square. It is south of Seneca Township, west of Grafton Township, north of Kane County, and east of Riley Township. Its soil is fertile and especially well adapted for dairy purposes. The territory is well watered by Kiswaukee Creek and its small tributaries.

EARLY SETTLEMENT

The records show that Coral was among the first townships in the county to be settled. Its first settler was William Hamilton, who located near the present site of Coral Village, in November, 1835, but he did not long survive his migration here from Ohio, as he died in the following spring from injuries sustained assisting Calvin Spencer of Marengo, to raise a log cabin. The next to locate were Benjamin Van Vleet and his father, and they built a cabin near the old Indian camping ground, but they were not permanent settlers, for in 1836 they sold to William Jackson and moved to Pecatonica, where both later passed away. O. P. Rogers settled here March, 1836, upon a claim entered for him by J. Rogers in 1835, and his wife was the first white woman in the township. At that time the Rogers' home was the only one between Dundee and a residence three miles west of Elgin. For many years Mr. Rogers lived in Coral Township, but finally removed to Marengo. Frank Diggins and Enos A. Pease came to this township in 1836, to settle on a claim made for them the preceding year. Other settlers of 1836 were: L. Thompson, Clark P. Thompson, Joseph Bullard and

379

Proctor Smith. A. Thompson came in 1837, as did John Jab, Robert Eddy, A. F. Randall, Sebas Frisbie, John Denison and Ira Nichols.

INDIAN VILLAGE

Prior to the white settlement in Coral Township, there stood near the present site of the village of Coral, a scattering village of Indian wigwams. From one of the earliest publications on McHenry County, the following, bearing on this Indian village, is quoted:

"Among these wigwams of various architectural descriptions, stood one of peculiar formation, being conical in form. This round building was about fourteen feet in diameter. Inside were placed seats which were about thirty inches wide, and formed of split sticks. It is believed that these were used during the daytime at council meetings as places to sit on, and at nighttime as bedsteads, upon which they spread skins of animals. The walls presented a picture gallery of a one-idea artist. Here was presented the picture of an Indian in full rig, on a march, followed by a squaw on a pony and a dog in the rear. This trio was produced over and over again till the walls were literally covered with its production. Though these lands had been purchased of the Indians, the time for giving possession had not arrived when the aggressive white man put in his appearance. Those who settled in Coral Township in the autumn of 1835, were visited the following spring by the inhabitants of this Indian village. They had spent the winter elsewhere and had returned to take up their abode and stay the balance of the time allotted them. Upon their return they found that much of the material comprising their wigwams had been taken by the white men and made a part of their shanties. They called upon Mr. Hamilton and secured their copper cooking pots, which he had found and was preserving as curiosities. They then opened up a pit of corn, which they had buried the year before, and commenced housekeeping in their way. These Indians only knew enough of our language to swear."

PIONEER EVENTS

The first marriage in Coral Township was that uniting Samuel H. Bullard and Samantha Dunham, by Beman Crandall, a justice of the peace, on August 25, 1839.

The first white child born here was Mary Eddy, a daughter of Robert Eddy and his wife, who was born in 1837.

John Hamilton, who died within this township in the spring of 1836, was the first white person to die in the township. The first cemetery was not laid out till 1838, hence he was buried in private grounds. A little later a cemetery was provided in Harmony; also another one at Union, after the latter became a fair sized village.

VILLAGE OF CORAL

Coral was the first village in Coral Township. It was laid out or rather settled on in the northwest quarter of section 8, by Fillmore & Anderson who opened a store there, which was burned and never rebuilt. The post office, which was the first established between Chicago and Galena, was given to the township in 1837, and kept at first at the house of William Jackson, who was its first postmaster. He was succeeded by a Mr. Smith, and he was followed by Harriet Dunham. W. J. Fillmore then secured the appointment and moved the office to Coral village. Other postmasters at Coral were William Ross, Mr. Cleaver, Mr. Valentine Alstine, Mr. Morris and Henry Stoddard. A large nursery was started at Coral, but it was later removed to Marengo. J. H. Ocock, William Boice, T. Ross and W. L. Morse were among the first dealers at Coral. With the coming of the railroad, other towns were laid out and Coral never grew much more.

July 16, 1866, was the date on which Coral village was platted in regular and legal form.

VILLAGE OF UNION

Union village is located on the Chicago & Northwestern Railroad, in section 4, township 43, range 6, east. It was platted in 1851 by William Jackson, with the idea of having it made a station point on the proposed railway when it should be constructed through the county. He really hit it nearer than men seldom do, for he secured a station. The first house was erected in 1851 by F. M. Mead, and it was later occupied by the station agent. The first store in Union was opened in 1852 by one Hathaway who acted as agent for Mr. Kimble of Elgin. Hungerford & Smith had the first drug store in Union, opening it in 1857. Cutler & Van Pelt and J. A. Crandall were among early merchants there.

INCORPORATION

Union has been an incorporated village since August, 1897, and the following is a list of names of those who have served as presidents: C.

L. Kremer, H. W. Kittenger, I. N. Muzzy, P. A. Ranie, H. W. Kittenger, E. H. Eggert, William D. Mallett, J. H. Calbow, P. A. Ranie, E. H. Eggert, P. A. Ranie, John Buchte.

PRESENT OFFICIALS

The following are the present officials of the village of Union: President, John Buchte; clerk, H. J. Miller; treasurer, H. F. Luhring; magistrate, P. A. Renie; marshal, L. F. Nulle; attorney, C. B. Whittemore; trustees, C. E. Guse, Fred Miller, August Kunke, Frank Trebes, Herman Trebes and William Clasen.

The village bonded itself in 1912 for a waterwork system. Good well water is their supply. A gasoline engine pumps the water to a pressure tank. The village maintains a volunteer fire brigade. The village is without debts at this date. Several years ago they purchased in conjunction with the Odd Fellows order, the old Universalist Church, a two-story stone structure built at a very early date. The Odd Fellows have the upper story, while the village has the first floor for its offices and meeting place.

POST OFFICE

The post office at Union dates back to the autumn of 1852 when its postmaster was a Mr. Cannon, who was succeeded in a year by S. A. Randall. Other postmasters have been: F. M. Read, Mr. Sheldon, S. A. Randall, William H. Alden, William M. Baldwin, J. D. Bliss, N. C. Gardner, Homer Darling, L. D. Fillmore, Mrs. E. E. Fillmore, and present postmaster, W. C. Null, who was appointed in February, 1915. This is a fourth-class office; has one rural route of thirty miles in length, with John Schneider as carrier.

DEFUNCT HARMONY

Harmony was the name given a little community in this township. It was never dignified by being platted, but it was an early community center where church and school privileges might be had by the pioneers. Here was built the first church within the township. In 1885 a store, a cheese factory, a school and church constituted the hamlet. It now exists in memory largely, for its commercial days are forever gone.

Chas. Kruse.
Anna Kruse

POPULATION

The population of Coral Township for four United States census periods have been as follows: In 1890 it had 1,432; in 1900 it reached 1,451; in 1910 its population was 1,354; and in 1920 it was 1,296.

TOWNSHIP OFFICIALS

The following are the township officials of Coral Township: Supervisor, Charles Ackman, Jr.; assessor, Herman Trebes; clerk, C. M. Siems; highway commissioner, Chris Fritz; justices of the peace, A. S. Peak and William Wertz; constables, L. F. Wilde and C. T. Cau.

CHAPTER XXVIII

DORR TOWNSHIP

BOUNDARIES

Dorr Township is bounded on the north by Greenwood Township, a portion of which is included in the city of Woodstock; on the east by Nunda Township; on the south by Grafton Township, and on the west by Seneca Township. Originally this township contained some very fine timber, but no prairie land, although it is level. It is watered by Hanley Creek, and a branch of the Kishwaukee.

ORIGIN OF NAME

The township was named in honor of Governor Dorr, of Rhode Island, who opposed the English laws governing that state.

EARLY SETTLERS

The first white man to settle in Dorr Township was Uriah Cattle, who came here from Virginia in the fall of 1834, and made his claim, after which he returned to his old home. The following spring he came back to this region, accompanied by William Hartman, Charles and John McClure, and John Walkup, who composed what was known in the early days as the "Virginia Settlement." These pioneers showed such energy after their arrival on Monday morning, that by the end of

384

the week they had their log shanties up and roofed, although there were no floors for a number of months. Mr. Cattle continued to reside in the township until his death, either late in the seventies, or early in the eighties. Charles McClure died in the township in 1844. These original settlers were later joined by Christopher Walkup, John L. Gibson, James Dufield, and William Hartman.

PIONEER EVENTS

The first death in this township was that of the three-year-old daughter of Uriah Cattle, in September, 1836. In the fall of that same year, a little daughter of James Dufield also died.

Martha McClure was born in the fall of 1835, and she is conceded to have been the first white child born in the township. She died at the age of seventeen years.

The first wedding was that solemnized between Oscar H. Douglass and Sarah Gaff by Rev. Joel Wheeler, May 13, 1839.

CEMETERIES

Ridgefield Cemetery, the oldest burial ground in the township, was laid out in 1835 by Charles McClure as a private cemetery, but later he permitted the interment of outsiders. It is divided by the eastern line of Dorr Township, and the greater part of it lies in Nunda Township. Originally it comprised only two acres, but subsequently was increased to the present size.

Oakland Cemetery, located at the western limits of Woodstock, was purchased by the corporation, December 20, 1859, of M. T. Bryan, and then comprised ten acres. Two additional acres were added for a Potters' Field, and other additions have since been made, as increasing space was needed. The Catholic Cemetery, known as "Calvary," is located just south of Oakland, across the highway, and both are kept in beautiful condition.

RIDGEFIELD

Ridgefield is located on section 25, township 44, range 7, and was platted by William Hartman, January 8, 1855, and it occupies the lands originally owned by members of the Virginia settlement. It came into being as a result of a station being located at this point, when the railroad was built through the county. Lots were sold so low by Mr. Hartman, in order to induce outsiders to come here, that he failed to realize any profit. He erected the first building, in which a store was established by George K. Bunker. J. G. Hartman opened a wagonmaking shop; Miles Graff was the first blacksmith; Daniel Root was the first shoemaker, and David Graff opened a hotel, but soon thereafter sold to a Mr. Holmes. Ridgefield is now the center of one of the large milk plants of the county.

Ridgefield post office was established in 1837, and was located a mile and a half west of the present village, at the residence of Christopher Walkup, who was the first postmaster. After the building of the railroad the office was moved to Ridgefield, and Isaac Hamilton was appointed postmaster. He was succeeded by A. F. Davis. During the subsequent years the post office has been kept by the owner of one or other of the stores at this point, and is now located in the Economy store.

POPULATION

According to the United States census the population of Dorr Township has been as follows: In 1890, 1,113; in 1900, 968; in 1910, 1,004, which was exclusive of Woodstock, which in the latter year had a population of 4,331; and in 1920, 6,408, including a portion of the city of Woodstock, the remainder of the city, with its population of 5,523, lying in Greenwood Township.

TOWNSHIP OFFICIALS

The following are the township officials: Supervisor, F. A. Walters; assessor, A. J. Murphy; clerk, J. C. Pierce; highway commissioner, Fred Menges; justices of the peace, T. J. Rushton and C. E. Lockwood; constables, F. G. Behringer, William Conney and P. W. Murphy.

WOODSTOCK

Woodstock, county seat of McHenry County, and one of the most beautiful of the smaller cities of Illinois, was laid out by Alvin Judd, in 1844. After the plat had been executed, Mr. Judd sold his interests to George C. Dean, who, in June, 1844, had the plat recorded. At that time the village was named Centerville because of its geographical position in almost the center of the county, but in February, 1845, through

SOLDIERS' MONUMENT AND BAND STAND, WOODSTOCK

the influence of Joel II. Johnson, the name was changed to Woodstock by Act of Legislature. This name was selected because Woodstock, Vt., was the birthplace of Mr. Johnson and other prominent men of the county, who sought to perpetuate pleasant memories of their old home, in their new one.

Woodstock has the highest altitude of any place in the state, the survey, made many years ago, giving it at 373 feet above the waters of Lake Michigan, and 954 feet above the sea level of the Atlantic Ocean. An inscription on the face of the basestones of the courthouse testifies to this interesting fact.

Bradford Burbank built the first log house in 1843, and the first frame one was put up by Alvin Judd in 1844. The latter was opened as a tavern. During the winter of 1844-5, Mr. Judd built another frame house. The first store was opened in 1845 by Josiah Dwight and Oscar L. Beach. Henry Petrie opened another store that same year. In 1848 A. W. Fuller established his general store, and the fourth mercantile establishment was conducted by William Dunning and Alfred Dufield.

Other very early business men were as follows: Neill Donnelly, John Donnelly, Ira C. Trowbridge, Leonard Burtchy, Jr., A. W. Tappan, L. B. Converse, Joseph Hatch, L. T. Salisbury, John Bunker, J. J. Murphy, George W. Bentley, J. C. Choate, F. C. Joslyn, C. B. Duffee, Joseph Golder, L. T. Hoy, J. S. Wheat, A. S. Wright, George F. Mills, George Sylvester, M. Sherman, E. W. Blossom, Eddy Brothers, II. P. Norton, and Ira C. Trobridge.

The commercial and industrial growth of Woodstock has been in keeping with the expansion throughout the county, and a history of its industrial interests, past and present, is given in the chapter devoted to this subject.

As above stated, the first tavern, or hotel, at Woodstock was the one put up by Alvin Judd in 1844. Others were the Exchange Hotel, kept for a long period by Mr. Trall; the American House, located on the west side of the Square, kept by Messrs. G. H. Griffing, White and McMasters; the Waverly, built by Roswell Enos, in 1856, on two lots which cost him $7 each; the Woodstock House, built by Alonzo Anderson in 1852-3; and the Richmond House, built by E. H. Richmond, in 1874, which was conducted for some years by Mr. Richmond.

PUBLIC SQUARE

Woodstock is beautifully laid out, many of its business houses being located on the streets surrounding the City Park, at the head of which stands the courthouse. To the right is the city hall. On the hottest of days, the delightful shade afforded by the little park is never lessened, and the drinking fountain furnishes artesian water and a mineral water. In the center of the park is the monument erected in honor of the soldiers of the Civil War, through the efforts of the Woman's Relief Corps, No. 223, of Woodstock. It is about twenty-five feet in height, and bears these inscriptions:

"Auxiliary to Woodstock Post No. 108, Grand Army of the Republic," on the north front; "Erected to the Soldiers of 1861-65," on the east front; "Erected in 1909 by the Woodstock Woman's Relief Corps No. 223," on the south front; while on the west front is "In Honor of Our National Defenders."

Surmounting this shaft is a granite statue of heroic size, representing a private soldier holding the Civil-War type of musket. The monument is guarded by four large brass cannon, secured from the war department, one being placed near each corner of the base of the monument, but there is a wide walk between the cannon and the monument. A little to the west of the center of the park is the band stand, and in the eastern part of the park is the drinking fountain. The trees in the park and throughout the city are principally elm, and were planted more than sixty years ago, when the public square was graded by the civil engineer of the Northwestern Railroad in 1856-7, and it was in accordance with his suggestion that these trees were set out promiscuously, instead of in rows. Many of these trees are now over sixty feet in height and afford a delightful shade.

POST OFFICE

The Woodstock post office was established in 1844, and Alvin Judd was the first postmaster. When he resigned in 1845, he was succeeded by Martin Thrall. Joseph Dwight succeeded him and remained in office until 1853, when F. D. Austin was made postmaster. Since then the following have served as postmasters of Woodstock: Dr. O. S. Johnson, 1857-61; A. E. Smith, 1861-66; William E. Smith, 1866; Mr. Crandall, 1866-67; Mr. Irwin, 1867-69; William E. Smith, 1869-75; Asa W. Smith, 1875-79; G. S. Southworth, 1879-87; Joel H. Johnson, 1887-91; Simon Brink, 1891-96; John A. Dufield, 1896-1900; C. F. Renich, 1900-1911; W. S. McConnell, 1911-15; G. G. Frame, 1915 to the present time.

The Woodstock post office belongs to the second class, and nineteen smaller post offices in the county are required to make their reports to this office, and purchase their supplies from it. On October 15, 1909, the Woodstock office was made a free delivery office. There are six rural free delivery routes out from Woodstock, the length of each one being thirty miles.

Since 1866 the Woodstock office has been a money order office, and the first order issued through it was on August 21, 1866, by E. Barton to A. A. Kelly & Co., of Chicago, for $9. The first order paid was on August 7, 1866, to John D. Short for $40, and it was issued by Dr. Asa Horn, of Dubuque, Iowa.

INCORPORATION

On June 22, 1852, Woodstock was incorporated as a village under Act of Legislature, and the governing power vested in a president and board of trustees. The original charter was amended several times, as needed. From 1852 until 1873 when Woodstock became a city, the following served it as village president: Alvin Judd, 1852-3; Enos W. Smith, 1854; Neill Donnelly, 1855-6; Melvin W. Baldwin, 1857; M. W. Hunt, 1858; H. B. Burton, 1859; Neill Donnelly, 1860; M. L. Joslyn, 1861; H. S. Hanchett, 1862; William Kerr, 1863-4-5; M. L. Joslyn, 1866; John S. Wheat, 1867; B. N. Smith, 1868; M. D. Hoy, 1869; E. E. Richards, 1870-71; and L. H. Davis, 1872-3.

The original village officials were: Alvin Judd, president; and Joseph Golder, L. S. Church, C. B. Durfee, J. C. Trowbridge, and George H. Griffin, trustees; Charles Fitch, clerk; John Brink, surveyor; L. W. McMasters, constable; and Charles Fitch, treasurer.

The last to hold position as village officials were: L. H. Davis, president; John A. Rarrish, assessor and treasurer; S. Van Curan, constable; S. Brink, clerk; and T. J. Daey, J. S. Wheat, George L. Sherwood, M. D. Hoy, G. K. Bunker and E. E. Thomas, trustees.

An election was held March 24, 1873, to decide relative to city incorporation, and the vote stood 109 in favor, none against the proposition.

The first city officials were: John S. Wheat, mayor; T. L. Maher, clerk; J. J. Murphy, treasurer; M. C. Johnson, attorney; and W. H. Stewart, G. K. Bunker, A. Badger, E. E. Richards, T. J. Dacy, F. Arnold, aldermen; S. Van Curan, marshal; A. J. Murphy, street commissioner.

The following have served as mayor of Woodstock: John S. Wheat, 1873; Neill Donnelly, 1874; R. C. Jefferson, 1875; Neill Donnelly, 1876; L. H. Davis, 1877-78; John J. Murphy, 1879-80; M. L. Joslyn, 1881-82; George H. Bunker, 1883-88; Erastus E. Richards, 1888-94; John D. Donovan, 1894-97; E. C. Jewett, 1897; E. E. Richards, 1899; E. C. Jewett, 1900-03; F. A. Walter, 1903-07; George H. Hoy, 1907-09; J. D. Donovan, 1909-10; A. J. Olson, 1912-14; he died in office, and Alderman H. J. Dygert completed his term; S. E. Olmsted was elected in 1916.

PRESENT OFFICIALS

The following are the present officials of the city of Woodstock: Frank J. Green, mayor; H. G. Fisher, clerk; William Freeman, health commissioner; Walter E. Conway, treasurer; T. H. Brown, magistrate; David Joslyn, Jr., attorney; and Frank Brown, Joseph Peacock, Henry Johanson, Lester Nogle, F. J. Wienke, T. B. Merwin, W. H. Hobbs, and T. B. Owens, aldermen.

PUBLIC IMPROVEMENTS

The first steps to secure public water works for Woodstock were taken in 1894 when a bond issue of $10,000 was made to secure funds; and another bond issue was made for $25,000 in 1902 for the improvement of the system already installed. The high water-tower tank in the western part of the city gives direct pressure and thus affords proper protection to the city in case of fire. The water is drawn from wells of the purest water, dug by the city for this purpose. The system of mains and street hydrants is complete throughout the city. A complete sewer system was not constructed until 1907-8.

Electric lights were installed in the city in 1904, bonds having been floated for this purpose to the amount of $3,000. Again in 1910 another bond issue was made for $8,000 for the extension of the service. Since then other improvements have been made as required.

The city of Woodstock granted the Western United Gas & Electric

Company a franchise to lay gas pipes and supply the city with gas in 1909.

The history of the telephone development is given elsewhere, in the chapter devoted to industrial activities.

The city hall was built in 1889-90, under Mayor E. E. Richard's supervision, and it is a three-story and basement, brick structure. It has an opera hall on the top floor, and contains the city offices, council chamber, fire department, public library and reading room.

CHICAGO INDUSTRIAL HOME FOR CHILDREN

The Chicago Industrial Home for Children is located on Seminary avenue, Woodstock, and is one of the ornaments of this progressive city. The institution was established here in 1894, when Mrs. Roxy D. Stevens, a widow, without children, seeing the importance of the work being done by the home, which had been incorporated March 4, 1889, and was being conducted in the private residence of its founder, Rev. Thomas B. Arnold, of Chicago, under great difficulties, offered her own pleasant and commodious home for the purpose. This residence was styled by the builder and original owner, Mr. Galister, an English villa. Mrs. Stevens offered this property to the institution, only stipulating that she be given a home to dwell in and an annuity until her death. Upon these conditions the property was transferred to the institution, and has continued to be the home of the undertaking ever since.

From this center have gone out many children who were born to a spring without flowers, a summer without sunshine, and an autumn of early frosts, with naught but a harvest of poverty, shame and disgrace before them, to homes of affluence, comfort and refinement, to become good citizens, noble men and women, and useful members of society. The acquisition of this property gave the institution an excellent start in its good work. Not having been built for institutional work, this home was not suited to the ever-increasing demands. In 1912 it was practically rebuilt, and made into a modern building, so that it is now well adapted to and equipped for the purposes of its incorporate demand, and which its charter sets forth to be: "To provide a home for homeless, orphaned, deserted, destitute and dependent children; to educate them and instruct them in industrial pursuits; also to aid such children in obtaining suitable Christian family homes."

The scope of the work of the home is two-fold, home saving and home finding.

"Home Saving. If the home is of the right character, it is better to extend temporary aid and preserve it than to suffer it to be broken up. In many cases by reason of sickness, death, the desertion of a parent, or some other cause, it is impossible for the home to continue. In such cases if we extend temporary aid to the children by bridging over the emergency, the home may be rebuilt, and the children have the rights and privileges that belong to every child, the right of home life and living.

"Home Finding. Through this department the institution finds homes in Christian families, for such children as are surrendered to it by parents, guardians, or by the courts. Hundreds of children have been given tender care, comfortable sustenance, good educational advantages, excellent training, wholesome moral and religious instruction, and many have been placed in Christian family homes for adoption, and by these means have been saved from becoming subject to those circumstances which are almost sure to result in viciousness and criminality."

The management of the home is vested in a board of eleven directors, and its offices are in Chicago. The institution is supported principally by voluntary contributions of charitably disposed people. Its accounts are audited by a public accountant at the close of each fiscal year. Its work is important and is measured by the amount of its contributions.

OLD PEOPLE'S REST HOME

The Old People's Rest Home occupies a site adjoining the grounds of the Chicago Industrial Home for Children, at Woodstock, and both are under the care of Rev. J. D. Kelsey. In 1903 Samuel K. J. Chesboro, Burton R. Jones, James D. Marsh, Thomas B. Arnold, John D. Kelsey, William P. Ferries, John E. Coleman, Esmond E. Hall, William E. Bardell, Freeborn D. Brooke incorporated the Old People's Rest Home, and opened it for occupancy that same year.

The object of this institution is to provide and maintain a home for aged people of both sexes, who are in a measure dependent, where they may have the advantages of good accommodations, agreeable associations, pleasant surroundings, comfortable sustenance and tender ministrations when needed, amid which to spend the closing years of life. Certainly its objects are both philanthropic and Christian, and as such can but appeal to the sympathies and aid of generous people everywhere.

The doors of the Rest Home are ever open to aged people, who need such a place of rest and care, without respect of nationality, race, creed, or religion. Many have already found shelter, care and comfort in their last years within its enclosure, and the managers are only sorry that their limited room does not admit of their taking in many more. The home inmates usually number in the neighborhood of twenty, which with the matron and other helpers constitutes quite a large family to be maintained. The capacity of the home is for about twenty-four inmates.

Rev. J. D. Kelsey has had charge of the home since it was established, and his wife was its matron until her health failed, the position now being held by Florence Walcott.

WOODSTOCK COUNTRY CLUB

The Woodstock Country Club was organized in 1915, and its membership has steadily increased. A tract of about fifty-seven acres was purchased by the club. These grounds, formerly the farm of the late Mr. McNulty, lie about two miles east of the courthouse, and are beautifully situated. There is considerable timber, and an artesian well over 1,000 feet deep. This well was sunk and suitable frame buildings have been erected. A golf course has been laid out, and other improvements are projected.

WOODSTOCK COMMERCIAL AND COMMUNITY CLUB

On February 26, 1913, the Woodstock Business Men's Association was founded, and in the spring of 1918, to meet conditions arising out of the war, a new constitution, by-laws and name were given the club, which has since been known as the Woodstock Commercial and Community Club. This was incorporated under the laws of Illinois, October 11, 1918. This organization has two objects, the promotion of business interests, and the furnishing of social diversions, or to use their own definition: "the furtherance of the social, civic, mercantile and industrial advancement of the city of Woodstock and the surrounding community."

The club is placed under the charge of a board of directors numbering fifteen, five of whom are elected annually. Among other benefits accruing from membership is the issuance of weekly reports showing the judgments given at the courthouse each week, in printed form. Retailers are also given a credit-rating book for the city of Woodstock and environments. This club takes in all honorable professional and business men of the community, and plans in the near future to become a still greater factor in advancing the best commercial and social interests of this section.

CHAPTER XXIX

DUNHAM TOWNSHIP

BOUNDARIES—TOPOGRAPHY—EARLY SETTLERS—ORIGIN OF NAME—PIONEER EVENTS—CEMETERIES—SCHOOLS AND CHURCHES—CYCLONE OF 1883—POPULATION—TOWNSHIP OFFICIALS.

BOUNDARIES

Dunham Township is bounded on the north by Chemung Township; on the east by Hartland Township; on the south by Marengo Township, and on the west by Boone County. It comprises all of congressional township 45, range 5. This township is about equally divided between timber and prairie land, or at least was when the county was first settled. It is naturally adapted to stock raising and many are the fine herds that have been grazing from its sweet grasses in the decades that have passed since its surface was first used by the white race. It is well watered and reasonably drained by Rush and Piskasaw creeks, with their several small tributaries.

TOPOGRAPHY

Rush Creek, a branch of the Kishwaukee, crosses the township from northeast to southwest, passing out from section 34, and the Piskasaw courses through the northwest corner.

EARLY SETTLERS

The first white man to locate in this township, with a view of becoming a permanent settler, was John Diggins, who came here in 1836, locating in section 10 and section 11, a farm later owned and occupied by O. C. Diggins. The latter named came to the township in March, 1837, and his family joined him as soon as he had a cabin prepared for them. While N. K. Jerome made a claim in 1837, he did not take up his residence upon it until 1838. Two unmarried men, Baker and Dun-

Claude C. Lace.

ham, were the next two to arrive, and they were followed by Joseph and James Metcalf. Before 1841, the following had taken up residence in Dunham Township: A. Joslyn, R. Latham, Joseph Diggins, J. F. Moore, Dexter Barrows, J. Snowden, R. and D. Linton, and W. R. Heath.

ORIGIN OF NAME

The original name of this township was Byron, but when the post office was established, it was discovered that another "Byron" existed within the state, hence the name was changed to Dunham, in honor of pioneer Solomon J. Dunham, a very prominent resident, then serving as a justice of the peace.

PIONEER EVENTS

Josephine Diggins was the first white child born in this township. She was the daughter of Mr. and Mrs. John Diggins, and she died when aged seventeen years.

In 1839 occurred the first death in Dunham Township, when Walter Walton passed away, and was buried in section 3 of this township.

The earliest marriage was that uniting Jacob A. Davis and Miss Helen M. Diggins, on New Year's day, 1839.

In 1840 a log schoolhouse was built by School District No. 1, in section 1, and a school was immediately opened.

The only church ever erected in this township was that of the Methodist Episcopal denomination known as the County Line Church. This building cost $2,000. Rev. P. M. Huffman was the first to serve as pastor.

There are about two miles of railroad in this township, the Chicago & Northwestern line running through Harvard from the southeast.

In 1874, a cheese factory was built in section 35, and was still being successfully operated in 1885. At one time Latham Corners had a general store, but its existence was brief.

Sheep raising as far back as 1870 was a large industry among the farmers of this township. The land it was believed then, was better adapted to stock than grain. There were more sheep killed by dogs in this township, along in the seventies, than in any other part of the county.

CEMETERIES

The first cemetery in this township was laid out either in 1841 or 1842, near the old Jerome log schoolhouse.

In the western part of the township around the Methodist Church, is another early burying ground.

Mt. Auburn Cemetery was laid out late in the seventies. It is about three-quarters of a mile southeast of the city of Harvard, taking the place of the old Harvard Cemetery, abandoned on account of low ground, the bodies being transferred to the new burial place.

SCHOOL AND CHURCHES

The first schoolhouse in Dunham Township was built in 1838 on the farm of Mr. Jerome. Here schools were kept and here the elections were held many years during the pioneer days. Here it was that the first term of school in the township was taught by Miss Edna Jewett.

The first religious services in this township were held in the Jerome schoolhouse in 1838 or 1839, and were conducted by Elder White and Rev. Jewett.

CYCLONE OF 1883

On June 11, 1883, Dunham Township had the misfortune to be visited by a cyclone, which first struck the residence of Richard Downs. The Moore schoolhouse was literally blown into splinters. Benjamin Phelps, Josiah Goodsell, Proctor Russell, D. R. Wyant, Arthur Thompson, Mr. Jerome, N. A. Clark, John Mohelus and Michael Sullivan, all suffered from the fury of the storm.

Being near to Harvard, with the county seat not far distant, there never has sprung up a village within this township. Neither has it a railway station nor has there been a post office in recent years, but a good rural mail route service delivers the mail for this section of the county.

POPULATION

In 1890 Dunham Township had a population of 919; in 1900 it had 859; in 1910 it had 849; and in 1920 it had 857.

TOWNSHIP OFFICIALS

The following are the township officials of Dunham Township: Supervisor, H. E. Whipple; assessor, D. A. Barrows; clerk, Herbert Kieskowski; highway commissioner, Thomas Green; justices of the peace, D. A. Barrows and L. O. Higgins; constables, C. M. Downs and David Fitch.

CHAPTER XXX

GRAFTON TOWNSHIP

BOUNDARIES—ORIGIN OF NAME—EARLY SETTLERS—PIONEER EVENTS—CHOL-
ERA—CEMETERIES—TOWNSHIP OFFICIALS—VILLAGE OF HUNTLEY—EARLY
BUSINESS INTERESTS—POST OFFICE—INCORPORATION.

BOUNDARIES

Grafton Township is in the southern tier of townships in this county, and is bounded on the north by Dorr Township; on the east by Algonquin Township; on the south by Kane County, and on the west by Coral Township, and is described in surveys as congressional township 43, range 7, east.

When first settled this township was very wet and swampy, and by many the land was believed to be next to worthless, the lowest point being in its center; but modern and more scientific methods have come to the rescue and drained out most of these lands, which are now among the finest, most productive of any in the country. Here one sees many beautiful, well improved and highly valuable farms. Crystal Lake covers one-fourth of section 1, and the Kishwaukee Creek and its branches drain the land and furnish ample water supply at all times of the year.

ORIGIN OF THE NAME

The name Grafton was given to this township by Prescott Whittemore who thus honored his old home back in New Hampshire, which was also called Grafton Township.

EARLY SETTLERS

The first settler was a Mr. Grinnell, who only remained a short time, and then sold his land to Lewis Holdridge, the second man to select Grafton Township as a place of residence. The third settler was Prescott Whittemore, who arrived in 1838, from New York state, and he

397

lived here for more than twenty years. Another pioneer was Mr.
Stowell, from Massachusetts, who made Grafton Township his home
for about fifteen years, and then went to California, where he died in
1870. William Robb was a settler of 1839, coming from New Haven,
Connecticut, locating in section 30, where he died many years ago. For
a time John Curren lived in this township, but finally sold to Thomas
Huntley and moved to Iowa. Richard Hadley came to Grafton Township about 1839-40, and James Winney and John Conover were here
about the same date last mentioned.

PIONEER EVENTS

The first white child born in Grafton Township was Marion, son of
William Robb and wife. He was born in 1839.

Death first invaded the home of Charles Stowell and wife and claimed
a two-year-old daughter, and she was laid away beneath the prairie sod
in the eastern edge of the village of Huntley.

The first to unite in marriage in this township were Sanford Haight
and Miss Mary A. Sprague. They were made man and wife by Beman
Crandall, a justice of the peace of this township.

The first hotel in Grafton was kept by Prescott Whittemore. It was
in fact his residence, but he had to care for the land and home-seekers
as they flocked into the county. He carried this on for ten years, more
for accommodation than for profit. When the village of Huntley was
established Mr. Whittemore sought to retire, but it was well known that
his "latch-string" always hung outside and anyone who desired might
here find a welcome hand and something good to eat.

CHOLERA

While Grafton was still in its infancy as a settlement, three soldiers
traveled on their way to territory further west, having been with General Winfield Scott in the War with Mexico. They were stricken with
that dread disease, cholera, and died, and were buried in the vicinity
where later stood the Free Methodist Church, at the north side of the
Township of Grafton.

CEMETERIES

In the early fifties the Protestants, of Huntley village laid out a
cemetery south of the place, the same being originally two acres. In

1882 the Catholics laid out their cemetery just to the south of the one just named above.

POPULATION

Grafton Township had a population in 1890 of 1,589; in 1900, 1,484; in 1910, 1,437; and in 1920, 1,475.

TOWNSHIP OFFICIALS

The following are the township officials of Grafton Township: Supervisor, John Conley; assessor, W. S. Conover; clerk, E. H. Cook; highway commissioner, John F. Weltzien; justices of the peace, John Donahue and Emil Arnold; constable, John French.

VILLAGE OF HUNTLEY

In 1851 Thomas S. Huntley laid out the village which bears his name. This was the same year thé railroad went through the township and this village was made a station on the line, and thus it soon began to be known abroad, and commenced to thrive as a small, but very enterprising place. Mr. Huntley built the first house and used it as dry-goods store. This building stood for many years as a monument of pioneer days in the village so well known now. Later it was used as a drug store, but at last disappeared from the village as a thing of the past. The first hotel was erected by Sanford Haight, and later the structure went into the construction of Glazier Hall. The first hotel was abandoned soon after it was built, and a second one put up by Lewis Holdridge, and conducted by a Mr. Johnson, then by Mr. Fletcher, who sold it to Byron Thornton, in whose hands it ceased as a hotel. H. B. Brown built the third hotel, and after two years sold it to Peter Ferris. Finally the property was burned. The next hotel was built by George Scheler in 1878; it was sold to Cummings Brothers and Haight, who hired O. P. Mason to run it. After going into many other hands it finally became a storehouse. The well known Ellis House was established by B. F. Ellis who conducted a model modern American plan hotel many years.

EARLY BUSINESS INTERESTS

The first general store in Huntley was opened by T. S. Huntley, who after one year sold it to Hoyt & Brown, who enlarged the building and greatly added to the size of the stock. Henry Dunn opened the second store in the village, and a Mr. Grist the third business place. A Mr. Hill was also engaged in mercantile pursuits here for a short time. In 1862, the first hardware store was opened by Mr. Marshall, who continued three years and sold to William Schemerhorn, and he conducted it five years, and then turned it over to his son, Theodore. About 1867 a grist mill was operated at this point. It was a steam plant built by the Jewells, in the southeastern part of the village. Subsequently, it became the property of a Mr. Schaffler, and under his proprietorship, in 1871, there was a serious accident which resulted in the killing of the engineer, William Benedict. Mr. Schaffler was also injured, but not so seriously. He rebuilt the mill and sold to a Mr. Spaulding, who conducted it till 1876, when it was burned. Spaulding rebuilt it and sold it to David Williams, who conducted it as a feed mill.

The first harness shop in this village was started by F. J. Glazier, and the first shoe shop in 1856 by Brown & Van Hoozen. A wagon shop was opened in 1857, and Dwight Ramsdell was the first blacksmith.

John S. Cummings shipped the first car of hogs from Huntley, and as there was no weighing scales in the place he "guessed" them off, paying three cents a pound, but when he reached Chicago with his load, he found his estimate a little too high. He also shipped the first car of cattle from Huntley to Chicago, and received only from $10 to $15 per head.

The Huntley Cheese Factory was an important factor in the community in its day, during the eighties. It was built by D. E. Wood & Co., in 1876-7. At the same time D. E. Wood and John Weltzine owned four other factories of this kind in McHenry County. When this cheese industry flourished at Huntley, some of the business men were: William Hackett, S. Haight, George Van Valkenburg, F. O. Dain, Patrick Duffy, Thomas Fenwick, J. G. Kelley, P. McNinney, Wood & Waltzine, A. Disbrow, T. R. Ferris, W. G. Sawyer, A. Oakley, B. F. Ellis, M. D. Hadley, Smith & Oakley, Teeple & Co., Devine & Skells, Hawley & Tappen, Ellis & Ballard, M. J. Kelley, D. M. Williams, Dr. O. K. Griffith and Otto Gaupner.

POST OFFICE

The post office was first established here in 1851, before which time people in this neighborhood went to Coral post office for their mail. Stewart Cummings was the first postmaster at Huntley and following him were Peter Miller, John Wales, Miss Izanna Bridge, H. B. Williams, John S. Cummings, Edward Haight, T. R. Ferris, John Donahue, T. R. Ferris, E. H. Cook and J. F. Wendt. This is a third class post office and has two rural routes going out into the surrounding district. Route No. 1 has as its present carrier, J. M. Venard; for Route No. 2 Thomas Frederick.

INCORPORATION

Huntley was incorporated as a village under the state laws in 1872 with officers as follows: John S. Cummings, president; John P. Skells, clerk; H. B. Brown, treasurer; F. J. Glazier, city marshal; D. E. Wood, Charles Bruckman, and S. S. Sprague, trustees. Since that date the various presidents have been: Thomas Grimley, Jackson Wood, O. K. Griffith, A. W. Nash, Henry Sinnett, W. G. Sawyer, Henry Sinnett, John Wiltzien, James Sheldon, D. M. Williams, John Wiltzien, John Donahue, John Wiltzien, John Donahue, F. A. Fisher, John Donahue, Henry Mackaben, J. F. Wiltzien.

The following are the officials of the village of Huntley: President, John F. Wiltzien; clerk, Frank McNeeney; treasurer, W. F. Barlett; magistrate, W. P. Whittemore; marshal, John C. French; attorney, F. B. Bennett; trustees, T. R. Ferris, Henry Williams, Claud Williams, James Marsh, Walter Butler and E. H. Cook.

PUBLIC IMPROVEMENTS

In 1910 the village bonded itself for water works. They now have three deep wells; an eighty foot steel tower; a twenty-foot tank surmounting the tower. Pumping is effected by means of an electric motor. The fire department is equipped with two hose carts, 1,000 feet of hose, and a hook and ladder outfit. The village owns a small frame hall, with a jail in the rear of it. A small, neat park adorns the opposite side of the chief business street, and good paving obtains throughout several streets.

CHAPTER XXXI

GREENWOOD TOWNSHIP

BOUNDARIES—TOPOGRAPHY—EARLY SETTLERS—CEMETERIES—MILLS—BUT-
TER AND CHEESE FACTORIES—VILLAGE OF GREENWOOD—EARLY INTERESTS
—POST OFFICES—HARVEST PICNIC—POPULATION—TOWNSHIP OFFICIALS.

BOUNDARIES

Greenwood Township is bounded on the north by Hebron Township;
on the east by McHenry Township; on the south by Dorr Township;
and on the west by Hartland Township. It comprises all of congressional township 45, range 7. It was named by C. M. Goodsall, and this
name was confirmed by township trustee, J. N. Barber.

TOPOGRAPHY

This township is gently rolling land, the soil is extremely fertile and
well cultivated, and the farms are exceedingly valuable. At at early
day, the valley of Nippersink Creek was heavily timbered but this growth
has long since largely disappeared at the hands of the settlers who have
cut it down for fuel and fencing. The main stream of the township is
the Nippersink Creek which has several branches.

EARLY SETTLERS

Probably Henry Weston was the first white man to settle permanently
in what is now Greenwood Township. He came in 1833, Queen Ann
Prairie was named in honor of his wife, who was the first white woman
in the township, and she was the first person to die in this township.
Soon after her death, Mr. Weston was married (second) to a Miss
Watson, and this was the first marriage in the township, although the
first recorded marriage is that between Charles Frame and Mary Dufield
on February 1, 1838, the ceremony being performed by Rev. Joel
Wheeler.

402

THOMAS LINDSAY

Following Mr. Weston the settlers were: Alden, Almon and William Stone, Lewis Boone, Henry Westerman, Elijah Slafton and James Watson, all of whom made claim to their land in 1837.

Lewis Boone took up many acres of both timber and prairie land, and a Mr. McCollum laid claim to a portion of this land and built a cabin on it. This action was resented by Mr. Boone, who tore down the cabin and cut the logs in two, accusing McCollum of jumping his claim. Finally, the two men resorted to a personal encounter, in which Mr. Boone was the conqueror. McCollum and his friends then attacked the Boones and drove them from the land. A lawsuit resulted, the same being the first filed on the McHenry County docket. Lewis Boone remained in the township until his death, and was buried in Greenwood cemetery. His son, Eldridge Boone, was the first white child born in the township, and when he died in 1838, he was buried in Greenwood Cemetery, his being the first body to be interred there.

George Weller, Amos Scofield, Daniel Cattle, Nathan Dufield, Jacob Eckert, Michael J. and Peter J. Herdklotz and their father Eldod Taylor, Squire Baldwin, and O. J. and A. P. Murphy, all of whom came prior to 1839. These settlers all located in the eastern portion of Greenwood Township. Another very early settler was Neill Donnelly who came in 1838.

CEMETERIES

About one-half mile south of the village of Greenwood lies Greenwood cemetery. It is the oldest burying place in Greenwood Township. Here repose many of the pioneers of the township.

Another cemetery was early laid out near the Methodist Church in southern part of the township.

What is known as the Soldiers' Monument Cemetery in this township, originally contained one acre of land, but was subsequently enlarged. In its midst stands the monument erected in memory of the soldiers and sailors who lost their lives during the Civil War. This was dedicated July 4, 1880.

Near the center of the township there was platted a small cemetery by the German settlers, and surrounding the Norwegian Church the people of that faith laid their dead to rest.

MILLS

In 1841, Lake & Scofield built a saw-mill on section 11, it being run by the waters of the Nippersink Creek. For more than a quarter of a

century this mill was active, or until late in the seventies, when it was
torn down and today no trace of a millsite can be seen.

The second mill of this kind was built by Toles & Brown, a mile
below the first one just named. It was also a water-mill. In 1845 they
also erected a grist-mill at an expense of $5,000, but this mill was
destroyed by a fire in 1862. Job Toles built a grist-mill in the village
of Greenwood at a little later date. The flour-milling industry has long
since been left to the great milling centers, near to the supply of
northern wheat and the farmers all buy their flour.

BUTTER AND CHEESE FACTORIES

It is of no little interest in these days of high-priced butter and
cheese, almost prohibitive on account of prices, to read of the many early
creamery and butter and cheese stations and factories in this county,
including the plant of Abbott & Thompson, who built the first cheese
factory in the township in 1848, and its capacity was more than 100,000
pounds of cheese annually. The second cheese factory in the township
was built in 1870, by Job Toles, in the village of Greenwood. These are
all obsolete industries, for today all of the surplus milk is bottled and
shipped to Chicago and other great cities for direct consumption, while
other sections of the United States manufacture the butter and cheese
which McHenry County farmers used to make in such quantities.

VILLAGE OF GREENWOOD

Greenwood is an inland village which was surveyed in 1842, and
platted into lots by Job Toles. He made an addition to the place in
1845. It is finely situated on the south branch of Nippersink Creek on
section 11. The first residences here were erected by Lake & Scofield.
The first store was started by C. M. Goodsell, who carried a very large
stock for so early a time. Burr & Co. started a wagon shop about as
soon as the place was established.

Greenwood contended for the county seat when it was removed from
McHenry to Woodstock in 1843. Not succeeding in that the village has
not grown commercially as have the railroad towns of the county, but
is a beautiful place of residence.

EARLY INTERESTS

In 1854-55, Weller & Hamilton planted several acres of apple trees,
and Greenwood had a nursery which was continued for a number of
years, but Hamilton finally sold and moved to Ridgefield, while Weller

closed out the business at Greenwood. Later Garrison Bros. conducted a business in furnishing fruit and ornamental trees, garden seeds and flowers. The first orchard in the township was set by Andrew Murphy, on Queen Ann Prairie, in 1842, the trees coming from Will County, this state.

The first store was opened in Greenwood Township, at Boone's Mill, in 1847, by a Mr. Lockwood who soon moved away, being succeeded by C. M. Goodsell, at the village of Greenwood.

Since the days of rural mail delivery, and near-by railroad stations, the trade of Greenwood has not even held its own, there now being but a small country store trade there.

Near Greenwood and in section 10 there are several Indian Mounds in which early excavations revealed the presence of numerous human skulls and other remains and instruments of domestic use, supposed to be the work of Mound Builders.

The first post office in either township or village of Greenwood was established in 1850, and was kept in the store of C. M. Goodsell, the first postmaster. Other postmasters were: Messrs. Robbins, Martin, John M. Barber, J. H. Garrison and D. W. Soper. Postal matters have all been changed of later years, for nearly every farmer has his mail dropped at his door every week-day morning, hence has little use for post offices.

HARVEST PICNIC

During the summer of 1877 the people of Queen Ann Prairie and the surrounding neighborhood inaugurated an annual outing which became for many years very interesting and attractive. It was known as the "Harvest Picnic." The first one occurred August 23, 1877, in the fine grove owned by Michael Senger. A big dinner and excellent literary program was enjoyed by a large gathering. It seems too bad that this custom was not kept up perpetually.

POPULATION

The census reports show that this township had in 1890 a population of 899; in 1910, 908; and in 1920, 858.

PRESENT OFFICIALS

The following are the present officials of the village of Greenwood: president, L. W. Thompson; clerk, M. C. Doolittle; treasurer, L. W. Thompson; magistrate, J. N. Barber.

TOWNSHIP OFFICIALS

The following are the township officials of Greenwood Township: supervisor, L. W. Thompson; assessor, M. Dassow; clerk, N. C. Doolittle; highway commissioner, O. H. Aavang: justice of the peace, John N. Barber; constable, Oscar Anderson.

CHAPTER XXXII

HARTLAND TOWNSHIP

BOUNDARIES

Hartland is the second township from the northern line of the county as well as the second from the west. It is bounded on the north by Alden Township; on the east by Greenwood Township; on the south by Seneca Township and on the west by Dunham Township, and comprises all of congressional township 45, range 6, east. When it was first settled by white men, its surface was nearly all covered with good timber, but by the time of the Civil War all of the heaviest first growth had been cut off. Grain and stock raising are callings largely followed by the land-owners in this township. The name Hartland was given the township in 1840, in honor of a town in New York by that name. The name "Antrim" was proposed by the many Irish settlers, but was not adopted by those in authority.

FIRST SETTLERS

It matters not, but here is a conflict in history, three factions of pioneers contending, one claims that the first to locate within this town-ship was F. Griffin; another set up a claim that the honor belongs to George Stafton, and still a third faction is sanguine that to such honor should be attached the name of John Quinlan. It is certain that all three came here at about the same date. Right on their heels was P. W. Tower, and a Mr. Smith, who gained the nick-name of "Whisky" Smith, arrived not long thereafter. P. M. Dunn, William Fanning, Alvin Judd, Andrew J. Haywood, Appolos Hastings, and Alonzo Golder were among the pioneer band in Hartland Township.

This township was settled almost entirely by Irish Catholic people,

407

who, strong in their faith, have made excellent citizens and built up thrifty and large congregations. Here, as in other townships in the county, a few of the settlers made their claims before the land had been surveyed by the government. Such claims gave rise to many disputes as to rights and titles, to settle which, meetings were held, attended by men with arms in hands, ready, if necessary, to maintain their rights by force. All such disagreements were finally adjusted without the spilling of blood, or creating of feuds, as has often been the case in other sections of the country.

PIONEER INCIDENTS

John Short, later known as "squire" in Woodstock for many years, a son of Mr. and Mrs. Francis Short, was the first white child born in this township. The date of his birth was sometime in 1836. His father lived in Hartland Township until his removal, early in the eighties, to Woodstock.

Mrs. Debbit, who died in 1840, was the first white person to die within Hartland Township, and her remains were buried in Hartland Cemetery.

The earliest marriage in the township, celebrated at the residence of a Catholic priest, was that of Walter Gibbs and the widowed Mrs. Sutton, but the first recorded marriage was that uniting William Fanning and Catherine Donnelly, the ceremony being performed by Father J. Gregory, a Catholic priest, on February 4, 1842.

CEMETERIES

Up to 1844, a rail or pole pen surrounded a single grave, and this constituted the only cemetery in Hartland Township, but during that year Mr. Brocken gave to the township a piece of land in section 13 to be used for burial purposes, and about it is now located Hartland Cemetery. There have been other small burying plots within the township.

BROOKDALE

During the year 1840, Wesley Diggins built a saw-mill on the banks of Kishwaukee Creek, and for a number of years a flourishing business was carried on at that point. About it grew up a tiny community, known as Brookdale, and for a time it was believed by some that here was the nucleus of a city, but with the clearing off of the timber, and the end of the immense lumbering business, the trade was drawn away to Harvard and Woodstock, and this generation knows of "Brookdale" only by hearsay. A store was maintained there for several years, as was one also at Oliver's Corners, but it too died a natural death. Other little communities of Hartland Township prospered for a time but soon fell into that "dreamless sleep that knows no waking." The little hamlet of Hartland is the only village now within the township.

POST OFFICE

For some years after Hartland Township was settled the people had to go to McClure's Grove, a distance of twenty-five miles, for mail. Later they received their mail at Crystal Lake, and finally a post office was established at the residence of Alvin Judd, about the center of the township. Eden post office was established in the eastern part of the township, with Henry Oliver as its first postmaster, and Peter McFarland was its second. At Deep Cut a post office was established in 1855, and there maintained until 1865. From 1865 to 1879 the people had to go to either Woodstock or Harvard for mail, but in the latter year a post office was established at Kishwaukee, and Philip Gafner was postmaster for many years. The people of the township, outside of the circuit around Hartland village, are furnished their mail by the rural free delivery system, daily, except Sundays.

EARLY COUNTERFEITERS

At an early day Hartland Township harbored a gang of counterfeiters. These daring men had their outfit in a kind of natural cave in the timber, which was covered with planks and sod. In it the counterfeiters were found to be entering into competition with the government in the production of silver coins. A mile away was a shanty in which the men spent their time when not working at their unlawful task. The excellent citizens were not backward in expressing their disapproval of these methods, and the gang, taking the hint so openly expressed, disappeared and were never again seen in this county.

POPULATION

In 1890 Hartland Township had a population of 960; in 1900, 874; in 1910, 905; and in 1920, 860.

RAILROAD

The Chicago & Northwestern Railroad traverses this township from the southeastern to the northwestern part, through the central portion. In 1877 a depot established near Deep Cut was first called Kiswaukee, now is called Hartland.

VILLAGE OF HARTLAND

Hartland was platted in the southwest part of section 13 and in the southeast of section 14, township 45, range 6, July 26, 1878. It is the only railroad station within the township. It is a small shipping point and in the midst of a very fertile agricultural section. A few stores and shops comprise the business interests of this place.

PRESENT OFFICIALS

The following are serving Hartland in an official position: president and treasurer, Earl C. Hughes; clerk, John H. Haley; and magistrate, Daniel H. Desmond.

TOWNSHIP OFFICIALS

The following are the township officials of Hartland Township: supervisor, E. C. Hughes; assessor, Frank Sullivan; clerk, J. H. Haley; highway commissioner, C. R. Cooney; justice of the peace, D. H. Desmond.

GEORGE LOWE

JESSIE WATSON LOWE

CHAPTER XXXIII

HEBRON TOWNSHIP

BOUNDARIES—ORIGIN OF NAME—FIRST SETTLERS—PIONEER EVENTS—CEMETERIES—EARLY INDUSTRIES—VILLAGE OF HEBRON—POST OFFICE—INCORPORATION—EARLY HISTORY OF HEBRON—POPULATION—TOWNSHIP OFFICIALS.

BOUNDARIES

Hebron Township lies along the northern line of the county, and is bounded on the north by Wisconsin; on the east by Richmond Township; on the south by Greenwood Township; and the west by Alden Township. It comprises congressional township 46, range 7, east. It is one of the best watered and drained townships in this county. Nippersink creek and its tributaries, with Goose Lake form a magnificent natural drainage system and supply unlimited water at all seasons of the year. While the greater part is prairie land, considerable timber was originally found growing along the streams. Grain, stock raising and dairying are profitably carried on here. Verily he who owns a farm home in this township is an independent man.

ORIGIN OF NAME

The story surrounding the naming of Hebron Township is so interesting and unusual that it is here given at length. The first white woman to live in Hebron Township was Mrs. Bela H. Tryon, and as is usual in such cases her home was the gathering place for lonely pioneers who came from far and near to her for motherly advice, and help in their affairs. It was the custom for them to engage in singing during the Sunday afternoons and evenings, and upon one occasion after they had finished singing Old Hebron, she suggested that Hebron would be a good name for the new township. Her selection was approved and the name adopted. On the Sunday following the adoption, the settlers gathered at her home, and to prove her pleasure, she fried a bushel of

411

cakes for them, all of which were eagerly consumed by the hungry men, the best of their own efforts at culinary operations. This is the only instance in McHenry County of the name being given by a woman to a township division.

FIRST SETTLERS

The honor of being the first settler in this township belongs to E. W. Brigham, who made his original claim in 1836, and built the first house in the township, constructing it of poles. He was a native of Vermont, as was Josiah H. Giddings, the second settler, who erected the first frame house, and long continued to occupy it, although he later added to its original proportions. Bela H. Tryon was the third settler, coming here in 1836, and residing here until his death in 1848. He was from New York state. From that same state also came in to this township, R. W. Stuart, A. H. Parker, and John Sawyer, very early settlers. G. W. Giddings and C. S. and John Adams were settlers of 1836.

PIONEER EVENTS

The first white child born in Hebron Township was Mary Robbe, who lived many years in her native township. Arabel Hibbard died in September, 1852, when eighteen years old, and hers was the first death in the township. She was a daughter of William and Julia Hibbard. On September 7, 1840, was celebrated the first marriage of the township, when Rev. Samuel Hall united George C. Hopkins and Rebecca Tuttle in marriage.

CEMETERIES

The first burying place within Hebron Township was set apart in 1844, two miles northwest of the village of Hebron, at the Presbyterian Church, and a Mr. Duncan, a Scotchman, was the first person to be buried in it. Another early cemetery was in the eastern part of the township, and there several burials were made before the place was abandoned. This was really a private burying ground on the farm of Robert Stuart.

During the sixties, the cemetery at the village of Hebron was laid out and has since been used. This is located right south of the main village and is handsomely cared for.

EARLY INDUSTRIES

In the sixties and early seventies cheese factories sprung up here and there all over this county, including those in and near the village of Hebron. The leading ones were those of H. W. Mead, George Conn, Robert Stuart, a Mr. Perrin and a Mr. McGraw.

VILLAGE OF HEBRON

Hebron village is situated in Hebron Township, in sections 16 and 17, township 46, range 7, east. It is situated on the line of the Chicago & Northwestern Railroad running from Rockford to Kenosha, and now has a population of more than 700. Its churches are the Methodist, Presbyterian, Baptist and the German Lutheran. The village has fraternal societies—the Masons, Odd Fellows and Modern Woodmen of America.

At first Hebron was named Mead Station from the fact that Henry W. Mead had been appointed depot agent at this point when the road first went through. The place was platted on the Mead lands, they having been the first settlers to locate here.

POST OFFICE

Prior to the building of the railroad the township of Hebron had two country post offices, one of which was situated at the house of Bela H. Tryon, who was the postmaster, the date of establishment being 1839. Mail was brought from Chicago and thence to Jaynesville, Wis. The mail was carried on horseback. Another office was established in 1842 in the west part of the township, and kept at John Adam's place, he being postmaster. The list of postmasters at Hebron office established in 1856, is as follows: J. H. Giddings, Munson Goodsell, Frank Rowe, John Pettibone, Frank Rowe, George Boughton, M. W. Merry, who held it three full terms; Dr. E. A. Mead, Henry Earl, who was commissioned in 1913. This is a third-class post office and has two rural free delivery mail routes going out from it six days each week. Route No. 1 is now in charge of carrier Ed Hawthorne, while No. 2 is under Clyde Trow.

INCORPORATION

Hebron was not incorporated as a village until October 21, 1895. The presidents of the village council since the first have been: G. W.

Conn, W. C. Hyde, G. W. Conn, Frank Rowe, Z. H. Young, L. A. Nichols and F. C. Slavin, and M. B. Spooner.

In the month of June, 1906, a system of waterworks had been installed and were on that date accepted by the Council. Bonds were sold to provide this needful internal improvement.

PRESENT OFFICIALS

The following are the officials of the village of Hebron: president, M. B. Spooner; clerk, C. E. Bieren; treasurer, Wilder E. Smith; magistrate, K. Woods; attorney, D. R. Joslyn, Sr.; trustees, J. M. Trueson, M. C. Clark, G. Phillips, Frank Holmes, M. B. Brooks and A. G. Dickerson.

EARLY COMMERCIAL INTERESTS

The first store built in Hebron was opened by M. S. Goodsell, and the first wagon shop was that conducted by George Colburn. The first "village blacksmith" was a Mr. Risden, while the first shoemaker was James Rowe. Among the dealers who came in a little later were: William O. Broughton, J. O. Reynolds, Lund & Johnson, C. F. Prouty, D. S. Blodgett, J. W. Webster, E. F. Hews, H. W. Mead, Frank Rowe, G. L. Phillips and Taylor Bros.

EARLY HISTORY OF HEBRON

By Cyrus L. Mead

Recollections of one of the oldest residents, dating from 1853 up to the early sixties.

It is with pleasure that we present to the readers of The Tribune a brief history of reminiscence of the early days before Hebron became a town. This information is given us by Mr. C. L. Mead, of our village, who has been a resident of this section since 1853. Although in his ninety-second year, his memory is very keen and his physical condition most wonderfully preserved. Following is the story dating from that time on until recent years, just as it was dictated to the editor by Mr. Mead.

"On the fifteenth day of March, 1853, I came to Woodstock, Illinois, from Oswego County, New York, town of Sandy Creek. My early arrival in that then small and unattractive place was made on that memorable day and well do I remember the weather. The sun shone brightly and the roads were as dry as in mid-summer.

"Not being favorably impressed with the village of Woodstock, I decided to walk to Richmond, a distance of some sixteen or seventeen miles. I carried a large satchel or carpet bag in which I carried my wearing apparel. Show me today the young man not yet in his twenty-sixth year who would attempt to walk this distance and carry a heavy parcel.

"I arrived in Richmond about the noon hour and took dinner at the hotel then owned and operated by Colonel Gibbs. In the afternoon I walked to the house of Barney Burdick, about a half a mile northeast of Richmond and there spent the time until the next day.

"On the following day I journeyed on foot to the neighborhood of Gena Junction, northeast of where my brother, Henry W. Mead, was then employed as teacher in the Gibbs district or Mound Prairie.

"Myself and brother had purchased the 400-acre tract of land now lying north of the Hebron townsite, which we came into possession of in the fall of 1853. After taking possession of our newly acquired farm, my brother Henry again resumed the teaching of school and I busied myself with the arranging of the buildings, there being a fair-sized house already built. This is the first house that was built in Hebron and stands today, except for some remodeling, with many characteristics of its original outlines. In later years it was moved and now stands as a part of the home in which James Roan lives.

"In the year 1854 together with my brother, we broke forty acres of sod, using seven or eight yoke of oxen to draw the plow. We sowed wheat and barley and had a fairly good crop. The harvesting was done with an old style cradle and grass scythe.

"Our sister, Mrs. Emily Conklin, kept house for us and together we toiled to gain a footing in this new country.

"In the fall of 1854 we purchased some twelve or fifteen head of hogs which we began feeding and by December were ready for the market. We killed and dressed them and hauled the meat to Milwaukee by wagon. We received $3.25 per hundred for the dressed meat.

"About the sixteenth of January, 1855, I concluded to return to New York, and although we had experienced a very open and mild winter the snow began to fall as I left and we had the heaviest snow and most severe winter weather up until April.

"I reached my destination and was united in marriage to Miss Finett Carman, in Wayne County, N. Y., on the 29th of January. We spent the next few weeks in New York, when we came to our new home in Hebron, arriving here about the middle of March. The snow was yet on the ground and the weather very severe.

'That spring we prepared our forty acres of new broken ground and put in wheat. In the harvest time we received thirty-five bushels to the acre. This occurred in the time of the Crimean war and we received all the way from seventy-five cents to $1.25 per bushel for the grain. Other crops were of a fairly good yield and times were very good.

"In the year 1856, April 1st, we sowed wheat, which looked like a promising yield, but a late frost occurred about the first of June, and although the grain was of good height it only yielded an average of nine bushels of poor wheat to the acre.

"Here I wish to speak of some of the early pioneers and neighbors who resided in this country and helped to subdue the vast prairies of this fertile township. To the east were: Eden Wallin, Alphonso Tyler, Fred Smith, L. D. Seaman and a man by the name of Farman, who owned the Simes place at that time. To the west we had 'Pappy' or Zenus Pierce, Colonel Ehle, John Adams, Whitney Brigham, Deacon Tower, Sheldon Sperry, Deacon Sawyer, Wm. Woodbury, Capt. Stone, Chas. Wright, Squire Giddings, Volney Phillips. To the south were Rowel Carney, John and Peter O'Dell, living on the farms now owned by A. J. Cole. We had no neighbors within two miles to the north, there being no road in that direction.

"The first post office was at the home of John Adams located where the present home of Charles Nichols, Sr., now stands, two miles west of town. We received mail twice a week from McHenry to Big Foot, the trip being covered by a mule team conveyance which also hauled freight, etc.

"Dr. Giddings built a residence on the present site of the R. D. Sill residence, which has also undergone many alterations and repairs, although the original part of the structure is still standing. This was the first house built in Hebron after my coming here.

"After Dr. Giddings built this house, the post office was moved to his home and even after the post office was moved to the Goodsell store in 1861, it still went under the name of Giddings and all business of the government was done through his name.

"At that early time there was no envelopes, although they were soon adopted, but at that time we simply folded our letter and placed some sealing wax on the fold to hold it securely. The postage at that time was five cents and we didn't send very many letters.

"In the year 1855 the first schoolhouse was built and is the building now occupied by the Hebron bakery. David Rowe was the carpenter who done the building. Miss Rebecca Lord taught the first school in the summer of 1855 in a granary on the Rowel Carney (George Francisco) farm and in the fall the school was resumed in the new building.

"The first board of directors were C. L. Mead, Henry Ehle and Rowel Carney. I served on the school board continuously from 1855 until 1880, except one year.

"In the year 1855 there was no road leading either north or south, all travel being done in an easterly and westerly direction.

"In the fall of 1855 I purchased the eighty-acre farm which I now own, for $22.50 per acre.

"In 1856 we purchased fourteen head of steers and fed them on meal and corn fodder. The meal was secured by taking corn to Richmond to the mill and having it ground. I had no previous experience with cattle feeding, notwithstanding I had very good success and by April 18, 1857, we sold these steers for $3.25 per hundred. Eggs and butter at that time sold at a low price. Butter was twelve and one-half cents to fifteen cents per pound and eggs were five cents and six cents per dozen, which was taken in trade at the stores.

"The crops in 1856 were just fair for a new country and we did not have much money.

"In the summer of 1857 we purchased some steers and a few head of sheep and began dealing in stock to some extent, also putting in our usual crop of wheat, oats and barley and some corn.

"By October we had selected about fifteen head of steers which we had intended to feed, we also had a good drove of seventy-five or eighty fat sheep. About the 29th of October, a cattle dealer came along, a Jew, and wanted to buy our herds. My brother had purchased a carload of hogs and together with the sheep and steers, we sold the entire lot to the Jew and did not feed any stock that winter, delivering our stock to Richmond, where they were loaded onto the trains.

"In the year 1858 the regular farm work was done and crops raised were not extra good, prices were also very low. In November I drove seventeen head of steers to Milwaukee, walking the whole distance and without the aid of help. I marketed the bunch for $3.00 per hundred and came home by rail as far as Springfield, Wis., thence by stage to Lake Geneva, and walked the balance of the way home.

"About the first of the month of December I again drove a herd of one hundred head of sheep to Milwaukee, this time covering the distance on foot and alone as before, receiving in the neighborhood of $3.00 per hundred.

"About the 10th of January, 1859, I drove some fourteen head of cattle to Milwaukee, which I had purchased of different farmers. These steers were in good condition and made the trip as well as our previous herds. In about two weeks I again made the trip on foot to Milwaukee, with some nine or ten head of fat steers. The country was new and it was difficult to find a place to shelter myself and stock for the night. About the first of March, I went for the fifth time with a herd of sheep, which were in very poor condition and my experience was very costly, realizing very little if anything on this trip. During my whole business transactions I was never held up or robbed, although forced to carry the proceeds of my herds home in money, checks were unheard of at that time. The five trips to Milwaukee covered over 300 miles and would be considered an impossibility or a rare undertaking on foot in the winter months at least.

"Our farming activities had so increased that we employed two men, my brother teaching school in the winter months, and in the following year of 1859 and 1860 we were very actively engaged. The steers we sold this year brought a better price and were sold to a Mr. Knowles, of Marengo.

"In the year of 1860 my brother went with a shipment of cattle to the Chicago market, then situated about six miles west of Chicago known as 'Bull Head Market.' At that time there were also a market and slaughter house located at Twenty-second Street. The Merrick Yards, near Cottage Grove, was the third yards and slaughter pens.

"The Methodist Church was built in the year 1861 and dedicated in the year 1862, in September. Elder Jewett was the promoter and besides being a good organizer, his ability as a horse trader is also recalled.

"In the year 1860 I raised and fattened a carload of hogs and had them ready for shipment over the new railroad, which reached Hebron in 1861. About the last of May the hogs were loaded onto a flat car and shipped to Milwaukee. This was the first car of stock out of Hebron. The railroad was of light construction and very little stock was shipped at that time.

"Henry W. Mead was appointed agent of the local station and the first station was built at that time. My brother continued to be the agent until after years, when the road installed telegraphy. The station was known as Mead's Station, but was changed to Hebron.

"In the year 1867 the Linn-Hebron Church was built and is still

PEHR H. LUNDGREN

FRANZ E. LUNDGREN

MRS. PEHR H. LUNDGREN

standing as first erected. Elder Lord was the first minister and previous to the building of the new church, held services in the residence now occupied by Willis Brown, which was then the Elder's home.

"The Baptist Church was built in 1876 and cost about $3,000. The Presbyterian Church was built in 1877. The cemetery in Hebron was laid out in 1860. Volney Phillips being one of the promoters and to my recollection, the first man buried in the new place. The German Lutheran Church was constructed in 1900.

"In the year 1862, Henry W. Mead was married to Miss Anna Turner, and myself and family moved from the north side of Hebron to the eighty-acre tract which I still own, my brother occupying the original farm, thereby dividing our interests and embarking separately.

"In going along I failed to mention the fact that in 1853 the only persons owning a buggy with steel springs were B. Tryon and Colonel Ehle. Buggies were just coming into use in this section at that time.

"The first cheese factory was built by William and Robert Stewart on the farm now owned by John J. Stewart in the year, as I recollect, 1865. In 1868 Henry W. Mead built a factory just north of the town site on his farm.

"The first schoolhouse was moved from the original site to Main Street in the year 1878, and is now occupied by the bakery. A brick building was erected which was the first half of the original building which was discarded for the new modern structure which now adorns the site. The first brick structure was built by Beek and Strowler. The board at that time were: E. R. Phillips, C. L. Mead and D. A. Clary.

"The only man now living who was here at that time is George W. Seamon, we being the two oldest residents.

"Our wheat crop in 1860 went thirty bushels per acre and with the 1855 crop of thirty-five bushels per acre were the only two which paid us for the raising.

"The first teachers in the new brick schoolhouse were: Friendly Strong and Miss Mary Brigham, the latter being a resident of Hebron at this time."

POPULATION

The census gives the population of this township in 1890 as 1,430; in 1900 it was the same number; in 1910 it was 1,167; and in 1920 it was 1,363.

TOWNSHIP OFFICIALS

The following are the township officials of Hebron Township: supervisors, H. M. Turner; assessor, Charles Hawthorne; clerk, L. K. Rowe; highway commissioner, Fred Peterson; justices of the peace, Carlton Hunt and F. E. Woods; constables, G. M. Housholder and Lyle Pierce.

CHAPTER XXXIV

MARENGO TOWNSHIP

BOUNDARIES

Marengo Township is bounded on the north by Dunham Township;
on the east by Seneca Township; on the south by Riley Township; on
the west by Boone County, and it is described as congressional township
44, range 5. The Kiswaukee and Rush creeks together with their numerous small tributaries furnish abundant water and drainage. Originally,
this township was almost entirely a prairie section, the soil is of a rich,
fertile character, and the farms of today are among the highest priced
and most valuable of any within this county. This is the only township
in McHenry County that has a stone quarry of any considerable importance; and it is located on section 31.

EARLY SETTLERS

Calvin Spencer came here from Seneca County, Ohio, in the spring
of 1835, and made his claim in what later became Marengo Township.
He was accompanied by his sister, and she was the first white woman
to keep house in the township. Soon after locating here Mr. Spencer
was married to Miss Mary Hance, and they became the parents of eight
children. He lived until 1875, when he died in Marengo Township. In
the autumn of 1835, Moses Spencer, father of Calvin Spencer, joined
his son and daughter, and in November that year his wife died, hers
being the first death in the township.

During the winter of 1835-36 Ward Burley located in Marengo Township, and he was the third settler. His claim was the present site of the

421

city of Marengo, and it is interesting to note that he traded his now extremely valuable land to Frank Stafford for a stock of dry goods, and dealt in merchandise for a time, and practiced medicine. He was the first doctor to locate within the township, and was actively engaged in medical practice until his death in 1847. John Sponsable located here in 1836, coming in from Garden Prairie, Boone County, Ill., where he had made a claim, but only remained there a short time, then located in Marengo, and there died in 1846. His brother, William Sponsable, came in the fall of 1835. His claim had formerly been taken by Richard M. Simpkins, but the latter removed to Coral Township. William Sponsable, after buying the Simpkins claim, later sold it to another settler, and moved to Seneca Township. In the fall of 1835, I. Bache came in from Pennsylvania, and purchased a claim upon which he resided until 1840. Amos B. Coon came to Marengo Township October, 1835, from Bradford, Penn., but after a short stay went to some one of the Southern states. In 1837, however, he returned and for very many years was engaged in an active practice as an attorney. Theophilus Renwick was another settler of 1836, and in 1837, M. B. Bailey arrived in Marengo, and opened a small store in the village of Marengo, which he conducted for a short time. He lived here until 1882, when he died. George R. Page, George Bennett, J. A. Davis, William and Charles Barnes, Timothy McNamara, and H. H. Chapman were all pioneers of Marengo Township.

ORIGINAL NAME

Originally this township was called Pleasant Grove, but when the post office was established it was called Marengo, and when the township was organized by the county board, for convenience sake, the same name was given it as the post office held; hence the civil township, the village and its post office are all known by one and the same name, Marengo.

PIONEER EVENTS

Dr. Ward Burley and wife had a son born to them soon after coming to the township, and it is believed that he was the first white child born within Marengo Township. This child only lived two years.

The first marriage ceremony performed was that by Justice of the Peace M. B. Spencer, January 14, 1838, when he united in wedlock M. B. Bailey and Miss Lydia Hance.

The earliest grist-mill, built in 1846, was located one and one-half miles northwest of Marengo. No traces of this mill have been seen for more than thirty-five years.

CEMETERIES

A little burial ground lying north of the village of Marengo was platted by the Scotch people living in that vicinity, and used by them.

The Catholic cemetery of Marengo lies in the northern part of the place and was laid out late in the seventies.

The Marengo Cemetery proper is directly north of the railroad, and was laid out in 1861. It originally comprised ten acres, but later was expanded. There are other small burying grounds in various parts of the township.

POPULATION

The census for 1890, 1900, 1910 and 1920 gave the following as the population of Marengo Township: In 1890, 2,702; in 1900, 2,859; in 1910, 2,250, and in 1920, 2,442. The corporation of Marengo had in 1900 as high as 2,005 inhabitants.

TOWNSHIP OFFICIALS

The following are the township officials of Marengo Township: supervisor, D. M. Wright; assessor, J. G. Kitchen; clerk, J. T. Beldin; highway commissioner, J. F. Wilson; justices of the peace, J. C. Tanner and A. G. Beath; constables, Willis Jobe and M. M. Wilson.

CITY OF MARENGO

Marengo was platted in 1846 by Damon & Spencer, and at a time when there was a small community settlement. The surveyor was A. B. Coon. It is situated in the extreme southeast corner of the Township of Marengo, in sections 25, 26, 35, 36. It is described as being all within congressional township 43, range 5, east.

The first house erected on the townsite of Marengo was that of Joseph Bryton, which was built in 1835. Moody Bailey opened the first store in 1837; A. M. Canon opened the first wagon shop, and Mr. Blakesley was the first blacksmith.

Among the men and concerns to be engaged in business at Marengo later than 1880 may be recalled with certainty the following: F. G. Vail, Skinner & Treat, Farmers & Drovers Bank, B. S. Parker, First National Bank, C. V. Wells, William Dougherty, P. T. Parkhurst, William Blood, Alexander Walling, John Kelley, John Arlington & Co., Tillman Gallaway, Reuben Miller, N. L. Jackson, Cady, York & Thompson, John Miles, C. H. Hance, F. W. Alderman, Arthur Wilbur, C. I. Boyington, M. A. Webb, William Stewart, Asa Wood, F. W. Patrick & Co., William F. Abbott, Casely & Fillmore, Vail, Otis & Co., A. S. Norton & Co., Gilbert Metcalf, C. W. Ingersoll, W. H. Sanders, Pacific Hotel, L. G. Buck, Almon & Ryder, C. F. Renwick, W. A. Treat, S. A. Srissey, G. W. Saunders, J. H. Bulard, Almon & Ryder, Henry Underwood, George Crego, Rodgers Brothers, Teeple & Co., E. P. Persons, A. R. Coon, Ira R. Curtiss, George Sampter, J. A. Read, H. E. & F. A. Patrick, P. B. Smith, A. P. Abbott, David Johnson, W. P. Pringle, Metcalf & Brown, A. L. Derry, George Stanford, Bartholomew & Co., W. H. Mesick, S. C. Wernham, L. C. Nutt, J. W. Green, C. N. Clark, O. L. Sherman, Marengo Pickle Manufacturing Company, J. J. Wilson, C. Fraidrich, J. Griffin, H. D. Storms, Frank Gaskell.

MUNICIPAL HISTORY

Marengo was incorporated as a village February 24, 1857. The first officers were as follows: F. Stafford, president; Calvin Spencer, Fletcher Lindsley, A. R. Parkhurst, I. P. Warner, trustees, and J. B. Babcock, clerk.

The village history extended down to September, 1893, when it became a city incorporation. The first officers under city incorporation were—E. D. Shurtleff, mayor; C. P. Fillmore, clerk; A. S. Norton, treasurer; J. M. Marks, attorney; aldermen—H. H. Blair, N. L. Jackson, H. G. Otis, E. P. Vail, J. H. Patterson, S. C. Wernham.

The present city officers are—C. B. Whittemore, mayor; Clifford Woeben, clerk; A. C. Smith, treasurer; E. D. Shurtleff, attorney; councilmen—Fred Dunker, A. E. Thompson, J. E. Heath, C. W. Wilke, Willis Job, C. J. Coarson.

PRESENT OFFICIALS

The following are the present officials of the city of Marengo: mayor, W. C. Woodward; clerk, C. A. Woleben; treasurer, Carlton S. Robb;

FIRST NATIONAL BANK OF MARENGO

health official, W. S. Eshbaugh; magistrate, J. H. Kitchen; marshal, Byron Miller; attorney, R. D. Donovan; aldermen, J. E. Heath, W. S. Seronguer, F. R. Ocock, A. E. Thompson, F. D. Piper and C. E. Kelley.

PUBLIC IMPROVEMENTS

A system of waterworks was installed in 1894. Wells were sunk and a good supply of pure water was obtained and this system continues to the present. It was piped throughout the city, a standpipe erected and has been a blessing to the place ever since. The city bonded itself for this and other improvements, but all such debts are paid off, and the city government, aside from a few small bills, is free of any debt. In 1905 a sewer system was commenced and later completed; paving followed in 1908, and now one sees and appreciates a beautiful, even brick paving instead of former black dirt roads. A volunteer fire company keeps the city safe from the fire ravages of former years. They have an auto-truck and hose wagons, bought at an expense of $2,000. At present the lights of the city are provided by a private corporation. Before 1908 electric lights were furnished by a local municipally owned plant.

FIRE DEPARTMENT

The Marengo Fire Corps was organized October 29, 1883, by H. B. Smith, J. Teeple and A. W. Kelley, with a charter membership of fifty-two. The need of such an association of men was felt on many former occasions, but never more than on March 5, 1876, when the Ryder House and adjoining stores were destroyed. There was also a large fire January 4, 1867. When this fire corps was organized A. S. Gormon was made its secretary; E. A. Vandevere, treasurer; and H. D. Otis, Charles Ingersoll and J. Teeple, directors. For a number of years this company was maintained and did fine work, but as the place grew and times changed, it was finally superseded by other organizations. It is now the ordinary volunteer fire company, named above.

PLACES OF AMUSEMENT

It was in April, 1883, that the Marengo Opera House was built by R. M. Patrick at a cost of $30,000. At that day it was among the finest playhouses in all Northern Illinois.

At present the places of amusement consist of occasional home talent plays, and the moving picture entertainments.

HOTELS

The first hotel at Marengo was built by Calvin Spencer in 1835, at the corner of State and Main streets. This was constructed of logs from the nearby forests, and was but sixteen feet square. When it was erected it was not with the intention of using it for a hotel, but Mr. Spencer soon found that he could not turn away the stranger, so engaged in the hotel business. In the spring of 1836 he built two more log houses about 18x26 feet in size; these served until 1838, when he added a frame structure 16x18 feet. Mr. Spencer continued in the hotel business until 1842.

In 1841 David Hammer built a log hotel, and conducted it a short time. In 1842 a Mr. Basford bought the Spencer Hotel, and took David Hammer as a partner. The firm of Basford & Hammer subsequently erected a frame hotel of considerable proportions, and it was used many years for hotel purposes by various persons. Later it passed into the hands of D. Johnson who converted it into a private residence.

About 1853, or possibly a year later, Jacob A. Davis built a hotel on the site later occupied by the Ryder House, and this was used as a hotel until 1876, when it was destroyed by fire. At that time it was the property of A. Ryder, who immediately rebuilt and gave the new structure his own name. This and other hotels have been built, served a good purpose and been abandoned, while other more modern hotels have taken their place and serve the traveling public today.

POST OFFICE

The first post office in the vicinity of Marengo was established in 1841, and was kept by Alfred King, at his residence, one mile west of the present city of Marengo. David Hammer succeeded King, although for a time the post office was kept at the home of Joseph Deitz, but was then removed to the corner of State and Main streets. Colonel Cornelius Lansing was the third postmaster, and William F. Combs was the fourth, he keeping the office in a store on the site later occupied by the Free Methodist Church. The office was then moved to the southwest corner of State and Main streets, where the postmaster was L. L. Crandall. As the fifth postmaster, Anson Sperry was appointed in 1853, and held the office until 1861, it being in the meanwhile moved to the site later occupied by the Marengo Opera House. From 1861 to 1873 Dr. O. S. Jenks was postmaster and he had his office in a building later used by William C. Stewart as a dry goods store. Mr. Stewart succeeded to the office, was postmaster from 1873 to 1882, and kept the office in the same building as did his predecessor. In 1882 J. Q. Adams was appointed postmaster, and he removed the office to the southwest corner of State and Washington streets. From that date to now it will hardly be of interest to trace the many homes had by this post office. The postmasters since the administration of the above named men have been: J. Q. Adams from 1882 to 1894, F. M. Mead from 1894 to 1898, then he was succeeded by J. Q. Adams, and he in turn in 1902 by Charles Scofield. In 1915 came James Cleary and in 1919 Charles Gilkerson. This newly appointed postmaster wisely kept the old clerks, who had been efficient in their places. They are as follows: Miss Bertha Rowe, assistant postmaster, and Miss Lucretia Marshall, clerk. The rural carriers are: L. D. Sheldon, route 1; Mrs. Ina Coonradt, route 2; Lee Grover, route 3; D. E. Echternach, route 4.

The Marengo office sold Thrift Stamps during 1917 to the amount of $31,204.36.

The Marengo office was a second class office up to about 1917 when it was set back to a third class, when the general cry at Washington was "retrenchment."

COMMUNITY CLUB

In the summer of 1916 E. D. Patrick remodeled the Marengo Opera House Building, and at that time submitted a plan to furnish and fit up on the third floor of this building a hall and clubrooms consisting of a hall 48 by 70 feet with 20-foot ceilings, billiard room, reception rooms, kitchen and dressing rooms with lavatory and toilet fittings, install lights and heat the same for an annual rental of $360.00.

Accordingly, a committee was appointed to organize the Community Club of Marengo, and they perfected such an organization, whose purpose it was to furnish clean and healthful entertainment and physical training and exercise to the members and families of the Community Club. The membership fee was fixed at $5 and $6 per year in advance.

The club is managed by a president, vice president, secretary and treasurer and five trustees. Monthly meetings are held by the officers, at which all matters pertaining to the management of the club are submitted and disposed of. The detail management is carried out through several committees, as: House Committee, Athletic Committee, Educational. Entertainment and Membership Committees, all reporting to business meetings each month, for council and advice, as well as giving suggestions for the betterment of the club. The membership age limit is eighteen years and over. Men are admitted only, however, the ladies use the Halland Gym one night each week. The Boy Scouts also are given a place one night each week, at a nominal fee. This club has no connection, whatever, with any religious sect or creed, and holds no religious services in their hall. The members rather seek to demonstrate the true spirit of Christianity and democracy, in a practical, everyday way. It certainly has filled a common community need in the place and is growing stronger each month. Members of this club work in perfect harmony with the various women's clubs, public school management and other societies of the city of Marengo. "WE" is the big word with this club. No cliques or anything of the kind, or politics is allowed to obtain within the club.

It has come to make the place a better, safer, pleasanter one in which to live and labor for the higher uplift of the general community.

REMINISCENCES ACCOUNT OF MARENGO

The subjoined is a sketch made up from recollections of that sturdy pioneer, Calvin Spencer, who dictated these "early-day notes" to his daughter who wrote them down at the time he gave them, hence may be relied upon as authentic history:

The first settler in what is now known as Marengo was Calvin Spencer who arrived here with his ox-teams November 17, 1835. The previous year he had been here and cut logs for a cabin, also cut and put up stacks of hay with a scythe. The scythe needing grinding he walked about eighteen miles further west to Big Thunder Mills on the trail to Galena. Mr. Spencer recalled seeing the body of Big Thunder sitting upright, facing the east in a pen built by the Indians to keep the animals away. It so remained there until the skull dropped off.

Mr. Spencer built on present site of the Gault Building, where he conducted a public house or tavern as then called. A large part of land was included in what is now the city of Marengo. The first post office was kept by Alfred King, who kept the office one mile west of the Spencer tavern. The post office was called Pleasant Grove, but finding another post office by that name, it was changed to Marengo, so named by Thomas Thorne. The first store was by Moody Bailey, on the site of the present Ellison garage. Fink & Walker Stage line covered the road to Galena up to the building of the railroad in 1851. It was the Galena & Chicago Union Railroad. Miss Spencer, daughter of Calvin Spencer, now has a way-bill dated Chicago, March 11, 1852, for lumber shipped to her father and which was used in enlarging her present house, which he had erected in 1844. This building stands some three blocks east of the central corners, on the road to Chicago.

The first justice of the peace was Moses Spencer, father of Calvin, who died in 1861 in his eighty-first year.

The first marriage was that of William Sponsable and Rachael Chatfield, both of whom were life-long residents of Marengo.

The first sermon was preached at the Calvin Spencer home in 1836, by Elder Southworth, an itinerant, the text being: "And he sat down and talked to the people."

The first medical doctor of Marengo was Dr. Burley Mason.

The first birth was Dr. Mason's son William, who died an infant.

The first school was taught in the summer of 1837 by Caroline Cobb, who became the wife of Spencer Flanders and she spent her life near Franklinville. The school in the fall of 1838 was taught by O. P. Rogers, who died only a few years ago. For many years he was a partner of L. Woodward in the nursery business.

The first newspaper at Marengo was the *Marengo Journal* in 1856, owned by Edward Burnside. The issues for the first few years ending in 1861 are now in possession of Miss Spencer in a bound volume.

The first water-mill was the Kishwaukee mill—it being on that stream; it was conducted by Smith Bros.

The first cemetery was a part of the present one which was later enlarged to the north side of the railroad. The first body buried there in the new part being George House, who died June, 1861.

The first Sunday school was conducted in the present Spencer residence.

Botsford & Howe operated the first steam-mill. Early merchants were Mr. Vawter, Kasson & Safford, Mr. Hyde and others.

Mr. Spencer was born in Cayuga County, N. Y., October 6, 1807, and died April 17, 1898. He was the son of Moses and Esther (Albee) Spencer. Calvin Spencer arrived at Marengo, with ox teams November 17, 1835. His parents also came west about that date, but the mother was taken ill en route and died the tenth of that month before reaching their destination. His brother-in-law Joseph Brayton, and wife, and a couple of young men came at the same time. The fear of Indians so worked on the mind of Mrs. Brayton that they could not be induced to remain in the country and they went back to La Porte, Ind.

Mr. Spencer was always an active man till well passed eighty years and retained his mentality and physical vigor up to near his death. His wife was born in 1810 and died in 1875.

Politically, he was identified with the Republican party. Originally he voted with the Whig party, and cast his first vote in 1828 against Andrew Jackson. He never missed an election. He heard the great debate between Lincoln and Douglas in Chicago, in 1856. In church affiliations he was of the Baptist denomination.

Of the seven children of Mr. and Mrs. Spencer, the survivors are: Orson, of Washington County, Ill., and Mary, widow of John Lambden, who was born February 25, 1841, in the old tavern at Marengo, still lives at the old homestead; and Edna Sophronia, born in the present Spencer house, May 27, 1849. She is known as a great lover of home and a zealous worker in the Baptist Church, and a liberal contributor to benevolent causes.

FIFTY YEARS AND MORE AMONG THE BEES

"As busy as a bee" certainly applies to Dr. C. C. Miller, the venerable gentleman of Marengo, who is now eighty-six years of age, and who has had to do with honey bees and flowers for almost three score years and has been associate editor of the well-known publication the "American Bee Journal" for many years. Doctor Miller was among the pioneer physicians of Marengo and vicinity, but about Civil war days abandoned his medical practice, and since then has been an active student and busy worker among the honey-bee hives, and occupied in imparting his knowledge by tongue and pen concerning the keeping of bees and the best methods of producing honey. His is no small, stinted knowledge of that most ingenious and wonderful of God's creatures, the honey bee. To be brief, in the introduction of this talented and universally respected veteran of the bee and honey industry, we will simply quote a short biography of him found a few years since in the biographical dictionary of notable persons in the United States, "Who's Who in America."

Miller, Charles C., apiarist, writer; born in Ligonier, Pennsylvania, June 10, 1831, son of Johnson J. and Phoebe Miller; A. B., Union College, Schenectady, N. Y., 1853; M. D., Medical Department University of Michigan, 1856; married Miss Helen M. White of Marengo, Illinois,

August 12, 1857 (died 1880) ; married Miss Sidney J. Wilson of Marengo, Illinois, November 15, 1881. Began keeping bees at Marengo, 1861; and at one time four hundred colonies of bees, now fourteen, and produced many tons of honey: extensive writer for bee and agricultural journals; department editor of Gleanings in Bee Culture, 1890; associate editor American Bee Journal, 1894; Prohibitionist, Presbyterian, Member National Bee Keepers Union (twice president). Member Beta Kappa. Author: "A Book by P. Benson," 1874; "A Year Among Bees," 1886, "Forty Years Among the Bees," 1902; "Fifty Years Among the Bees," 1911. Editor "Apiary Terms" in Standard Dictionary; home, Marengo, McHenry County, Illinois.

His chosen profession, medical doctor, was too trying on his sensitive nature; it worried and chafed him, and for this reason he was content in withdrawing from that profession for which he had well fitted himself, and for a time he was a musical instructor in the old "Marengo Collegiate Institute" whose existence is now but a faint memory among the older members of McHenry County society. He has knowingly remarked in recent years that his "chair" there netted him $50 and some old lumber.

For a time Doctor Miller taught school and gave piano lessons and conducted singing school. He is full of music and at one time was a regular contributor of both words and music to the famous "Song Messenger." He was the efficient chorister in the Moody Church of Chicago and even in his old age still may be classed among the "sweet singers."

His great achievements have been in that of an expert apiarist. At one time he had 400 colonies of bees and a careful estimate places the amount of honey he caused to be produced by these bees to be in round numbers 100 tons.

His writings on the honey bee, its habits, customs, and value have found their way into the Country Gentleman, Youth's Companion, Gleanings In Bee Culture, and every book of importance on bees in this country, and he has drawn from his knowledge of bees in his productions. He was editor of the department on bees in the Standard Dictionary, and his writings have been translated into the French, German, Swiss, Italian, Russian and Japanese publications. Doctor Miller is known far and wide, and by the bee publications in Texas, he is styled the "Sage of Marengo."

Doctor Miller is a religious man, and has been a ruling elder in the Presbyterian Church of Marengo since 1857. Through his religion, he sees the hand of the Creator in Nature. The sunshine, wind, rain, the grass and the flowers all appeal to his religious nature and in these elements he recognizes sublime beauty. Even the modest daisy is not too insignificant to be noticed, examined and talked about. So well is he acquainted with flowers that he was elected secretary of the Northern Illinois Horticultural Society, and still later was its president. He is truly a many-sided man. Whether one views him from the standpoint of scholarship, science, art, composition, Christian manly virtues, a home-lover and home-maker, or as the plain, everyday, hard-working enthusiast over bees and the production of the extract of all sweetness—"honey and the honey-comb," it matters not, he stands out in the open, high above and far removed, from but few, if any, in the various roles in life, in which he has been so conspicuous a figure for more than a half century in one place, McHenry County, Ill.

CHAPTER XXXV

McHENRY TOWNSHIP

BOUNDARIES

McHenry Township is bounded on the north by Richmond and Burton Townships; on the east by Lake County; on the south by Nunda Township; and on the west by Greenwood Township, and it is congressional township 45, range 8. The Fox River traverses it from north to south, and it contains half of Pistaqua Lake, which is in the northeastern part; one-half of Lilly Lake, which is in the southeastern part; and McCollum's Lake, which is near the center of the township; while two branches of Boone Creek which is the main stream of the Nippersink, as well as many smaller water courses supply ample water and drainage. It is one of the most fertile and productive townships of McHenry County, which has long had the reputation of being one of the leading agricultural sections of the state. McHenry County is one of the oldest settled townships in the county, and in it the county seat was located not only before Lake County was separated from McHenry, but for some time thereafter, as is given in another chapter.

EARLY SETTLERS

The first settler of McHenry Township was Dr. Christy G. Wheeler, who came here in 1836, and opened a small store. He was a brother of Elder Wheeler, who lived to attain the distinction of being the oldest living pioneer of McHenry Township. Dr. Wheeler was a medical practitioner and also a local preacher, and alternated between his mercantile pursuits and his two professions. His health was very frail, he

433

in fact having come to Illinois in the hope that the change would prove beneficial, but he did not improve, and at length died only a few years after his settlement here. Some of the other pioneers were as follows: Henry and John McLean; Louis and John Boone, William and David McCullum, Wesley Ladd, Samuel Walker, Allen and Freeman Harvey, B. B. Brown, Jonathan and Mike Sutton, Rev. Joel Wheeler, William H. Hankins, and his aunt Mrs. Valentine and her son, and also a man by the name of Teabout. The Harkins party came to McHenry Township in September, 1837, having made the journey in an emigrant wagon, which they used as a shelter until their cabin was erected. In December, 1837, Young Valentine fell from a tree and was instantly killed. Mr. Teabout lost his life while hunting not long thereafter through the accidental discharge of his gun.

PIONEER EVENTS

Rev. Joel Wheeler performed the first marriage ceremony in McHenry Township in November, 1839, when he united Joseph Fellows and Christiana Robinanlt, that is recorded. The first child born in the township was Christy Wheeler.

The first death was that of William Herrick. He was crossing the Fox River on the ice, his horse broke through, and in some way his rifle was accidentally discharged, causing his death. His body was interred on the banks of the river, and there remained for many years, but in the early eighties, when a cellar was being dug on the site of his grave, his remains were disinterred and laid to a final rest in the McHenry Cemetery.

CEMETERIES

The "silent cities" of the township, the cemeteries, are numerous. At first the dead were buried near the old mill-dam, one mile to the north of the village of McHenry, but as other cemeteries were opened up, the bodies were removed from it and placed where the graves would receive better attention. Among the township's burying grounds are these: Thompson's Burying Ground, the Ringwood Cemetery; one located just west of Ringwood; and others both public, and church-burying grounds. The Catholics have a large cemetery near their church at Johnsburg; the Woodland Cemetery is at McHenry village. This last named was laid out in 1858, and is a Protestant cemetery, while the Catholics have another one located near the village of McHenry also.

At the point on the Fox River where the city of McHenry now stands, in the days long before the white man set his foot on McHenry County soil, the Indians built a ford of broad, flat, square-cut stones of sandstone, which were regularly laid and secured by other stones in such manner that the swift current of the stream would not dislodge them. The pioneer white men removed these stones and used them for hearth-stones, and some of them are still to be found. It has never been ascertained the source from which the Indians obtained these stones, as no similar formation has been found anywhere in this locality.

The Village of McHenry is distinguished as having been the county seat for so many years, and also as being the first town that was organized in McHenry County. It was laid out by a Chicago surveyor, named Bradley, in 1837, through the efforts of Henry McLean, and the latter built the first house in the place, a log one, 12x16, near the site of what later was known as the Riverside House. For several months after this little building was erected it served as a gathering place for the settlers and a wayside tavern. Dr. Christy Wheeler opened and conducted the first store. The first wagonmaker was Richard Bishop, who opened his shop in 1840. Nathan Haight was the first blacksmith. The first saw-mill was built in 1837 by a man named Barnum, who later sold it to H. O. Owen and James Salisbury who completed the work of construction, John McOmber doing the actual work. Mr. McOmber afterwards built himself a house from the first lumber sawed by this mill. Not long after this mill was completed, James Salisbury went below to correct some error with reference to its action, and not having notified the millman, he had scarcely placed himself in the machinery, than the gate was hoisted, the mill put in motion, and Mr. Salisbury was crushed and killed almost instantly. He was buried by Rev. Joel Wheeler in the first cemetery by the mill dam.

In 1851 E. M. Owen and his brothers H. A. and O. W. Owen, built a grist-mill at McHenry that was for a long time the best in the county. They ran it in partnership until 1858, when E. M. Owen bought the interests of his brothers, and sold it to R. Bishop for $20,000.00. Mr. Bishop immediately added the roller process at a cost of $10,000.00, and for a number of years this mill was one of the leading industries of Mc-Henry.

The old mill site is pointed out by the old settler as one of the important land-marks of by-gone days. The race that conveys the water to the mill is still overflowing and the water wastes itself away from day to day, but its utility seems forever gone for milling purposes. In fact there are but few of the early mills in use anywhere, on account of the milling center for flour making has long since changed and it is conducted on a different plan, perhaps a better plan, at least the farmer sells his wheat and buys his supply of flour now!

FACTORIES

There was a day when McHenry bid fair to become a place of much manufacturing interest, in fact it is related that the village had an opportunity during the early sixties to secure what is now known the world over, as the Elgin Watch Factory, but business men did not pull together in harmony, and they let the prize slip away to Elgin, which made concessions and some sacrifices, in order to build up that great plant when its stock holders most needed aid.

In the early eighties a pickle factory was established at McHenry. It was founded by that well-remembered pioneer and excellent citizen, Richard Bishop, who for many years operated this factory with profit to himself and the surrounding country, but in time this business shifted to large city centers, Pittsburg, Cincinnati, Chicago, etc., and the small town plants were put out of commission. However at this time there are hundreds of acres of land in and around McHenry, Richmond, Spring Grove and other eastern McHenry County points which produce cucumbers which are placed in salting plants near where they are grown and later in the season, are shipped to Chicago, where they are made into pickles. It has come to be a large industry.

In 1868 George Gribbler built a brewery at McHenry. He commenced in a small way but eventually possessed a large paying plant where lager beer was produced in great quantities. It had a large local and a fairly large shipping sale.

One of McHenry's earliest industries was the wagon factory of Richard Bishop, whose well equipped plant was totally destroyed by fire in 1878, but was rebuilt upon a much larger scale, with improved machinery for turning out farm and light wagons. But this, too, like other small town factory interests, had to succumb to the inevitable and in time gave way to the great wagon factories in the country, with which small places were unable to compete, hence had to close down.

BUSINESS FACTORS IN 1885

By reference to old publications, paper files, etc., it is learned that the following constituted the majority of business men, firms and professions in McHenry from 1880 to 1885:

Richard Bishop, E. M. Owen & Son, Amos D. Whiting, Francis A. Herbard, Isaac Wentworth, Charles B. Curtiss, Gottlieb Boley, Nordquist & Weber, Barbeau Brothers, L. D. Lincoln, John B. Blake, Henry Madden, William M. Yager, E. M. Howe, Mathias Englen, O. W. Owen, J. P. Smith, H. E. Wrightman, Perry & Owen, Mayers & Bartlett, Edwin Lawless, Henry Colby, Dr. H. T. Brown, Dr. C. H. Fegers, I. E. Bennett, John Karges, E. G. Smith, George Dimmel, Anton Engelen, J. J. Gillis, John Heimer and Thomas Knox. Many of the above named business factors had been residents of McHenry prior to and during the Civil war period, and bore well their part in sustaining the Union at that time.

INCORPORATION

It was incorporated August 10, 1872, with the following officers: Richard Bishop, president; J. B. Perry, J. M. McComber, H. C. Smith, John King, and Frank K. Granger, trustees; and Michel Keller, clerk.

The subjoined have served as presidents of McHenry village from date of its incorporation: 1872—R. Bishop, 1873—J. B. Perry, 1874—C. B. Curtis, R. Bishop, F. K. Granger, R. Bishop, Smith Searles, R. Bishop, Anthony Webber, Rollin Howard, R. Bishop, B. Gilbert, F. K. Granger, Rollin Howard, J. Van Slyke, Simon Stoffel, J. Van Slyke, (1891), (No record for several years), 1897—John I. Story, 1898—W. A. Christy, John Evanson, P. J. Freund, F. J. Wattles, John H. Miller, Simon Stoffel, D. J. Wells, R. G. Chamberlain, John Olson, and Simon Stoffel.

PRESENT OFFICIALS

The following are the present officials of the village of McHenry: president, Simon Stoffel; clerk, W. G. Schram; treasurer, J. C. Holly;

magistrate, John W. Kimball; marshal, John Walsh; attorney, A. H. Pouse; trustees, Peter Doherty, Louis Erickson, John R. Knox, Albert Krause, R. I. Oaten and Frank Wetten.

PUBLIC IMPROVEMENTS

The village voted to issue bonds and construct a system of water works in August, 1897, and this was carried out, and today the village has a fine system of waterworks, including a deep artesian well from which is ever flowing a large stream of health-giving water. The water is pumped to a ninety-foot steel water tower which has a large holding capacity as reserve in case of fire or other emergencies. The water is distributed through the scattered village, and most all neighborhoods will soon have water in front of their very door.

At the pumping station, a combined water plant building with its gasoline pump and other fixtures, are housed within one building together with the "City Hall," as the brick structure, near the center of the village is known. Here the council meets, and here, in a large fire-proof safe, is kept a good set of public municipal records.

An ordinance was passed the village board March 9, 1908, by which a Chicago electric company was granted a franchise to distribute electricity throughout the village for a term of twenty years. This was carried out, and thus it was that McHenry was soon illuminated by the brightest of modern lights.

POST OFFICE

McHenry has two post offices. One at the old original village and another near the depot, in what is styled West McHenry, about one mile apart. The original McHenry post office was established in 1837, with Christy Wheeler as postmaster. When West McHenry sprang into existence, at the time the railroad was built, there was soon a bitter rivalry between the two town sites and indeed the spirit has not altogether died out, however generally speaking peace obtains between the two sections. It was during one of these hard-fought rivalry battles that by some "hook or crook" the office was moved from the old to the newer part of town. So, for more than a year, the people at the old village had no postoffice, but through Congressman Elwood, a man came from the department at Washington, and looked the field over and as a result a new post office was established, since which date, 1883, the two parts

of McHenry have each had a post office, one mile apart. Certainly Uncle Sam is a peace maker! The postmasters names for the earliest years are not a matter of record, save in the Department at Washington, hence only those of a later period can be given. At the original Mc-Henry they have been in the order given: J. B. Perry, Captain Snow, Rollin Waite, J. C. Holly, T. J. Walsh, who was commissioned in 1915. This is a third class postoffice; has three rural routes cared for as follows: No. 1 by carrier H. H. Fay; No. 2, D. I. Granger; No. 3, Joe N. Miller. The U. S. leases the brick building in which this postoffice has been kept several years.

The West McHenry post office has had for its postmasters: C. V. Stevens, J. W. Kimball, Simon Stoffel, H. C. Mead, E. E. Bassett, who was commissioned in 1914. This is a third-class post office and sends forth one rural delivery or mail on a twenty-nine mile route, the carrier being James N. Sayler.

"West McHenry" is the direct result of the building of the Chicago & Northwestern railroad through this section. The place was laid out by George Gage and it was largely through his influence that West McHenry was made a station on the road. At first the village was called "Gatetown," but soon took the name of West McHenry. Some of the second lot of business men at this point were: William Hanley, Oatman & Sons, Amos D. Whiting, Smith & Snyder, Curtis & Walker, W. A. Cristy and W. H. Wiswell.

EARLY HOTELS

The first hotel in the township was built in 1837, by B. B. Brown, at McHenry. It was a rude, although very comfortable log house, and served as a hotel more than twenty years. The second hotel was the Mansion House, at McHenry, built by Horace Long, and used for the old courthouse until the county seat was removed to Woodstock. It was built in 1838, was a frame structure 40x60 feet, and two stories in height. Early in the eighties it went out of commission as a hotel.

The Fremont House was erected in 1851, but was burned about seven years later.

The old Riverside Hotel was built in 1864 by John W. and David Smith. This was counted a fine structure in those days. It was built of brick and was three stories high, with dimensions 40x60 feet. It served its day and generation and passed out of use.

The Parker Hotel of West McHenry was built in 1858 by George

Gage, and for a time bore the owner's name. Its first landlord was Mr. Van Doozen, who opened it New Year's Day with a grand ball. He was succeeded by William Murray, and he in turn by a Mr. Holmes. Later, came Landlord Edson, who after two years was followed by W. Parker and L. D. Lincoln. On August 4, 1881, F. A. Parker, son of W. Parker, took charge of the hotel, but, in 1884, resigned in favor of his father.

The principal commercial hotel of the village is now known as the Park Hotel, an old building, but the hotel is conducted on modern plans, as far as possible in so small a place where the customers stop but for an occasional meal, and possibly over night.

JOHNSBURG

This is a small hamlet situated on the northeast corner of section 13, of McHenry Township, three miles southeast of Ringwood, a station on the railroad in this township; and it is also about two miles northeast from McHenry village. This hamlet was settled by the Germans in 1852, and was named in honor of their leader, for the settlement was really a colony. His Christian name being John the place was called Johnsburg. It has ever been known almost exclusively as a German settlement. St. John's Roman Catholic Church was established here by Father Portman in 1845, when the membership consisted of but three families, but today it is among the largest churches of any denomination within McHenry County. About 1880 a $45,000 stone edifice was constructed here, and then its membership (1880 to 1885) was 275 families. The present business interests are not large, this hamlet being away from any railway, and the greater number of the people trade at larger places in and out of this county. A large parochial school is conducted here, by the Catholics.

There are doubtless many of the present day citizens of Johnsburg who are sons and daughters of pioneers whose names here follow, and who were in the early vanguard and among the settlers, later thrifty Germans who claimed as their heritage this portion of McHenry County, in the fifties and sixties. Henry Hatterman, Martin May, Charles Mathew, Peter Rothermel, John Weber, Peter Werfs, Charles E. Buchanan, Theodore Mayer, Charles Kuhnert, Ley & Adams, Simon Nichols, Mathias Hohlman, Henry Miller, Mathew Heimer, Frank Miller, William Akthoff, Joseph Palmer, Steffen Thelen, Peter Adams, Martin Boughner, L. N. Freund, John Molitur and John Thelen, were the most prominent.

RINGWOOD

This village is a station on the Chicago & Northwestern railroad, in sections 9 and 10 of McHenry Township. It was settled in 1837 by Dr. Luke Hale and William H. Beach. Doctor Hale was a physician engaged in active practice at Ringwood for many years. Both of these men came from Vermont, bringing their families with them. The village was platted and recorded in 1844. Owing to the fact that the entire plat was surrounded by a ring of woods, the appropriate name "Ringwood" was given to it by its proprietors. Elder Wheeler held the first religious services in what is now McHenry Township, in a log house erected by H. W. McLean.

The first school was taught in this township in a log building which stood on the banks of Fox River.

SPECIAL FEATURES

Every Township has its own peculiar features, distinct from all others. Here in McHenry Township it may be said of its special characteristics that it is the oldest organized settlement of the county; it was the home of the original county seat when Lake and McHenry were all in one large sub-division of Illinois. The old land-marks which to the older generations presented hourly reminders of an honor this division of the county once possessed, but today these reminders are mostly gone and the story is handed down from father to son. But this township and her beautiful villages and hamlets may well boast of the progress they have made with the passing years.

POPULATION

McHenry Township had a population in 1890 of 2,555; in 1900, 2,673; in 1910, 2,679; and in 1920, 2,825.

TOWNSHIP OFFICIALS

The following are serving as the township officials of McHenry Township: Supervisor, Stephen H. Freund; assessor, John W. Kimball; clerk, Charles B. Harmsen; highway commissioner, William B. Tonyan; justices of the peace, W. J. Welch and E. C. Hawley; constables, W. H. Kelley and John Walsh.

CHAPTER XXXVI

NUNDA TOWNSHIP

BOUNDARIES

Nunda Township comprises congressional township 44, range 8 and one third of range 9. It is bounded on the north by McHenry Township; on the east by Lake County; on the south by Algonquin Township; on the west by Door Township. This subdivision of McHenry County is among the finest agricultural sections of the northern portion of Illinois. Dairying is now the chief industry of the farms. The Fox River courses through the township. As originally known Lilly and Clear Lakes were in the center of its territory, but these lakes are gradually disappearing. Hanley's Creek crosses the northern portion, and Stickney's Run, with lesser streams make Nunda one of the best watered in McHenry County.

ORIGIN OF NAME

For a short period after Nunda Township was settled, it was known as Brooklyn, it being so named by William and C. Goff. But when a post office was petitioned for, it was discovered that another Brooklyn was already in existence in Illinois. A public meeting was called, and the name was changed to Nunda in honor of the birthplace of Col. William Huffman, a leading man in the community, who was born in Nunda, N. Y.

EARLY SETTLERS

The first white man to invade the confines of what is now Nunda Township was George Stickney, who came in December, 1835, locating on section 6, where he erected the first house in the township. This

442

primitive cabin contained no iron of any description, wooden pegs being used instead of nails. Benjamin McOmber, who arrived a short time after Mr. Stickney, lived in his log house. Samuel Terwilliger, came in June, 1836 and was the third settler. Cameron Goff was the fourth, and he arrived in October, 1837.

Prior to 1840 these made Nunda their permanent settlement: George T. Beckley, Abram Vincent, De Witt Brady, Joseph Walkup, Charles Patterson and his four sons, William Huffman and his four sons, Wm. St. Clair, Fred Bryant, J. Gracy, G. A. Palmer, John Fitzsimmons, J. E. Beckley, A. Colby, D. Ellsworth and W. Musgrave.

PIONEER EVENTS

The first plowing in this township was executed by Samuel Terwilliger.

John Terwilliger, son of Samuel Terwilliger and wife, was the first white child born in Nunda Township. He lived on the same farm on which he was born, until he passed from earth in 1876.

An infant son of the Terwilligers was the first child to die in the township. His remains were laid away in the Holcombville burying ground.

In 1845 James and Samuel McMillen erected a saw-mill on section 22, which was the first in the township. After 1863, at considerable expense it was fitted over into a grist-mill and as such used many years. A carding-mill was constructed there in 1846, by Mr. Truesdell, but two years later it was abandoned as it would not pay. The first real grist-mill was built at Barryville by T. J. Ferguson, at a cost of $6,000; this was used many years. McHenry County paid the large sum of $15 for every wolf scalp which was taken within the limits of the county. This custom obtained until 1850. It is related that certain hunters of Nunda Township distinguished themselves by capturing cubs and caring for them until they were six months old, at which time they killed and scalped them, and then claimed the bounty.

OLD VILLAGE OF NUNDA

What is now within the incorporation of the city of Crystal Lake, but was originally known as the village of Nunda, was platted in August, 1868. It was situated on section 32, township 44, range 8. A man named Reed conducted a general store there as early as 1855. The first depot for the railroad at this point (Chicago & Northwestern system now) was shipped out from Chicago on flat cars. That was in 1856. It was set down carefully, just where the old Fox River Valley crossed the "Northwestern." Then, Nunda the village had not even been thought of. This station house was for the accommodation of the workmen, and being fearful of the high winds, it was staked down to the right-of-way. Finally Nunda sprung up and flourished under that name many years, and was finally incorporated as a village, but with the several Crystal Lake corporations it was decided at an election not long since that Nunda should be merged with the Crystal Lake villages, and so it is today.

BARREVILLE

This was the name given to a collection of houses or hamlet in this township. Thomas Combs built a store there, and about it grew the small place. A mill was built in 1857 and carried on successfully by its proprietor, Mr. Ferguson, until his death in 1865. Patterson Bros. owned the mill later, and still later it was owned by Messrs. McCord and J. F. Thompson. It was finally owned by Louis Munch, who in 1884 remodeled it and made "patent flour" there.

In the spring of 1881, a butter and cheese factory was built at Barreville by E. F. Matthews at a cost of $3,000.

In 1854 a post office was established on Silver Lake Prairie, and the first postmaster was Russell Stanton. About 1864 the office was moved to Barreville, with Fred Bryant as postmaster.

The early business and professional men of Nunda included the following: Crystal Lake Pickling and Canning Co., G. H. Clayson, Nunda Flour Mills, Gilbert & St. Clair, E. Beckley, J. Goodwin, Philip Roberts, J. A. Sheldon, Piatt & Pinney, C. H. Stone, Smith Bros., Dr. George Horn, G. E. Dickinson, M. M. Hulburt, W. T. Hamilton, Hartman & Barnes, Edgar Beckley & Son, A. M. Clark, D. W. Wattlers, F. W. Stark, O. C. Colby, J. N. Powell, P. A. England, D. Williams, J. F. Wheaton & Son., Dr. E. Ballou, Dr. C. C. Watson, and Robert Rowley.

The history of the village corporation is included in that of Crystal Lake and will be found in the township history of Algonquin. Of the post office, it may be stated in this connection that one was established at Nunda Center about three miles north of the village, and James McMillen was the postmaster. The office was moved to the village in 1855, and called Dearborn, but the name was later changed to Nunda.

TERRA COTTA

Terra Cotta, a station on the Chicago & Northwestern Railroad, located on section 21 of Nunda Township, is home of the third largest terra cotta plant in the United States. This plant is the principal interest of the settlement, employment here being given to an average of 300 people. An account of this industry and the American Terra Cotta and Ceramic Company, is given in the chapter on Railroads and Industrial Enterprises.

POPULATION

In 1890 Nunda Township had a population of 1,805; in 1900 it was 1,965, in 1910 it was at 2,110, including parts of Crystal Lake and North Crystal Lake corporations, and in 1920 it was 2,321.

TOWNSHIP OFFICIALS

The following are the township officials of Nunda Township: Supervisor, A. H. Hale; assessor, George L. Bryant; clerk, H. A. Rowley; highway commissioner, John Pierson: justice of the peace, P. F. Hunt; constable, George J. Chlert.

CHAPTER XXXVII

RICHMOND TOWNSHIP

BOUNDARIES—FIRST SETTLERS—PIONEER EVENTS—VILLAGE OF RICHMOND—POST OFFICE—PUBLIC IMPROVEMENTS—MUNICIPAL HISTORY—SOLON MILLS—ORIGIN OF SWEET BY AND BY—POPULATION—TOWNSHIP OFFICIALS.

BOUNDARIES

Richmond Township in the northeastern part of McHenry County, is bounded on the north by the State of Wisconsin; on the east by Burton Township; on the south by McHenry Township; and on the west by Hebron Township. It is a well-watered township, its streams being the North and South Branches whose waters find their way into the Fox river. Twin Lakes have a small outlet which flows into the Nippersink. The surface of this portion of McHenry County is nearly level and is well adapted to general agriculture. Where needed, there has been considerable tile drain put into the land and this is annually being carried on.

FIRST SETTLERS

To Hon. William A. McConnell belongs the distinction of having been the first pioneer to invade the prairie wilds of this township. He located here in 1837 and built a log cabin 16x18 feet. Following him came Charles A. Noyes, John Purdy, Todd Francis, Daniel Newcombe, William and Alexander Gardner, Stephen Pardee and R. R. Crosby, the majority of whom arrived in 1838.

PIONEER EVENTS

The first white person to die in this township was Francis Purdy, who passed away in August, 1839, and was buried in the Richmond Cemetery. One week later, Hannah Thomas passed from earth. She was the daughter of Briggs and Amy Thomas.

446

Clara B. Mason

Fred A. Mason

The first white child born in the township was Sarah, daughter of John and Pamelia Purdy; the date of her birth was July 4, 1839.

The earliest marriage of parties living within this township was that of Andrew Kennedy and Laura Warner, in 1844.

Alexander and David Williams commenced erecting a sawmill in 1838, on the Nippersink Creek. Later this mill became the property of Henry and John W. White. The last two mentioned built a gristmill at Solon in 1840, the first of its kind in the county.

The oldest burying ground in this township is the one at the village of Richmond. Another cemetery was established at Solon very soon after the one at Richmond. Another in the White schoolhouse district, was among the first to be in general use.

VILLAGE OF RICHMOND

Richmond was platted in 1844 by Charles Cotting and Theodore Purdy. It is situated on sections 9 and 16, and is on the banks of Nippersink Creek. The same year that the village was platted, Messrs. Cotting and Purdy built a gristmill, and at its frame raising (a great event those days) the offer was made by its owners that whoever climbed to the top of the building could have the naming of the new village. Isaac M. Reed reached the top of the building and named the place Richmond, after a favorite town of his in Vermont. At first this township was named Montelona, but later it took that of Richmond.

Charles Noyes erected the first house in the village of Richmond. This was built of logs and was 20x24 feet in size. Ralph Andrews was the pioneer wagonmaker, and David C. Andrews was the first blacksmith; the first lawyer was C. K. Young and the pioneer physician was Dr. Hessett.

Of a somewhat later date, the business and professional factors in Richmond were as follows: F. W. Mead, George Alfs, Robert Johnnott, H. Chevillin, A. P. Gray, Dr. I. B. Rice, A. R. Alexander, Downing & Dennison, John West, C. E. Culver, H. F. Boutell, Milan Hicks, C. F. Paxton, Aldrich & Burton, C. F. Hall & Co., D. A. Potter, Smith & Haythorn, John Billings, Cropper & Co. With the many changes in the passing of multiplied years down to the present, the village has never ceased to progress with other parts of the county.

A fine modern public school building was erected in 1910. It is a two-story and basement structure. It has six main rooms and there are seven teachers. Its first session was held, commencing January 1, 1911.

This building was built at the cost of $25,000, but it is stated that $40,000 would not build such a structure today.

POST OFFICE

The post office here is a third-class one and has two rural free delivery routes connected with it—No. 1 in charge of Clyde Wilson; No. 2 in charge of F. G. Motley. These routes are about twenty-nine miles in length. The postmasters, since the establishment of the office, have been: William McConnell, appointed 1838, who was succeeded by William Adams, D. Bennett, Luther Emmons, Dr. Stone, Allen Potter, J. V. Aldrich, D. A. Potter, Marcus Foot, J. V. Aldrich, J. T. Bower, J. V. Aldrich and W. P. Stevens, who was commissioned in 1914.

PUBLIC IMPROVEMENTS

The village erected a large town hall for general public purposes in 1900 at a cost of $15,000, and it is known as "Memorial Hall." It was named for Charles DeWitt McConnell who donated $10,000 toward its building.

MUNICIPAL HISTORY

Richmond is an incorporated village and has been so ever since 1872, when its first officials were elected as follows: Dr. F. S. Bennett, president; A. R. Alexander, clerk; J. V. Aldrich, treasurer; D. A. Potter, magistrate; Alanson Brown, constable; and Dr. S. F. Bennett, John Haythorn, George Purdy, William Purdy, John Halian and J. R. Hyde, trustees.

The presidents and clerks for the village from 1884 (no record prior to that date) have been as follows:

Presidents

Richard Wray	1884
J. W. Haythorn	1885-86
Daniel Dennison	1887
L. W. Howe	1888-89
P. K. Wright	1890
F. E. Holmes	1891
J. T. Bower	1892-1900
George McConnel	1894-98
G. W. Eldridge	1898-01
E. C. Covell	1902-19

Clerks

F. W. Mead	1884
Charles S. Green	1885-86
E. R. Bennett	1887
William Sherman	1888
L. W. Nichols	1889-90

Clerks—Continued		F. B. McConnell.........1902-07
G. E. Eldridge 1891		R. G. Scott 1908-15
John Holian 1892-97		R. F. Parsons 1917
H. J. Kimball............1894-96		J. T. Bower.............1918-19
H. W. Aldrich...........1898-16		E. C. Covell...................

PRESENT OFFICIALS

The following are the village officials of Richmond: president, E. C. Covell; clerk, J. T. Bower; treasurer, J. N. Burton; magistrate, J. F. Brown; marshal, W. H. Reed; trustees, J. B. Richardson, Fred Arp, W. A. McConnell, F. H. Bell, Robert Walkington.

SOLON MILLS

Solon Mills was among the first settled communities in this county. It is situated on section 26 and 27. A flour mill was built there at a very early date, but the property became entangled in endless litigation and was of little value to the community. The old mill still stands a monument to legal folly and poor business judgment. The property and twenty acres of land on which it stands are now held by Chicago parties. It is on the bank of Nippersink Creek. With the failure of the milling interests, and the springing up of other villages near by, Solon has never taken on much commercial importance, but has a few business interests. It is in a splendid farm and stock country. Lands are selling for high prices and the demand for substantial commodities is steady.

ORIGIN OF "IN THE SWEET BY-AND-BY"

To but very few who have heard since childhood's happiest hour that now immortal song, "In the Sweet By-and-By," is it known that this popular song was composed and set to music in Richmond, but such is the fact. Dr. S. E. Bennett, for so many years one of Richmond's foremost citizens, is the author. He located here in 1859 at the age of twenty-three years, taking charge of the public schools as principal, and held that position for two years, then going to Elkhorn, but returned in 1871 and again took charge of the school work for one year. He then attended Rush Medical College, Chicago, from which he was graduated in 1874, when he began the practice of medicine, continuing it for more than twenty-five years or until his death in 1898. During his residence in Richmond he became associated with J. P. Webster, a musical composer. They were associated together for several years, during which time they published a number of hymns, the leading one being that immortal one, "In the Sweet By and By," now translated in all languages of the civilized world.

It appears from writings of Mr. Richards, in his Woodstock Reminiscences, that "Doctor Bennett and Professor Webster, a musician, were in a corner store at Richmond and that something was said in desponding mood. Someone said, 'Oh, that will be all right in the sweet by and by,' whereat Doctor Bennett turned to his desk and in a few minutes handed the poem to Professor Webster, saying 'how will that do?' Professor Webster took his violin and in a little time composed the music. It was then sung and approved by those present, and given to the world."

POPULATION

Richmond Township had a population in 1890 of 1,212; in 1900, 1,498; in 1910 its population was 1,472; and in 1920, 1,448.

TOWNSHIP OFFICIALS

The following are the township officials of Richmond Township: supervisor, F. B. McConnell; assessor, John Collison; clerk, J. T. Bower; highway commissioner, Henry Vogel; justice of the peace, William H. Rotnour; constables, John Collison and W. H. Reed.

CHAPTER XXXVIII

RILEY TOWNSHIP

BOUNDARIES AND TOPOGRAPHY

Riley Township is the southwestern subdivision of the county, and comprises congressional township 43, range 5. It is bounded on the north by Marengo Township; on the east by Coral Township; on the south by Kane County, and on the west by Boone County. Coon Creek, with two of its tributaries, furnishes the water courses for the territory within the township. The streams are small and not as numerous as in other parts of the county, but the township is among the best agricultural sections. It is almost exclusively prairie land and even as long ago as fifty years, the farms were spoken of as being among the best in Northern Illinois.

EARLY SETTLERS

This township was first settled by T. W. Cobb, Roswell Bates, N. E. Barnes, Jenkins Underwood and Osborn Underwood. These persons came in between 1836 and 1843. Whitman Cobb arrived here in 1836, and possibly several more of the men just named were pioneers of the same year. Cobb continued a resident of the township until 1874, when he moved to Warren, Ill. Three years later, however, he returned to Riley Township, and died here soon afterwards. Samuel Smith came in 1837, and Russell Baily in 1838. All of these men made permanent homes within the township.

PIONEER EVENTS

The first white child born within this township was Ezra O. Knapp, a son of Mr. and Mrs. Charles Knapp.

The first death was that of Samuel Smith in 1837.

451

Spencer Flanders and Caroline Cobb were united in marriage by Ward Burley, a justice of the peace, August 19, 1841, this being the first wedding in the township.

Dr. Albert E. Smith was the township's first physician. He settled here in 1837, remained several years, and was followed by Dr. John Wentworth, who was in active practice until his death.

It was said of this township in 1877: "Having plenty of facilities in adjoining townships, they have erected no church buildings within its limits. The population for many years was about evenly divided between the Congregationalists and the Methodists. Meetings were frequently held in nearby schoolhouses."

From the start, this township has been alive to the value of a good common school system and has improved every opportunity given it along this line.

The township was among, if not the very first in the county to provide itself with a good town hall, centrally located, where it held its elections and transacted all business, while other townships put up with the schoolhouse that happened to be situated nearest by for all such affairs.

It had a cheese factory in the early seventies. It also was early among the townships of the county to set out fruit trees and reaped the reward of such action by later harvesting large crops of luscious apples and cherries.

CEMETERIES

The earliest cemetery was laid out at a very early date, nearly in the center of the township.

Another small burying ground was laid out close to the Kane County line.

SOUTH RILEY

What was known as South Riley post office was established very early in the southwest quarter of section 27. A store and blacksmith shop were maintained there for a time. With the coming of the free rural mail delivery system the post office was discontinued, since which time the people of the township have traded at Marengo or other nearby points.

POPULATION

In 1890 Riley Township had a population of 830; in 1900, 915; in 1910, 822; and in 1920, 717.

Rev. D. J. McCaffrey

TOWNSHIP OFFICIALS

The following are the township officials of Riley Township: supervisor, H. H. Barber; assessor, C. Mackey; clerk, Cleo Anthony; highway commissioner, H. H. Dunbar; justices of the peace, Roy Griebel and R. W. Metcalf; constables, A. Stockwell and Frank Griebel.

CHAPTER XXXIX

SENECA TOWNSHIP

BOUNDARIES

Seneca Township is one of the central subdivisions of the county, being composed of all of congressional township 44, range 6, and is bounded on the north by Hartland Township; on the east by Dorr Township; on the south by Coral Township, and on the west by Marengo Township. As an agricultural section it has no superior in all this part of Illinois. The fertile, gentle rolling land has been put in a high state of cultivation. Originally, this township was heavily timbered on the west side of its domain, and nearly all of the houses of the early times were built of excellent varieties of solid oak cut from the nearby forests.

ORIGIN OF NAME

Seneca was the name of a powerful Indian tribe in western New York, from which many of the first settlers to this township came, hence they named the township to which they moved after that Indian tribe of the far away Empire State.

FIRST SETTLERS

It is stated on good authority that the first white man to invade what is now known as Seneca Township was E. Pettitt, who came in 1835. His selection of land was subsequently known as the Sponsable farm. John Belder also arrived that year from La Porte, Ind., and he lived here for many years. Jedediah Rogers, a Vermont Yankee, was another settler of 1835. In 1836 Russell Diggins moved from St. Lawrence County, N. Y., to Seneca Township, and his wife died soon after their arrival in this township. Her death was the first known within the

454

township. A claim was taken up by a Mr. Woodard in 1836, but he left it before the Civil War period. Another permanent settler was Robert G. White, who came in 1836 and remained until his death in 1871. It was he who built the first saw-mill in the township. Eli Craig came in 1836, and in 1838 was elected a constable. During the latter year came to the township as settlers the following: Amos Damon, Captain Silas Chatfield, Joseph Hanna, Solomon Baldwin, Christopher Sponsable, Whitman Cobb and Ephriam Rogers. The next season the arrivals to the township were: M. Dickenson, John Ackerson, Peter Deitz, Clark Wix and Spencer Flanders. In 1840 the permanent settlers were: Leander Bishop, John White, William Sponsable and Salem Stowell. Another account given of the township's settlement says that the first band of settlers included Jasper Havens, Levi Morsey and Joseph Hanna, all of whom came from Virginia in 1835-36. A Mr. Albro was the first settler at Franklinville, coming there in the autumn of 1836.

PIONEER EVENTS

A Mr. White and his family came into the township in about 1836, settling in section 29, where soon after White & Son put up a saw-mill at the junction of the Middle and North branches of the Kishwaukee. A little later George Smith & Co. erected a flour-mill on the same stream on section 30, and this was doing a good business late in the eighties. The township had another saw-mill, built by Anderson & Graves in 1844. From quite an early day the principal business of the township was its dairy industry. A cheese factory was erected at Franklinville in 1868. Later this was bought by Doctor Stone and moved to a site not far distant, and was there used as a feed store. Still later it was converted into a feed-mill and butter and cheese factory. The next year Mr. Bigelow put up a second factory on his farm a mile to the west of the village of Franklinville. Subsequently this was sold to I. Boies of Marengo.

In literary affairs Seneca Township, from a very early time, has been second to none in the county. A literary society was organized and met semi-monthly, its object being largely to procure good books as cheaply as possible. When the books had been well read by the community they were auctioned off and more new ones provided.

As to the market prices in this township between 1836 and 1850, let it be stated for a fact that those who dealt at Franklinville (known a long time as "Snarltown") sold their eggs at five cents a dozen and their butter at ten cents a pound, in trade. Corn brought a shilling a bushel, in barter.

In putting down the rebellion in the Civil War, Seneca took an active part, one family named Penman, within the limits of the township, sending every member, to wit: father, mother, four sons, daughter and son-in-law. And what is still more wonderful, every member of that household returned in safety.

Perhaps the crowning glory of the township took place on Fourth of July, 1876, Centennial Year, at which time Mayor Donnelly, having offered a flag to the township bringing the biggest delegation to the Woodstock celebration, Seneca brought in nearly eight hundred people, and carried away the coveted prize.

CEMETERIES

The first burial place was between Woodstock and Franklinville.

Franklinville Cemetery was laid out in 1839 by the common consent of the pioneer settlers, but especially by the members of the Methodist Episcopal Church. Mrs. Lazarus was the first to be buried at that place.

SCHOOLS AND CHURCHES

The first school in Seneca Township was taught by Mrs. Stevens, the wife of G. B. Stevens, at their residence, one mile south of Franklinville, in 1840. The first schoolhouse was erected in Franklinville.

The earliest religious meetings were held at the home of G. B. Stevens in 1839, by Rev. Leander Walker, and he and Rev. Nathaniel Jewett preached alternately every four weeks at private residences until 1849, when the Methodists built their church at Franklinville.

FRANKLINVILLE

This is a little community or hamlet, situated in section 22, about four miles southwest of Woodstock. It was first known as Snarltown, but the name was later changed to Franklinville in honor of Franklin Stringer, a spirited, highly enterprising citizen of the township. The reason assigned for the first and peculiar name of this hamlet is said to have been on account of a man named George Albrow, who immigrated hither from New York State. He possessed so contrary a nature that had he lived in later days he probably would have been termed a 'grouch.' In those days, his habit of snarling at everyone gained for him the name "Snarl" Albrow. Hence the village that grew up around him was called after him, but fortunately this nomenclature was soon abandoned in favor of one given in honor of a much worthier personage.

A Mr. Lockwood opened a store on section 22, and began trading with the neighboring farmers, and after one year he exchanged his store for one owned by a Mr. Robinson of Geneva, Ill. Robinson was in time succeeded by Harley Wayne, who in 1843 took in George T. Kasson as a partner. Kasson bought out Wayne and formed a partnership with U. T. Hyde, and they opened a second store. Norman Brebhall was the first blacksmith to kindle his glowing forge in the hamlet. In 1843, through the efforts of "Long" John Wentworth, then congressman from this district, a post office was established at Franklinville, which at first was called Belden, and Sylvester Mead was appointed postmaster. He was followed by H. Wayne, and he by G. T. Kasson. The office was abandoned in 1866, and for six years there was no post office, but in 1872 Carrie Deitz was appointed as postmistress. Franklinville is now served by rural free delivery.

The community still known as Franklinville has a Methodist Episcopal Church, a charge out from Woodstock; a store and blacksmith shop. In its early days it had high hopes of becoming the seat of justice and ranking among the best places of the county, but time changes the best laid plans of men.

The Seneca Ladies' Literary Society of this hamlet was organized in 1855, and has been in continuous service ever since. The first work undertaken was to help raise funds at a charge of five cents each two weeks, for the Mount Vernon Association. It early established a library and exerted an influence for good in various ways. It has now adopted and is supporting a French orphan. Mrs. Martha Rose, now of Marengo, was an early librarian there and is still an honorary member on its rolls.

POPULATION

In 1890 Seneca Township had a population of 1,046, including a part of Union village in Coral Township; in 1900, 1,105; in 1910, 1,023, and in 1920, 940.

TOWNSHIP OFFICIALS

The following are the township officials of Seneca Township: supervisor, E. F. Knecker; assessor, R. M. Bean; clerk, Roy Andrews; highway commissioner, Henry A. Russell; justice of the peace, Philip Andrews; constable, James Welch.

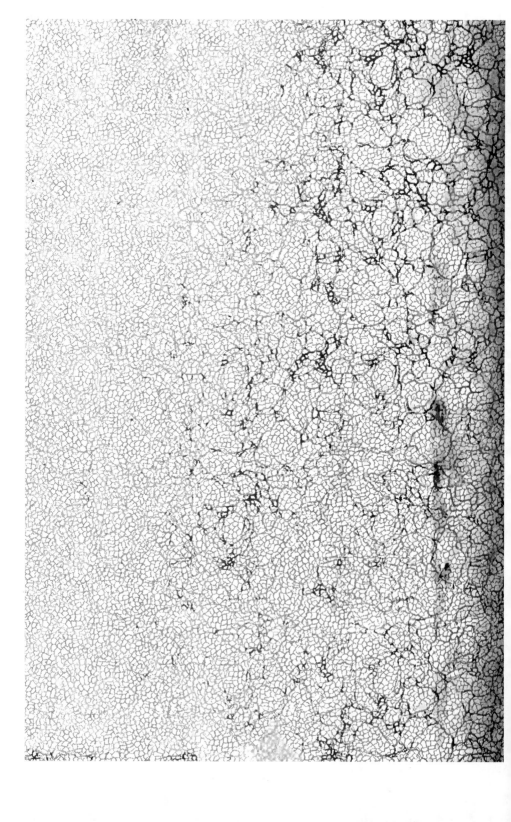

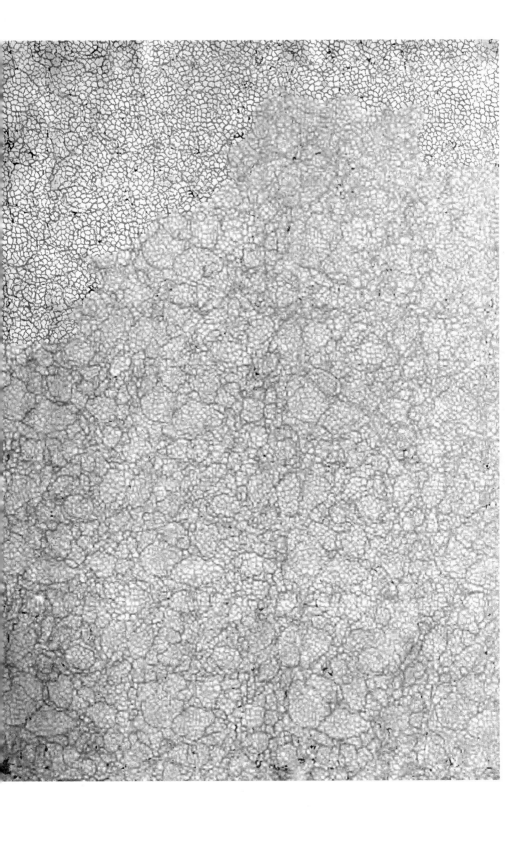

Printed in the USA
CPSIA information can be obtained
at www.ICGtesting.com
LVHW011101311223
767829LV00011B/423